Expelling the Poor

D1557561

Expelling the Poor

*Atlantic Seaboard States and the
Nineteenth-Century Origins of
American Immigration Policy*

Hidetaka Hirota

OXFORD
UNIVERSITY PRESS

OXFORD
UNIVERSITY PRESS

Oxford University Press is a department of the University of Oxford. It furthers
the University's objective of excellence in research, scholarship, and education
by publishing worldwide. Oxford is a registered trade mark of Oxford University
Press in the UK and certain other countries.

Published in the United States of America by Oxford University Press
198 Madison Avenue, New York, NY 10016, United States of America.

Library of Congress Cataloging-in-Publication Data
Hirota, Hidetaka-author.
Expelling the poor: Atlantic Seaboard states and the nineteenth-century origins of American
immigration policy / Hidetaka Hirota.
Includes bibliographical references and index.
Identifiers: LCCN 2016035614 (print) | LCCN 2016054116 (ebook) |
ISBN 9780190619220 (Updf) | ISBN 9780190619237 (Epub) |
ISBN 9780190619213 (hardcover) | ISBN 9780190055561 (paperback)
Subjects: LCSH: Deportation—Government policy—United States—History—19th century. |
Irish—Government policy—United States—History—19th century. |
Poor—Government policy—United States—History—19th century. |
Immigrants—Government policy—United States—History—19th century. |
Prejudices—Political aspects—United States—History—19th century. |
United States—Emigration and immigration—Government policy—History—19th century. |
Atlantic States—Emigration and immigration—Government policy—History—19th
century. | United States—Ethnic relations—History—19th century.
Classification: LCC JV6483 .H57 2017 (print) | LCC JV6483 (ebook) |
DDC 325.7309/034—dc23
LC record available at https://lccn.loc.gov/2016035614

For Megumi

CONTENTS

ACKNOWLEDGMENTS

In the course of researching and writing this book I received assistance, guidance, and encouragement from many people and institutions. I have long looked forward to the moment when I can thank them for training and supporting me. I am very glad that it has finally come.

This book began as a doctoral dissertation at Boston College. I owe my biggest debt to Kevin Kenny, who has mentored me since my first year of graduate school. He read all versions of the manuscript with unflagging commitment and patience while giving me the best advice at every stage of my scholarly career up to today. The education I received from him is my most important intellectual asset. Heather Cox Richardson has been exceptionally supportive and enthusiastic about this project over the years. Her insightful suggestions decisively helped me conceptualize this book and formulate its main arguments. Cynthia Lynn Lyerly always generously spent her time answering my questions during my countless sudden visits to her office. Her careful reading of the manuscript saved me from embarrassing factual errors. I would like to express my special gratitude to David Quigley for teaching me how to frame historical questions from broad perspectives at the early stage of my graduate education. His words stayed in my head throughout the course of writing this book.

My teachers I met as an undergraduate laid my intellectual foundations. At Sophia University in Tokyo my advisor, Kazuyuki Matsuo, not only introduced me to the study of American history but also strongly recommended I pursue an American doctorate. My interests in America's past were also developed through Makoto Tanno's seminars in American studies and literature as well as Noriko Ishii's courses on American women's history. My gratitude to Cecelia Bucki and David McFadden at Fairfield University, where I spent an academic year, has never waned. By taking their courses, I decided to come back to the United States for graduate work in American history.

A postdoctoral fellowship from the Society of Fellows in the Humanities at Columbia University enabled me to turn the dissertation into this book. I am deeply grateful to the board members of the Society of Fellows, especially Christopher L. Brown and Eileen Gillooly, for having me as a Mellon Research Fellow for three years and providing me with an almost utopian intellectual environment that could not be found elsewhere. Their friendship and scholarly mentorship were indispensable to the completion of this project. During my time at Columbia, I had the opportunity to offer seminars on wealth and poverty in America and on American nativism in the Department of History and the Center for the Study of Ethnicity and Race. Conversation with undergraduate and graduate students in these courses substantially furthered my thoughts on the relationship among nativism, political economy, and immigration policy. I thank my students for their valuable input to this book.

A vast array of friends, colleagues, and scholars in various disciplines have read parts of the manuscript. For their comments, suggestions, and constructive criticism, I would like to thank Vanessa Agard-Jones, Tyler Anbinder, Teresa Bejan, John Belchem, Stefan Berger, Marcelo Borges, Benjamin Breen, Maggie Cao, Christopher Capozzola, Daniel Carey, Muzaffar Chishti, Elizabeth Clemens, Mimi Cowan, Ian Delahanty, William Deringer, Souleymane Bachir Diagne, Hasia Diner, Gilberto Fernandes, Brian Goldstone, David Gutiérrez, David Gutkin, Ruth-Ann Harris, Masako Hattori, Ai Hisano, Murad Idris, William Jenkins, Marilynn Johnson, Walter Kamphoefner, Daniel Kanstroom, Yuko Konno, Yo Kotaki, Paul Kramer, Alan Kraut, Anna Law, Gabriel Loiacono, Ian McCready-Flora, Gráinne McEvoy, Laura Madokoro, Yoshiya Makita, Malgorzata Mazurek, Seth Meehan, Melissa Milewski, Kerby Miller, Gerard Moran, Satoshi Nakano, Frances Negrón-Muntaner, David Northrup, Brendan O'Malley, Kevin O'Neill, Sherry Olson, Nicholas Parrillo, Dan-el Padilla Peralta, Mary Anne Poutanen, Bruno Ramirez, Carmel Raz, Lucy Salyer, George Sánchez, Ian Shin, Rogers Smith, Hiroshi Takei, Evan Taparata, Van Tran, John Tully, David Wagner, Rebecca Woods, Grant Wythoff, and Elliott Young. I would also like to thank Kornel Chang, Catherine Clinton, Mary Dudziak, Eric Foner, Cybelle Fox, Hendrik Hartog, Martha Hodes, Rebecca Kobrin, Stephanie McCurry, Timothy Meagher, Hiroshi Motomura, José Moya, Mae Ngai, Kunal Parker, Christina Duffy Ponsa, Gautham Rao, and Seth Rockman for encouraging me or expressing their endorsement of my work on various occasions.

At Oxford University Press, Susan Ferber kindly and professionally guided me through the publication process. Her sharp editorial suggestions thoroughly refined the manuscript, bringing it to a fundamentally higher level. I feel extremely fortunate to receive the benefit of her extraordinary editing for my first book. It has been a genuine privilege to work with her. I also want to thank Susan for making the whole process a very pleasant experience by giving me warm and encouraging words at various stages of this book's development. My sincere thanks equally go to all other Oxford staff involved in the production of this book. Without their devotion and assistance, the book's publication would have simply been impossible. My gratitude extends to two anonymous readers who offered me a number of helpful suggestions for the improvement of the manuscript in their incredibly enthusiastic and supportive reports.

Fellowships and grants from many organizations and institutions allowed me to start, develop, and complete this project. For generous financial assistance, I am grateful to the American Historical Association, the American Society for Legal History, the City College of New York, the Cushwa Center for the Study of American Catholicism at the University of Notre Dame, the Gilder Lehrman Institute of American History, the Immigration and Ethnic History Society, the Institute for Political History, the Japan-United States Friendship Commission, the Massachusetts Historical Society, the Moore Institute for Research in the Humanities and Social Studies at the National University of Ireland-Galway, the Society of Fellows in the Humanities at Columbia University, and the William Nelson Cromwell Foundation. Funding from the Clough Center for the Study of Constitutional Democracy, the Department of History, the Graduate School of Arts and Sciences, the Graduate Student Association, and the Irish Studies Program at Boston College is equally appreciated. I would particularly like to acknowledge that the publication of this book is supported by the Paul L. Murphy Award from the American Society for Legal History.

Research for this transnational project took me to archives and libraries in four countries on both sides of the Atlantic. I would like to thank the archivists, librarians, and staff members at the following institutions for their friendly and professional assistance: the American Antiquarian Society, the Archdiocese of Boston Archives, the Boston College Libraries, the Boston Public Library, the Bowdoin College Library, the City of Boston Archives, the Columbia University Libraries, the Harvard University Libraries, the Historical Society of Pennsylvania, the Library of Congress, the Massachusetts Archives, the Massachusetts Historical Society, the National Archives and Records Administration in College Park, Philadelphia, San Bruno, Waltham, and Washington, DC, the New York Municipal Archives, the New York Public Library, the New York State Archives, the New York State Library, the Philadelphia City Archives, the State Library of Massachusetts, the Wisconsin Historical Society, the Library and Archives Canada, the

Provincial Archives of New Brunswick, the British Library, the British National Archives, the Liverpool Records Office, the Public Record Office of Northern Ireland, the Cork City and County Archives, the Galway County Archives, the National Archives of Ireland, and the National Library of Ireland. Special thanks are due to the Sophia University Institute of American and Canadian Studies for generously providing me with workspace whenever I was in Tokyo.

Parts of this book have previously been published. An early version of chapter 7 appeared as "The Moment of Transition: State Officials, the Federal Government, and the Formation of American Immigration Policy" in the *Journal of American History* 99, no. 4 (March 2013). Portions of chapters 2, 3, 4, 5, and 7 were published as "'The Great Entrepot for Mendicants': Foreign Poverty and Immigration Control in New York State to 1882" in the *Journal of American Ethnic History* 33, no. 2 (Winter 2014). I am grateful to Oxford University Press and the University of Illinois Press for allowing me to reprint these articles here. Images in this book are reproduced with generous permission from the American Antiquarian Society, the City of Boston Archives, and the Columbia University Butler Library.

I owe my deepest thanks to my family. My parents, Tsuneo and Ikuko, have given me many forms of irreplaceable support since the moment when I decided to pursue a career as a historian of the United States. My sister Tomoko's almost annual visits first to Boston and later to New York City always gave me a pleasant break from work. Three of my grandparents passed away while I was writing this book. Their deaths gravely saddened me, but the birth of Haruhisa brightened my whole world with boundlessly multiplying joy. His growth added unforgettable pleasant memories to the days I spent preparing the final manuscript.

Finally, I would like to thank my wife, Megumi, who witnessed the genesis of this project and has helped me in more ways than she will ever realize. Her support, faith, and patience are just what made this book possible. She shared with me all excitement, laughter, and difficulty that came with its evolution. Nothing is more important to me than life with her—my partner, best friend, and love. I dedicate this book to her.

Expelling the Poor

Introduction

Thomas Green and Edward Boyle started out their journeys as typical emigrants from mid-nineteenth-century Ireland. Both laborers, they each embarked from Liverpool en route to North America. In the summer of 1850, Green arrived in Boston on the *Trimountain* with 224 other Irish passengers. Four years later Boyle followed the same course as Green, arriving in Boston in the winter of 1854. In Massachusetts, Green married a woman named Elisa Brady and secured employment in Boston, at least for a while. After separating from his wife because of a "quarrel," Green lost all means of self-support and entered a Massachusetts state almshouse in Bridgewater. Boyle's prospects were even worse than Green's. Debilitated by "ship fever" caught during the voyage, he became an inmate of the Bridgewater almshouse just two weeks after his arrival. The admission of the destitute Irish into public almshouses was not uncommon in nineteenth-century Massachusetts. But the experiences of Green and Boyle diverged from those of the majority of Irish immigrants in America in one critical respect. Under Massachusetts state law, which allowed for the deportation of any foreign pauper to "any place beyond [the] sea, where he belongs," Green and Boyle were removed from the almshouse and sent back to Ireland by state officials on April 13, 1855.[1] While most nineteenth-century Irish immigrants, including those who became inmates at almshouses, remained in the United States, Green and Boyle made a second transatlantic voyage, this time from the United States back to Ireland as deportees.

This book tells the story of people like Green and Boyle, Irish immigrants deported from the United States due to their poverty under state

law. It provides the first sustained study of immigration control conducted by states prior to the introduction of federal immigration law in
the late nineteenth century. Based on an analysis of immigration policies
in major American coastal states, including New York, Massachusetts,
Pennsylvania, Maryland, Louisiana, and California, it examines the origins of immigration restriction in the United States, especially deportation
policy. By locating those origins in cultural prejudice against the Irish and,
more essentially, economic concerns about their poverty in nineteenth-
century New York and Massachusetts, this book fundamentally revises
the history of American immigration policy, which has largely focused
on racism in the West. It also places the implementation of American
deportation law in a broad context that extended from the United States
to Ireland, Britain, and Canada. Beginning with Irish migrants' initial
departure from Ireland, this study traces their transatlantic movement
to North America, the process of their expulsion from the United States,
and their postdeportation lives in Britain and Ireland. Using a rich array
of archival sources collected on both sides of the Atlantic, the narrative
brings together the evolution of nativist sentiment, the development
of state immigration policy, the social realities of law enforcement, and
human stories about deportees' experiences. In short, *Expelling the Poor*
presents a transnational social and legal history of American immigration
control.

During the first half of the nineteenth century, New York and
Massachusetts received a growing influx of poor Catholic Irish immigrants. The newcomers' religion triggered an outburst of anti-Irish nativism in these states, but so too did the immigrants' poverty. Impoverished
at home and sickened during the transatlantic passage, a significant portion of the Irish arrived in the United States without the physical strength
and financial resources to support themselves and thus had to enter almshouses and lunatic hospitals as paupers soon after landing. Calling Irish
paupers "leeches" who consumed public charity funds supported by citizens' taxes, nativist Americans advocated the closure of America's borders
against indigent immigrants from Europe, especially Ireland.

To reduce Irish pauperism, New York and Massachusetts built upon
colonial poor laws for regulating the local movement of the poor to check
the landing into the state of destitute foreigners. In Massachusetts, an
exceptionally strong anti-Catholic and anti-Irish tradition inspired the
state legislature to go beyond merely setting entry regulations, or excluding the unacceptable. Rather, Massachusetts developed laws for deporting foreign paupers already resident in the state back to Ireland or to
Britain, Canada, or other American states. Between the 1830s and the

early 1880s, at least 50,000 persons were removed from Massachusetts under this policy. State policies applied to all destitute foreigners, and German immigrants attracted their fair share of nativism. Those expelled from Massachusetts also included American paupers who originally came from other states. Yet it was Irish poverty that generated the principal momentum for the growth of state immigration policy. No other coastal state engaged in passenger control with the same level of legislative effort and success as New York and Massachusetts, the major receiving states for Irish immigration. Maryland and Louisiana had little interest in restricting European immigration throughout the nineteenth century, while Pennsylvania and California failed to establish sustainable systems of immigration regulation. *Expelling the Poor* thus provides a national history of state-level immigration control and reveals the centrality of New York and Massachusetts in this history. Ultimately, it argues, regulatory measures in the two states laid the foundations for American immigration policy.

State officials enjoyed sweeping powers over foreigners in both New York and Massachusetts. As symbolized in the commonly used provision in state law restricting the landing of aliens "*likely* to become a public charge," state passenger policy allowed officials to use their discretion in determining the admissibility of the immigrants in question. Other categories of excludable people under state passenger laws were people with mental and physical defects, such as "lunatics," "idiots," and "infirm persons." Insanity and infirmity in the nineteenth century were never well-defined or self-evident conditions, but always subject to fluid and arbitrary interpretations by those who diagnosed them.[2] In this medical milieu state officials adopted the widest possible definitions of insanity and infirmity, applying exclusion provisions to foreign passengers as they saw fit. The massive discretionary power vested in law enforcers characterized deportation as well. Massachusetts' law, which provided for the removal of any foreign pauper to any place "where he belongs," gave officials complete freedom in deciding destinations for deportation. State officials ruthlessly applied deportation law to foreign paupers without considering the circumstances of their lives, expelling them regardless of how long they had lived in the United States or what form of attachment to the community they had established.

The enforcement of deportation brought about harsh, often tragic consequences for expelled immigrants. Some deportees pleaded not to be sent back to Europe, but their pleas usually fell on deaf ears. Irish immigrants removed from Massachusetts included elderly people who had spent as long as forty years in the United States as well as those who had siblings

and relatives in the state. Fearing that her four-year-old boy would not survive the return passage, one immigrant mother decided she had to leave
her child in Boston before her deportation. On one occasion, state officials
went so far as to place the children of destitute Irish immigrants on board
a Liverpool-bound ship even after their parents ran away. Moreover, officials routinely ignored the welfare of deportees in the process of removal.
Those with mental illness received little care and protection during the
transatlantic return passage. Upon arrival in Britain or Ireland, American
officials abandoned deportees on the streets without basic provisions such
as food, clothes, and money. Some deportees perished during the deportation voyage, while others died soon after their arrival in Europe.

Immigration control in New York and Massachusetts, when combined with the officials' own nativist prejudice, often crossed the line
into illegality. In New York, state law permitted the return to Europe of
foreigners who were denied landing upon arrival, but it prohibited the
postentry removal, or deportation, of people who had once been admitted. Frustrated with the absence of state deportation law, municipal
officials in New York City forcibly and unlawfully sent destitute immigrants in the city back to Europe at their own discretion. Unauthorized
deportation was exercised in the Bay State as well. Massachusetts state
law required officials to put immigrant paupers on a trial and obtain
court warrants for removal before they deported these people. But officials often bypassed this process, seizing foreign inmates from charitable
institutions and placing them on board deportation ships for the sake
of expediency and convenience. At the height of nativism in the 1850s,
Massachusetts officials deported abroad some American citizens of Irish
descent—American-born children and naturalized immigrants—despite
the fact that state law explicitly limited overseas removal to noncitizens.
The experience of indigent immigrants described in this book illuminates
the nearly complete absence of rights and protection for those deemed
excludable and deportable—especially non-naturalized ones but also
sometimes citizens—in the execution of state-level immigration control.
Given the colossal power vested in enforcing officers under state laws and
their habitual violations of limitations and procedures provided by these
laws, to be an immigrant pauper in nineteenth-century New York and
Massachusetts rendered one rightless in a practical sense.

Expelling the Poor is not exclusively a study of the two northeastern
states' regional response to mid-nineteenth-century Irish immigration,
but a work that contextualizes the critical significance of this reaction in
the history of American immigration policy. Officials in both New York
and Massachusetts fundamentally influenced the development of national

immigration policy in the late nineteenth century by playing a central role in the making of the federal Immigration Act of 1882. Passed three months after the enactment of the federal Chinese Exclusion Act of 1882, which suspended the immigration of Chinese laborers, the Immigration Act was the first general legislation that applied to all foreigners at a national level and set the groundwork for subsequent federal immigration laws. It banned the landing of undesirable aliens, such as paupers and people with mental defects, and included a deportation clause for criminals. Modeled on existing immigration policies in New York and Massachusetts, these provisions came from a draft bill that the two states' officials created. In addition, the act left the enforcement of its provisions to the hands of state officials. Under the federal act of 1882, officials in other states as the agents of national immigration law simply excluded paupers upon arrival. Yet officials in New York coerced indigent immigrants, after their initial admission, into returning to Europe, and those in Massachusetts also deported paupers under their own state law. The 1882 act limited postentry compulsory removal to criminals. Not until 1891 did the federal government introduce a more general deportation policy that applied to all excludable people. By making the deportation of people other than criminals a practical reality in the operation of national immigration law, state officials in New York and Massachusetts established the environment for the federal government to start general deportation in 1891. Immigration control in these Atlantic seaboard states thus molded the legal and administrative frameworks of national policy for excluding and deporting foreigners from the United States.

State-level actions in New York and Massachusetts—especially officials' abuse of deportation power—had profound implications for national immigration policy. Federal control from the late nineteenth century onward gave inspecting officers almost unlimited power over foreigners with the rise of what immigration scholars call the "plenary power" doctrine. The doctrine assumed that Congress possessed absolute power over the admission and removal of aliens and that its immigration policy was not subject to judicial scrutiny for constitutionality. It thereby allowed United States officers to determine aliens' excludability and deportability in ways which minimized their constitutional protections such as due process.[3] In this respect the later federal policy borrowed liberally from the experiences of the two east coast states, which had struggled with the immigration of the Irish poor in the decades before the Civil War. *Expelling the Poor* traces the roots of this aspect of federal control back to mid-nineteenth-century New York and Massachusetts, where officials operated with little constraint as they put in place harsh deportation measures against those foreigners whom they deemed unde-sirable. Principles of immigration policy were fashioned not only by laws and court opinions but also through the actions of people who carried out border control. Nativist state officials' earlier coercive and illegal prac-tices set precedents for American officers' assertion of unrestricted power against foreigners, laying the social groundwork for the plenary power doctrine. New York and Massachusetts officials' administration of the 1882 federal act transplanted the styles of immigration control developed in their states to national immigration policy during its formative period. Having guided state-level regulation, antipathy to the destitute Irish in turn set the direction of federal immigration control.

Analyzing the role of anti-Irish nativism in the development of immi-gration policies in New York and Massachusetts underscores the cen-trality of economic considerations in the hostile sentiment against the Irish. Nativism, as it is used in this book, refers to a set of hostile ideas, attitudes, and actions against foreigners, which were founded upon the fear of their impact on American society. One of the major tenets of anti-Irish nativism in nineteenth-century America was that Irish immigrants' belief in hierarchical and seemingly despotic Catholicism would corrupt American republican democracy and predominant cultural values rooted in Protestantism. Irish immigrants' drinking habits and supposed predis-position to criminality and violence reinforced Protestant Americans' con-viction that the Irish were unsuited for American society. Furthermore, anti-slavery Americans in the North regarded as a threat to American freedom Irish immigrants' tendency to support pro-slavery Democratic politicians and oppose the anti-slavery movement. While these tenets of anti-Irish nativism set the context within which immigration restriction unfolded on the Atlantic seaboard, antipathy to Irish pauperism was the most critical aspect of anti-Irish nativism when it came to the develop-ment of state immigration policy. Simply put, nativists resented many Irish immigrants' lack of money to support themselves and the immigra-tion policy they developed aimed to expel the indigent Irish dependent on public relief. This book fundamentally demonstrates how American immi-gration regulation emerged as a matter of class.

From the viewpoint of proponents of immigration restriction, the problem of Irish pauperism was not simply a financial one; it also had grave ideological dimensions. Irish immigrants' dependency on charity violated predominant economic ideals in nineteenth-century America that expected every white person to support himself through independent productive labor. Originating from the poor law, state immigration policy developed in tandem with other public policies for poverty regulation that made paupers social outcasts. Deportation was therefore a policy intended to ensure that the United States was a nation of self-sufficient workers by eliminating foreigners who deviated from this vision. At the same time, nativists in New York and Massachusetts despised Irish immigrants as degraded and barbaric people. They viewed Irish pauperism as particularly odious compared to that of Americans and other immigrant groups, including Germans. When nativists called for immigration restriction, they clearly targeted the Irish not only because of the disproportionately large number of Irish paupers in their state but also because of their prejudiced presumptions about the Irish. This book, then, traces the institutionalization into regulatory immigration policy of an economic logic that considered paupers the antithesis of American citizens and alienated them as such—a process driven by intense bias against people of Irish ancestry.

Although both were at the center of state-level immigration control, immigration policies in New York and Massachusetts differed in some important respects. New York relied on exclusion as the primary method of immigration control, at least as formal policy, and the state legislature resisted introducing deportation law for most of the nineteenth century. In addition to excluding foreigners of undesirable character, immigration officials in New York provided admitted newcomers with care and social services. By contrast, Massachusetts policy stood out for its purely restrictive features. Massachusetts always pursued aggressive measures against destitute Irish immigrants with the combination of exclusion and deportation, and its regulatory policies constantly expanded throughout the nineteenth century.

Regional political culture lay at the heart of this difference. The Puritan and English origins of Massachusetts led to a particularly strong sense of anti-Catholicism and superiority to Irish people among Anglo Americans in the state. This cultural heritage directly affected politics in the region. New England, especially Massachusetts, was a stronghold of the pro-English Federalists at the turn of the nineteenth century, and the Massachusetts Federalists maintained anti-Irish nativism as part of their core principles. Throughout the antebellum period, the political power of Irish immigrants in Massachusetts remained weak in the face of the dominant Whigs, who tended to uphold nativism, and the anti-slavery Free Soilers, many of whom hated the Catholic Irish as much as southern slaveholders. During the 1850s a nativist party enjoyed extensive control of Massachusetts politics, drastically expanding the scale of pauper removal. Massachusetts' strict approach to immigration control thus developed to a great extent on the basis of the anti-Irish political culture that allowed nativist immigration policy to flourish.[4] Immigrants in New York, by contrast, found it far easier to participate in politics and influence immigration policy. Since the days of Dutch rule in the colonial period, New York had cultivated an environment relatively tolerant of ethnic and cultural diversity. The Democrats in New York were more enthusiastic about mobilizing immigrant votes than their partymen in Massachusetts, and New York politicians, regardless of their party affiliation, generally hesitated to alienate foreign-born voters by explicitly endorsing proscriptive immigration policy. Opponents of immigration repeatedly called for tighter immigration restrictions, especially the introduction of deportation law, but their legislative proposals often had to be compromised due to the visible political power of immigrants.[5] It was precisely the absence of formal deportation law and the perceived laxness of state immigration policy that drove nativist public officials in New York toward radical and unauthorized actions, including illegal deportation.

This story of poor Irish immigrants and state deportation policy has significant gender dimensions. State officials never provided the statistical information about the ratio between men and women among deportees, but a disproportionate number of deportation cases involved Irish women, especially those with children. The substantial presence of women among deportees must be understood as a consequence of women's particular economic vulnerability in nineteenth-century America, making them an overrepresented population among charity recipients and almshouse inmates. As a group, Irish women enjoyed good job opportunities, especially as domestic servants, but their ability to earn wages remained fragile and could be easily cut off by various family circumstances. Pregnancy and obligations to raise children severely limited their employment prospects, and for pregnant women and those with children, abandonment and widowhood practically meant admission into almshouses. Even when their husbands were loyal to marriage and alive, their temporary absence during their search for jobs in distant places forced wives and children to enter charitable institutions. Deportations from almshouses were arranged within this gendered structure of poverty and dependency in nineteenth-century America. In many ways, therefore, the history of deportation is especially a story of immigrant women and their children.[6]

Nineteenth-century nativism against European immigrants, especially the Irish in the antebellum period, tends to be interpreted merely as a form of bigotry. While immigration scholars have extensively analyzed the ideological and cultural dimensions of anti-Irish nativism and how these led to sporadic outbreaks of mob violence and harassment against the Irish, they often failed to see how hostile sentiment escalated into concrete, state-backed action.[7] Yet this anti-Irish nativism had concrete and enduring impacts. In New York and Massachusetts, anti-Irish nativism was grafted onto existing poor laws, giving rise to a series of new immigration laws that physically removed foreigners and their children from the United States. The Know-Nothing movement in the 1850s, the radical anti-Catholic and anti-immigrant political movement, represented the pinnacle of nativism in antebellum America, but state officials retained their determination to expel foreign paupers after the demise of Know-Nothingism.[8] Immigration policies in New York and Massachusetts even expanded during the Civil War and Reconstruction, and these state measures exercised a seminal influence on federal exclusion and deportation laws. Nativism against the Irish in nineteenth-century New York and Massachusetts was more than just a set of hostile sentiments. It left tangible consequences at the level of immigration law and policy that had profound and long-lasting effects on the lives of foreigners from many parts of the world in the United States.

This history forces a reconsideration of the origins of immigration control in the United States. Discussions of immigration regulation in the United States have long rested on what legal scholar Gerald Neuman calls an "open borders myth," the assertion that "the borders of the United States were legally open until the enactment of federal immigration legislation in the 1870s and 1880s."[9] Historians have conventionally identified as the foundation of American immigration control two federal laws that emerged in the late nineteenth century largely as a result of racism against Chinese immigrants to the West Coast, especially California. These were the Page Act of 1875, which prohibited the entry of convicted criminals, Asian laborers brought involuntarily, and women imported for prostitution (a provision designed chiefly against Chinese women); and the Chinese Exclusion Act of 1882.[10] The latter can be regarded as class legislation for its focus on laborers, but anti-Asian racism indisputably stood at the core of federal Chinese exclusion. The sentiment underlying Chinese exclusion, its advocates in Congress manifested, was that "the Caucasian race of California," while having no "objection to European immigration," could not tolerate "people possessing the worst elements of civilized society" from China. "The Chinese race and the American citizen," as anti-Chinese congressmen asserted, "are in a state of antagonism."[11] In the matter of European immigration and its relation to government control, attention has usually been focused on the federally operated Ellis Island landing station, which did not open until 1892.[12]

The policies of New York and Massachusetts, however, show that American borders were never really open and immigration control functioned actively on the East Coast at the state level with Europeans as the targets, long before federal Chinese exclusion and before Ellis Island. *Expelling the Poor* places the Irish squarely in the discussion of the origins of American immigration control in a novel way. While anti-Asian racism is critical in the nation's immigration history, the origins of immigration control lay in economic and cultural nativism against the Irish in Atlantic seaboard states. Further, integrating state-level dimensions into the historical narrative of American immigration policy exposes aspects of this history that cannot be seen solely at the federal level.

The state-level control that developed in response to Irish immigration enables federal Chinese exclusion to be understood in a new light. One of this study's objectives is to situate Chinese exclusion in a broader history of American immigration policy that includes earlier state legislation. California's ultimately unsuccessful effort to check Chinese immigration in the 1850s demonstrates how opponents of Chinese immigration regarded policies for regulating destitute Europeans' admission in New York and Massachusetts as precedents for immigration control and consciously mentioned them as a rationale for their own policies against the Chinese. In 1852, anti-Chinese California Governor John Bigler justified the banning of Asians by referring to the fact that the Atlantic seaboard states had already exercised some forms of regulation and that the United States Supreme Court had endorsed these states' right to exclude any person whom the state deemed "dangerous or injurious to the interests and welfare of its citizens."[13] In the late 1870s, in support of federal policy for suspending Chinese immigration, one restrictionist brought up Atlantic seaboard states' ongoing campaign to nationalize state passenger policy and claimed that Chinese exclusion was "of the same class, in principle, with this general legislation sought by New York."[14] Atlantic seaboard states' policies and federal Chinese exclusion were therefore not separate developments but constituted a single story of immigration control in the United States.

The conventional focus on federal immigration law does not mean that scholars have entirely neglected prior state-level control. Previous generations of historians and some recent immigration scholars have explored colonial and state legislation that restricted the entry of people on the grounds of poverty, contagious diseases, criminal records, and race, as well as various laws that can be regarded as antecedents for deportation law, such as the fugitive slave laws that provided for the forcible return of runaway slaves to their masters.[15] These works provide crucial insights into local and state policies for the admission and removal of people before the age of federal control. Yet many of these studies limit their analysis to some representative state laws without explaining the evolution of policy over time. Consequently, the development of state control before the 1880s and, more critically, the relationship between state policies and later federal regulations remain unclear. Also, their primary focus often lies on legal doctrines and theories of immigration policy, rather than on how officials enforced those laws on a quotidian basis and how the enforcement affected the lives of the men and women who fell into the clutches of the state and its agents. It was one thing for a state to pass a law or keep it on its statute books, but quite another for that state to implement the law. Louisiana, for example, had a law restricting the landing of passengers unable to support themselves. But the state rarely implemented this provision, given its overriding interest in securing white settlers in order to maintain whites' racial dominance over blacks. Louisiana therefore continued to admit destitute European immigrants who would surely have been excluded at northern ports.

Expelling the Poor pays particular attention to the law's practical implementation, highlighting the intersection of law, nativist sentiment, and human experience. Its analysis of law enforcement suggests that the expansion of state officials' legal authority over immigration control fostered coercive treatment of destitute immigrants, including their illegal removal. A closer look at nativist officials' execution of deportation also opens a window into the meaning of American citizenship in the nineteenth century, especially in the period before the Civil War.[16] Nativists in antebellum Massachusetts, in their treatment of Irish American pauper citizens, overrode certain rights and liberties later taken for granted in the operation of state immigration law. Prior to the ratification of the Fourteenth Amendment in 1868, American citizenship was fragile and relatively insignificant as a marker of people's liberties, and its attendant rights remained inchoate. In the mid-nineteenth century, moreover, nativism was so powerful that citizenship did not provide an effective check on nativist officials' aggressive action against citizens of Irish descent. Massachusetts law made noncitizenship the criterion for overseas deportability. In reality, state officials in the 1850s made no such distinction in their view of Irish American paupers, whose dependency seemed to undermine republican society regardless of which side of the Atlantic they were born on. They therefore had little hesitation in deporting even Irish American citizens.

A transnational approach adds an important layer to this study's analytical and methodological originality. Scholarship on American nativism has taken a decidedly domestic approach that focuses on Americans, governments, and foreigners within the United States. Likewise, historians of American immigration policy often artificially separate the American segment of a broader migratory route, beginning their analysis with the arrival of migrants and ending it with their deportation from the United States.[17] Yet expelled people's lives as migrants obviously did not cease at the point of expulsion; they endured a return journey to their country of origin and perhaps even further internal migration within that country when they returned.[18] In order to illuminate the full panorama of deportees' complex migration paths, this study trails actual people as they moved not only from Ireland to the United States through Britain and Canada but also back again to Europe, thereby exposing a lesser-known stream in nineteenth-century global migration from the United States to Ireland. By following this circular migration, this book incorporates a transnational framework into its narrative. *Expelling the Poor* takes the passage from Ireland as the starting point in the migration process, but also considers the fate of the deportees after they were shipped back to Europe. Between these two stages of migration—departure and return—the immigrants encountered American nativism and confronted state power as they went through the process of deportation. Situating Irish migrants at the center of the story, this book as a whole encompasses the history of American deportation law at multiple levels— local, state, national, and transnational.[19]

The experiences of deported paupers in Britain and Ireland uncover how American immigration policy functioned in a transatlantic context. After all, Massachusetts deported masses of Irish paupers to Liverpool. At the same time, the British government enforced its own policy for the compulsory removal of these Irish paupers from Britain to Ireland. Workhouse officials in Ireland, meanwhile, insisted that these paupers did not belong to their community and even proposed sending the deportees back to the United States. Irish paupers were therefore subjected to expulsion not only in the United States but also in Britain, and treated as unwanted strangers in every place they reached in their migration process, including Ireland. The postdeportation story also displays the transnational influence of the concept of the "undeserving" poor. Immersed in the ethos of nineteenth-century industrialization that demonized the transient poor who allegedly refused to participate in production due to their laziness and moral failing, American, British, and Irish officials placed Irish migrant paupers into a shared category of undeserving poor. The officials' view of Irish migrant paupers as the undeserving poor facilitated their banishment from the United States and Britain and their social marginalization in Ireland. The ways the laws of settlement and removal shaped the fate of Irish deportees in Britain and Ireland, as well as in the United States, demonstrate that American deportation policy operated as part of a broader legal culture of excluding nonproducing members from societies in the north Atlantic world.

At the heart of this transnational social and legal history lies an integrated analysis of diverse archival materials collected in the United States, Canada, the United Kingdom, and Ireland. Legal documents, legislative reports, and immigration officials' annual reports are probed for the legal and administrative aspects of state-level immigration control and factual information about state policies. Personal and published writings by opponents of immigration, their petitions to governments, political cartoons, and the records of private charitable organizations are the basis for examination of the relationship between anti-Irish sentiment, economic ideals, and immigration law. Ethnic newspapers and migrant letters convey immigrants' views of widespread nativist sentiment and their strategies to protect themselves from state deportation law. Some scenes of exclusion and deportation are reconstructed from fragmentary pieces of information from American passenger records, British consular records, and the admission registers and inmate reports of charitable institutions in the United States, Britain, and Ireland, as well as American, Canadian, British, and Irish newspaper reports on the departure and arrival of migrants. The records of Irish estates that sent many destitute Irish tenants to North America provide details of the social profiles and migration histories of Irish paupers who became deportees in the United States. Parliamentary papers and the minutes of workhouse officials in Britain and Ireland elucidate postdeportation episodes and the transnational legal culture of pauper regulation.

Expelling the Poor traces transatlantic Irish migration and the social and legal history of state-level immigration control in the United States over the course of the nineteenth century. The narrative starts by observing Ireland's impoverishment during the first half of the nineteenth century and the exodus of the poor Catholic Irish during the potato famine in the 1840s. While the high level of poverty generally characterized Irish famine immigrants, Americans were shocked by the arrival of destitute tenants and paupers who emigrated to British North America and the United States with financial assistance from local landlords and Irish workhouses—the poorest of the poor, who could not otherwise leave Ireland. Economic concerns about the poverty of these Irish immigrants, as chapters 2 through 5 demonstrate, determined the development of state immigration policy to the 1870s. In New York and Massachusetts, where passenger control had been conducted at the local level since the eighteenth century, the influx of famine-stricken Irish immigrants during the 1840s led to the introduction of state-led passenger control. For the next three decades, the two states developed the most advanced and sustainable systems of state-level immigration control in the United States. Despite their different trajectories, New York and Massachusetts engaged in the same larger process of developing mechanisms of state-level immigration control. From this process the move toward federal regulation emerged. Chapter 6 completes the transatlantic circle by exploring the process of deportation from the United States and its aftermath in Europe. Deportees' experience in Britain and Ireland reveals that while American nativism provided the driving force for the deportation of Irish paupers to Europe, the policy unfolded within a wider system of pauper restriction and forcible removal that transcended national boundaries. The final chapter examines the critical moment when state immigration laws developed into national policy, highlighting the influence on later federal immigration policy of New York and Massachusetts officials' participation in the administration of the Immigration Act of 1882.

Exclusion and deportation laws in Atlantic seaboard states intersected with a number of social, ideological, and legal issues of fundamental importance in nineteenth-century America. They included ethnic prejudice and cultural intolerance, social welfare and political economy, the notion of the "deserving" and "undeserving" poor, citizenship and civil liberties, American state development, and the relationship between states and the federal government. Most importantly, the evolution of state immigration policy derived its ideological justification from the sanctity of freedom based on economic self-sufficiency and the fear of dependency—beliefs that shaped Americans' conception of their nation as a republic of independent, industrious workers and had a far-reaching impact on major debates of the time, including the debate over slavery. The story that follows is therefore fundamentally about nineteenth-century Americans' vision of the nation and their effort to realize that vision by selecting which immigrants would be admitted and allowed to stay. New York and Massachusetts led the charge to exclude and deport those who were deemed particularly unsuited for American society, such as Irish paupers.

Contemporary American immigration policy is characterized by militant border control; the zealous, and often wrongful, enforcement of deportation law and resultant hardship on immigrants and their families; the aggressive and disrespectful attitude of Immigration and Customs Enforcement agents toward deportable foreigners; and the harsh system of immigrant detention, as well as tension between federal authority and state governments over immigration.[20] State-level immigration control in nineteenth-century New York and Massachusetts prefigured the current problems of American immigration policy. Indeed, the experience of poor Irish immigrants, including heartbreaking cases of forcible expulsion and tragic aftermaths of deportation in Europe, foreshadowed to a remarkable extent those of other European, Asian, and Latin American immigrants in later periods.

In 1849, commenting on an "agitated national topic" concerning the "foreign poor," Herman Melville wrote in his semiautobiographical novel *Redburn* that "if they can get here, they have God's right to come; though they bring all Ireland and her miseries with them."[21] Melville's view on immigration proved to be far too progressive. In the reality of nineteenth-century America, "God's right to come" had to be constrained by man-made policy. By the 1890s, the regulatory approach to immigration—admission control at the border and removal after entry—that New York and Massachusetts had developed over the previous century became normative in the American reception of newcomers. This book uncovers the origins of these practices, which laid the groundwork for subsequent federal control and enormously affect the lives of immigrants to the United States today.

CHAPTER 1

⌀⌀

Shovelling Out

Ireland and the Emigration of the Poor

Almost a decade after the onset of the potato disease that led to the so-called Great Famine in Ireland, Irish workhouses in the mid-1850s still remained busy dealing with local poverty and destitution. The destruction of the potato crop and the government's inadequate reaction to it had brought about mass starvation and death. A sailor who delivered a cargo of food to a village in County Cork during the famine described what he had witnessed: "The people build themselves up into their cabins so that they may die together with their children and not be seen by passers-by. Fever, dysentery and starvation stare at you in the face everywhere."[1] Faced with the gloomy prospect of death, desperate Irish men and women, including those who had been evicted by landlords due to their inability to pay rent, poured into local workhouses in search of immediate food and shelter. Workhouses by no means offered comfortable solutions to malnutrition and destitution. Severe overcrowding and poor ventilation facilitated the spread of diseases among inmates and kept the mortality rate at these institutions high. Nevertheless, people found workhouses a better option than helplessly waiting for a miserable death at home or on the street.

Still better than staying at workhouses as paupers for an indefinite period of time, many inmates concluded, was to emigrate and build a new life abroad. Workhouse officials had their own reasons to support the idea of overseas emigration—the reduction of destitution in their districts and the long-term cost of maintaining paupers. Thus workhouses in Ireland sponsored the emigration of their inmates to British North America and the United States throughout the famine decade. The Cork workhouse sent a group of one hundred paupers to Quebec on the *Satellite* in June 1854. A year later, the workhouse spent £3 to help four inmates go to Boston. In the spring of 1855, County Galway's workhouse supported the emigration of three pauper children named Barry to New York City via Liverpool.[2] These are just a few examples from numerous cases of the assisted emigration of paupers from famine Ireland. Between 1846 and 1855, Irish workhouses aided about 20,000 persons to emigrate. Besides the workhouses, local landlords also paid the passage for their destitute tenants, assisting 50,000 to 100,000 persons to cross the Atlantic. These assisted paupers comprised a segment of the 1.8 million Irish who left Ireland for North America during that period.[3]

This chapter analyzes the people who emigrated from Ireland to North America in the first half of the nineteenth century, with a focus on their material conditions. Until the early nineteenth century Irish emigrants chiefly consisted of Protestants, especially Presbyterians. By the 1830s Catholics, who were markedly poorer than their Protestant predecessors, had become the dominant group among Irish emigrants. The chapter examines in depth how the practice of assisted emigration allowed extremely indigent tenants and paupers, who could not otherwise afford the trip, to leave Ireland during the famine. In the mid-nineteenth century, a growing number of Irish emigrants to North America either appeared outstandingly wretched or were unable to support themselves without becoming public charges in the new world. The poverty of the Catholic Irish, along with their religious faith, stimulated anti-Irish nativism and played a critical role in the development of immigration control policy. This marked the initial phase in the circular migration of those who would eventually be deported from the United States to Ireland under American immigration policy.

An examination of the character of Irish migrants whom antebellum Americans encountered must start with the transformation of Ireland in the early nineteenth century and the related changes in the composition of Irish migration in the 1830s. Irish migration to North America dated back to the seventeenth century. The first wave of what could be called a mass migration brought 50,000 to 100,000 people, three-quarters of whom were Catholic, to the American colonies. The stream of emigration continued in the eighteenth century, followed by 100,000 Catholics, mostly young, single male soldiers, sailors, convicts, and indentured servants. In addition to voluntary migrants, at least 10,000 convicted Irish vagrants and criminals were deported to America between 1700 and 1775. Yet the major emigrants from Ireland in the eighteenth century were as many as 250,000 Protestants, about 70 percent of whom were Presbyterians from Ulster, a northern province of Ireland, descended from Scottish settlers. In pursuit of economic mobility and greater religious freedom from the intolerant Anglican Church, Ulster Presbyterians left Ireland for the new world in families and congregations. New England, especially Massachusetts, became the first place in America that these Ulster migrants settled.[4]

The arrival of Ulster Presbyterians in Massachusetts created immediate friction with their Puritan predecessors of English origin. Besides religious differences, the poverty of Irish migrants irritated the Puritans, who detested them for being "unclean, unwholesome, and disgusting." Noting that "great numbers of Persons have lately bin Transported from Ireland into this Province," Boston authorities complained in 1723 that too many of them would "become a Town charge." At one point in the eighteenth century, the Irish accounted for two-thirds of the inmate population of the almshouse in Boston. The Puritans also resented the perceived inclination of the Irish to drunkenness and violence, attaching to Ulster Presbyterians the label "Wild Irish," a derogatory term that would continue to be applied to later migrants. The Puritans' animosity to the Irish was sometimes expressed in the form of mob action. In July 1729, for example, a group of Bostonians caused a loud disturbance in trying to prevent the landing of Irish migrants, making the town authority call for the police force to restore order.[5]

The hostile environment of Puritan Massachusetts drove the Presbyterian Irish to leave the region and seek settlement elsewhere. While some of them migrated to other parts of New England, the majority settled principally in Pennsylvania and the Carolina and Georgia backcountry. No more than 10 percent of the Irish from Ulster remained in New England. The Presbyterian Irish in the eighteenth century were thus subject to intense hatred from their Puritan neighbors, but their economic and social conditions eventually improved. Although earlier Ulster migrants included indentured servants and poor laborers, the majority of them were farmers, artisans, and petty professionals such as physicians by the turn of the nineteenth century, forming an urban elite class in America. Despite this upward mobility, the experience of the Presbyterian Irish in eighteenth-century Massachusetts illustrates how unfriendly the region was to the Irish from early on and prefigured the outbreak of more drastic anti-Irish movements in later periods.[6]

The traits of eighteenth-century Irish migrants in America, such as Protestant faith and upwardly mobile status, gradually but significantly changed in the first few decades of the following century. The population of Ireland grew substantially at the turn of the nineteenth century, presumably owing to early marriages and high marital fertility. Between 1788 and 1841 Ireland's population almost doubled, rising from 4 million to 8.1 million. Protestants contributed to the population growth, but for a country whose inhabitants were three-quarters Catholic, this demographic explosion created a vast pool of potential Catholic migrants.[7]

Population growth in itself would not have been a problem were it not for an ongoing crisis in the Irish land system. Since the sixteenth century, Catholic Ireland had been under the colonial rule of Protestant Britain. The Catholic Irish owned only 5 percent of Irish land by 1750. In the early nineteenth century, the land was owned by British landholders and the Crown, while there were a small number of wealthy Catholic Irish landlords. The vast majority of the Irish rented the land as tenants. It was common for wealthier tenants who could produce surplus crops and raise livestock for commercial sale to sublet the land they rented to smaller farmers or hired landless laborers who earned daily wages through manual work. By 1841 landless laborers comprised the largest portion (56 percent) of Ireland's rural population. Even though small farmers enjoyed a higher economic standing than landless laborers, their lives were also precarious, firmly bound to the obligations for rent, tithes, and taxes.[8]

In multistratified agrarian Irish society, economic fluctuations in the early nineteenth century prompted a large-scale emigration of rural Catholics. Between 1750 and 1814, British demand for food and textiles for domestic consumption boosted the Irish economy. The process of commercialization, however, made the Irish population vulnerable to instabilities in the international economy. In 1815, at the end of the Napoleonic Wars, crop prices in Ireland, which had gone up during the war, plummeted to almost half the wartime prices. Until then, landlords had been promoting tillage to produce crops for sale, which provided steady employment for laborers, but they switched their principal business from tillage to grazing, reducing the land for crop production and enclosing common land. This change in landlords' policy resulted in higher rents and the eviction of tenants, making the precarious lives of smallholders and landless laborers even more insecure. Scottish traveler Henry D. Inglis, who visited Ireland in the 1830s, noted that "a visible deterioration has taken place in the condition of the laboring classes and of the small farmers." Widespread economic displacement, unemployment, and impoverishment led rural Catholics to emigrate in search of a better life.[9]

The departure of Catholics transformed Irish migration to North
America. In the period between 1783 and 1815 (from the end of the
American Revolutionary War to the end of the Napoleonic Wars), 100,000
to 150,000 people migrated from Ireland to North America, most of them
Protestants. Yet the proportion of Catholics expanded steadily, and by the
1830s it surpassed that of Protestants. Protestant farmers and artisans
remained dominant among migrants from Ulster, but Catholics' representation increased, especially in impoverished and overpopulated counties
such as Tyrone, Monaghan, and Cavan. In the other provinces of Ireland—
Leinster, Connacht, and Munster—four-fifths of the migrants between
1827 and 1837 were Catholics. During the three decades after 1815,
between 800,000 and one million Irish people left for North America,
but the proportion of Protestants to the entire migrant population was
reduced to 10 percent by 1840.[10]

The material conditions of nineteenth-century Catholic migrants were
considerably worse than those of eighteenth-century Presbyterians.
Historians agree that the early nineteenth-century Irish were poorer than
people in other parts of Europe and becoming poorer toward midcentury.
Gustave de Beaumont, a French traveler who visited Ireland in the 1830s,
remarked: "Irish poverty has a special and exceptional character, which
renders its definition difficult, because it can be compared with no other
indigence. Irish misery forms a type by itself, of which neither the model
nor the imitation can be found anywhere else." He also noted the ubiquity
of poverty in Ireland: "In all countries, more or less, paupers may be discovered; but an entire nation of paupers is what was never seen until it
was shown in Ireland." Another contemporary observer described Ireland
as "the very empire of mendicity."[11]

Catholic Irish migrants of the 1830s were undoubtedly poor, but the
level of their poverty should be examined with caution. The fact was that
the poorest of the Irish did not leave the country in the prefamine years.
Such people simply could not afford to purchase a ticket for the passage to
cross the Atlantic. Those who left for North America were at least financially capable of arranging their trip either with their own savings or
with the assistance of their families or friends who had emigrated earlier.
People at the very bottom of the economic structure had no choice but to
remain. By revealing the relatively decent economic status of most of the
migrants in the early 1840s, historian Kerby Miller argues that "many
emigrants only *appeared* destitute after long ocean voyages."[12]

At the same time, the range of poverty within Ireland might have had
little meaning for Americans, and the destitute appearance of many newcomers provided sufficient soil for the growth of anti-Irish sentiment in

the United States. Philip Hone, a former mayor of New York City, wrote in his diary in 1836 that these immigrants "increase our taxes, eat our bread, and encumber our streets" and that "not one in twenty is competent to keep himself."[13] Even though the prefamine Catholic migrants did not come from the poorest class, their economic standing was already below the American living standard, and they looked wretched enough to convince Americans that many Irish migrants were beggars and paupers abusing American poor relief and threatening the public health of American society.

A glance at the migration process allows for a better understanding of Americans' perceptions of migrants' material conditions. Most ships for the transatlantic passage in the early nineteenth century were designed to carry commodities rather than human passengers. Some companies began to run ships devoted to the passenger trade in the 1830s, but these vessels were far from adequate to accommodate human beings. Individual passengers were allotted only a limited amount of space below deck. Shippers often packed in as many passengers as possible by deceiving port officials and evading passenger regulations that set limits on the number of passengers one vessel could carry. Passengers had to endure poor ventilation in the packed steerage throughout the voyage, often suffering from contagious diseases known as "fevers," such as smallpox, dysentery, cholera, and typhus. Poorly stored food and water were unfit for human consumption. Due to suffocating congestion, sickly air, viruses, unhealthy diet, and frequent storms, the passengers emerged mentally demoralized and physically weakened by the time their ship reached the North American shore.[14] The transatlantic voyage thus contributed to the deteriorating appearance of migrants, buttressing Americans' bias against the poverty of the Irish.

The foreign observer who dubbed Ireland in the 1830s "the very empire of mendicity" would find the title even more appropriate for the country in the following decade. The living standard of the Irish rural poor continued to decline in the 1840s. Visitors to Ireland then hardly failed to notice the prevalence of "decay, rags, beggary, and want."[15] Rural impoverishment was plainly reflected in Irish people's diet. By the mid-1840s, the Irish had become increasingly dependent on a single crop, the potato. Already in 1835 a Scottish traveler noted from Westport, County Mayo that "potatoes were raised for the family consumption; grain, to pay the rent."[16] According to one study, at least 1.5 million people were totally dependent on the potato, and 3.5 million were nearly so, out of the 8 million population of the early 1840s.[17] Under these circumstances, any ecological change that would disrupt the potato supply would lead to demographic catastrophe. The realization of this frightening scenario in the middle of the decade not only devastated the Irish population but also triggered the emigration of the Catholic Irish on an unprecedented scale, which would fundamentally change the demography of the United States.

In the fall of 1845, a potato blight that modern scholars believe originated in Peru and reached Europe through the United States hit Ireland. The disease, biologically named *phytophthora infestans*, quickly engulfed Ireland through airborne spores. The potato crop had occasionally failed in Ireland before 1845 on a local basis, at least eight times in the 1830s and three times in the 1840s, but the 1845 potato blight was unrivaled in its duration and scale of devastation. In 1846 nearly the entire potato crop was ruined, and the year 1847, known as "Black '47," was the worst moment of the famine period, with the harvest dropping to as low as 10 percent of the prefamine level. In the decade between 1846 and 1855, 1.1 to 1.5 million people in Ireland perished because of starvation and various famine-related diseases.[18]

Ireland's subordinate status to Britain greatly affected the impact of the famine on Irish people. Being a colony of the United Kingdom, Ireland never received as much sympathy from the authorities in London as people in Britain could expect in a similar situation. The British government offered some relief measures, such as a supply of imported Indian corn and public work projects, to let the poor purchase food. These measures, however, were far from sufficient and were ultimately impeded by the prejudiced conviction of the British that the "lazy" Irish should recover from hunger and destitution that were supposedly brought about by their moral degeneration. In 1847 Parliament passed the Poor Law Extension Act, which imposed the responsibility for famine relief upon the Irish themselves. The act required local workhouses in Ireland to levy a tax on holders of property equivalent to £4 or more, in order to provide the needy with relief. The tax heavily burdened smallholders, who were already living on the edge, often compelling them to give up their land and emigrate. The law also propelled landlords to aggressively evict impoverished tenants, as it required the landlords to pay taxes on behalf of these tenants exempted from the tax obligation. A section in the poor law act known as the Gregory Clause, which prohibited any tenant holding more than a quarter-acre of land from receiving public poor relief, also virtually forced Irish people to abandon their land. Many chose emigration over admission into workhouses as paupers. Others retained their holdings but starved to death. John Mitchel, an anti-British nationalist leader, proclaimed from exile in the United States in 1861: "The Almighty, indeed, sent the potato blight, but the English created the famine."[19]

Numerous accounts of poverty, destitution, and eviction in famine-stricken Ireland appeared in newspapers, travelers' journals, and British official reports. When English philanthropist James H. Tuke visited Mayo, one of the most devastated counties, in the fall of 1847, he witnessed "a crowd of almost naked perishing creatures" congregating on the streets "in a state of 'perfect destitution.'" "'Feed us or we die,' seems written on the countenances of every one," wrote Tuke. Confessing that he had seen the residence of a "noble Red Man" and the "negro quarter" in North America, Tuke remarked that "never have I seen misery so intense or *physical* degradation so complete," as among the people in Mayo.[20]

Descriptions of the famine reached the United States in various forms. In addition to the reports produced in Ireland and Britain, some Americans visited Ireland and provided their own accounts. Abolitionist Frederick Douglass, who was visiting Dublin in 1846, wrote to his colleague William Lloyd Garrison about the "painful exhibitions of human misery": "The streets were almost literally alive with beggars, displaying the greatest wretchedness—some of them mere stumps of men, without feet, without legs, without hands, without arms." Barefooted and bareheaded women whom Douglass saw were "only covered by rags which seemed to be held together by the very dirt and filth with which they were covered." At an Irish hut, he could find all of "human misery, ignorance, degradation, filth and wretchedness." The condition of the Irish people compelled this radical abolitionist to admit that they were "in much the same degradation as the American slaves."[21] Elihu Burritt, a philanthropist from New England, recounted the scene of emigrants' departure from Cork for Liverpool. Hundreds of "the famished laborers of Ireland" were on the dock, and "men gaunt, and clad almost in rags, embraced each other's necks."[22] Catholic priests in Ireland asked Boston Archbishop John Fitzpatrick to raise relief funds and provisions to help the dying rural population through Boston newspapers.[23]

The overwhelming magnitude of destitution, starvation, and death resulted in the exodus of people from Ireland. Out of the prefamine 8.5 million population, 2.1 million people left Ireland while more than 1 million died between 1846 and 1855, reducing the population to two-thirds of its prefamine level. Of the 2.1 million emigrants, 1.5 million went to the United States and 340,000 left for British North America. Between 200,000 and 300,000 people who belonged to the poorest class among the emigrants went to the nearest place from Ireland, Britain, and several thousands more departed for Australia and New Zealand. Catholic predominance continued through the famine period. Protestants, who made up a quarter of Ireland's population, accounted for only 10 percent of the emigrants. Not surprisingly, famine migrants were poorer and less skilled than their predecessors. The percentage of laborers among Irish migrants arriving in New York had already expanded from 60 percent in 1836 to 75 percent in 1846. Between 1851 and 1855, the proportion of laborers and servants remained 80 to 90 percent.[24]

As in the prefamine period, the very poorest could not afford the passage and did not leave, and the migrants included better-off farmers. But once again, this spectrum of Irish poverty mattered little in North America, where all the Irish migrants seemed desperately poor. The *Edinburgh Review* in January 1848 captured this gap between the migrants' economic standing within Ireland and their condition on the other side of the ocean. The complaint in Ireland, the periodical pointed out, was that those who emigrated "belonged to the best and most substantial class of the agricultural population," and they actually were smallholders "above the level of the prevailing destitution" who could finance their self-removal from Ireland. The complaint in Canada, however, was "that those who came were the helpless and destitute."[25] In the United States the poverty of the famine Irish was often equated to that of African Americans, who were forced into the poorest and most degraded condition in northern society. Famine migrants might have been less poor than the poorest in Ireland, but as they entered the United States, their relative financial capability within Ireland ceased to carry any meaning under the American economic structure. In America, these migrants constituted the poorest class in society.

For the majority of the famine migrants, their journey started with going to one of the port cities in Ireland, such as Dublin, Galway, Cork, Waterford, Londonderry, or Belfast, where they would embark on a passage either to Liverpool or direct to North America. The internal migration could be as uncomfortable and demoralizing as a sea voyage. During the famine, when migrants had to camp on the grassy verges enclosed by stone walls on each side of the road, they often found casual burials and decaying corpses accompanied by the smell of the putrefying potatoes, as well as starving stragglers all around. Mud, sharp stones, dampness, wet winds, and ground frosts also afflicted the travelers, whose outfits were hardly adequate for such conditions.[26]

Upon reaching an Irish port, most famine migrants took a short passage to Liverpool either by steamships or smaller conveyers such as fishing boats. Earlier in the century, Irish ports functioned as the primary places of embarkation for the transatlantic voyage. Emigrants also usually headed for British North America rather than the United States, because of the British government's taxation on American-bound ships, which made American routes more expensive than those to Canada. As the Liverpool–New York line emerged as a safer and faster route than the one between Ireland and Canada, however, migrants increasingly departed for North America from Liverpool instead of Irish ports. During the famine decade, Liverpool sent four to five times more migrants to North America than all Irish ports combined.[27] Though short in distance, the journey from Ireland to Liverpool could be hazardous and physically too demanding for passengers who had already been weakened by starvation and malnutrition. Shippers placed priority on baggage and livestock for British importation, and they often packed passengers on the deck without shelter. Seasickness afflicted them on almost every voyage, and during the stormy weather they were exposed to cold seawater and vomit. One priest who travelled on a Liverpool-bound packet testified that "we were sea-sick before we were quite out of sight of Ireland."[28]

Little improved upon arrival in Liverpool. From the moment of their arrival, migrants had to protect themselves from the vicious and unhealthy environments of the Merseyside. Despite the shipping companies' advertisements guaranteeing a prompt departure for North America,

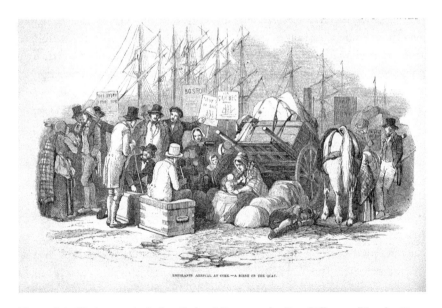

Figure 1.1: "Emigrants Arrival at Cork—A Scene on the Quay," *Illustrated London News*, May 10, 1851. The Liverpool–New York line was the major route for Irish migrants to North America during the famine, but they also embarked on the transatlantic voyage directly from Irish port cities such as Cork.
Courtesy of Butler Library, Columbia University in the City of New York.

migrants often had to spend weeks waiting for their ship. More than the psychological stress of not being able to embark, human vice plagued the helpless migrants. They were subject to wicked tricks and frauds by those who sought to prey upon the naïve travelers. Swindlers, known as "runners," approached poor migrants to deceive them with valueless expired or fake passage tickets and trick them into going to the boarding houses of predatory landlords who exploited the migrants with arbitrary rates.[29] An Irish man named Patrick Carley, for example, handed over his valuable £2.10s to the men he ran into on the streets of Liverpool under the false promise that with the payment, he could take a passage to the United States on the *Siddone*. The men told Carley that £2.10s was a bargain price and that Carley would have to take care of the livestock on the vessel during the voyage. Pleased that he won a good deal that would bring him to America at a minimum cost, Carley went to the quay, only to find that the men's arrangement, including the livestock supervision, was a complete fiction.[30]

Even if they managed to distance themselves from the runners, the migrants still had to endure overcrowded and foul-smelling slums around the waterfront while waiting for their ship. Those weakened by starvation and the initial voyage easily caught contagious diseases and perished. Irish destitution and beggary were ever-present on the streets and docks of Liverpool. American writer Herman Melville, who himself had visited Liverpool as a cabin boy of a packet ship, wrote about seemingly ubiquitous Irish beggardom on the streets of Liverpool: "In these haunts, beggary went on before me wherever I walked, and dogged me unceasingly at the heels. Poverty, poverty, poverty, in almost endless vistas; and want and woe staggered arm in arm along these miserable streets."[31] The scene of poverty in Liverpool shocked Nathaniel Hawthorne, American consul in the city, who remarked that "the people [around the docks] were as numerous as maggots in cheese; you behold them, disgusting, and all moving about, as when you raise a plank or log that has long lain on the ground, and find many vivacious bugs and insects beneath it."[32]

The Atlantic crossing had been perilous enough in the prefamine period, but conditions worsened considerably during the famine. The overcrowded steerage was unventilated and unsanitary, leading to outbreaks of fever. The London *Times* described one steerage quarter as "a noisome dungeon, airless and lightless."[33] The mortality rate among the famine passengers could be extremely high. In 1847, the worst year of the famine, 32 percent of 97,000 passengers heading for British North America died either during the transatlantic voyage or shortly after their arrival, while the rate for US-bound passengers was 9 percent. Overall,

20 percent of all the emigrants who left Ireland for North America in that year perished on board ship or soon after disembarkation. Because of the horrifying mortality rates, the ships transporting famine passengers became known as "coffin ships." In February 1847, the United States government sponsored a federal Passenger Act to guarantee fourteen square feet of clear deck space per passenger out of a concern for passenger welfare. This reduced the number of passengers a single vessel could carry at one time, which raised the price of the fare to the United States. As a result, poorer, usually more fragile migrants chose to take the cheaper Canadian passage. In Quebec, ships with the starving and sickened Irish poured into a quarantine station located on the island of Grosse Isle on the St. Lawrence River. Weaker passengers died in the steerage before the ship's landing. Historians estimate that at least 12,000 Irish migrants perished on Grosse Isle in 1847.[34]

Mortality rates dropped sharply after 1847, but Irish migrants continued to bear poverty and disease throughout the famine decade. Comparing the year 1849 with 1847 and 1848, a Boston port official remarked, "The condition of passengers, so far as relates to their health . . . has been better than the two preceding years, but their poverty is full up to the *usual standard*."[35] In 1851, a London periodical concluded that "the Atlantic is 'bridged over' for Irish paupers, or, at any rate, it will be soon."[36] Americans horrified and disgusted by the poverty of arriving Irish passengers routinely used adjectives such as "ragged" and "naked" to describe them. Historian Robert Scally points out that these terms were adopted to refer to extreme cases, but also "often to those clothed merely as they had always been, shoeless and bareheaded."[37] This reinforces the view that the famine migrants, though diverse in their economic standing, looked uniformly poor to American eyes.

Such were the experiences of Irish migrants in the first half of the nineteenth century. From leaving their homes to landing at North American ports, every phase of journey could have an adverse effect on the appearance and health of migrants. Even if they survived the entire process, their financial and physical conditions were often too delicate to proceed farther from the port. The debilitated migrants frequently entered local almshouses or lunatic asylums soon after their arrival. Among those migrants were many future deportees from Massachusetts. Bridget Flynn, for example, landed in Boston on the *Madore* in 1848. As an indication of her fragile physical state, she was recorded to have been "at Hospital of Ireland" for two years before her emigration. Upon landing in Boston she entered an almshouse at Deer Island in Boston harbor, where she spent three years. Flynn later became an inmate at a public almshouse in Bridgewater, Massachusetts, from which state officials deported her to Ireland on April 13, 1855.[38] The massive influx of the destitute Irish during the famine decade also led New Yorkers to repeatedly call for the introduction of state laws to "ship back at any time any and all immigrants to the country from whence they came" if they were paupers.[39] The emergence of state-level immigration control on the Atlantic seaboard of the United States in the late 1840s was a direct response to Irish famine migration.

Although most Irish migrants in the first half of the nineteenth century did not come from the poorest class, the migrants did include the poorest of the poor. Certain extremely impoverished tenants and paupers who would not be otherwise able to leave Ireland emigrated to North America with financial and material assistance from the British government, landlords, and local workhouses. This assisted emigration immensely affected the way Americans saw Irish migrants in general. The extensive newspaper coverage of assisted paupers' arrivals with an alarming tone, as well as their wretchedness that caught particular public attention, made Americans assume that their poverty represented the material condition of Irish migrants as a group or even that most migrants from Ireland had been paupers at home. Such an assumption—though incorrect— hardened the attitude toward the Irish of Americans, who believed that foreign authorities were unjustly imposing upon the United States the tremendous financial burden of supporting non–self-sufficient people. The scale of assisted emigration was in fact limited. Nevertheless, much more than the arrival of indigent migrants who managed to pay for their own passage or came to America with the support of their families, this form of migration inflamed anti-Irish nativism and advocacy for immigration restriction in Atlantic seaboard states.

Assisted emigration from Ireland to North America was practiced before impoverished Catholics became a dominant migrant group in the 1830s. When the economic depression and ensuing evictions after the conclusion of the Napoleonic Wars created a large destitute population in Ireland, the British government sought a means to dispose of the people in Ireland whom it regarded as "surplus" or "redundant." One of the solutions the government came up with was state-aided emigration to British North America of the poor who could not afford the fare. Assisted emigration was also intended to expand colonial settlements in Canada as markets for British manufactured goods. And the British hoped that it might reduce agrarian violence in Ireland. One of the most extensive assisted emigration schemes took place in 1823 and 1825, when about 2,600 destitute residents of the Blackwater region of Counties Cork and Limerick were sent to various parts of Ontario through Quebec. Between 1815 and 1826, the British government financed the emigration of 10,500 to 11,000 people from Ireland to British North America. The government continued the scheme modestly during the 1830s by providing funds to individual landlords who wished to remove insolvent tenants from their estates.[40]

The idea of assisted emigration revived as the famine produced widespread evictions and pauperism. The British government hesitated to sponsor assisted emigration due to its laissez-faire policy toward the famine and the costs, but a number of destitute tenants on properties in Ireland owned by the British monarch, known as Crown estates, received passage tickets and provisions from the government to emigrate to North America. In the Crown estates of Boughill and Irvilloughter in Galway, when tenants sent memorials to Parliament on the necessity of public works and their inability to pay rents, the Commissioners of Woods, Forests and Land Revenues of the Crown decided to send the impoverished tenants to Quebec. In June 1848, the first party of 253 emigrants left the port of Galway on the *Sea Bird*. During the passage they were provided with foodstuffs such as biscuits, beef or pork, butter, tea, and sugar. The first wave was followed by an additional 158 emigrants. In the summer of 1849, the Crown estate of Kingwilliamstown in Cork sent 119 tenants on the *Nimrod* to Liverpool, where they would embark for New York. The emigrants were selected from a list filed by the estate's Crown agent on those tenants prepared to leave the estate voluntarily and those whose compulsory removal would be necessary for the estate's "improvements." The estate sent two more batches to New York within two years, resulting in a total number of 191 assisted emigrants from Kingwilliamstown.[41]

Assisted emigration from the estate of Ballykilcline in the parish of Kilgrass in County Roscommon illustrates how the famine overwhelmed tenants' lives. During the 1830s, the tenants of Ballykilcline launched a rebellion against the Crown agents by refusing to pay rents they regarded as too high, supposedly with the help of the Molly Maguires, a secret agrarian society that violently resisted coercion against tenants. When Crown officials tried to enter the estate to evict the recalcitrant tenants, the tenants refused to leave their houses and attacked the bailiffs. The physical and moral devastation of the famine, however, deprived the strike of momentum. The tenants' rebellion was ultimately defeated by a detachment of 60 police, 25 cavalry, 30 infantry, and a stipendiary magistrate in May 1847. The evicted tenants petitioned the Commissioners of Woods for the permission to restore their possessions or "the means of emigration." The commissioners agreed to finance the emigration of the evicted tenants and others who wished to emigrate with basic provisions such as clothes, shoes, cooking utensils, and landing money. A total of 366 Ballykilcline tenants, including infants, children under the age of six, and aged dependents, embarked from Liverpool for New York in seven vessels between September 1847 and April 1848. With the exception of twenty-two persons who declined the offer for assisted emigration but would be eventually evicted, the entire tenantry left the estate, making the lands "perfectly untenanted" by May 1848.[42]

The Crown emigrants were not the only tenants who received assistance from their estate owners. Individual landlords also assisted the emigration of destitute or evicted tenants. Financing assisted emigration was never cheap, but most of the landlords came to the conclusion that sending away poor tenants who could not pay their rents would cost less than maintaining them.[43] Some tenants also sought assisted emigration to flee destitution at home. Pat Dullard, a tenant of the Prior-Wandesforde estate in County Kilkenny, for instance, petitioned in January 1842 for his family's emigration to the United States. His family was "in the utmost and extreme indigence." He had rented a cabin but his landlord evicted him, he noted, "and I know not where to go." Another tenant begged his landlord to "send me out of this miserable land to America where I hope to earn a support for my self and my distressed family."[44]

Landlord-sponsored emigration followed a procedure similar to that for assisted emigration from the Crown estates. Estate agents usually furnished emigrants with minimal clothes, food during the voyage, and some cash upon landing, though the amount and quality of provisions varied.[45] The tenants also received passenger contract tickets or vouchers. A contract ticket used in the estate of Sir Robert Gore-Booth in County Sligo specified the terms of passage, such as fare, destination, space guaranteed for a passenger, and provisions of water and food.[46] A voucher from the Shirley estate in County Monaghan to be given to the estate's passenger agent in Liverpool contained a note stating that "you will please give the party mentioned on the back hereof, credit in the Passage to America."[47] Kerby Miller estimates that landlords cleared their estates by shipping over 50,000 tenants and laborers to North America between 1846 and 1855. Gerard Moran, in his synthetic work on assisted emigration, states that the number could have been as high as 100,000.[48]

Landlords and their agents usually selected recipients of assistance out of the applicants who expressed their wish to leave. Although some self-sufficient farmers applied, landlords tended to finance the emigration of poorer laborers. Landholders held much less interest in fulfilling their better-off tenants' desire to emigrate than removing the surplus population from their estates.[49] Especially after the enactment of the poor law amendment of 1847, landlords had to pay poor rates for tenants whose holdings were valued at £4 or less, which encouraged them to clear such tenants from their estates.[50] In March 1847, an agent of Lord Palmerston's estate in Sligo compiled a list of 900 poor tenants whom the estate was supporting and recommended to Palmerston shipping all of them "on the principle of profit and economy."[51] The estate's emigrants were "the poorest class of farmer, very little better than paupers."[52] Gore-Booth also preferred to send aged tenants, widows, and orphans, since their prospects of contributing to the permanent improvement of their holdings were quite low.[53] The majority of the 1,300 emigrants from the Shirley estate in the decade up to 1852 belonged to the poorest class who possessed little or no furniture, bedding, clothing, or footwear. In May 1849, a Liverpool agent for the estate depicted a batch of the Shirley emigrants as a "ragged pack."[54]

An agent of the Marquis of Lansdowne's estate in the parish of Kenmare in County Kerry, William Steuart Trench, portrayed the situation of assisted emigration in rare detail. Kenmare was one of the areas hit hardest by the famine, and the Lansdowne tenants were among the poorest in Ireland.[55] Trench recalled the condition of Kenmare: "As the potato melted away before the eyes of the people, they looked on in dismay and terror.... Kenmare was completely paralyzed."[56] By the winter of 1849–1850 starvation had passed its peak, but pauper tenants who had lost their holdings "were dying nearly as fast of fever, dysentery, and scurvy within the walls of the workhouse," which was already overcrowded beyond its capacity.[57] When Trench failed to solve the congestion of the workhouse through public work projects, he recommended that Lansdowne "adopt an extensive system of voluntary emigration" as the only practical and effective way to reduce the large expenses the estate had to pay "unless these people died or left." Upon obtaining Lansdowne's approval, Trench announced to the tenants that he would offer free emigration to every person in the workhouse who wished to be sent to North America. After some initial skeptical hesitation among the tenants, "a rush was made to get way at once" by workhouse paupers and impoverished smallholders who gave up their holdings. Trench sent out 200 persons every week from Cork, and within a year he emptied the workhouse, shipping nearly 3,500 paupers to America through Liverpool.[58] Reporting on the emigration scheme, Trench told Lansdowne that "We have not lost one single man I should wish to keep.... We lost none but abject Paupers."[59] Trench continued assisted emigration after 1851, sending about 1,100 more destitute tenants to the United States at Lansdowne's expense by 1855.[60]

There are two conflicting views on the nature of landlord-sponsored emigration. On the one hand, landlords and their agents almost unanimously emphasized the voluntary nature of assisted emigration. William Steuart Trench claimed that he never "sent one person away, except by the earnest entreaty of the emigrant himself."[61] Gore-Booth swore that "no man was compelled to go by me."[62] The tenants on the Prior-Wandesforde estate were reported to be assisted "at their own earnest request," as "nothing can exceed their desire to emigrate and the desire of their friends to induce them to leave."[63] Certainly, a large number of tenants voluntarily petitioned their landlords for assistance to emigrate.[64]

On the other hand, assisted emigration can be seen as a form of forcible expulsion. To begin with, as historian James Donnelly Jr. has noted, "it was a pretence to say that a pauperised tenant without the ability to pay rent or to keep his family nourished had a 'free' choice in the matter."[65] Denis Mahon of Roscommon used force to send 1,000 tenants to Quebec.[66] Estate bailiffs in Counties Fermanagh and Leitrim declared that no relief would be provided to pauper tenants who did not accept the offer for emigration.[67] When the agent of Earl Fitzwilliam's estate in County Wicklow arranged the emigration of 1,600 tenants in 1847, he issued an order: "cabin to be thrown down," whether the tenant accepted the offer or not. The list of assisted emigrants from the Fitzwilliam estate also shows that the estate sent away some tenants despite their declaration that they "will not go."[68] To prevent insolvent tenants from returning to vacated places, landlords often required recipients of assistance to level their houses or had their hired agents demolish them.[69]

Some landlords might have been more benevolent than others, but once again the landlords' priority lay in eliminating surplus tenants from their estates with minimum costs. Assisted emigration was designed not as a humanitarian project to improve the quality of tenants' lives but as a method of alleviating landlords' financial burden. For this reason, landlords preferred to send their tenants to Canada, rather than the United States, as a cheaper destination. Also, some landlords, including Lansdowne and Palmerston, shipped their tenants in fall when the vessel fare was relatively cheap, though summer would be ideal for emigrants to find employment and means to support themselves before winter.[70]

Regardless of the degree of benevolence or coercion involved in assisted emigration, the schemes usually ignored the welfare of emigrants. Gerard Lyne's study of Trench's statistical returns reveals that the Lansdowne estate failed to provide at least 2,206 emigrants with clothes for the transatlantic voyage and that 1,681 passengers received no provisions beyond the ship's utterly insufficient allowances. To a Cork newspaper's accusation that Trench shipped away "illprovided" emigrants, Trench himself had to admit: "This is to a certain extent true but it would have cost thousands more to do it otherwise."[71] Palmerston's agents attributed the alleged nakedness of the estate's emigrants to the condition of passage: "Large sums were expended in providing clothing . . . but we suppose the hardships of a rough sea voyage were too much for the inferior kind of clothing to which the inhabitants of the west of Ireland are accustomed."[72] Poorly equipped ships could cause human catastrophe. Of the 476 passengers from Denis Mahon's estate on the *Virginius*, 158 died during the voyage and 109 more perished at Grosse Isle in August 1847, despite Mahon's claim that he supplied his passengers with lavish provisions such as tea, coffee, sugar, and rice as well as usual foodstuffs.[73]

One indisputable consequence of assisted emigration was the repeated arrival in Canada and the United States of large numbers of exceptionally impoverished and destitute people. Reporting on the arrivals of 420 and 230 paupers on two vessels from the Palmerston estate, a newspaper of St. John, New Brunswick, noted that "not more than two had shoes or stockings to their feet, while many of the females were in a state shocking to decency."[74] Enraged by the arrival of assisted paupers, the residents of St. John resolved in a public meeting "to ship back to Ireland the decrepit, aged, and naked children and women" transported by Palmerston.[75] Similarly, writing to Gore-Booth that his former tenants who could not support themselves "would in all probability be sent back again to Sligo," a government emigration agent at St. John anticipated the possible deportation of paupers, a practice once done by the city's overseers of the poor earlier in the century. The agent stated that "a large number of those who remain [in St. John] have become a public charge, from their inability to work, and utter destitution." "This 'shoveling out' of helpless paupers, without any provision for them here, if continued," he protested, "will inflict very serious injury on this colony."[76] Denis Brennan, an emigration agent hired by the Lansdowne estate, complained that the cost of shipping the paupers far exceeded his salary from the contract. In New York, Brennan had to provide extra money to port officials for the pauper passengers considered "ineligible" for landing.[77]

A significant portion of the assisted tenants who landed in Canada migrated to New England and New York in search of better economic opportunities. The emigration agent at St. John observed in the fall of 1847 that one-third of the emigrants who had arrived from the Gore-Booth estate "have re-emigrated to the United States."[78] The Henigans, one of the families assisted by Gore-Booth, testified: "We left miserable St John. It is almost as bad as Ireland. We are getting on very well since we came to the state of Maine."[79] One historian estimates that half the assisted tenants sent from the Palmerston estate to St. John in the famine period migrated to the United States, noting that proceeding to Boston after waiting for a while was an established pattern. Some members of households left for America in the hope that they could secure employment there and later remit money to those remaining in Canada so that the entire family could reunite in the United States.[80] The authorities in Canada also provided some incentive to migrate southward. When the residents of St. Andrews, New Brunswick, implored the colonial government to meet the needs of the more than 300 impoverished Fitzwilliam emigrants until they could be "got rid of," the government offered the emigrants free or assisted passage to Boston, Portland, or Bangor, Maine. About 40 percent of the former Fitzwilliam tenants in St. Andrews migrated to the United States as a result of what might be called double assisted emigration.[81]

In addition to the British government and individual landlords, workhouses in Ireland either wholly or partly financed the emigration of their pauper inmates to North America. In 1838 the Irish Poor Law Act introduced a system of poor relief to Ireland, modeled on the 1834 British Poor Law Act, which replaced the traditional custom of parochial outdoor relief—a form of charity that directly gave provisions such as money, food, and clothes to the poor—with a centralized system based on locally administered workhouses. The Irish poor law divided Ireland into 130 districts known as poor law unions. The Board of Guardians, who were elected by ratepayers in each union, administered the workhouse with the rates collected from property holders under the supervision of a central authority, the British Poor Law Commissioners. While organizing poor relief in Ireland, the act of 1838 permitted the Boards of Guardians to levy an emigration rate with the consent of the ratepayers and to assist the emigration to one of the British colonies of those who had been in the workhouse for at least three months. In the prefamine period workhouses conducted assisted emigration only modestly, partly because the law disqualified people outside workhouses, though as destitute as paupers, from assistance and partly because local ratepayers and the Poor Law Commissioners frowned at the introduction of an emigration tax.[82]

The famine altered the poor law unions' attitude toward assisted emigration. Poverty had been mounting before the famine, but most workhouses had still retained space for additional inmates. By the fall of 1846, however, needy people, including evicted tenants, filled up the workhouses in Ireland. The countryside was flooded with wretched people who could not even enter workhouses. These circumstances led the Boards of Guardians to assisted emigration as a means to reduce pauperism in their unions. The famine posed a dilemma for the guardians. They wished to conduct more assisted emigration, but they lacked financial resources to do so because of the ratepayers' inability to pay the rates. The 1847 Poor Law Extension Act, which created an independent poor law commission for Ireland, enabled the unions to aid the emigration of the poor outside the workhouses, but it did not fundamentally improve the situation. Only relatively well-off unions sent their paupers to North America until 1849.[83]

The British government implemented a major change in the relief system in the summer of 1849. After the select committee on the Irish poor law made repeated recommendations that "the means of facilitating emigration under the provisions of the poor laws should be increased," Parliament modified the rules so that the Poor Law Commissioners could provide loans to the guardians to defray expenses for assisted emigration. With this change, workhouses started to send their paupers to North America by financing the inmates' whole emigration or subsidizing the emigration of those who had received some assistance from their landlords, families, or friends.[84] The Limerick workhouse secured a loan of £500 and paid for the passage of 103 paupers to New York, providing 15 shillings for each between December 1849 and January 1850.[85] The government's decision in 1853 to appropriate the remainder of the extra rates levied earlier throughout the United Kingdom for famine-related purposes to assisted emigration further facilitated the workhouses' involvement in the scheme. In March 1854, for instance, the Mountbellow Poor Law Union in Galway spent £5 for Honor and Thomas Braydon to "defray the expenses of their emigration" to New York, where they had friends to receive them.[86]

Assisted emigration from the workhouses contributed to the flow of Irish chain migration. By the mid-nineteenth century, chain migration—whereby people who had emigrated and established social and economic foundations in the new world in advance guided or financed the emigration of family or friends—had become an established pattern in Irish emigration to the United States. The poor law unions often expended cash to support emigration costs partly paid by remittances from the inmates' relatives or friends in the United States. In April 1855 the Cork Poor Law Union provided a sum of 30 shillings to Catherine McDonnell and her four children to purchase clothes, with "their passage to America having been paid for."[87] The emigration of the three pauper Barry children was financed both by the Galway Poor Law Union, which paid their fare from Galway to Liverpool, and by their friends in America, who paid their passage from Liverpool to New York. In total, about 5,000 workhouse inmates received assistance in the late 1840s, and Irish workhouses and orphanages sent about 15,000 more to the United States between 1851 and 1855.[88]

Equally noteworthy is the participation of Canadian workhouses in the assisted emigration of indigent Irish people. Presumably by way of reducing the number of nonlocal inmates, workhouses in British North America sponsored the journey of Irish pauper migrants to the United States. Sally Rodgers and her three-year-old daughter, Ann, were among the Irish migrants who went to the United States with assistance from Canadian workhouses. A widow from County Donegal, Rodgers entered the St. John almshouse with her daughter on March 20, 1849. The alms-house register recorded the mother's condition at the time of admission simply as "destitute." After supporting Rodgers and her daughter for four months, workhouse officials sent them to Boston on July 16.[89] Whether they had been paupers in Ireland or they became so in St. John remains unknown. Yet their experience suggests that the arrival of Irish paupers in the United States was a consequence of assisted emigration schemes not only by Irish workhouses but also by charitable institutions in British North America.

Although recent studies challenge the sweeping generalization of the fam-ine Irish as a group permanently lacking mobility, revealing that some of them eventually accumulated remarkable wealth in the United States, at least upon arrival, the perceived and actual destitution of these migrants appalled Americans.[90] Irish migrants in reality included those who could support themselves, but their level of self-sufficiency mattered little when they first arrived. Their visual appearance had a profound consequence for Irish migrants, as Atlantic seaboard states responded to mid-nine-teenth-century Irish immigration by developing a practice of restricting the landing of foreigners who seemed likely to become public charges in America. Under this arrangement, the admission of migrants depended less on their realistic ability to support themselves than on the way they appeared to American inspecting officers.

The immigration of the impoverished Catholic Irish provoked intense anti-Irish nativism in the United States, but Americans constructed their attitude toward the Irish not only through the experience of directly seeing them but also by hearing about the situation of famine-stricken Ireland. Newspaper reports on the famine and eyewitness accounts by American travelers significantly influenced how Americans viewed Irish migrants. These reports and accounts tended to highlight the exceptionally misera-ble scenes of poverty and destitution. People deformed by malnutrition, or "stumps of men," for instance, drew the attention of Frederick Douglass.

Such descriptions of the people in Ireland, when read alongside reports on arrivals of noticeably indigent passengers, predisposed Americans to imagine that all the migrants were as poor and destitute as the most impoverished in Ireland. As a result, Americans perceived the level of the migrants' poverty to be greater than it actually was.

A similar analysis can be made for assisted emigrants. These migrants might have been generally more wretched and more likely to become public charges than other Irish migrants, but assisted emigrants' material conditions resisted monolithic characterization. Some of the work-house emigrants looked more decent than destitute voluntary migrants and those sent by landlords. With public funding for assisted emigration, some poor law guardians took the welfare of their inmates more seriously than landlords did of their tenants.[91] Although the workhouse emigrants were technically categorized as paupers upon departing Ireland, not all of them became public charges in America. Many of them were simply join-ing families or friends who had already emigrated to the United States. Some self-supportive people deliberately entered workhouses in Ireland to obtain a free ticket to the new world. One woman from Limerick even per-suaded the workhouse officials to finance her passage to the United States by threatening to spend the money she had received from her daughter in America and enter a workhouse as a pauper.[92] Thus the workhouse emi-grants had more complicated socioeconomic realities than their legal sta-tus as paupers could have implied. Furthermore, the ratio of the assisted emigrants (100,000 sent by landlords, 20,000 by workhouses, and 1,000 from the Crown estates at most) to the 1.8 million people who emigrated from Ireland to North America during the famine decade appears to be quite small.

Assisted emigration nevertheless had a much bigger psychological impact on Americans than its size may have warranted. The actual level of poverty of the assisted emigrants arguably counted less for Americans than the fact that they were paupers transported from foreign poorhouses as well as the image of a flood of Irish paupers into the United States. Americans viewed assisted emigration as the British Empire's conspiracy to dump its "surplus population" in the United States. In addition, with their seemingly chronic dependent status and low likelihood of becoming productive citizens, assisted paupers perfectly fit into the category of the "undeserving" poor in American society. Consequently, Americans reacted to the arrival of assisted emigrants more attentively and negatively than to ordinary migrants' landing. Americans were also exposed to newspaper headlines such as "more arrivals" of assisted paupers and "more paupers coming" on a regular basis.[93] In April 1851, a Boston newspaper wrote

BOY AND GIRL AT CAHERA.

Figure 1.2: (this page) "Boy and Girl at Cahera," *Illustrated London News*, February 20, 1847. **Figure 1.3:** (facing page) "Bridget O'Donnel and Children," *Illustrated London News*, December 22, 1849. The poorest of the poor generally did not emigrate abroad during the famine, but illustrations and reports of extreme poverty led Americans to assume that all Irish immigrants had belonged to the most impoverished at home.
Courtesy of Butler Library, Columbia University in the City of New York.

that "thousands upon thousands of Irish paupers were yearly sent to our shores." "These paupers are often diseased, almost always old and unable to labor," the newspaper stressed, "and are therefore thrown directly upon our charitable institutions."[94] Media reports like this popularized a simplified image of masses of paupers from Irish workhouses flowing into the United States to be burdens on local communities. Although historians

BRIDGET O'DONNEL AND CHILDREN.

know figures for the relatively small scale of assisted emigration, contemporary Americans did not know this. The sporadic but sustained landing of destitute tenants and paupers shaped a distorted portrait of assisted emigration as if it was the dominant form of Irish migration and most migrants had been paupers in Ireland. When nativists condemned the wretchedness of Irish famine migrants, they embraced an exaggerated and somewhat universalized image of Irish poverty.

If Americans regarded Irish poverty as more extensive and alarming than it actually was, how in practice did they react to Irish migration and how were the migrants treated in the new land? Non-Irish paupers, and criminals, arrived in the United States as assisted emigrants from various parts of Europe in the nineteenth century. The British government sent English and Scottish paupers to North America as well, and from the 1850s onward, local authorities in Germany and Switzerland routinely sponsored the assisted emigration of paupers and criminals.[95] These assisted emigration schemes from Europe exasperated Americans, but their harshest criticism was reserved for Irish paupers. When destitute Irish migrants arrived, nativists in New York and Massachusetts quickly called for strict immigration restriction against them, including their deportation to Ireland. Legal devices of regulating the admission of foreigners and banishing unwanted outsiders had existed in the two states since the colonial period. Yet it was the growth of Irish pauperism in the 1830s and 1840s that prompted the institutionalization of immigrant exclusion and deportation as state policies.

CHAPTER 2

Problems of Irish Poverty

The Rise of State Control on the Atlantic Seaboard

In July 1843, Henry David Thoreau was daily observing the arrival of European immigrants in a quarantine station on Staten Island in New York during his temporary residence on the island. On the fourth of July, Thoreau wrote in a letter to his sister, 1,600 immigrants arrived, and "more or less every day since I have been here." During the cleansing of vessels, immigrants exhausted from the transatlantic voyage were "washing their persons and clothes." Men, women, and children also "gathered on an isolated quay near the shore, stretching their limbs and taking the air, the children running races and swinging—on their artificial piece of the land of liberty." After temporary detention for a day or two during cleansing, Thoreau noted, immigrants "go up to the city."[1]

Thoreau's impartial description of arriving immigrants hardly represented Americans' attitude toward foreigners in mid-nineteenth-century Atlantic seaboard cities. Almshouse officials in New York City provided a more prevailing sentiment of the period when they declared that "we protest most strongly against the free admission to our territory of the outcasts and vagabonds" from abroad.[2] Since the eighteenth century, immigrants to the United States had been generally poor and included a large number of paupers dependent on public charity. Yet no immigrant group generated more concerns about imported poverty among Americans than the Irish. The increased immigration of impoverished Catholics from Ireland in the 1830s, and the even larger influx of the famine-stricken Catholic Irish in the 1840s, infuriated Protestant Anglo Americans, provoking an anti-Catholic and anti-Irish nativist movement. Many native-born Americans regarded the Irish as culturally inferior and felt that their Catholic faith was incompatible with republican principles. But Irish immigrants' pauperism stimulated nativist hostility as well. In addition to harassing immigrants with street violence and anti-Catholic propaganda, nativists called for banning the landing of destitute immigrants and deporting those already in the nation back to Europe.

This chapter examines the early development of immigration control in Atlantic seaboard states. It first examines how the British poor law, especially its principles of legal settlement and belonging, was introduced to colonial America, serving as a model for colonial laws to regulate the admission of outsiders and expel the transient poor. The colonial law developed into state laws for controlling the landing of foreign passengers and deporting indigent immigrants after the American Revolution, but the small scale of immigration at the turn of the nineteenth century had made the implementation of the laws loose. These state laws, however, drew renewed attention in the 1830s, when nativists realized their utility as a vehicle for restricting pauper immigration from Ireland.

When the overwhelming scale of Irish famine immigration during the 1840s disrupted coastal states' passenger policies, nativist citizens in Massachusetts and New York, the major receiving states of the famine Irish, demanded the introduction of more stringent and thorough measures against pauper immigration. In New York, supporters of immigrants also sought to use state power for the protection of newcomers from fraud and exploitation. As a result the Massachusetts and New York legislatures centralized authority over passenger regulation, which had been administered by municipal officials, at the state level, creating new state agencies charged with immigration control. Massachusetts and New York had established their positions as the most committed states in the sphere of immigration control by enforcing passenger policy most rigorously among Atlantic seaboard states since the colonial period. The two states perpetuated these positions through the creation of state-run immigration bureaus in their responses to Irish famine immigration. Anti-Irish nativism, in short, guided the formation of state-level immigration control in the first half of the nineteenth century.

The roots of immigration law in America dated to the British poor law, a seventeenth-century set of poor laws that established each parish's financial obligation to support the local poor and its right to refuse to relieve the transient poor who did not belong to the parish. This arrangement allowed parishes to return wandering beggars back to their own neighbor-hoods.[3] Transplanted to America during the colonial period, the British poor law became the foundation of American immigration law. The story of early American immigration control, therefore, is about how British laws for regulating the movement of the poor were transformed into laws to restrict the admission of particular foreigners and deport them, and economic considerations for immigrants' poverty were paramount in this transformation.[4]

Following their mother country's practices, British colonists in America enacted poor laws that operated on the principle that paupers should be taken care of in their towns of legal settlement. One could acquire the right of settlement by living within the town's territory for a certain period of time. By meeting the residency criterion, the person was regarded as legally settled in the town and considered to belong to the community. The colonial poor law required every town to recognize the claims for relief of the legally settled poor. If a person sought aid without having settlement in the town, local authorities could reject the request. By making settle-ment a qualification for relief, town residents protected their treasuries from being spent on outsiders who did not belong to their communities.[5]

If a person became destitute in a town where he did not have legal set-tlement, the outsider was not only ineligible for public relief but also sub-ject to expulsion from the town or even from America. In Massachusetts, the colonial government passed in 1639 an order that authorized local courts to "determine all differences about the lawful settling and provid-ing for poor persons" and to "dispose of all unsettled persons into such towns as they shall judge to be most fit for the maintenance and employ-ment of such persons and families for the ease of this country." Under this order, each town could remove paupers who sought poor relief from the town but had legal settlement elsewhere.[6] Likewise, New York's first general poor law of 1683 authorized local officials to send transient beg-gars to "the county from whence they came."[7] In both Massachusetts and New York, if the transient pauper had no settlement in the colony, he could be expelled to a neighboring colony or sometimes back to Europe. On April 26, 1720, for example, New York City's Common Council ordered that "James Lowry an Ancient Man do Transport himself to Bristol."[8] Various colonies from New England to the South, including Connecticut, Rhode Island, Pennsylvania, Delaware, and Virginia, had removal laws, expelling destitute persons roaming without settlement to other colonies or to Europe.[9]

Towns in colonial New England also removed strangers coming from other towns by a practice called "warning out." If outsiders entered a town

without the consent of residents, they would receive a notification order-
ing them to leave town within a certain number of days, whether or not
they requested poor relief. If the outsiders remained, they would be compelled to leave the town by its constables. For example, in 1763 the town
of Peterborough, New Hampshire, authorized constable James Templeton
to "warn Jean Culberson now in this place forthwith to Depart out of this
town." Technically, warning out applied to all unsettled persons. Yet New
England colonists practiced it mainly to remove from the community destitute transients who seemed likely to become public charges.[10]

As a device to prevent the consumption of the town's treasury by transients, warning out functioned in particularly discriminatory ways against
women. Town officials were generally more enthusiastic about expelling
transient women than their male counterparts because of women's potential to give birth to children. Town authorities realized that a pregnant
transient woman would incur large expenses from delivery and the subsequent care of the mother and the baby. Any indication of pregnancy thus
motivated town officials to expedite the removal of the transient woman,
especially when she was unaccompanied by a man. Town residents also
often quickly notified authorities of the presence of transient women
upon discovering their pregnancies. This gendered consideration of economic burdens of outsiders would have enduring significance, as the same
concern made destitute immigrant women with children particularly vulnerable to state deportation policy in the nineteenth century.[11]

Warning out served not simply as an economic measure to protect the
town's treasury but also as a means of social control. An order for warning
out was usually issued based on a "respectable" (i.e., land-owning) inhabit-
ant's complaint about an unsettled transient. The source of complaint could
be the person's apparent destitution, but it could also be behavior that
appeared objectionable to respectable residents. Constables in Providence
removed Olive Goddard and her two children to Newport, Rhode Island, in
January 1763 when respectable town folks informed Providence officials
that she was "a lewd woman."[12] New Englanders used warning out as an
omnibus measure to control the quality of people who would reside in the
community, and its enforcement was highly discretionary. These aspects of
warning out were later succeeded by state and federal immigration laws,
which allowed inspecting officers to exert a significant amount of control
over the admission and deportation of undesirable foreigners.

The colonial practice of pauper removal laid the foundations for state
policies for the compulsory return, or deportation, of destitute foreigners
already in America to their countries of origin, but these policies emerged
largely as a legacy of the Massachusetts poor law. Although various

colonies expelled transient paupers, pauper removal practically became a dead letter in statute books or was abolished entirely in most states except Massachusetts by the early nineteenth century. In Rhode Island, for example, historian Ruth Wallis Herndon notes how the practice "trailed off in the nineteenth century." "Never again were town leaders swamped, as they were in the 1780s and 1790s," Herndon concludes, "by the business of interviewing and removing transient people in need."[13] New York retreated from pauper removal too. In February 1824, as a result of an investigation of the condition of poor relief in the state, the legislature abolished pauper removal due to high costs for its implementation and unnecessary complications between officials in different towns involved in removal processes. Thereafter, all destitute people in New York, including foreigners, were to be supported at county almshouses instead.[14]

Massachusetts, by contrast, developed a unique system of pauper removal after the American Revolution that was deeply connected with citizenship status and continued to enforce this system during the nineteenth century. In 1794, the legislature enacted Massachusetts' first comprehensive poor law as a state. The act defined the eligibility for acquiring legal settlement in the state. Except for cases where eligibility was based on preceding legal connections with the town (such as marriage, parentage, public service, ministry service, approbation by the town, and apprenticeship), citizenship became a prerequisite.[15] Shortly afterward, the legislature passed another act, which provided that all unsettled persons in the state who were paupers or likely to become public charges would be removed to their places of legal settlement. Upon a complaint about a transient pauper by a town's relief officers, known as the Overseers of the Poor, a justice of the peace in the county would summon the pauper in question to the court for a trial. When the justice confirmed the location of the pauper's legal settlement, he would issue a warrant for the pauper's removal to his or her town of settlement. If the pauper had no settlement in any town within the state, the justice could "cause such pauper to be sent and conveyed by land or water, to any other State, or to any place beyond [the] sea, where he belongs" at the expense of the state.[16] The 1794 acts made destitute foreigners particularly vulnerable to banishment. Anyone without legal settlement in Massachusetts would be expelled from the state, and only American citizens could acquire it.

At a time when immigration still remained a minor issue in the state, Massachusetts lawmakers did not design the acts of 1794 explicitly as immigration legislation. Pauper removal during the eighteenth century sought chiefly to regulate the movement of the transient poor who had legal settlement within Massachusetts. Of 1,039 people warned out of

Boston in 1791, 740 possessed settlement in other Massachusetts towns and only 237 were born outside the United States.[17] Nevertheless, by making non-naturalized foreigners ineligible for settlement and thus subject to removal when destitute, the acts of 1794 set the legal framework of policies for the deportation of immigrant paupers.[18]

In addition to removing destitute outsiders from the community, Atlantic seaboard colonies and states built upon the British poor law's strong sense of vigilance against the transient poor to develop passenger laws for prohibiting the landing of, or excluding, immigrants of undesirable character. In March 1701, Massachusetts introduced its first passenger act with an exclusion clause. The act required captains of vessels to procure bonds for passengers who were "impotent, lame or otherwise infirm, or likely to be a public charge." Port towns would use collected bonds to protect their treasuries from expenses incurred from supporting these passengers. If shipmasters failed or refused to provide bonds, they could not land the passengers and in most cases had to bring them back to the place of embarkation.[19] In 1820, the Massachusetts legislature prohibited the landing of any passengers, American or foreign, who "may be liable to become chargeable for their support to the Commonwealth," without a bond not exceeding $500. If the bonded passengers entered public almshouses as paupers within three years of arrival, local authorities would use the bonds for their maintenance.[20] In 1831 the legislature amended the law to apply only to "alien passengers." The new law also allowed shipowners to choose either to provide a bond of $200 for each foreign passenger who might become a pauper or to pay a commutation fee of $5 for each foreign passenger in lieu of bonds. An aggregate of the fees, just like bonds, would help municipal governments defray expenses related to the care of needy immigrants.[21]

A similar form of passenger control developed in New York. In 1683 the colonial government enacted New York's first passenger law, which declared that any passengers who could not provide for their "well demeanor" would be sent back to their places of origin. In 1788, in response to the growth of pauperism in New York City due to urbanization and the immigration of poor Europeans after the American Revolution, the state legislature passed a poor law that required shipmasters arriving in the port of New York to report to the mayor the names and occupations of the passengers they landed within twenty-four hours of arrival. If any passenger could not give "a good account of himself or herself" or appeared likely to become a pauper chargeable to New York City, shipmasters had to either bring the person back to the place of embarkation within one month or provide to the mayor or aldermen a bond of £100 with surety that the person would not become a public charge. In 1797, the legislature modified the bonding policy so that bonds should be provided prior to the landing of passengers. To meet the realistic necessity of accommodating sick seamen and alien passengers, the legislature also opened a marine hospital on Staten Island, which would be run by capitation taxes collected from all passengers and crews on board each vessel coming from a foreign port. Immigration policy in New York became extremely rigid in 1824, when a new state passenger law applied a bond of $300 to each alien passenger regardless of his or her condition. The city of New York, however, subsequently enacted an ordinance to permit shipmasters to pay much cheaper commutation fees for the landing of nonpauper passengers. As a result, passenger control in New York, as in Massachusetts, operated on the basis of the combination of bonds and commutation fees.[22]

As the policies of Massachusetts and New York suggest, colonies and states conducted entry regulation at ports by compelling shipmasters to bring back destitute passengers unless they prepaid their costs in the form of bond and commutation fee. Most of the seaboard colonies and states adopted an exclusion policy of this kind, following the Massachusetts and New York models. Under Delaware's 1740 law, shippers had either to pay for any expense involved in supporting "infant, lunatic, maimed, aged, impotent, or vagrant" passengers or to take them back to the place "whence such person or persons were imported." Sharing the same language, the states of Pennsylvania and Maryland required masters of arriving vessels to provide a bond or pay a commutation fee for the landing of "each passenger not being a citizen of the United States" in order to "indemnify and save harmless" the treasury of Philadelphia and Baltimore, respectively.[23]

The history of the poor law in the colonial and early republic periods suggests that the transatlantic spread of the British poor law planted on America's eastern seaboard region the seeds of two forms of immigration control, deportation and exclusion, both of which operated on the basis of people's economic conditions. Yet the necessity of enforcing the rules remained minimal until the 1830s. Massachusetts continued to operate under its 1794 pauper removal law. But the implementation was sporadic and aimed primarily to return American paupers to their towns of settlement within the state, rather than deport foreigners to Europe. In short, pauper removal law was not yet immigration law in the early nineteenth century. Enforcement of the exclusion policy also remained mild at best. By 1827 the bonding system in the passenger law had become a "mere form," as Boston mayor Josiah Quincy put it. A New York official retrospectively admitted in 1870 that the collection of bonds under the

1824 act was not a serious problem "so long as emigration was small."[24] Implementation of regulatory measures became much more stringent, however, when impoverished Catholic Irish immigrants began to enter the United States in large numbers in the 1830s and most decisively during the Irish famine of the following decade.

When it came to immigration policy, the poor law was not the only thing that early America inherited from Britain. Protestant British colonists brought with them a strong animosity to Catholicism and to Irish Catholics in particular. By the early nineteenth century the United States had established itself as, in effect, a Protestant nation ruled by people of Anglo Saxon descent. The substantial inflow into the United States of the Catholic Irish during the first half of the century frightened many Protestant Americans, who thought that these immigrants would overrun American society. Americans also considered the poverty and wretchedness of the Irish a significant financial drain on poor relief funds and a threat to the public health of their community. Out of these concerns emerged intense anti-Irish nativism in antebellum America. In Atlantic seaboard states, anti-Irish sentiment stimulated the more active enforcement of poor laws to exclude and deport destitute Irish immigrants and the modification of these laws to regulate immigration more effectively. In other words, Protestant Americans' nativist sensibilities, rooted in their aversion to the Catholicism and poverty of the Irish, were translated into concrete social policies. If the British system for regulating the movement of the poor provided legal and institutional foundations for immigration control, anti-Irish nativism played a critical role in the development from these foundations of immigration restriction policies in the mid-nineteenth-century United States.

Hostile sentiment against the Catholic Irish had long existed in America. Since the Reformation, many Protestants had looked down on Catholics as corrupt Christians whose religious life was guided by superficial formalities and superstitions, rather than genuine, individual faith. While religious prejudice of this kind was a central ingredient in British conceptions of Irish Catholics as inferior people, British Protestants despised them even as pagans and barbarians, due to the peculiar nature of Christianity in Gaelic Ireland, which incorporated elements of pre-Christian traditions and customs. Furthermore, according to historian Nicholas Canny, in the eyes of Britons, the Irish practice of transhumance indicated that Irish people were nomads, who stood at "the opposite pole of civilization from themselves." Protestant British settlers in America transported these biases to the colonies, and nineteenth-century Anglo

Americans inherited their ancestors' prejudice toward Catholicism and the Irish.[25]

Although Anglo Protestant repulsion for Catholicism and the Irish characterized nineteenth-century American society, it grew stronger in Massachusetts, especially Boston, than anywhere else. Among British settlers in colonial America, Puritans in the Massachusetts Bay Colony had expressed the harshest hostility to Presbyterian Irish immigrants, forcing them to leave New England and settle in Pennsylvania and the South. With their stringent adherence to Protestant values and sense of cultural superiority, Massachusetts Puritans cultivated even sharper hatred of the Catholic Irish, whom they contemptuously called "St. Patrick's Vermin."[26] Owing to this Puritan background, many nineteenth-century Anglo Bostonians harbored exceptionally intense anti-Catholic and anti-Irish worldviews. The Englishness of Boston appeared in the city's architecture. In 1839, British consul Thomas Grattan described Boston as "far more English-looking than New York [City]," which had a mixed heritage of Dutch and English cultures. Also, as Sven Beckert points out, the ruling class of New York City, merchants, had diverse ethnic backgrounds, and they perceived the ethnic diversity as "a point of pride, not contention."[27] By contrast, as Thomas O'Connor has argued, Boston was "an American city with an intensely homogeneous Anglo-Saxon character, an inbred hostility toward people who were Irish, a fierce and violent revulsion against all things Roman Catholic." The Irish who settled in New York City and Philadelphia "lived among social, economic, and ethnic groups that were much more diverse in their origins and more receptive in their attitudes."[28]

The anti-Irish cultural background of Massachusetts was reflected in politics. At the turn of the nineteenth century, New England, especially Massachusetts, was a stronghold of the Federalists. Endorsing the idea of strong central government controlled by members of the elite class and holding pro-British views, the Federalists despised Irish immigrant radicals, who promoted more egalitarian republicanism in the United States. The Federalists' anti-Irish sentiment was further enhanced by these Irish immigrants' affiliation with their political rivals, the Republicans. In 1798, in the midst of mounting diplomatic tension with France, the Federalists passed the Alien and Sedition Acts, which included provisions for immigrant deportation. Federalist leader Harrison Gray Otis, a congressman from Massachusetts, made it clear that the passage of these laws in part arose from the Federalists' sentiment that they "did not wish to invite hordes of wild Irishmen." When the New England Federalists held the Hartford Convention in 1814 under the leadership of Massachusetts members, they advocated the prohibition of naturalized citizens from serving in Congress and any United States office, an action designed to weaken the political power of Irish immigrants. After the decline of the Federalists, their nativism was inherited by the Whigs, who enjoyed a dominant position in Massachusetts politics by occupying the governor's office and controlling the state legislature and the municipal government of Boston for most of the 1830s and 1840s. Massachusetts had therefore cultivated the distinct cultural and political environments for anti-Irish nativism to flourish by the time of the arrival of Catholic Irish immigrants.[29]

The considerable growth of the Catholic population in the United States arising from Irish immigration during the first decades of the nineteenth century triggered an anti-Catholic movement. According to historians' estimates, the population of Catholics in the United States was limited prior to 1800, numbering about 35,000. By 1840, however, the exodus of the Catholic Irish to North America had boosted the Catholic population to 663,000. In New York City, the number of Catholics expanded from 15,000 to 90,000 between 1815 and 1840. In the decade between 1825 and 1835, the Catholic population of Boston grew fourfold from 5,000 to 20,900.[30] The Catholic presence still remained much smaller than the Protestant, but it was large enough to arouse the hostility of native-born Protestants, who believed that Catholics' allegiance to the pope in Rome and the hierarchical structure of the Catholic Church would corrupt freedom and democracy in America. And, given that the growth of the Catholic population stemmed from the mass immigration of the Catholic Irish during this period, the anti-Catholic movement was in essence a manifestation of Protestant Anglo Americans' nativism against Irish immigrants.

The anti-Catholic movement unfolded in the form of street violence and propaganda. On the night of August 11, 1834, a mob of forty or fifty workingmen burned down an Ursuline convent in Charlestown, Massachusetts, where nuns ran a boarding school for girls. Harassment of Catholic Irish immigrants occurred frequently, and immigrants' resistance only added fuel to Protestants' anger. Three years after the burning of the Ursuline convent, when a band of Protestant firemen and Irish immigrants started a fistfight on Broad Street in Boston, the conflict developed into a riot that engulfed the city in anti-Irish furor.[31] Nativists fulminated against Catholic immigrants' alleged schemes to overturn American society and replace it with despotic papism. Nativist activists and Protestant preachers, such as Samuel F. B. Morse, Lyman Beecher, and William C. Brownlee, published anti-Catholic propaganda to "warn our Protestant friends of the insidious Jesuitical working of that abomination, showing its demoralizing, debasing character."

Catholicism, Morse declared, "is opposed in its very nature of Democratic Republicanism."[32] Maria Monk's 1836 *Awful Disclosures of the Hotel Dieu Nunnery of Montreal*, which sensationalized the alleged immoral life at a Catholic nunnery, became a national bestseller. These publications drove toward the nativist cause even moderate Protestant Americans, who would otherwise tolerate the Catholic Irish, by exaggerating the Catholic threat and the immigrants' incompatibility with American society.[33]

Underlying the religious questions that sparked the outbreak of the anti-Catholic movement were deep concerns about immigrant poverty and pauperism. As the material conditions of Irish immigrants declined in the 1830s, their poverty emerged as a chronic social problem in American cities. In search of cheap rents, most Irish immigrants resided in congested slums, such as Five Points in New York City and those in the North End and Fort Hill in Boston.[34] The Irish also accounted for a significantly disproportionate share of charity recipients. In 1833, the Boston Free Dispensary aided 1,331 foreigners and 854 Americans. Of the 1,331 foreigners, 1,234 were Irish.[35] In 1834, half of the alien inmates in the almshouses of New York City and Philadelphia were born in Ireland.[36] Destitute and often disease-stricken, Irish immigrants on the streets were already a hazard to public health. But in nativist eyes, those seeking relief and admission to charitable institutions were even worse in that they abused welfare funds supported by Americans' taxes. At a public almshouse, as a Massachusetts nativist put it, a lazy "Irish tramper" engaged in self-indulgence and "smoke her pipe at the expense of the Commonwealth of Massachusetts."[37]

Opponents of the Irish found the arrival of assisted paupers sent by landlords and workhouses in Ireland particularly troublesome. They regarded assisted paupers not as voluntary immigrants who would contribute to the development of society, but as useless surplus populations dumped on America by the Old World. Phrases such as "dumping" and "importation" of foreign paupers appeared frequently in newspapers and public discourse. John Davis, a congressman from Massachusetts and the state's former governor, asked in the United States Senate in 1836: "Is it morally right for Great Britain to attempt to throw upon us this oppressive burden of sustaining her poor?"[38] In 1837, almshouse officials in New York City reported to the Common Council that "this metropolis [was] forced to be the recipient of the poor objects" sent from foreign countries.[39] The voluntary arrival of penniless immigrants was irritating enough, but the shipment of people who were destined to become public charges from the moment of landing in the United States struck many Americans as unjust and unacceptable.

Native-born Americans resented Irish pauperism not only because it drained public treasuries but also because it violated prevailing economic ideals in antebellum American society. In other words, Irish pauperism was ideologically, as well as financially, problematic. By the tenets of the "free labor ideology," in the influential explanation of historian Eric Foner, opportunity for property-owning independence was the distinctive quality of northern society as compared to the slaveholding South. The colonial experience of British oppression had implanted the sanctity of independence and the fear of unfreedom and dependency in Americans' minds. After the Revolution, the continued presence of chattel slavery, a symbol of the denial of self-ownership, enhanced this conception. Free labor ideology assumed that, in a free society which technically guaranteed independence and upward mobility for everyone, citizens would engage in productive work. Pauperism, more than mere poverty, embodied a form of dependency that was not supposed to exist in free northern society. Those in temporary poverty due to uncontrollable financial misfortunes received sympathy as the "deserving" poor, but middle-class Americans tended to view the chronic poverty of able-bodied persons as an individual failing arising from the personal laziness and moral defects of the "undeserving" poor. In the ethnically biased eyes of Anglo Americans, the dependency of Irish paupers, all of whom belonged to the undeserving poor, destabilized the integrity of American free labor society more seriously than that of the native-born poor. Convinced that Catholicism made people docile and unprogressive, nativists also considered the Catholic Irish predisposed to willful dependency and undeserving poverty.[40]

Free labor ideology derived part of its intellectual foundation from the notion of American exceptionalism. Applied to free labor discourse, the notion celebrated the availability of supposedly boundless economic opportunity and its relatively fair distribution among free white men as American society's unique assets that distinguished the United States from the Old World, where peasants were permanently oppressed with little mobility. Adherents of this view regarded the undeserving poor imported from the Old World, such as Irish paupers, as a foreign threat that would poison American free labor society by demoralizing industrious, independent workers. Many Americans also believed that the assisted emigration of paupers was a scheme of rulers in Europe to weaken democratic America as a way of legitimizing their authority in hierarchical Europe.[41]

The impact of industrialization in the early decades of the nineteenth century further hardened Americans' attitude toward immigrant paupers. The introduction of mechanization in industries such as textile manufacturing and shoemaking disrupted traditional artisanship and bound workers to factory-based wage labor, causing a decline in workers' social status and income. As economic self-sufficiency became increasingly elusive, many working-class Americans felt that they were coerced into lives of dependency and unfreedom, which they called "wage slavery."[42] The introduction of a cheap foreign labor in the form of destitute Irish immigrants provided a convenient scapegoat on which to blame the deterioration of the social and economic conditions of American workers. Poor but self-sufficient immigrant laborers were quite different from foreign paupers in almshouses, but nativists readily collapsed the distinction. Dreading job competition and the further decline of wages, American workers complained that they "cannot labor for the same prices that the pauper populace of foreign countries can, and still support their elevated stand in society." Deprived of their jobs by foreigners, American workers and their children would "descend to a level with the cast-off paupers of Europe."[43]

Nativist Americans responded to burgeoning Irish pauperism by calling for the restriction of pauper immigration through state legislation. The influx of the destitute Catholic Irish during the 1830s made states confront the necessity for the rigid enforcement of their passenger laws. At this point people in Massachusetts realized the usefulness of the state's pauper removal law as immigrant deportation policy. In 1835, members of a legislative committee on pauper immigration in Massachusetts reported that they "find a law in existence, relating to the disposition that may be made of foreign paupers, which they think a salutary one, and are somewhat surprised that it has not been more availed of."[44] Quoting the language of the pauper removal law of 1794, the Superintendent of the Boston House of Industry urged the state legislature to "send any foreign pauper, by land or water, to any other State, or to any place beyond the sea where said pauper may have come from."[45] When Harriet Martineau, a British social theorist, visited the United States in 1836, she quickly noticed the clamor for shipping Irish paupers back to Ireland.[46] As "the tax upon our citizens has become odious," a Baltimore newspaper claimed, measures should be taken to "send this refuse of other cities back to the places from whence they came."[47]

Advocates of state immigration control in the 1830s found the United States Supreme Court endorsing their cause. Under the influence of Federalist Chief Justice John Marshall, who supported the idea of a strong national economy, the court had ruled in *Gibbons v. Ogden* (1824) that the regulation of passenger carriage fell under the federal commerce power. This decision thus approved the superiority of Congress to state governments in the sphere of immigration.[48] In the case of *City of New York v. Miln* (1837), however, the Supreme Court (now with Democrat Roger B. Taney as Chief Justice) reversed its position, upholding the constitutionality of New York State's 1824 passenger law. The law required shipmasters upon arrival to file a report on the condition of their alien passengers to the mayor or alderman of New York City and levied a fine on those who did not submit such a report. Municipal officials used the reports to identify paupers and prevent their landing without bonds. Dismissing the claim of the master of the ship *Emily* for the law's supposed violation of federal commerce power, the Supreme Court ruled that New York's passenger act was not "a regulation of commerce, but of police," intended to prevent the state from being burdened with foreign paupers. Just as states had a duty to protect the safety of their people from "physical pestilence which may arise from unsound and infectious articles imported," they must provide precautionary measures against "the moral pestilence of paupers, vagabonds, and possibly convicts." Internal police power of this kind "rightfully belonged to the states" and was not "surrendered or restrained by the Constitution of the United States."[49] By validating state passenger legislation as an exercise of internal police power, the *Miln* ruling legitimized immigration control by states.

The Taney Court's decision in the *Miln* case needs to be understood as part of a broader ongoing debate over states' right to control the admission of people whom they deemed undesirable. By the time of the case, the rise of radical abolitionism in the North had incited the aggressive defense of slavery by southern states. White southerners also increasingly worried about slave insurrection after a series of mutinous attempts and actuals revolts, including Denmark Vesey's ultimately unfulfilled scheme in South Carolina in 1822 and Nat Turner's bloody rebellion in Virginia in 1831. Furthermore, international events such as the Haitian Revolution at the turn of the nineteenth century and the abolition of slavery in the British West Indies in 1834 horrified southern slaveholders, who feared that the resultant influx of black revolutionaries and emancipated blacks into the United States would subvert American slavery.[50]

Southern states reacted to the external and internal challenges to slavery by passing laws for prohibiting the admission of free blacks who did not reside in the state. After the Vesey conspiracy, South Carolina passed the so-called Negro Seamen Act, which required black seamen arriving on a vessel to be detained in jail until the ship's departure, a policy followed by other southern states, such as Georgia and Louisiana.[51] From the perspectives of slaveholders, by minimizing the presence of free blacks from the North and abroad, who could transmit incendiary abolitionist ideas to local blacks, these laws protected white citizens from slave insurrection. The governor of South Carolina declared in 1824 that his state "has the right to interdict the entrance of such persons into her ports whose organization of minds, habits, associations, render them peculiarly calculated to disturb the peace and tranquility of the state." Southern states thus considered their anti-black laws measures for public safety and self-preservation, in the same way as northeast states justified their passenger laws as a practice of police power against foreign paupers.[52] In this situation, southern states frowned upon any potential federal encroachment on their authority to control the admission of outsiders. New York passenger law owed the Supreme Court's endorsement in the *Miln* case to the desire of southern Democrats, including Chief Justice Taney himself, to preclude federal intervention in southern states' policies for free blacks.[53] The recognition of state immigration policy as an exercise of police power emerged in close relation to the national debate over slavery and states' rights.

Encouraged by the Supreme Court's support for New York policy, Massachusetts legislators passed a new alien passenger act in April 1837. The act authorized officers appointed by a port city or town to board incoming vessels from outside the state and examine the condition of passengers. If the officers found "any lunatic, idiot, maimed, aged, or infirm persons, incompetent in the opinion of the officer so examining to maintain themselves, or who have been paupers in any other country," no such passenger would be allowed to land until the shipmaster paid a bond of $1,000 that remained effective for ten years after arrival. The previous state passenger law had required a bond of $200, effective for three years, for the landing of a destitute passenger. The introduction of a larger bond extending over a longer period must have reflected policymakers' intention to discourage shipmasters from preparing bonds and to pressure them to bring destitute passengers back to their places of embarkation instead. As for nonpauper passengers, the shipowners had to pay to the treasury of the city or town a two-dollar capitation tax, known as head money, for the landing of each one. The aggregate of the tax would be used for the support of foreign paupers in the state. Earlier law had charged shipmasters only when they brought alien passengers likely to become public charges, with no bond or capitation fee required if all foreigners on the ship appeared self-supporting. But the 1837 act set up a compulsory landing fee for all nonpauper passengers. Even if the ship carried no paupers, every alien passenger was now subject to the capitation tax.[54]

Citizens in Massachusetts had not forgotten about the removal provision of the 1794 poor law. In September 1837, the Boston City Council appropriated parts of the funds collected as head money for the purpose of deporting foreign paupers to their places of origin under the removal law. This policy was instigated partly by the Panic of 1837, which wreaked havoc on the economy of New England and expanded dependency on public charity among foreigners in Boston.[55] Between 1837 and 1845, according to the census filed in 1845, the city of Boston spent a third of the head money collected during these years to expel from the state 4,706 paupers without settlement in Massachusetts and to return 715 paupers back to Ireland in particular. Nothing indicates the importance of Irish immigration in the revival of pauper removal policy in Massachusetts more palpably than the fact that the state's official statistics listed only Ireland as a distinct destination for deportation.[56]

The state of New York also moved to check Irish pauper immigration by actively enforcing its exclusion law. Unlike Massachusetts, New York neither implemented deportation nor modified its existing 1824 passenger law, which banned the admission of any destitute alien without a bond of $300. But antipathy to Irish pauperism was so intense that foreign observers anticipated the wholesale deportation of immigrant paupers from New York. Reporting to the United Kingdom Foreign Office in the fall of 1843, Anthony Barclay, the British consul in New York City, stated he had received information that municipal officials were "about to ship back to Liverpool, perhaps directly to Ireland ... all such native British subjects" who were or would become charges upon the city. Referring to New York's pauper exclusion policy, Barclay reported that he had seen the rejection of the landing in New York of twenty-six passengers in one ship and their subsequent return to Liverpool "by the order and at the expense of the city authorities," and that "great numbers were being sent by other vessels at the same time by the same authority." Barclay's fears about the prospect of deportation were exaggerated, as New York had abolished laws for removing paupers from the state almost twenty years earlier. Yet the growing tension over Irish paupers and the active enforcement of exclusion policy in New York City raised the possibility that deportation laws might be revived.[57]

Meanwhile, officials in Atlantic seaboard states collectively sought federal intervention to supplement their regulatory passenger policies. In 1837, the mayor of Boston invited the mayors of New York City, Philadelphia, and Baltimore to submit a joint petition to Congress, "praying for its interference to prevent the great evils arising from the influx of paupers among us." A Massachusetts representative later submitted the resolution to Congress, along with petitions and memorials on foreign pauperism from various states and cities.[58] Urged by these actions, Congress appointed a select committee to file a report on pauper immigration, which was submitted to the House in 1838. Delivering the nativist sentiments of diverse bodies of citizens in Washington, DC, Massachusetts, New York, and other states, the report strongly protested against the assisted emigration of "the outcasts of foreign countries; *paupers, vagrants,* and *malefactors*" arranged by European poorhouses and suggested the passage of a law that would "effectually prevent the introduction of paupers and convicts from foreign countries into the United States."[59]

The report condemned pauper immigration regardless of nationality, but it confirmed that Irish immigration lay at the core of the problem of imported poverty. The report was accompanied by a series of letters from American consuls in various European cities regarding the practice of assisted pauper emigration. Those in Germany denied the existence of such practice, though some of them pointed out local governments' policies for sending criminals to the United States. The consul in Dublin, by contrast, admitted that it was "by no means an uncommon occurrence" for individual landlords to send their impoverished tenants to America. The report also highlighted the disproportionate presence of the Irish among the foreign pauper population. In Philadelphia, foreigners accounted for about half the people admitted to the city's almshouse in 1836, and 70 percent of the alien inmates were born in Ireland, making the Irish proportion more than six times larger than that of the English, the second biggest immigrant inmate group.[60] The report did not bring about any immediate congressional action, but its findings reminded the American public that the problem of immigrant poverty was essentially that of Irish poverty.

Social and political nativism against the Irish escalated on the eve of the Irish potato famine. In Philadelphia, anti-Catholic sentiment and Irish immigrants' determination to resist intolerance sparked a three-day riot in the Irish neighborhood of Kensington in May 1844, resulting in the destruction of more than thirty homes, two Catholic churches, and a Catholic seminary. During the riot, nativists agitated for mob violence by proclaiming that "these paupers, beggars and naked starvelings have in their hands deadly weapons."[61] Opponents of immigration also sought to minimize foreigners' influence on electoral politics. In 1841, a group of citizens calling themselves "Native Americans" formed a political organization in New Orleans. Their goal focused on the restriction of officeholding to native-born citizens and the extension of the waiting period for naturalization to delay immigrants' participation in elections. The organization soon spread to New York City, Boston, Philadelphia, St. Louis, and Charleston. In New York City, the Native Americans, who named their branch the American Republican Party, successfully placed their candidate, James Harper, in the mayoral office between 1844 and 1845. The party disappeared by 1847 without achieving any of its agenda.[62] Nevertheless, the emergence of nativist organizations, as well as anti-Irish street violence, suggests that state immigration policy in the 1830s and the early 1840s operated in tandem with various attempts to exclude the Irish from American society. Having originated from the British poor law, American states' laws for restricting the admission of destitute outsiders and banishing them increasingly assumed the character of immigration control, rather than the regulation of domestic pauperism, toward the mid-nineteenth century. The catalyst for this development was cultural and economic antagonism toward Irish immigrants.

If Americans found the arrival of the Catholic Irish in the 1830s shocking, nothing prepared them for the scale of Irish famine immigration in the following decade. When the famine exodus started in the 1840s, states found their existent passenger policy utterly ineffective to prevent the landing of destitute foreigners and check the growth of Irish pauperism. State immigration policy had hitherto been implemented at the local level by town and city officials. The arrival of the famine Irish, however, compelled Massachusetts and New York, the two major destination states for them, to centralize the authority over immigration at the state rather than municipal level for a stricter supervision of foreign passengers. By the 1840s, both Massachusetts and New York had pioneered measures for pauper deportation and exclusion. Irish famine immigration stimulated the formation of state-level immigration control, and it was during the famine period that Massachusetts and New York solidified their leading positions in immigration control in antebellum America by establishing specialized state immigration agencies ahead of other coastal states.

The exodus of the impoverished Irish affected the Atlantic seaboard region extensively, but famine immigration struck Massachusetts and New York harder than any other states. Numerically, New York received the largest number of famine immigrants, followed by Pennsylvania. In 1850 there were approximately 343,000 Irish-born people in New York and 151,700 in Pennsylvania, while the number of the Irish in Massachusetts was 116,000.[63] Yet the proportional presence of the Irish in the entire state population was larger in Massachusetts and New York (11 percent) than in Pennsylvania (6.6 percent). This trend continued at the city level. Irish immigrants' proportion of the total population in 1850 was 26 percent in Boston and New York City and 17.7 percent in Philadelphia.[64] The Irish presence in the famine era was therefore more visible in Massachusetts and New York, especially Boston and New York City, than anywhere else in the United States.

Famine immigration enhanced the distinct presence of Irish pauperism in Boston and New York City. The flood of destitute Irish immigrants contributed to a threefold growth in annual expenditures for pauper aid in the city of Boston in the period from 1845 to 1850, when the number of paupers who had local settlement decreased.[65] Irish-born inmates accounted for 57 percent of all inmates, and 87 percent of the foreign inmates, who entered the Boston House of Industry in 1847.[66] The fact that the section on pauper statistics in the city's 1845 census had a column for "Born in Ireland," independent of those for "Born of American Parents" and "Born in other for'n [foreign] Places," highlights how exceptional Irish poverty was in Boston.[67] In New York City, of 5,700 foreign-born patients who were admitted to the municipal Bellevue Hospital in 1847, 4,863 persons, or 85 percent, were born in Ireland. In 1849, the city's almshouse admitted 1,006 Irish immigrants. This evidence is striking given that the number of the English inmates, the second largest foreign-born group, who entered the institution in that year was merely ninety-two.[68] The Irish were so overrepresented in the pauper population that "Irish," "immigrant," and "pauper" became virtually synonymous.

The extraordinary wretchedness of famine immigrants exacerbated Americans' already negative view of Irish poverty. Nativists attributed the pauperism of the Irish to their supposed "ignorance," "total inability, even when in perfect health, to adapt themselves to the requirement of society here," "moral debasement," and "want of self-respect."[69] Allegations of pervasive Irish drunkenness and criminality reinforced the prejudiced association between Irish immigrants and the undeserving poor. In an anonymous letter to the Boston City Council, one nativist wrote that "we shall be driven from our houses by the Lazy, Ungrateful, Lying and Thieving population of old Ireland." He claimed that he had witnessed Irish people sitting on the streets in Ireland and Liverpool, "picking the vermin from under their arm pits in fact that they are too lazy to wash themselves." "Instead of giving them bread," he continued, "provide a scrubbing brush and a cheap comb for each person and compel them to clean up daily."[70]

Assisted emigration was never a dominant form of Irish famine migration to North America, but Americans found the constant arrival of assisted paupers in the 1840s simply overwhelming. "They are so numerous," Massachusetts officials commented on assisted paupers, "that the expectation of transporting the whole of them, will never be realized." They noted that "this heretofore unprecedented kind of emigration from

Ireland" was bringing into North America destitute half-starved people "in such masses." These Irish immigrants were "paupers in the truest sense of the word," who were destined to be public charges in the state until the end of their lives.[71] Almshouse officials in New York City declared that "we must do what we can do as a city to protect ourselves ... by a rigid enforcement of salutary municipal laws." Otherwise they would "continue to be overrun by the worthless and dissolute" transported from Europe to the United States.[72]

Throughout 1847, the most devastating year of the Irish potato famine, anti-immigrant tension remained extremely volatile. When an American visitor to an almshouse in New York and his daughter died of "ship fever" contracted from foreign-born inmates, nativists insisted on "the necessity of taking immediate measures to protect our city against these evils."[73] Antagonistic sentiment of this sort sometimes came close to inciting violence. The arrival in Boston of destitute immigrants on the ship *Thomas W. Sears* in April 1847 stimulated "considerable excitement" among the residents of Boston who almost started a riot against the ship.[74] When the Boston city government decided to erect a quarantine hospital on Deer Island in Boston harbor for the reception of immigrants the following month, anti-Irish citizens threatened to destroy the institution, circulating handbills that declared: *"American citizens of Boston!* The honorable Fathers of this City, have thought expedient to erect a HOSPITAL on Deer Island, for the protection of FOREIGN PAUPERS! ... AMERICAN CITIZENS! BE IN AT THE DEATH!!"[75] Tensions between nativists and the Irish exploded again in June, when several hundred Irish immigrants expressed their intention to use violence to oppose the implementation of exclusion policy by the authorities of Charlestown, Massachusetts, so that all foreign passengers would be allowed to land.[76]

In Massachusetts, antipathy to the famine Irish, especially assisted paupers, crystallized in the form of direct advocacy of their deportation. The Boston City Council received countless petitions, from groups of thirty to two hundred Bostonians, demanding the stringent enforcement of the removal provision in state law. The petitioners requested that the city execute every applicable law to "cause all paupers in our Alms Houses to be sent or conveyed to the places beyond seas or otherwise, to which they may belong."[77] Disgusted by the British government's assisted emigration schemes, Abbott Lawrence, former congressman from Massachusetts, reportedly declared that "I would send the foreign paupers back! ... but not to Scotland, not to Ireland, not to Wales. I would send them up the Thames to London, and land them opposite the Parliament House, *under its very eaves, if possible, while Parliament was in session!*"[78] These voices did not fall on deaf ears; Boston officials enforced pauper removal law to expel the Irish poor. In July 1846, the *Newburyport Herald* reported that the authorities of Boston deported on the ship *Joshua Bates* between seventy and eighty Irish paupers, "who have been sent out here probably from pauper houses in Ireland." Reflecting the prevailing nativist sentiment, the article remarked that "we think no one will complain" about their removal.[79]

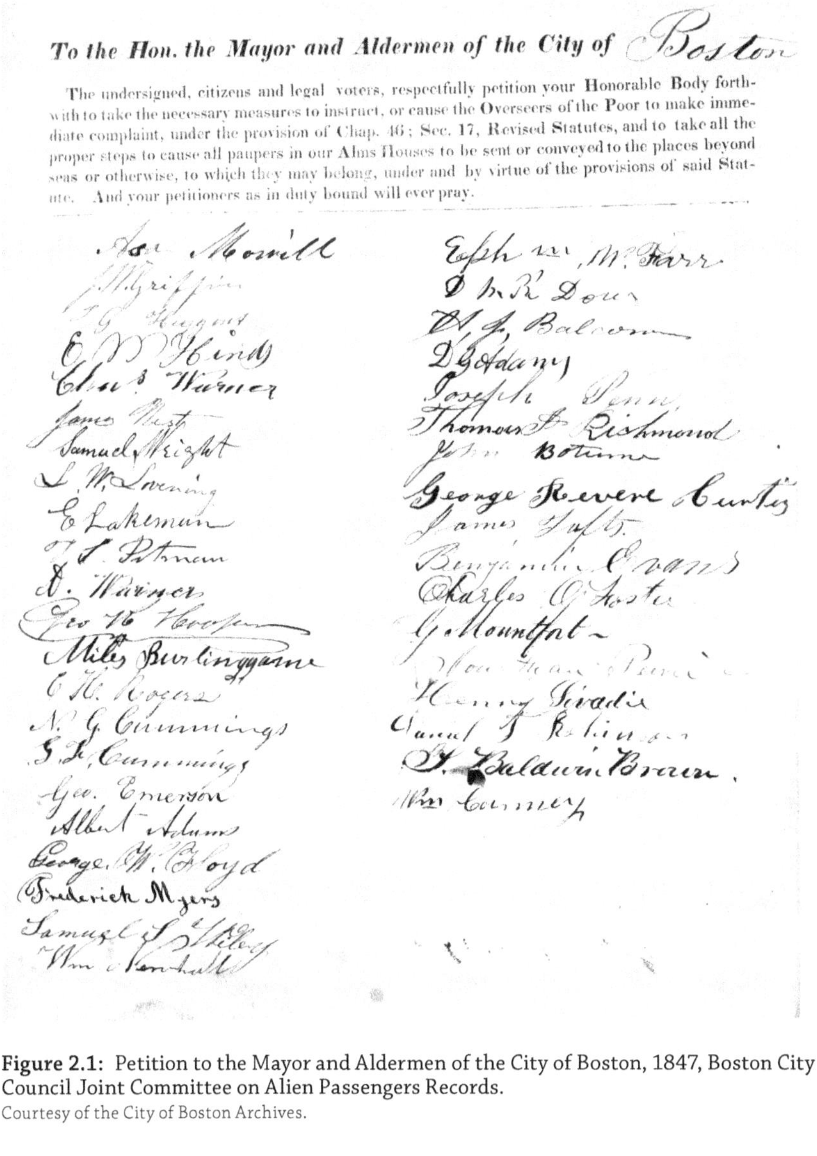

Figure 2.1: Petition to the Mayor and Aldermen of the City of Boston, 1847, Boston City Council Joint Committee on Alien Passengers Records.
Courtesy of the City of Boston Archives.

During the famine years the vast majority of the immigrants were allowed to land in Boston, but port officials excluded unbonded pauper passengers through the provisions of the 1837 alien passenger act. In July 1847, for instance, 190 passengers who arrived in Boston from Liverpool "in a most destitute and wretched condition" were "ordered off" to return to Europe because of the captain's failure or refusal to prepare bonds for them.[80] By keeping a sharp eye on pauper passengers and strictly demanding bonds for them, the officials tried to exclude as many paupers as possible, or at least make sure that the city of Boston would not suffer the expenses caused by the foreign poor. In the port of Boston, a municipal officer called the Superintendent of Alien Passengers directed the examination of passengers and the collection of bonds.

The superintendent's activities were supported by the municipal health commissioner. When a vessel arrived at the quarantine on Deer Island in Boston harbor, a port physician would board and examine the passengers. Upon confirming their healthy condition, the physician issued a certificate that the vessel "is not foul, or infected with any malignant or contagious disease . . . and in my opinion there is no objection to a permission being granted for her to be removed" from the quarantine. The superintendent's approval of the certificate would permit the landing of the healthy passengers if the shipmaster paid a capitation tax for each of them. Persons with contagious diseases would not be allowed to disembark.[81] In this way, the regulation of public health was an integral part of immigrant exclusion policy.

Quarantine policy operated in ways that regulated immigrant admission in other states as well. In New York, for example, a state law of 1827 allowed the Health Officer of New York City to determine which passengers should be confined to the quarantine on Staten Island and how long they should remain there. Without the officer's permission, no passengers with contagious diseases hazardous to public health would be released for landing.[82] In a strict sense quarantine regulation was a policy for delaying—rather than permanently prohibiting—the admission of passengers. Nevertheless, as legal scholar Gerald Neuman has pointed out, the strict implementation of quarantine laws could lead to the death of diseased passengers during isolation before their landing, a consequence tantamount to immigrant exclusion.[83]

The enforcement of exclusion could be tumultuous. On May 17, 1847, the British brig *Mary* arrived in Boston from Cork, Ireland, with forty-six passengers. The Boston Superintendent of Alien Passengers decided that none of the passengers would be allowed to land without bonds, "owing to their destitute condition." When the captain of the ship failed to provide the required bonds, the superintendent ordered him to bring the passengers to Halifax, Nova Scotia. Infuriated by the arrangement, the passengers assaulted the captain with handspikes and held the windlass under control as the ship was about to depart for Halifax. One newspaper describing the incident reported: "The resistance of the unfortunate passengers is not to be wondered at, when it is considered that they were not landed at the termination of the voyage, but forced to go in an entirely different direction from what they contemplated." The captain requested help from the captain of another vessel and his crew to restore order, but the passengers fought back. During the disturbance, one of the passenger rioters was thrown from a height of several feet and fell on the deck. After another boat's crew, armed with cutlasses, joined the two captains, they finally suppressed the riot. The *Mary* eventually arrived in Halifax with all the forty-six passengers on May 26.[84]

This episode illuminates the centrality of American officials' discretionary power in the implementation of exclusion law. Port officers' priority lay in simply denying the landing of unbonded passengers, and it mattered little to the officials what would happen to excluded aliens once they left the American shore—whether they would be returned to their port of departure or sent somewhere else. A few days after the incident the Boston superintendent rejected another British vessel from Cork, the *Seraph*, and diverted it to St. John, New Brunswick, with one hundred fever-stricken passengers.[85] The Boston authorities judged that these vessels belonged to Britain and therefore they could be returned to anywhere in British territory whether it was Liverpool, Cork, or British North America. Officials' emphasis on the expediency of removal and their disregard for the fate of expelled paupers, as seen in the cases of the *Mary* and *Seraph*, were the recurring features of immigration policy in nineteenth-century Massachusetts.

Although the Massachusetts cases reveal that state deportation and exclusion laws were actively enforced in the 1840s, many Americans found their states' passenger policies inadequate to deal with Irish famine immigration. When the famine migrants began to arrive, the immigration laws of the Atlantic seaboard states were administered by city officials. Shipmasters of arriving vessels provided bonds or paid capitation taxes to municipal, rather than state, authorities, such as the Superintendent of Alien Passengers in Boston. In Philadelphia, the Board of Guardians of the Poor, the city's poor relief agency, collected bonds and head money under Pennsylvania law. The visible and constant growth of Irish pauperism during the first few years of the famine convinced Americans, especially those in Massachusetts and New York, that the local administration of state immigration law was insufficient for the purpose of blocking pauper immigration.

In Massachusetts, welfare officials who daily observed the admission of Irish paupers into public almshouses detected a critical structural problem in state passenger policy. When a bonded passenger entered an almshouse as a pauper after landing, the expense would be paid out of the bond. As long as bonded immigrants remained in their city of arrival, officials in the city could identify those who had been bonded among almshouse inmates. But when bonded immigrants left their place of arrival and entered almshouses in other cities or towns, local officials usually had no clue as to the bonding status of these immigrant paupers—whether they had been bonded at the time of arrival or landed as healthy passengers without bond. If the immigrant pauper had been bonded, the city or town technically did not have to draw on its own treasury for the maintenance of the person at its almshouse. In practice, however, without information about paupers' bonding status, local officials often had no choice but to reach into their own treasuries to cover the cost of bonded paupers.[86] Thus, the centrality of cities and towns in state immigration policy posed an obstacle to the efficient management of foreign pauperism.

New York had also developed a problem with its passenger policy. Prior to the 1840s, a New York official noted, immigrants "could be controlled," meaning that bonded passengers were accommodated at public charitable institutions when they needed relief after landing. Once the famine immigration started, however, "the law became susceptible of the most flagrant abuses." Under state law, shipmasters would lose the bonds that they paid upon arrival for destitute passengers if they entered public almshouses. To retain the bond money, shipowners sent their former passengers, when they became destitute, to private poorhouses or hospitals instead of public institutions. Filthy and overcrowded, these private facilities were often utterly ill-equipped for accommodating humans. Frauds such as the imposition of arbitrary rents by avaricious boarding-house keepers and their agents, or "runners," also often afflicted newcomers.[87] Under these circumstances, immigrant aid societies in New York City proposed to reform state immigration law from a humanitarian standpoint. Influential public figures who sympathized with the plight of immigrants, such as Whig leader and newspaper editor Thurlow Weed and Irish-born Catholic Archbishop John Hughes, endorsed the idea. These actions moved Mayor William V. Brady to hold a public meeting of citizens for the purpose of discussing immigration reform in March 1847. At the meeting, participants resolved to establish a body of nonpartisan state immigration commissioners, who would supervise the collection and appropriation of bonds as well as the treatment of needy foreigners with broader authority than that of municipal officials.[88]

Nativists in Massachusetts and New York were highly frustrated by the incompetence and irresponsibility of some local officials. For both states, securing bonds and capitation taxes was crucial to minimizing the public expense of maintaining foreign paupers. Precisely because of this importance of bonds and head money, New Yorkers were outraged when a municipal investigation of the bonding system revealed that the mayor's clerk, who was responsible for keeping account of the bonds, had been pocketing the money collected from shipmasters since 1836, causing a significant drain on the city's treasury.[89] Also, the Democratic aldermen in New York City, whose electoral power base lay in Irish immigrants, administered landing regulations loosely in return for their votes.[90]

A similar type of scandal shocked citizens in Massachusetts. In the spring of 1847, the legislature discovered that "either from the inefficiency of the officers appointed to execute them, unpleasantness of the duty, or some other operating influence," provisions of state passenger law "have been disregarded" by municipal port officials. Calvin Bailey, the Superintendent of Alien Passengers for the port of Boston since 1837, confessed that he had permitted the landing of sick and aged passengers "without requiring any bond of indemnity." The superintendent also let disabled passengers land without bonds if they proved that they had friends who could take care of them, neglecting his duty to obtain a bond for every infirm passenger. Asked why he knowingly evaded the law, Bailey answered, "My only plea is humanity; and if you were to see them dying and suffering, as I do, on their arrival, I doubt whether you could deny them the privilege of landing." The investigating committee suggested the replacement of municipal immigration officers with state officials who should be appointed by the governor and should act "under oath and bonds for faithful performance" of their duty.[91]

The superintendent's neglect of state passenger law enraged nativists in Massachusetts, where anti-Irish sentiment had already become volatile. Angry citizens sent a memorial to the City Council, complaining that "the rigid enforcement of the laws in relation to immigration, is the only safeguard against the too great influx of poor, depraved, vicious, and unfortunate fellow beings."[92] The nativist *Boston Daily Bee*, invoking an Old Testament image, warned against the further entry of "offscourings of Ireland—poor, worthless hacks, who come out as paupers, to curse our land with a curse compared to which the locusts of Egypt were a blessing." "And poor as our laws have been on this subject," the *Bee* lamented, "we have not even had officers, with patriotism to execute them."[93] Nativist citizens also demanded the removal of Bailey from the office of Superintendent of Alien Passengers, which led to his replacement by a new superintendent named Jotham B. Munroe.[94] In the meantime, between 1,200 and 1,300 citizens of Massachusetts petitioned the legislature for "a speedy and thorough revision of the whole scheme" of passenger regulation.[95]

Faced with an array of problems, the New York legislature introduced a monumental reform to state immigration policy in May 1847. In response to citizens' petition for a state immigration commissioner, the legislature founded the Board of the Commissioners of Emigration of the State of New York. Friedrich Kapp, who served as one of the commissioners in 1870, attributed the board's creation to the lobbying campaign inside and outside of the legislature by Thurlow Weed, who mobilized Whig members and his Democratic friends, and by Andrew Carrigan, a wealthy Irish American citizen who later became the president of the New York Irish Emigrant Society. The establishment of the state board signified the transfer of leadership over immigration issues from cities to the state. At the same time, however, municipal governments remained a vital part of immigration control in that the commissioners included the mayors of New York City and Brooklyn, in addition to six officials appointed by the governor. To ensure that the commissioners' activities would extend to the protection of immigrants, the presidents of the Irish Emigrant Society and the German Society were included as commissioners, giving the board ten members.[96]

The commissioners' foremost task was twofold: immigration regulation and immigrant protection. The commissioners were authorized to board ships arriving in the port of New York and to inspect the condition of passengers. If they found "any lunatic, idiot, deaf and dumb, blind or infirm persons, not members of emigrating families, and who ... are likely to become permanently a public charge," the commissioners were to require shipmasters to provide a bond of $300, which would be effective for five years, for the landing of each of these passengers. If shipmasters refused to provide bonds for these passengers, they were not allowed to land. Pauper exclusion through bonding was not a new policy, but legislators sought to tighten passenger inspection and admission regulation by creating a state immigration agency devoted to the matters of immigration. Besides bonds for those who might become dependent on public charity, shipmasters had to pay one dollar in head money for each healthy passenger.[97]

The other chief duty of the Commissioners of Emigration was the protection of immigrants. The officials were authorized to "provide for the maintenance and support" of the persons for whom shipmasters had paid bonds and head money upon arrival. The state-run marine hospital on Staten Island was placed under the commissioners' supervision for this purpose, and another immigrant hospital was established on Ward's Island in 1848. The commissioners would also assist newcomers in proceeding to other parts of New York or other states, where they could meet their relatives or friends or obtain employment by "writing and receiving letters for the uneducated" and by "providing the means of conveyance to distant places."[98] The aggregate of head money would cover the expense of the commissioners' activities, including their management of charitable institutions. In this way, the commissioners provided social services to those who were admitted to the United States.

Massachusetts followed a similar path a year later. The mass petitions from citizens led the state legislature to appoint a committee for the modification of the foreign passenger and pauper laws in January 1848.[99] Following the committee's suggestions, the legislature enacted "An Act Concerning Alien Passengers" in May. As New York's legislature did in 1847, the Bay State government centralized authority over immigration with this act. Under the passenger act, the governor would appoint a Superintendent of Alien Passengers in each city and town to execute the provisions of the act. When a vessel arrived in any Massachusetts port with foreign passengers, the superintendent, now a state official, would board the vessel and examine the passengers. If the official found any "lunatic, idiot, maimed, aged, or infirm person, incompetent, in the opinion of the superintendent so examining, to maintain themselves, or who have been paupers in any other country," the shipmaster needed to give the superintendent a bond of $1,000 for the landing of each of such passengers. For a passenger whom the superintendent judged as unlikely to become a public charge "by undoubted evidence," the shipmaster could land the person with the payment of two-dollar head money. The state government would distribute collected bonds and capitation taxes to cities and towns to alleviate the financial burden of supporting foreign paupers in their almshouses.[100]

Although New York and Massachusetts introduced similar systems of passenger regulation supervised by the state government, there was a significant distinction between the two states' policies. In New York, the rise of state control partly stemmed from humanitarian concerns about the welfare of immigrants. For this reason, the duties of the New York Commissioners of Emigration included providing social services and protection to newcomers who were allowed to land. In Massachusetts, by contrast, the centralization of immigration power occurred mainly out of a nativist impetus for stricter restriction on Irish pauper immigration and the Superintendent of Alien Passengers did not take any responsibility for immigrants' security. Massachusetts bonds under the 1848 act mirrored the state's rigid attitude toward immigrants. Compared to New York's $300 bond, which remained effective only for five years, Massachusetts' bond was much larger ($1,000) and stayed valid for the lifetime of the person in question.[101] Massachusetts legislators hoped that the removal of time limit for bonds would encourage shipmasters to stop landing destitute passengers and to return them to Europe. Thus compared to its New York counterpart, the Massachusetts policy was much more focused on achieving the nativist goal of physically reducing the number of undesirable immigrants in the state. The anti-Catholic and anti-Irish tradition, as well as nativist political culture, in Massachusetts allowed the state to develop an exceptionally harsh approach to Irish paupers.

During the 1830s, the immigration of the impoverished Catholic Irish provoked intense nativist movements in Atlantic seaboard states. Laws for the removal of transient paupers and the restriction of destitute passengers' landing had existed in these states, but this Irish immigration changed their primary objective from the regulation of indigent people's domestic movement to control of immigration. Anti-Irish nativism thus triggered the emergence of immigration law in the United States, and as parts of the same process, both cultural prejudice and economic concerns contributed to this development. The scale of the Irish famine influx during the 1840s starkly revealed that the states could no longer leave their immigration policies in the hands of city officials. Realizing the inadequacy of the existing system to regulate the admission of foreigners, New York and Massachusetts placed immigration control under direct state supervision. All Atlantic seaboard states encountered the problem of Irish pauperism, but New York and Massachusetts responded most determinedly by establishing state-run immigration agencies. In other major immigrant-receiving states, such as Pennsylvania, Maryland, and Louisiana, state passenger law continued to be enforced by local officials.[102]

Early poor laws left one critical legacy in state-level immigration control. Most of the colonial and early state poor laws had a provision that prohibited the landing of "persons likely to become a public charge" without bonds. A nearly identical phrase ("likely to become permanently a public charge") appeared in New York's 1847 act, which created the Commissioners of Emigration. Massachusetts' passenger act of 1848 used a similar formulation when it defined terms for head money. Shipmasters could land healthy passengers by paying head money if they were "not likely to become chargeable to any city or town" in Massachusetts.[103] The absence of concrete definitions of the term "likely to become" allowed inspecting officers to use their discretion in deciding who needed bonds for landing. Likewise, under the Massachusetts pauper removal law, an immigrant pauper could be deported to "any place beyond [the] sea, where he belongs." Again, officials had complete authority in determining where the pauper in question belonged—other American states, Canada, or Europe. Together, state exclusion and deportation laws equipped enforcing officials with tremendous power over the fates of aliens. When this legal power was combined with officials' own nativist sentiment, the implementation of immigration policy became exceedingly coercive.

CHAPTER 3

༺ঌ

Different Paths

The Development of Immigration Policy in Antebellum Coastal States

On May 13, 1848, the British ship *Albion* arrived in Boston harbor. The ship carried forty-four passengers from Skibbereen in County Cork, Ireland, and twenty-four passengers from Liverpool. All the passengers were born in Ireland. The passenger record listed all of them, including women, as laborers and their children, with the exception of one servant. As the crew prepared for the landing and the passengers became increasingly excited and uneasy about stepping on to American soil, someone unfamiliar appeared on board. This person, the governor-appointed Superintendent of Alien Passengers for the port of Boston, then started to examine the conditions of the immigrants. Finding several of them too destitute or sick to support themselves without becoming public charges, the superintendent demanded a bond of $1,000 for each of these Irish immigrants from the ship's Captain Driscoll so that the state did not have to expend public money for their maintenance. Either because he found the bonds too costly or because he hesitated to provide extra money in addition to the mandatory capitation tax for other passengers, Driscoll did not supply the required bonds. As a result, the superintendent prohibited the landing in Boston of six indigent passengers and ordered the captain to bring them back to Europe.[1] Cities and towns in Atlantic seaboard states had long excluded destitute foreigners in this way, but in the late 1840s, New York and Massachusetts began to regulate immigration under the direction of the state government, inaugurating a new era of state-level immigration control in the United States.

This chapter traces the development of state immigration policy between 1849 and 1854. Faced with the Supreme Court's challenge to state passenger law in 1849 and the intensive arrival of assisted paupers from Ireland during the early 1850s, legislators in New York and Massachusetts revised state immigration policies. In both states, the modification of policy included the enactment of new laws to minimize the pauperism of immigrants, especially the Irish. New York's reform focused on reinforcing existing exclusion policy, and the state government resisted deporting immigrants. Massachusetts, by contrast, expanded deportation policy by empowering the Superintendent of Alien Passengers to expel foreign paupers abroad and eventually by creating the Commissioners of Alien Passengers and Foreign Paupers, who possessed even broader authorities over removal than the superintendent. The two states adopted distinct policies, yet in a national context—specifically that of the other major immigrant receiving states, such as Pennsylvania, Maryland, Louisiana, and California—it is clear that they developed by far the most advanced systems of state-level immigration control. Building upon a system that emerged in response to the influx of the famine Irish in the late 1840s, the two northeastern states consolidated the state supervision of immigration in the early 1850s. Economic concerns about Irish immigrants' poverty, inflated by cultural prejudice against them, continued to lead this development.

Immigration regulation unfolded not only in a world of laws but also in complex social and political settings. This chapter explores how immigrants viewed nativism, state policy, and public officials. It also pays close attention to how state officials treated immigrants and actually enforced exclusion and deportation laws, revealing that the expansion of regulatory policy in this period provided grounds for nativist officials' abuse of their authority over foreigners. In Massachusetts, the threat of deportation for foreigners significantly increased with the rise of the nativist Know-Nothing movement on the eve of the national election in the fall of 1854. Law, human action, and politics all shaped the story of immigration control in antebellum America.

The establishment of state immigration boards in the late 1840s improved the quality of passenger regulation in Massachusetts and New York. Realizing that the introduction of state control stemmed from municipal officials' failure to secure bonds for the entry of destitute foreigners, Jotham B. Munroe, the Superintendent of Alien Passengers for the

Port of Boston, confirmed in his first annual report that "*bonds* have been required" for pauper passengers and they were not permitted to land otherwise.[2] During one week in November 1848, the *Boston Daily Bee* reported, the superintendent excluded five passengers, as "they were unable to support themselves, and the masters of vessels unable to bond them."[3] Similarly, the New York Commissioners of Emigration denied admission to unbonded paupers to the extent that the officials believed their activities had "had some effect in lessening the number of [the] aged and infirm shipped to this country by the local authorities of Europe."[4]

The officials' dutiful implementation of the law notwithstanding, state-level immigration regulation was soon confronted with problems. Steamship companies questioned states' legal right to collect the capitation tax, or head money, for the landing of nonpauper passengers. Shippers regarded head money as an arbitrary tax on their business. To protect their profits, steamship runners usually calculated the price of passage to include the head money that shipmasters had to pay upon arrival. Without the tax they could have offered a lower passage fare, thereby increasing their business. In *City of New York v. Miln* (1837), the United States Supreme Court had upheld individual states' right to protect themselves from objectionable outsiders, such as pauper immigrants, as an exercise of internal policy power. Thereafter, coastal states had justified the collection of head money as a means of police regulation to protect their treasuries from the cost of supporting foreign paupers. Shippers, however, remained skeptical about the constitutionality of seaboard states' taxation policy in light of the court's earlier ruling in *Gibbons v. Ogden* (1824) that the authority to regulate passenger carriage belonged to the federal government.

In 1849, the Supreme Court delivered a critical ruling on the constitutionality of state passenger law. James Norris, a shipowner from St. John, New Brunswick, arrived in the port of Boston in June 1837, with nineteen nonpauper passengers on his vessel *Union Jack*. Under the state passenger law, a Boston port official compelled Norris to pay two dollars in head money for each of his passengers. After some unsuccessful attempts in lower courts to regain his money, Norris carried the case to the United States Supreme Court in 1846. In January 1849, the court ruled in *Norris v. City of Boston* and a similar case from New York called *Smith v. Turner*, together known as the *Passenger Cases*.[5]

By a narrow margin (5 to 4), the Supreme Court decided that the statutes of Massachusetts and New York requiring head money for the landing of immigrant passengers infringed upon federal authority over foreign commerce, which was vested in Congress by the United States Constitution.

Justice John McLean, for the majority, asserted that the capitation tax was "a regulation of commerce, not being within the power of the State." McLean concluded: "Congress has regulated commerce and intercourse with foreign nations, and between the several States, by willing that it shall be free." It was beyond the power of individual states "either to refuse a right of passing to persons or property through her territory, or to exact a duty for permission to exercise it." The Supreme Court declared passenger laws in Massachusetts and New York unconstitutional and void.[6]

The Supreme Court decision confirmed the superiority of Congress to states in the sphere of passenger regulation, but it left certain ambiguities in the understanding of states' capacity for internal police regulation. Continuing his earlier support of state sovereignty in the *Miln* case by way of recognizing southern states' right to prohibit the admission of free blacks, Chief Justice Roger B. Taney brought up in his dissenting opinion the notion of internal police power to argue that the Massachusetts passenger law "only exacts security against pauperism," just as southern states "cannot admit emancipated slaves." The justices, including those in the majority, concurred with Taney on states' right to police power itself and agreed that states still possessed a legitimate authority to protect themselves from undesirable outsiders. "In giving the commercial power to Congress," Justice John McLean noted, "the States did not part with that power of self-preservation which must be inherent in every organized community." Justice Robert Grier remarked that the provision in the state passenger law in question was not bonds for pauper immigrants but head money as a tax that involved a commercial transaction between states and passengers. The invalidation of state head money did not undermine states' right to repel foreign lunatics, idiots, criminals, and paupers from their shores. Thus the Supreme Court permitted states to exercise internal police power through the exclusion of unbonded paupers and the deportation to Europe of destitute foreigners already in the United States.[7]

The Supreme Court's endorsement of state police power did little to compensate for what seaboard states lost by the decision. To begin with, the loss of the capitation tax signified the loss of revenues that funded the activities of state immigration agencies and the administration of marine hospitals for sick immigrants who were admitted to land. The invalidation of head money also invited what state officials called "unrestricted" immigration. The discontinuation of head money lowered the price of steamship tickets, allowing poor people who could not otherwise emigrate to cross the Atlantic. "The very almshouses in Europe would seem," the *Boston Herald* noted, "to have transferred their inmates directly to our own" since the Supreme Court decision.[8] Without alternative measures to prevent "the unrestricted influx of aliens, of all classes, into territory," Massachusetts Governor George N. Briggs warned, "the consequences to the treasury, morals, and health of the people . . . may be most disastrous."[9]

Besides the legal problem, state policy also suffered from the heavy volume of Irish pauper immigration, which simply made the strict enforcement of passenger regulation impossible. Landlords and workhouse officials in Ireland had assisted Irish paupers in emigrating since 1830s, but the most intensive phase of shipping destitute tenants and inmates to the United States came in the early 1850s. The passenger reports at the quarantine station on Staten Island in New York described with great frequency the figure of a destitute Irishman "sent out by his landlord." Many of the assisted emigrants were also recorded as "cripple," "deformed," or "paralyzed."[10] The New York Association for Improving the Condition of the Poor, a private charitable society, complained about the "systematic invasion of our country by the indigent."[11] The records of the New York City Almshouse reveal the consequences of state immigration officials' practical inability to prevent the landing of assisted Irish paupers. Between 1849 and 1854, foreigners accounted for 76 percent of the persons admitted to the institution, and 82 percent of these were born in Ireland.[12]

Assisted paupers came from various parts of Ireland, but a series of arrivals in the early 1850s from the estate of the Marquis of Lansdowne in County Kerry drew particular attention, as their level of wretchedness was exceptional even compared to the condition of other assisted paupers. Between December 1850 and March 1851, the estate financed the emigration of 1,700 famine-stricken tenants to the United States.[13] During this period, New Yorkers frequently witnessed Lansdowne tenants "in an almost naked and famishing state, in Broadway, begging the charity of the passers." Their destitution and raggedness stunned New Yorkers, who were no strangers to immigrant poverty. In New York City, the Lansdowne tenants settled in a neighborhood called Five Points, where they could find the cheapest housing, becoming the poorest inhabitants of the nation's poorest and most infamous slum.[14] Some of the Lansdowne immigrants continued their journey to Massachusetts. In May 1851, upon the arrival of 162 assisted paupers, including the Lansdowne tenants from New York, the nativist Boston Daily Bee proposed their immediate deportation: "A more miserable looking gang of human beings never were seen. They should be sent back at once to those who so unmercifully cast them away."[15] The newspaper stressed that Bostonians would soon realize the importance of an enhanced immigration law, "the end of which will be to keep the paupers of foreign countries at home, where only they can belong."[16]

Thus from 1849 to the early 1850s, state immigration officials struggled with two issues. The United States Supreme Court had struck down coastal states' capitation taxes, threatening the financial basis of state immigration policy. The incursion into New York and Massachusetts of assisted paupers from Ireland also paralyzed the existing mode of admission regulation, leading to increased foreign pauperism in New York City and Boston. Within a few years of the foundation of state immigration agencies, officials in New York and Massachusetts faced a necessity to overcome legal problems with the passenger policies and to improve their quality for the more effective restriction of pauper immigration.

In response to the *Passenger Cases* and the influx of assisted Irish paupers, New York and Massachusetts reformed their immigration policies. Both states fixed the constitutional problem with the capitation tax in similar ways, but New York and Massachusetts thereafter followed different courses. The New York legislature tightened surveillance over the entry of assisted pauper immigrants by expanding the category of excludable people. Yet it resisted any further action, rejecting demands from the Commissioners of Emigration and private citizens for the enactment of a deportation law. By contrast, the Massachusetts legislature passed a series of new laws to strengthen immigration control in the state much more drastically. It fundamentally enhanced exclusion policy by extending entry regulation to immigration by railroad, increased the number and authority of officials charged with deportation, and broadened the category of deportable people, instituting an extensive system to restrict pauper immigration by 1854.

After the invalidation of state head money in the *Passenger Cases*, New York and Massachusetts resolved the constitutional flaw in state passenger law by manipulating legal technicalities. Three months after the court decision, the New York legislature passed a new passenger act, which required shipmasters to provide a bond of $300 for the landing of every passenger regardless of his or her condition, with the option of paying a $1.50 fee for a nonpauper passenger in lieu of a bond. In March 1850, Massachusetts similarly changed state passenger law, establishing a bond of $1,000 applicable to every immigrant passenger. Shipmasters could commute the bond by paying a fee of two dollars for each immigrant passenger who was not judged a pauper by the Superintendent of Alien Passengers.[17]

These provisions were crafted very carefully to let the states virtually continue the collection of head money. Shipmasters found the requirement of bonds for all immigrant passengers impossible to meet because of the enormous amount of money they would have to prepare. If the ship-masters wanted to land their passengers, they therefore had to turn to the payment of the cheaper commutation fee, which in practical terms func-tioned as head money. Legally, the states received the fee not as a manda-tory capitation tax upon passengers but an option that the shipmasters voluntarily paid. By coercing shipmasters into choosing the commutation fee, this arrangement allowed New York and Massachusetts to collect head money without violating federal authority over foreign commerce.[18]

Once they fixed the head money system, policymakers in New York moved to strengthen the restriction of assisted pauper immigration. Under the law of 1847, the Commissioners of Emigration had prohibited the entry without bonds of people unable to support themselves, such as "lunatic, idiot, deaf and dumb, blind or infirm persons" and those likely to become public charges. In April 1849, legislators broadened the category of people who required bonds for landing by including persons "who *have been* paupers in any other country or who from sickness or disease, *exist-ing at the time of departing from the foreign port* are or are likely soon to become a public charge."[19] Clearly, the explicit emphasis on pauper status and the state of dependency at the time of departure was targeted against assisted pauper passengers. In July 1851, the legislature further extended the bonding category to "persons above the age of sixty years, or widow with a child or children, or any woman without a husband, and with a child or children."[20] Recent studies of Irish assisted emigration during the famine reveal the higher likelihood of assisted emigrants to have been in their fifties or older than the average Irish immigrant and the overrepre-sentation of women with children among assisted emigrants sent from workhouses.[21] Given these findings, policymakers must have designed the specification of particular passenger groups in the new bonding policy to identify assisted paupers. The Commissioners of Emigration admitted that the revision of the passenger law in 1851 gave "much greater efficacy" to the collection of bonds for "helpless persons sent from the poor-houses of Europe."[22] By setting up detailed rules for bonds, legislators made it difficult for shipmasters to evade bonds for assisted paupers and aimed to exert pressure on shipmasters to bring them back to Europe.

In addition to controlling the admission of assisted paupers, the New York Commissioners of Emigration sought ways to return immigrant paupers to Europe. New York state law did not permit the compulsory deportation of aliens from the state, but it did allow the officials to trans-fer immigrants to other parts of the state or other states by helping them reach their final destinations. Beginning in 1850, the Commissioners of Emigration used this power to send back destitute foreigners who expressed their wish to return home, by financing their passage to Europe. In 1853, for example, the officials sent 271 persons "back to Europe at [their] own request." By using "the power already given to them by the laws under which they act," the Commissioners of Emigration tried to reduce the number of foreign paupers in the state, especially those shipped to the United States by foreign authorities. Before the Civil War, the commissioners returned at least 2,505 persons back to Europe through this policy.[23]

Despite the New York commissioners' efforts to exclude assisted paupers and send voluntary returnees back to Europe, it became clear by 1854 that these policies were not extensive enough to curtail foreign pauperism. The state legislature, however, refused to grant the commissioners any further authority for the rest of the 1850s. The Commissioners of Emigration, if the law had permitted, would have happily removed destitute aliens against their will. The officials firmly believed that it would be "most desirable" to deport assisted paupers, but at the same time, they regretfully noted that "this direct power is not granted by the existing laws of this State."[24] The New York *Journal of Commerce* contrasted New York with Massachusetts, which had developed laws for the overseas deportation of foreign paupers. Unlike Massachusetts, the press lamented, "we have no law in this State by which European paupers, idiots, &c., can be sent back, without their consent."[25] Proponents of immigration control in New York increasingly regarded deportation as imperative to protect the state from foreign pauperism, but the state legislature remained extremely reluctant to authorize the Commissioners of Emigration to enforce such policy.

If the development of regulatory immigration policy in New York was a story of cautious progress, Massachusetts provided a story of active expansion. When the Massachusetts legislature modified the head money system in March 1850, it also substantially augmented the power of the Superintendent of Alien Passengers. The 1794 state poor law provided that upon the complaint of the Overseers of the Poor, any justice of the peace could order the removal of any transient pauper to the place where the person had legal settlement within the United States or "to any place beyond [the] sea, where he belongs."[26] In 1850, the legislature vested this authority to initiate deportation in the Superintendent of Alien Passengers. The 1794 law originally aimed to regulate the movement of the transient poor within the United States, but this legislative action reflected policymakers' recognition of immigrant deportation as the principal function of the pauper removal law.[27] The Superintendent of Alien Passengers began to supervise not only the admission of foreigners but also their deportation after initial entry into the state.

Two cases of pauper removal illustrate how the Superintendent of Alien Passengers processed deportation. In September 1851, Superintendent Munroe brought to the police court four immigrant inmates at the Deer Island almshouse to ask for their expulsion. In their trial, the justice upheld their status as foreign paupers without settlement in America and ordered the deportation to Ireland of William Hassett from County Kerry and Dennis Moran from County Mayo. The justice also ordered the return of John McKenzie from Dundee, Scotland, who became a "cripple" and public charge during his nineteen-month stay in Boston. The court dropped the charge against the other defendant, William Graham, who was "a respectable and well dressed Englishman," on the grounds that he had been sent to Deer Island for the offense of temporary drunkenness rather than pauperism.[28] In the same month, after a local court determined five destitute immigrants were unsettled foreign paupers, all of them were placed on board the Liverpool-bound *Plymouth Rock*.[29] As these cases show, the enforcement of pauper removal law took several steps. The Superintendent of Alien Passengers first physically took paupers to the court and put them on trial. Actual deportation took place after the court ordered their removal. Thus the superintendent had the power to initiate deportation, but he first needed to obtain the court's approval to expel foreign paupers.

The revision of immigration policy in Massachusetts extended beyond the empowerment of the Superintendent of Alien Passengers. By 1850, Massachusetts had established a notorious reputation among steamship companies for its stringent passenger law. In New York, the Commissioners of Emigration could retain bonds collected for pauper passengers for only five years after their arrival, but Massachusetts bonds remained in force during the lifetime of bonded passengers. Massachusetts officials also tended to require a bond for the entry of a passenger whom the New York commissioners would let land without bond as a nonpauper. Between 1848 and 1850, New York collected fewer than 300 bonds out of more than 600,000 arriving passengers. By contrast, Massachusetts secured over 4,000 bonds, even though there were fewer than 90,000 immigrants to the state.[30] The British consul at Boston noticed that shipowners found Massachusetts passenger law so difficult to comply with that he occasionally had to assist the owners of British vessels from Ireland in landing their passengers by providing required bonds on the owners' behalf.[31] The rigidity of Massachusetts policy drove emigrant agents in Europe to send Boston-bound passengers to New York first and then arrange their trip to Boston by railroad. Consequently, Massachusetts received a large number of pauper immigrants coming through other American states and Canada for whom neither bonds nor head money was obtained, among them the Lansdowne immigrants from New York.

In the spring of 1851 the Massachusetts legislature reorganized the state's immigration policy, introducing the regulation of immigration by railroad in response to shipping agents' practice as part of this reform. In May, the legislature established the State Board of Commissioners of Alien Passengers and Foreign Paupers as the first comprehensive state agency to administer immigration control and poor relief. Known as the Alien Commissioners, the board consisted of a member of the Executive Council, the State Auditor, and the Superintendent of Alien Passengers for the port of Boston. While the commissioners inherited all the duties and power of the superintendent over the exclusion of unbonded desti- tute passengers and the deportation of foreign paupers, they acquired new authority to regulate foreigners' admission into the state by railroad. The commissioners would appoint agents at train stations in Massachusetts to collect information from transportation companies about the names and conditions of all foreign passengers who arrived in the state "otherwise than by water," so that the state could identify the immigrants if they later became public charges. If the passengers became paupers within one year of arrival, the company that brought them would have the option to pay for the cost of supporting them at almshouses or take them back to their places of origin. When the passengers needed aid at the time of arrival, railroad companies could choose to bring them back instead of assuming the responsibility for their maintenance.[32] Thus the legislature made land borders sites of immigration control, just like ports. The regu- lation of admission by railroad, along with deportation, became a unique feature in Massachusetts' immigration policy compared to that of other states.

The creation of the Alien Commissioners also aimed to scale up depor- tation. To facilitate the removal of foreign paupers from almshouses, the commissioners would authorize their agents to visit all almshouses and other charitable institutions in Massachusetts at least once a year. The agents would then, "from actual examination and inquiry," ascertain the locations of inmates' settlements. Upon confirming a pauper's lack of settlement in Massachusetts, the commissioner agents would arrange deportation to the place "where he belongs" under the removal law.[33] By enhancing the activities of the Superintendent of Alien Passengers with more personnel and duties, Massachusetts policymakers refined the sys- tem of state-level immigration control.

Some evidence reveals that people expelled from Massachusetts by the Alien Commissioners included assisted paupers. In 1851, Superintendent

Munroe returned "a large number of the most unfortunate of Ireland's poor, from the estate of the Marquis of Lansdowne" in five batches to New York on the grounds that the state which admitted these indigent foreigners in the first place should take care of them.[34] In July of the year, the *Boston Evening Transcript* reported on the prospect of the deportation from the Boston House of Industry of a group of paupers originally "taken from the Almshouses of England and Ireland" or "sent to this country by heartless landlords," including the Lansdowne tenants, the "most wretched and helpless paupers we have seen this year."[35] In September 1852, according to the *Boston Daily Bee*, twenty-three paupers, who had been "sent here" by Irish officials, were deported to their homeland "on the same principle." These deportees got "the benefit of sea voyages, and the authorities in Ireland of paying double passages," which implies that the senders who had assisted the paupers' initial emigration were compelled to pay their return passage to Ireland.[36]

On the initiative of the Alien Commissioners, Massachusetts immigration policy went through further structural development. After their first year of operation, the commissioners persuaded the legislature to construct state-run almshouses in three parts of Massachusetts and an immigrant hospital on Rainsford Island in Boston harbor "for the accommodation of all aliens who become a public charge upon the Commonwealth."[37] In Massachusetts, foreign paupers without legal settlement in the state had hitherto been accommodated at city or town almshouses alongside local paupers at the expense of the state. The transfer of deportable foreigners to state institutions specifically designed for them, the commissioners believed, would make their removal more convenient. Administrators of the new state almshouses acquired the same deportation authority as the Alien Commissioners "in causing the inmates of said institutions to be returned to the place or country from which they came."[38]

The Alien Commissioners also expanded the category of deportable people to include aliens suffering from insanity. Many of the Irish immigrants during the famine period had some sorts of mental illness because of malnutrition, famine-related diseases contracted in Ireland or during the transatlantic voyage, and difficulties in adjusting to life in the United States. Unable to work, those who developed insanity often entered lunatic hospitals. In 1851, 70 percent of the newly admitted patients at the Boston Lunatic Hospital were born in Ireland.[39] In December 1853, officials at the Worcester State Lunatic Hospital complained that the institution "is fast filling up with a class of incurable foreign paupers, which circumstance is already seriously impairing its usefulness as a curative institution." In 1854, the Alien Commissioners decided to expel foreign

Figure 3.1: J. H. Bufford, *State Alms House, Bridgewater, Mass.* In 1854, three state-run almshouses were established in Bridgewater, Monson, and Tewksbury to accommodate paupers without settlement in Massachusetts, many of whom were immigrants.
Courtesy of the American Antiquarian Society.

patients at lunatic hospitals from the state, considering paupers and lunatics equally objectionable financial burdens on the state.[40] In April, the state legislature authorized the trustees and inspectors of state lunatic hospitals and local authorities such as the Overseers of the Poor to cause the removal of any lunatic who had no settlement in the state to "any other State, or to any place beyond [the] sea."[41]

The integration of insanity into state immigration policy was based on the Alien Commissioners' highly monolithic view of foreign patients at lunatic hospitals. By the mid-nineteenth century, medical superintendents had identified several potential causes for insanity such as religious anxiety, business failure, political excitement, ill health, and physical blows on the head, but they diagnosed insanity with varying definitions, rather than solid professional guidelines. In practice any behavioral pattern, including the lack of appetite or inability to talk, could be regarded as a manifestation of insanity. Historian David Rothman has thus concluded that "the barrier between normality and deviancy was very low." Additionally, physicians of mental illness, often middle-class Protestant Anglo Americans, customarily used their own cultural standards in making diagnoses, tending to view as deviants those with different cultural and religious values. The Catholic Irish were particularly vulnerable to this sort of bias.[42] In this medical milieu, lunatic hospitals had patients with diverse conditions, including those who would have been considered sane under different circumstances and discharged. Nevertheless, from the standpoint of nativist officials, all immigrants joined a singe group of foreign paupers who were nothing but drains on public relief fund upon entering lunatic hospitals, and such paupers should be expelled from the state.

Thus by 1854, Massachusetts had established an extensive system of state-level immigration control. At the center of the new state immigration policies stood the Massachusetts Alien Commissioners. They resembled the New York Commissioners of Emigration in some ways. But unlike their New York counterparts, whose duties included the protection of admitted immigrants, the Massachusetts Alien Commissioners focused exclusively on immigration restriction without hospitable purposes. Emerging from a combination of existing legal institutions for regulating the movement of the poor, deep-rooted cultural prejudice against the Irish in Massachusetts, and frustration with Irish poverty, the Massachusetts Board of Commissioners of Alien Passengers and Foreign Paupers was America's first public agency committed to border control and immigrant deportation.

Examining federal passenger policy elucidates how New York and Massachusetts officials viewed the situation of immigration control in the early 1850s. By then the federal government had passed two passenger laws, one in 1819 and the other in 1847. Political scientist Aristide Zolberg has argued that these federal laws, which reduced the number of passengers a vessel could carry for the humanitarian purpose of securing sufficient space for each passenger, operated as a form of immigration regulation by raising fares and preventing the emigration of poor people from Europe.[43] It is nevertheless worth underscoring that Zolberg's study focuses on the practical outcome of federal legislation, rather than its intentions, whereas most contemporary public officials clearly did not see federal passenger law as a means of immigration control. Chief Justice Taney, for example, referred to the absence of federal regulation when he defended state legislation in the *Passenger Cases* by noting that the federal passenger act of 1819 "says nothing about the landing of passengers, nor about their health or condition."[44] In the state-level discourse on immigration control, few if any officials saw federal law as something that could supplement state pauper policies. Given the repeated submission of petitions from Atlantic seaboard states for a federal law that would restrict pauper immigration, federal regulation was virtually nonexistent from the perspectives of state officials, or at best they regarded federal passenger law as simply inadequate. In the antebellum period, they viewed state law as the only tool to control immigrant admission.

Immigration control in New York and Massachusetts followed different paths in the first half of the 1850s. New York stuck with exclusion as the state's principal method of immigration regulation, with a strong focus on preventing the landing of assisted paupers. Massachusetts pursued a more rigid and comprehensive form of immigration control, with exclusion and deportation. The distinction between New York and Massachusetts, however, diminished when placed in the national context of state immigration policy. During the 1850s most coastal states had some laws to regulate the landing of passengers, yet they failed to—or did not even attempt to—implement state-level immigration control to the same extent New York and Massachusetts did. The experiences of other major immigrant receiving states, such as Pennsylvania, Maryland, Louisiana, and California, show that no state in antebellum America was more committed to immigration control and more successful in sustaining state immigration policy than New York and especially Massachusetts.[45]

As a northeastern state, Pennsylvania developed passenger policies very similar to those in New York and Massachusetts. Following these states, Pennsylvania originally developed an immigration policy as part of the state's poor law, and municipal officials, the Philadelphia Board of Guardians of the Poor, took charge of administering passenger regulation. The Pennsylvania state law of 1828 required shipmasters to pay $2.50 in head money to the Guardians of the Poor for the landing of each nonpauper alien passenger and prohibited the entry of any destitute passenger who appeared likely to "become chargeable to the said guardians of the poor" without a bond of $150. After the *Passenger Cases*, Pennsylvania again followed New York and Massachusetts, changing head money into a fee that shipmasters voluntarily paid to continue the collection of the capitation tax. The Guardians also assisted the voluntary return to Europe of foreign paupers, as the New York Commissioners of Emigration did.[46]

The Guardians of the Poor certainly recognized the problem of immigrant poverty in Philadelphia. During the height of Irish famine immigration, they frequently resolved to strictly enforce state passenger policy in order to reduce the number of Irish paupers, who accounted for half the inmate population at the city's almshouse.[47] In practice, however, the Guardians conducted pauper exclusion in much milder ways than New York and Massachusetts officials. They sometimes admitted foreigners unable to support themselves through private arrangements. The Philadelphia officials, for example, approved an application of Irish

immigrant Patrick Kiernan, who was already in the city, for the landing
of his deaf and dumb daughter on the condition that he would personally provide to the Guardians a bond for his daughter.[48] New York and
Massachusetts officials admitted pauper passengers as long as shipmasters prepaid the cost of maintaining them in the form of bonds. But this
policy's essential intention was to urge shipmasters to bring such passengers back to Europe rather than take pains to land them by securing
large bonds. Given that the Commissioners of Emigration and the Alien
Commissioners looked for every excuse to exclude or remove undesirable
aliens, officials in New York and Massachusetts would not accept private immigrants' requests for the entry of family members with physical
disabilities.

Tension between the Guardians of the Poor and a private immigrant society also hindered the development of immigration policy in Pennsylvania.
Under the act of 1828, all head money collected from shipmasters went into
the hands of the Guardians of the Poor. The aggregate of head money was
supposed to be spent on the support of destitute immigrants in the city,
but the Guardians regarded the money as general revenue for the board
and sometimes even rejected needy foreigners' request for admission to the
almshouse.[49] In this situation the Philadelphia Emigrant's Friend Society,
a private immigrant aid society formed in 1848, demanded a share of head
money to better support newcomers, based on the model of the New York
Commissioners of Emigration, who used head money for providing social
service programs to admitted foreigners. Believing that "this money ought
to be carefully economized and scrupulously employed for the benefit" of
immigrants, the society began to send petitions to the state legislature for
the distribution of head money to the society in 1851.[50]

By extension of its claim to head money, the Emigrant's Friend Society
proposed the introduction of a state-run immigration agency. In 1854, the
society sent a delegation to New York City to "investigate and examine the
system pursued in reference to emigrant passengers arriving at New York."
The delegation's report on the operation of the New York Commissioners
of Emigration convinced the society that the Pennsylvania legislature
"ought without delay to adopt similar laws, in relation to immigrants
landing at the port of Philadelphia" and "to appoint, after the example
of the State of New York, a Board of Commissioners." The commissioners would use head money for the welfare of immigrants and protect
the state from "the liability for their support and maintenance," which
implies that the officials' duties would include pauper exclusion through
bonds.[51] The society's plan would have established a counterpart of the
New York Commissioners of Emigration in Pennsylvania, a state board

devoted to immigrant protection and immigration regulation. Hoping to retain control over head money, however, the Guardians of the Poor adamantly opposed the immigrant society's proposal.[52] In the end, the poor law officials prevailed. The legislature never gave serious consideration to petitions from the Emigrant's Friend Society.

Perhaps most decisively, divisions among legislators impeded the growth of public policy for immigration control in Pennsylvania. In the mid-1850s, a nativist party known as the Know-Nothing Party occupied the offices of governor and Philadelphia mayor and held the majority in the state house of representatives. The popularity of the party in part lay in its ability to appeal to diverse groups of voters with the platforms of nativism, anti-Catholicism, temperance, and anti-slavery. Yet precisely because of this multifaceted nature of its agenda, as well as the rivalry among members along their prior party affiliations, the Know-Nothing Party in Pennsylvania suffered deep factional divisions to the extent that it could not pursue any particular legislative goal. The most crucial division emerged between those who insisted that the party concentrate exclusively on issues of nativism and those who advocated the promotion of anti-slavery and temperance besides nativism. Consequently, Pennsylvania legislators failed to elect anyone to the state's vacant seat in the United States Senate. As historian Tyler Anbinder has argued, this internal division prevented the Know-Nothings in Pennsylvania from "acting with even a semblance of unity" and "the resentment generated by this stalemate paralyzed the legislature for the remainder of the session."[53] Given the high level of anti-Irish sentiment in Philadelphia as expressed in the Kensington riots in 1844 and the strength of political nativism in the mid-1850s, state-level immigration control could have emerged in Pennsylvania, but such a policy never developed in the state due to the absence of political unity and leadership.

As a result, Pennsylvania maintained the local administration of immigration policy laid out in 1828 throughout the antebellum period, symbolizing the state's failure to keep up with the enthusiasm for state-level immigration control in New York and Massachusetts. In stark contrast with developments in these states, Pennsylvania continued to rely on the Philadelphia Board of Guardians of the Poor, a municipal agency, for the implementation of state immigration law. Passenger regulation by the Board of Guardians remained loose at best, because, after all, it was not an immigration agency and the officials identified poor relief, rather than immigration control, as their primary business. The Guardians continued to enforce passenger regulation, but its place in their activities remained minor.[54]

In the South, the immigration of destitute Europeans provoked the occasional emergence of nativist organizations, but racial politics in the region minimized the influence of nativism on state immigration policy.[55] Due to the large proportion of blacks in the population, southern policymakers regarded securing the settlement of European immigrants as a critical means to strengthen white racial solidarity and to sustain the institution of slavery. Accordingly, the Democrats, the region's dominant politicians, constantly checked attempts to discourage immigration to the South. Also, southern nativists themselves lacked determination to achieve their anti-immigrant agenda. Sectional tensions over slavery prevailed over concerns about immigrants' Catholicism or poverty. As historian David Gleeson points out, white southerners were much more preoccupied by "the abolitionist 'fanaticism' of their Protestant 'brethren' in the North" and the destiny of slavery in the United States.[56] Immigration regulation thus failed to take permanent hold in southern states.

Restrictionist goals were never prominent, for example, in Maryland's immigration policy. Immigrants to Baltimore had long been mainly German farmers who quickly moved out of Maryland to settle in the agricultural regions of the West. Irish immigration in the 1830s made foreign pauperism a visible problem in Baltimore, but concerns about imported poverty did not result in the enactment of an expressly regulatory immigration policy in Maryland.[57] Maryland's passenger law of 1833 required shipmasters to pay $1.50 in head money to the city of Baltimore for the landing of each alien passenger, with the option of providing a bond of $150 in lieu of the capitation tax. Unlike passenger laws in northeastern states, Maryland's 1833 law did not list persons likely to become public charges as excludable without bonds, allowing for the admission of any pauper passenger if the shipmaster paid a small amount of head money. While New York and Massachusetts tried to compel shipmasters to bring destitute immigrants back to Europe by demanding heavy bonds, Maryland made no effort to deter their landing, reflecting the dearth of interest in immigration control among lawmakers in the state.[58]

Embodying the southern reluctance to discourage immigration, Louisiana, too, stayed away from developing restrictive policies. As a major point of entry to the Old Northwest and Texas for settlers from Europe, New Orleans was the second busiest port in antebellum America, after New York.[59] The large volume of immigration, however, did not prompt the Louisiana legislature to enact laws to regulate the entry of newcomers. With whites outnumbered by blacks in Louisiana, legislators had no intention of impeding the inflow of European immigrants to the state.[60] In 1842, the Louisiana legislature instituted a capitation tax for the purpose of securing funds for treating sick and indigent foreigners at the municipal Charity Hospital, but it did not bind shipmasters with any bonding obligation for paupers. As Maryland did, Louisiana allowed shipmasters to land destitute passengers with the payment of cheap head money.[61]

Local business elites' desire to profit from the passenger trade through a wide-open port helped preclude the introduction of regulatory policy in Louisiana. Pressured by business leaders who promoted the unregulated passenger trade, New Orleans authorities ignored the problem of foreign poverty and even suppressed information about outbreaks of yellow fever epidemics in the city, which might have led some people to question the open port policy. When a yellow fever outbreak in New Orleans killed about eight thousand people from 1853 to 1854, legislators finally decided to establish quarantine institutions where foreign passengers would undergo health inspections before landing. Louisiana lawmakers' unwillingness to advance any form of entry regulation, however, delayed the completion of the facilities until 1859. And the health examination of immigrants remained extremely mild or virtually nonexistent, allowing sick and penniless passengers who would have been rejected at other ports to land in New Orleans.[62]

The weakness of regulatory impetus against European immigration in the South did not mean that the region was isolated from the antebellum politics of immigration control. Since the 1820s, southern states had implemented Negro Seamen laws for imprisoning black sailors from the North and abroad during their ship's stay at a southern port, for fear that the spread of abolitionist ideas from these free blacks to local slaves could incite slave rebellions. Even after the circuit court invalidated South Carolina's Negro Seamen law for breaching federal commerce power in *Elkison v. Deliesseline* (1823), southern officials continued to detain black sailors by justifying their action as the legitimate exercise of state police power against threats to public peace. State-level immigration control in the antebellum South, however, should not be overrated simply by the sustained enforcement of the black sailor law. In contrast to the expansion of immigration policy in New York and Massachusetts during the 1840s and 1850s, the southern policy increasingly yielded to diplomatic concessions toward midcentury. British consuls, for example, successfully persuaded Louisiana and Georgia to allow for the landing of black sailors with the permission of local authorities in 1852 and 1854, respectively.[63] Ultimately, the policies banning the admission of free blacks collapsed when the Civil War destroyed slavery, the institution that southern states had attempted to preserve through these policies.

The Northeast and the South by no means dominated the story of state immigration policy. The discovery of gold in 1848 transformed California into a receiver of ambitious migrants from various corners of the globe, including Asia, Europe, and the Americas. Shortly after the incorporation of California into the Union as a state in 1850, the legislature enacted the state's first passenger act in 1852. Politicians in California were familiar with the New York and Massachusetts passenger laws, and as one state official admitted, "that was the law that we adopted" in 1852.[64] California's passenger act extensively replicated immigration policy in these two eastern states. It required shipmasters to either provide a bond of $500 or pay $5 in head money to the state of California for the entry of each passenger. The act further banned the landing without an additional bond of $1,000 of "any lunatic, idiot, deaf, dumb, blind, cripple or infirm person," as well as any person who had been "a pauper in any other country" and who appeared likely to become a public charge "from sickness or disease existing either at the time of departure from the port of departure, or at the time of arrival in any part of this State." This lengthy definition of people requiring bonds was an exact replication of the New York passenger act of 1851, which tightened surveillance over assisted pauper immigrants from famine Ireland. The 1852 act also established a governor-appointed Commissioner of Emigration for the city of San Francisco, authorizing the official to implement the act's provisions.[65]

It would be hasty to conclude, nonetheless, that the passage of the 1852 act brought California to the same stage of state-level immigration regulation as New York and Massachusetts. In the absence of substantial pauper immigration, the passenger act of California was something of a formality, duplicating the New York policy for a new state. The impending issue in antebellum California was not the presence of foreign paupers but the participation of Chinese immigrants in gold mining. California had received only a modest wave of Chinese immigration before the 1850s, with 325 Chinese passing through the San Francisco Customs House in 1849. Yet news of the discovery of gold sparked a rush of Chinese gold seekers to California during the next few years. By the end of 1852 the number of Chinese in California reached 20,000, accounting for 10 percent of the total population and 20 percent of the mining population in the state.[66]

The growing presence of Chinese as miners, cooks, and laundrymen quickly provoked white Californians' antagonism to the immigrants from Asia, who they believed were stealing American gold. Echoing this anti-Chinese sentiment, Governor John Bigler proclaimed in 1852 that California should stop "indiscriminate and unlimited Asiatic emigration." From Bigler's point of view, European paupers in New York and Massachusetts "merely" endangered the public health, whereas Chinese miners in California more seriously threatened "the most vital interests of the State and people" by taking away "precious metals."[67]

White Californians' racial prejudice against Chinese immigrants as inferior and inassimilable reinforced the argument in favor of immigration restriction on the basis of race. Representing white voices in California, Governor Bigler emphasized that Europeans were "part of our own people, belonging to the same race" and he uniformly favored "liberal enactments" for European immigration. Asians, by contrast, "in a moral and political sense, are the very antipodes of our race" and could not assimilate into "any of the relations of civil or social life" in America. Members in the legislature joined the governor by proposing to "exclude all foreigners, except those of European nations or of European descent, from the State."[68] What lawmakers in California wanted was a racially restrictive measure against Chinese immigration, rather than class legislation against paupers. In 1852, California still lacked state-level policies that would explicitly pursue this goal.

For the rest of the 1850s, the California legislature attempted to restrict Chinese immigration through race-specific laws. In 1855, the legislature passed a passenger act which required shipmasters to pay $50 in head money to the Commissioner of Emigration for the landing of each passenger "so disqualified from becoming a citizen of the United States."[69] The act clearly targeted Chinese immigrants, based on the assumption that Asians were not entitled to naturalization as "free white persons" under the Naturalization Act of 1790. Applying to all unnaturalizable passengers regardless of economic conditions, the 1855 act aimed exclusively to discourage shipmasters from landing Chinese passengers with an exorbitant rate of head money, which never exceeded a few dollars in Atlantic seaboard states. California lawmakers also endeavored to compel Chinese miners already in the state to leave. In 1854 the legislature prohibited mining by foreigners unless they paid a monthly license tax, or so-called Foreign Miners' Tax. Exempting those who had started their naturalization process, the act sought to reduce the Chinese presence in mining regions without offending naturalizable European miners. It is critical to note that these anti-Chinese measures developed in tandem with governmental and private actions for purging California mining of Native Americans, people of Mexican descent who had long lived in California before it became an American territory, and Latin Americans. Immigration restriction against Chinese was therefore integrated into a larger scheme to make California a white man's state.[70]

To the disappointment of restrictionists, anti-Chinese legislation in California suffered repeated failures. The United States Supreme Court's decision in the *Passenger Cases* made shipmasters and even the Commissioner of Emigration doubt the constitutionality of anti-Chinese head money from the beginning. In 1857, shippers achieved an easy victory over the tax when the California Supreme Court declared it unconstitutional for infringing upon federal commerce power in the case of *People v. Downer*.[71] In 1858, the legislature passed another passenger act that plainly prohibited the landing of any persons of the "Chinese or Mongolian races."[72] But again, the California Supreme Court struck down the act within a year in an unpublished opinion before its first enforcement, on the grounds that the carrying of passengers came under the general denomination of foreign commerce and that the unconditional prohibition of foreigners' admission by a state was "as much as infringement upon the right delegated to Congress, as would be the imposition of a tax upon the same class of persons."[73]

The invalidation of the 1858 act forced California lawmakers to realize the impossibility of sustainable state-level restriction of Chinese immigration. The committee on immigration reported to the legislature in March 1859 on the "impracticality of framing" legislation directly preventing Chinese immigration "without clashing with high judicial decisions, and with the powers of Congress." With every immigration act struck down by the court, the committee felt that "the last barrier [against Chinese immigration] is thrown down" and "almost all peaceable and supposed legal measures have failed."[74]

Taxation of Chinese immigrants already in the state met challenges as well. In 1862, building upon the Foreign Miners' Tax, the legislature introduced a monthly tax of $2.50, which came to be known as the Chinese Police Tax, on all Chinese residents in the state, except those running businesses or working in the production of sugar, rice, coffee, or tea. The Chinese Police Tax did not last long. In the same year, a Chinese merchant named Lin Sing challenged the tax in *Lin Sing v. Washburn*. The California Supreme Court declared the tax a "measure of special and extreme hostility to the Chinese," which would reduce immigration from China and trade with that nation. The police tax's effect therefore came into conflict with federal power over foreign commerce, just like state head money. Taxation of residents belonged to the sphere of states' rights, but a state could not set particular immigrants apart from other residents as special subjects of taxation. For these reasons, the court invalidated the Chinese Police Tax. Finally, the Burlingame Treaty of 1868, which guaranteed free Chinese immigration to the United States, sounded the death knell of state-level

Chinese exclusion schemes in California.[75] Thus even though California established the Commissioner of Emigration in the early 1850s as the state immigration agency, the state ultimately failed to sustain measures to restrict Chinese immigration.

California's attempts nevertheless have important implications for the development of American immigration policy. In California, every legislative attempt to restrict Chinese immigration suffered legal constraints due to its clash with federal authority over foreign commerce. Emerging from the nationwide concern about the states' right to police power against various forms of external threats, this same question also shaped the course of passenger laws in northeastern states and stimulated southern states' opposition to federal encroachment on their policies for black sailors. State immigration policies everywhere stood in uneasy tension with federal power, whether they targeted destitute Europeans, free blacks, or Asians. In this sense, the situation in California provides one chapter in the national narrative of state-level immigration control. With the failure to limit Chinese immigration through legislation, however, police power in California was expressed in the form of physical violence against the Chinese by local white residents. Unable to overcome the formidable constitutional limitations on state policy, California lawmakers eventually turned to national legislation as the only way to check Chinese immigration. Developments in midcentury California laid the groundwork for the introduction of federal Chinese exclusion a few decades later.

Despite some differences in mode and nature, New York and Massachusetts developed the most stringent systems of state-level immigration regulation in antebellum America. As officials in these states acquired more authority over immigration, their attitudes toward foreigners simultaneously became harsher. The first half of the 1850s also witnessed the intensification of political nativism, which promoted the rigorous implementation of regulatory immigration law. Nativist officials' negative views of destitute foreigners, the anti-immigrant political atmosphere, and even immigrants' effort to counter nativist charges against them all contributed to the expansion of regulatory immigration policy. Conversely, the abusive treatment of immigrants by state officials would not have occurred without their legal empowerment. Thus to fully analyze state immigration policy during this period, it is crucial to look at the law, society, and politics as a whole. This nexus in immigration control appeared most dramatically in Massachusetts, but tension between foreigners and public officials who implemented state immigration law escalated in New York as well.

On the surface, the New York Commissioners of Emigration might seem to be entirely a benevolent agency, at least for admitted immigrants. The duties of the commissioners included the protection of naïve newcomers from fraudsters after landing as well as assistance to immigrants in safely reaching their final destinations. The inclusion of immigrant society presidents among the state's officials also reflected the hospitable intent of the commission upon its foundation in 1847. An exclusive focus on the social service programs of the commissioners presented in their annual reports, however, obscures admitted immigrants' increasing dissatisfaction with the officials in the early 1850s.

During the years of expansion in New York immigration policy, Irish American newspapers in New York City frequently reported on the rude treatment of foreigners by the commissioners and their agents. In January 1851, shortly after landing in the city, Cornelius Guinea, an immigrant from County Cork, went to the commissioners' office to ask for their assistance in reaching out to his brother in Boston. A clerk in the office, Guinea told the *New York Irish-American*, "refused to give me any." The clerk then "flung me outside the office, and raised his foot as if he were going to kick me."[76] When reporters from the *Irish-American* visited the commissioners' office, an official was yelling with a ruler in his hand at an immigrant woman who sought aid from the state agency: "If you say another word, I will poke this down your throat!"[77] The commissioners' agents also included nativists whose "sympathies are all anti-Irish" and who "threw the holy water of the people out of the window."[78]

The New York Commissioners of Emigration also gained notoriety for their hostile and inhumane treatment of debilitated foreigners at charitable institutions under their control, such as hospitals on Staten Island and Ward's Island. One Irish immigrant patient at the Ward's Island hospital witnessed how another Irish-born patient was "most unnecessarily assaulted by two watchmen" at the institution.[79] Furthermore, as the Irish American *New York Citizen* revealed, immigrants including women with infant children were "left destitute of food for days" and "sick passengers are very grossly maltreated." "Such," the newspaper ridiculed the officials, "is the protection afforded by the Commissioners of Emigration."[80] The commissioners certainly provided some welfare services to newcomers. Yet during the 1850s, the abusive aspect of their activities became conspicuous to the extent that the *Irish-American* perceived that "the entire city is full of anger" with "the blundering and inefficiency of the Commissioners and the barbarity of their officials."[81]

In Massachusetts, Irish immigrants did not passively endure anti-Irish nativism and the expulsion of their country men and women. To protect themselves from state deportation policy, for instance, the Irish promoted naturalization. In Massachusetts the lack of legal settlement, which only citizens could acquire, made immigrants subject to overseas removal when they became destitute. As long as immigrants remained noncitizens, they would never escape the possibility of being expelled from the United States. The *American Celt*, a Boston Irish American newspaper, pointed out Irish immigrants' vulnerability to restrictive state policy due to their noncitizen status: "Aliens are subject to the Police regulation of this country,—yet, not being citizens, they have no protection against the many abuses to which such Police is always and everywhere liable." Obtaining American citizenship through naturalization would exempt them from pauper removal law. Calling citizenship a "priceless jewel of self-protection," the *American Celt* urged immediate naturalization to its immigrant readers: "Why, therefore, don't you get naturalized?"[82] Naturalization would also increase the political power of the Irish as a group, which could allow them to overturn the deportation policy. "Had we more naturalized citizens," argued the *Boston Pilot*, "no longer would you have to record the fact that an Irish woman had been sentenced to be sent out of this commonwealth to Ireland, as a foreign pauper, aye, and that woman, too with a family of helpless children."[83]

The newspapers dropped their relatively even tone, however, in the sensational case of the deportation of an Irish woman in 1851. Eliza Sullivan, an Irish immigrant, had lived in the United States for eighteen years and as a resident of Southbridge, Massachusetts, for seven years. Two years earlier, her husband Jeremiah had deserted pregnant Eliza and their American-born child. Being unable to work due to her advanced pregnancy, Sullivan had requested a few times public assistance from the town, which was granted. In late April, several weeks after her latest request for relief, the selectmen of Southbridge arrested her and brought her to a local court "on the charge of being an incumbrance or expense on the town." The justice ordered her deportation to Ireland and gave a warrant for removal to a town official called Rogers, who "forcibly and against her will compelled her to leave the town." Rogers took Sullivan and her children to Boston, intending to put them on board a ship to Liverpool. When he found the ship full, he handed the deportees to another officer named Oxton, who brought them to New York City and arranged their deportation on the ship *Shannon*. Leaving her four-year-old boy in Boston for fear that he would not survive the transatlantic voyage, Sullivan went to New York City and got on the ship with her younger child. When the *Shannon* was about to depart, the story took an unexpected turn. The New York Irish Emigrant Society had become aware of the case and rescued the family from the ship under a New York state law that made it illegal to "forcibly seize and confine any other with intent to cause such person to be sent out of this State against his will." It was reported that Oxton, as soon as he heard of the rescue of the mother and her child, "fled from the city of New York, and she [Sullivan] has not seen him since."[84] Irish American newspapers alarmingly publicized the incident as a case of "kidnapping" or "abduction."[85]

While Sullivan's dependency stemming from the combination of desertion and pregnancy represented the economic precariousness in nineteenth-century America of immigrant women without family members to rely on, this case exposed the sweeping nature of Massachusetts deportation policy. Sullivan and her child were ultimately saved from deportation, but the case revealed that American-born children would be subject to overseas banishment with their immigrant parents. As the *New York Irish-American* put it, "They hurried her off to Boston and her children (Native born Americans too!), whom they tried to deport from Free America, (Oh Gracious God!)."[86] The whole process of the Sullivans' deportation, including their transfer from Boston to New York and embarkation in violation of New York state law, also illuminates officials' discretionary power in executing removal. The nativists among them clearly had no hesitation in resorting to unlawful action to expel Irish paupers. Oxton's flight suggests that he tried to deport the Sullivans from New York knowing that he was breaking the state's law. The *Boston Pilot* denounced the unlimited power that officials could assert under Massachusetts removal law: that "any citizen who happens to get into office, and who *may* be a rogue, or a fool, or both, should have and hold this power in our land is a thing which quite passes our comprehension."[87] The Sullivans' case shows how the expansion of deportation authority in the early 1850s could invite coercive and even illegal removal when the power was exercised by nativist officials.

After the Sullivan case the *Boston Pilot* once again called for immediate naturalization, but in much more extreme language than in previous calls. Given what happened to Eliza Sullivan, the necessity of naturalization left no space for hesitation. "To those foolish Irishmen who neglect the duty of naturalization we have a word to say," wrote the *Pilot*. "Do you not see that every one of you is in danger. Any one of you may be disabled, and the sick man may be compelled to go to the alms-house." The press highlighted the problem with the noncitizen status: "You see that eighteen years of residence will not save you. . . . What *will* save you then?" Naturalization. Without citizenship, no immigrant would be safe. In concluding the warning to non-naturalized immigrants, the newspaper swore that it would show no sympathy to any Irishman who failed to naturalize within a year and would be deported as a result: "We will not lift a finger to save him from being transported to the paradise of fools."[88]

Although local officials oversaw the removal of the Sullivans, newspaper reports on other deportation cases demonstrate that the Alien Commissioners could be equally ruthless. In September 1851 the commissioners forcibly placed an Irish pauper woman against her will on a Liverpool-bound deportation ship, even after she had made "several ineffectual attempts" to run away from the ship.[89] The removal of an Irish family of four in the same month further exposes the harshness of deportation by the commissioners. Earlier in September, the officials brought the family from the South Boston almshouse to the police court to obtain a warrant for their expulsion. After the court approved their deportation, the parents ran away, leaving behind their two children, one of whom was blind. The commissioners then decided to place only the children on board the Liverpool-bound *Parliament*. The *Boston Traveller* stated the Boston mayor ordered the suspension of their deportation for humanitarian reasons, though the press could not ascertain "whether or not the order was obeyed."[90] Regardless, the initial attempt to send away the children without their parents indicates the utter absence of consideration for deportees' lives in the operation of Massachusetts removal policy.

To the dismay of Irish immigrants, anti-Irish nativism in Massachusetts continued to grow, reaching a critical point in 1854. From 1845 to 1854, the United States received more immigrants than in the seven previous decades combined. In 1854 alone, 427,833 immigrants reached the American shore, a figure that would not be superseded until the 1870s.[91] This unprecedented influx of foreigners, especially poor Catholics from Ireland and the German states, created intense xenophobia in the northern states. In 1854, widespread nativist sentiment crystallized into the rise of the Know-Nothings as a political movement. Emerging from secret anti-immigrant societies in New York City, the Know-Nothings pledged to promote anti-Catholic and anti-foreigner legislation by running their own candidates from their official organization, the American Party. Owing to the failure of the Whigs and Democrats to settle the issue of slavery, the Know-Nothings attracted people's expectations not only as a nativist party but also as an alternative to the traditional parties. As the national election in the fall of 1854 approached, the Know-Nothings drew more public attention than either of the old parties.[92]

Massachusetts became the vanguard of Know-Nothingism. Having former Free Soilers as members, the Bay State Know-Nothings enjoyed support not only from nativist citizens but also from those who valued their anti-slavery dimension. Irish immigrants' overwhelming support for the proslavery Democratic Party also drove anti-slavery citizens to the Know-Nothings. Thus political nativism in Massachusetts grew out of fears that the political participation of Catholics, especially the Irish, would corrupt American republicanism and bolster pro-slavery forces. By the fall, the Know-Nothings had swept local elections in eastern Massachusetts towns and cities. In Boston, Know-Nothing Jerome Van Crowninshield Smith was elected mayor with the largest vote in the history of mayoral elections in the city. In Massachusetts, the American Party was clearly a party against Catholic Irish immigrants.[93]

As the fall election approached, nativists in Massachusetts tirelessly promoted their candidates by agitating against Irish pauperism. Anti-immigrant newspapers reminded the public of Lord Lansdowne's assisted emigration scheme in 1851 and maintained that "most of the danger that exists from the ravages of typhus and similar diseases, springs from the foul and disgusting habits of the Irish population."[94] They also demanded thorough enforcement of the deportation policy. One reader of the *Know-Nothing and American Crusader*, a Boston nativist newspaper, showed his irritation with the lax practice of pauper removal. For him, Massachusetts officials had exercised deportation "in such a lukewarm manner as to give the impression that it is of small interest or importance to the welfare of our country and her institutions."[95] One nativist sent an editorial to the anti-Irish *Boston Daily Bee* under the pseudonym REMEDY. Claiming that immigration restriction was the "remedy" for the problem of Irish paupers' supposed abuse of public charity, he urged his readers to vote for the Know-Nothings, who "will see all laws properly executed and executed to the very letter."[96]

Whenever the Alien Commissioners deported Irish paupers, nativists commended the policy and encouraged its continuation until they expelled all foreign paupers from the state. In September 1854 Albert G. Goodwin, who succeeded Jotham B. Munroe as the Superintendent of Alien Passengers in 1853, brought four Irish-born inmates of the Boston House of Industry to Justice Russell of the Police Court, including "a half witted fellow." Goodwin charged these immigrants as foreign paupers who obtained aid from the city of Boston despite their lack of settlement "against the peace of the Commonwealth." At the trial, Justice Russell ordered their prompt return to Britain. Upon hearing of this case, nativists praised the justice by saying "Good, Justice Russell did right" and wishing "every pauper sent to this country was immediately returned."[97] When Judge Russell delivered an order of deportation to another Irish-born pauper a few weeks later, the *Bee* applauded the decision as a "noble work."[98]

Irish leaders desperately promoted naturalization among immigrants to increase anti-Know-Nothing votes, but prospects in the upcoming election clearly favored the nativists. Judge George Bigelow told Charles Francis Adams that "this new organization [the Know-Nothing Party] . . . will make a complete revolution in the elections in the Autumn."[99]

One of the principal differences in immigration policy between New York and Massachusetts during the 1850s was the former's relatively moderate position on immigration control, including its reluctance to adopt deportation as state policy. Both the Commissioners of Emigration and nativist New Yorkers clearly wanted harsh measures against foreign paupers, such as their compulsory deportation. The New York legislature, however, did not move for that specific purpose throughout the 1850s, even though criticism of immigrant pauperism was as enthusiastic in New York as in Massachusetts. The New York Commissioners of Emigration returned immigrant paupers to Europe, but only at the paupers' own request, whereas Massachusetts immigration officials vigorously enforced deportation policy.

Part of the explanation for the different approaches to immigration regulation lies in the volume of immigration to these states. New York City alone received approximately 70 percent of all immigrants to the United States before the Civil War, while only 7 percent of immigrants arrived in Boston.[100] In light of the magnitude of immigration to New York, the rigid enforcement of immigration control through deportation would have been beyond the capacity of the state government. While deportation was much more manageable in Massachusetts, accommodating rather than removing newcomers was the realistic option in New York.

But differing political climates also profoundly affected the course of immigration control. The substantial size of the immigrant population in New York—about a quarter of the state's population and half of New York City's population—curbed the escalation of restrictive policies by politically empowering the immigrants. Political scientist Daniel Tichenor has demonstrated that the recurrent failure of nativist attempts to restrict European immigration in the nineteenth century was due to the value of immigrants as a voting bloc that "Democratic leaders and other politicians had a compelling interest in winning over."[101] When an election approached, agents of political parties in New York tried to accumulate political capital through their kindness to almshouse inmates, many of whom were of Irish birth, by visiting almshouses and providing paupers with food and clothes.[102] Democratic politicians, whose major constituency included European immigrants, and even Whigs, realized that the immigrant vote was too valuable to alienate by sponsoring restrictive policies such as deportation.

In Massachusetts, immigrants' political participation proceeded much more slowly than in New York. Bostonians had recognized the Catholic Irish as a voting bloc by the mid-1850s. Yet as historian Thomas O'Connor has noted, prior to the Civil War, "the Irish had not at all reached the point where they were capable of playing a decisive role in Boston's politics. They had no leaders, no political funds, and no machine of any sort to help them organize a campaign or to mobilize voters."[103] The strong anti-Catholic and anti-Irish traditions of Massachusetts, as well as the nativist inclination of dominant politicians in the state, undoubtedly delayed the political progress of the Irish. The division between the Catholic Church and Irish immigrants also contributed to the relatively weak political influence of the Irish in Massachusetts. A native-born citizen whose social views and political philosophy paralleled those of the Whigs, Boston Bishop John Fitzpatrick politically distanced himself from Irish immigrants by urging them to vote for Whig candidates rather than their Democratic favorites in elections.[104] In New York, by contrast, Archbishop John Hughes established a more harmonious relationship with immigrants than Fitzpatrick and succeeded in mobilizing state politics to their benefit, as seen in his involvement in the creation in 1847 of the Commissioners of Emigration, whose duties included the protection of newcomers.

At the same time, the smooth development of immigration control can be explained by the merger of nativism and anti-slavery in Massachusetts, where anti-slavery politicians enjoyed exceptional popular support compared to their colleagues in other states. In the Bay State, some of these politicians were opponents of immigration. As historian Bruce Laurie has shown, the exclusion and deportation laws enacted in the early 1850s were the projects of the anti-slavery Free Soilers, who included nativists. If politicians in New York generally hesitated to offend immigrants, the Massachusetts Free Soilers succeeded in building sizable constituency by attracting voters in the countryside, as well as nativists in Boston. While voters in rural and rising industrial towns had developed the strong sense of New England identity characterized by anti-slavery and anti-South mindsets, many of them also supported temperance under the influence of Protestantism and virtually integrated nativism into their regional identity. The Free Soilers drew wide support from these anti-slavery and nativist voters, enjoying sufficient influence on state politics to promote legislation of their design. Laurie thus asserts that it was the Free Soilers who "laid the legal and administrative groundwork for a crackdown on the poor and foreign born." This led to the radicalization of immigration restriction in Massachusetts when the Free Soilers' political successors, the Know-Nothings, seized control of state politics in 1855.[105]

New York and Massachusetts followed different paths, but the period between the late 1840s and the early 1850s as a whole marked a foundational moment in the history of American immigration control. Both states had had some measures for immigrant exclusion or deportation since colonial times, but immigration regulation in these states became firmly institutionalized under the command of state immigration agencies during this period. Once these states modified their immigration policies in response to the *Passenger Cases*, the policies remained legally unchallenged until the mid-1870s. The new policies enacted from 1849 to 1854 set in motion state-level immigration control in New York and Massachusetts, and it is precisely these policies that later developed into national immigration policy.

The expansion in the authority of state officials meant more than the establishment of legal and institutional backbones for subsequent immigration policy. The new duties and powers assigned to state officials increased their control over immigrants, resulting in the coercive and abusive treatment of undesirable foreigners and the practice of unlawful removal. The rise of the Know-Nothings fueled anti-Irish sentiment. The Know-Nothing ascendancy opened up a period of militant nativism when all paupers of Irish descent, regardless of citizenship status, became subject to overseas banishment.

CHAPTER 4

✧

Radical Nativism

The Know-Nothing Movement and
the Citizenship of Paupers

One day in the summer of 1855, T. McIntyre, an Irish immigrant, was composing a letter in his room in Boston to his family in Ireland. "There is nothing here but work hard to day [*sic*] and go to bed at night," wrote McIntyre of his life in America, "and work harder tomorrow." The nights he spent playing the fiddle by the fireside in Ireland had become distant memories. Should his brother John live in Boston for one week, McIntyre imagined, "he would have very little notion about fiddling on Saturday nights." A large number of Irish men and women daily arrived in the United States, but he stressed that "people need not expect a great deal of enjoyment when they come here." At one point in his letter, McIntyre mentioned a ship that would depart for Liverpool with about five hundred passengers the next day. The Irish immigrant then added that they included fifty-seven paupers who would be "sent home by government." The ship McIntyre referred to was Captain George W. Putnam's *Daniel Webster*, and the fifty-seven paupers were immigrants expelled under Massachusetts deportation law. Writing as if he was warning all people at home planning to leave Ireland for America, McIntyre commented on the deportation: "This will give you some idea of what sort of times are here."[1]

What sort of times were Irish immigrants in Atlantic seaboard states having in 1855? McIntyre's negative impression of prospects in the United States for immigrants might have been shaped primarily by his exhausting life as a laborer. But his remarks on deportation clearly emerged in response to the current social and political situation in Massachusetts. This chapter examines state-level immigration control during the period of radical nativism in the second half of the 1850s. Anti-immigrant sentiment in antebellum America reached its zenith with the stunning debut of the nativist Know-Nothings in American politics in 1854. Under the influence of the Know-Nothing movement, immigration control in New York and Massachusetts became extremely coercive. Inspired by nativist politicians' anti-foreigner language, pressure from nativist citizens for stricter immigration restriction, and the prevailing view of Irish paupers as undeserving of relief and sympathy, New York and Massachusetts officials disregarded legal constraints on deportation. In New York, nativists had limited influence on state politics, but the anti-immigrant atmosphere set by the Know-Nothings induced local authorities to expel destitute immigrants abroad, despite the absence of deportation law in the state. In Massachusetts, where the Know-Nothings dominated the state government, officials implemented deportation policy on an unprecedented scale, banishing Irish paupers mercilessly with force and sometimes illegally. And people unlawfully deported to Europe by the Know-Nothings included even American citizens of Irish descent.

As a political movement, Know-Nothingism did not last long, fading away by the late 1850s. Nevertheless, the Know-Nothings deeply influenced the ways American officials enforced immigration policy and treated foreigners. The harsh manner of removal and officials' aggressive attitude toward undesirable aliens remained after the downfall of the Know-Nothings, shaping the style of American immigration control in later periods. The deportation of citizens illuminates the disparity between Irish American paupers' legal status as citizens and their practical treatment as aliens in the pre–Civil War era, when American citizenship lacked national definition and rights later taken for granted had yet to be formulated, let alone guaranteed. Immigration control by the Know-Nothings thus played a vital role in defining the nature of American immigration policy and reveals the meaning of antebellum American citizenship.

The election of 1854 closed with the Know-Nothings' stunning achievements as a third party in northern states. In Massachusetts, the Know-Nothings' strongest hold, nativists captured the governorship, elected all the state officers, and occupied every seat in the state senate and all but three of the 378 seats in the house of representatives. In Pennsylvania, the Know-Nothings also won the governorship and a majority in the house. In Connecticut, Rhode Island, and New Hampshire, nativists secured control of the executive and legislative branches of state government. Even though they fell short of securing the governorship in New York, leaders of the party found their showing promising in future state politics. The Know-Nothings also made a sizeable impact in California, Indiana, Maine, and Ohio. By the end of 1855 the Know-Nothings had captured eight governorships, more than a hundred seats in Congress, and mayor's offices in Boston, Philadelphia, and Chicago.[2]

As they sat down in their new offices, the Know-Nothings started to pursue their nativist agenda based on two principal tenets. First, they believed that Protestantism defined American society and that Catholicism was incompatible with American values such as democracy, freedom, and individualism. Second, the Know-Nothings believed that only native-born Americans could understand and operate American republican institutions.[3] Following these convictions, the Know-Nothings proposed to extend the probationary period before naturalization from five years to twenty-one years in order to deter naturalization and curtail the political power of the foreign-born in the United States. In Massachusetts, the Know-Nothing legislature required all public schools to read the Protestant King James Bible every day and banned the use of public money for sectarian schools to make Catholic children attend public schools. Nativists further discriminated against Catholics by amending the state constitution to disqualify anyone who retained allegiance to "foreign prince, power, or potentate" (namely, the Pope) from holding public office in the state. In February 1855, the legislature went so far as to appoint a so-called Nunnery Committee to investigate Catholic priests' alleged sexual misconduct and torture of nuns at convents and Catholic schools. In an investigation of a convent school in Roxbury, about twenty men, only seven of whom were official committee members, disrupted the school to inspect the building. They poked into closets and cellars and terrorized nuns and children, only to find nothing after all.[4]

Other than Catholicism, the poverty of foreigners became the Know-Nothings' chief target. As earlier nativists, the Know-Nothings regarded foreign pauperism as a huge economic burden upon American taxpayers as well as a threat to the public health and morality of American society. Yet the particular situation of assisted pauper emigration from Europe in the mid-1850s made the Know-Nothings even more hostile and vigilant to immigrant pauperism than their predecessors. While assisted emigration from Ireland had still been continuing, the years between 1854 and 1855 witnessed an intensive influx of assisted paupers from various parts of continental Europe. Throughout these years, newspapers in coastal cities frequently reported on the arrival of German, Swiss, Belgian, and Italian paupers, and sometimes criminals, sent by local authorities in continental Europe.[5] The Know-Nothings interpreted assisted emigration as a sign of foreign governments' conspiracy to undermine American society. Erastus Brooks, a New York nativist, regretted that the United States had kept its gates wide open for foreigners to make it "the common Alms-House of the world."[6] For Thomas R. Whitney, a Know-Nothing congressman from New York, assisted paupers were "not merely useless, they are worse than useless." By sending their paupers to the United States, European authorities afflicted Americans with "a disease, both moral and physical— a leprosy—a contamination."[7]

The Know-Nothings in Congress enthusiastically sought to establish federal measures against assisted emigration. In August 1856, W. R. Smith, an Alabama Know-Nothing, introduced to the United States House a bill to "Prevent the Introduction in the United States of Foreign Criminals and Paupers." The bill required potential immigrants in foreign countries to file applications for immigration. Only those who passed the inspection by American consuls with a certificate that the person was neither a pauper nor a criminal would be allowed to enter the United States. The Know-Nothings, whose major political strength lay in municipal and state governments, could not push the bill any further, but its introduction in Congress indicated the momentum of nativism in this era. Some non–Know-Nothing members of Congress supported the idea of consular inspection because it reflected "the sentiments prevailing almost universally in Massachusetts, New York, and the other States" against foreign paupers.[8]

Additionally, the Know-Nothings built upon earlier nativists' economic critique of impoverished foreigners to aggravate native-born workers' fear of "pauper labor," or cheap labor of poor immigrants who would work for lower wages than Americans. Unless the United States restricted immigration, nativists warned, "the pauper prices of Europe" would become the standards for wages in America. An even worse consequence would be the degradation of American workers to the status of paupers as a result of losing job competition with "half-starved pauper-laborers from Europe, admitted *duty free* into the American labor-market."[9] At a time when industrialization had already brought about the sharp deterioration of working-class Americans' living conditions, the agitation for pauper labor increased native-born workers' anxiety about the potential loss of economic independence—a grave failure as free white American citizens. The actual presence of immigrant paupers reinforced this anxiety, fostering American workers' animosity toward such foreigners. Hostility to immigrant poverty was so central to Know-Nothing ideology that the *New York Times* called foreign pauperism "the great battle-cry" in the Know-Nothing movement.[10]

It is crucial to note here that assisted pauper emigration from continental Europe never threatened the centrality of the Irish in the problem of immigrant pauperism during the Know-Nothing period. By 1855 the German population in New York City had come close to half the Irish population, but the pauper population did not reflect this demographical difference. That year only 281 Germans entered the Bellevue Hospital in the city, while the hospital treated 4,242 Irish patients. The number of the Irish admitted to the New York City almshouse was thirteen times larger than that of Germans. In Boston, the number of Irish-born inmates at the Deer Island House of Industry in the same year was more than three times larger than that of all non-Irish immigrant inmates combined. German immigrants certainly included impoverished people and assisted paupers, but with greater financial resources and less physical debilitation than the Irish in general, Germans as a group proved to be much less likely to become public charges than people fleeing famine in Ireland.[11] Immigration from continental Europe contributed to the escalation of nativism in the mid-1850s, but the Know-Nothings recognized that the Irish remained the chief source of foreign pauperism.

The ascendancy of the Know-Nothings, especially their criticism of foreign pauperism, strongly affected public officials' view of state immigration policy. In New York, the political power of immigrants, who accounted for about a quarter of the state's population, hampered Know-Nothingism as a political force. The popularity of William H. Seward, the renowned anti-slavery senator and former New York governor who was supportive of immigrants, also worked against the Know-Nothings in state politics.[12] The nativists' political influence was thus relatively limited, but their arguments on immigrant poverty echoed the anti-pauper language that had developed in the state. They also spurred the idea of adopting more restrictive policies than admission regulation and consensual return, the principal methods of immigration control in New York. In January 1855, one state senator introduced a bill that would provide for the compulsory deportation of aliens who became paupers within one year of arrival, though the bill died before passage.[13] In August, upon learning of the recent landing of one hundred paupers from Liverpool, the New York Commissioners of Emigration resolved to deport all of them back to "the ports whence they came" without their consent.[14] In support of authorizing the commissioners to deport foreign paupers, poor law officials in New York urged the state legislature to "devise some method by which the Commissioners of Emigration can relieve the commonwealth from so unnecessary and so heavy a burden."[15]

While these voices advocated deportation in New York, the Know-Nothings in Massachusetts, who controlled state politics, successfully translated nativist sentiment into the active implementation of state deportation policy. In his inaugural address in January 1855, Know-Nothing Governor Henry J. Gardner devoted a large portion of his address to the cost of supporting foreign paupers, which accounted for about a third of the state's entire expenditures, and specified the deportation of foreign paupers as the party's primary agenda.[16] Gardner then called for new legislation that would make the implementation of pauper deportation law "imperative, not merely permissive." By demanding "stringent national laws regarding immigration, the imposition of an uniform and sufficient capitation tax, and the universal deportation of criminals and paupers shipped to our shores," the governor also expressed his wish to expand Massachusetts immigration policy on a national scale.[17]

The Know-Nothings' intense nativism accelerated pauper removal in Massachusetts during Gardner's three-year tenure between 1855 and 1857. Under the aegis of the governor, the Massachusetts Commissioners of Alien Passengers and Foreign Paupers (Alien Commissioners) and their agents first strengthened the restriction of pauper immigration by railroad. The 1851 alien passenger act provided for the return to their places of origin of passengers who had entered the state by railroad and who applied for relief within one year of arrival. In 1855, the commissioners realized that many of the inmates in state charitable institutions should have been sent back to New York and New England states under the 1851 act.[18] The officials left no record on how exactly they dealt with the situation, but presumably they pressured railroad companies to bring back their former passengers who entered almshouses after arrival. During the first four years after the passage of the act in 1851, the number of passengers returned annually never exceeded 200. In 1855, however, the number soared to 499, in 1856 it was 363, and in 1857 it was 263. This increase occurred despite the fact that the number of passengers coming into the state by railroad substantially dropped from 14,097 in 1854 to 5,501 in 1857.[19]

The Alien Commissioners also tirelessly deported immigrant paupers already resident in the state. The commissioners' agents visited all the state almshouses, the immigrant hospital on Rainsford Island, state lunatic hospitals, and local charitable institutions to personally examine inmates. Upon confirming their lack of legal settlement in Massachusetts or the existence of family or friends who could support them elsewhere, they banished such paupers from the state. On March 8, 1855, for example, a group of ten destitute immigrants, including nine Irish, were "sent to Europe" from the state almshouse in Monson. The almshouse registers reveal that some of these deportees suffered from sickness, "rheumatism," and "frozen" body parts.[20]

The efforts of the Alien Commissioners bore fruit. In 1854, only 319 persons were removed from Massachusetts. During Henry Gardner's governorship between 1855 and 1857, however, the commissioners expelled a total of 4,028 persons, including 611 paupers deported to Liverpool and numerous others sent to British North American cities such as Montreal, Quebec, and St. John.[21] Appreciating the commissioners' devotion to pauper removal, the superintendent of the Tewksbury state almshouse wrote in 1857 that they had been "able to relieve the State from the support of a large number of permanent paupers who have been a charge to the State for a long time, and would have remained so for years, had they not been sent to their homes."[22]

Massachusetts state law simply provided that the Alien Commissioners may deport foreign paupers from the state, but the records of almshouses show how the discretion of the commissioners and their agents brought about diverse consequences to immigrant inmates in the enforcement of removal policy. Destinations were determined based on an officer's perception of where the pauper "belonged." An Irish immigrant inmate could be deported to New York, Canada, or Ireland, depending on the officer's personal assessment of the pauper's migration history and his or her circumstances at the time of admission. If the foreign-born inmate had any family member or friend in another US state or Canada, the officer usually returned the person to these places.

If the inmate had no family or friend in either the United States or Canada, he would be sent to the place which the examining officer judged was responsible for the maintenance of the pauper. Mary Ryan arrived in New York from Ireland in September 1856. After stopping by Providence, Ryan reached Worcester, Massachusetts, and became a pauper. Both of her parents lived in Ireland, and her Irish husband had died of ship fever in New York two weeks after landing. The commissioners returned Ryan to New York on the grounds that New York, instead of Massachusetts, should support her as the place that had originally admitted her.[23] Immigrants with no acquaintances in North America could also be returned to Ireland. Bridget Flynn, for example, entered the Bridgewater state almshouse after landing in Boston and spending three years at the city almshouse at Deer Island. Flynn's complete lack of support in North America prompted a commissioner agent to write in her record, "Ought to be sent home." Flynn was deported to Ireland on April 13, 1855.[24]

Repeated admission to almshouses also increased the inmate's likelihood to be deported abroad. To the annoyance of almshouse officials, some paupers re-entered almshouses after being discharged or removed. An official of the Bridgewater state almshouse complained about the return of removed paupers "in a very dilapidated condition, requiring more care with less prospect of reform."[25] The Alien Commissioners handled the repeaters with a determination to expel them from the nation. Thomas Hill, one of the repeaters, had once been sent to New York, where he initially landed, from the Monson state almshouse. Within a year, however, he re-entered the same almshouse. Four months later, he was deported to Ireland.[26] Commissioner agents also predetermined the deportation of possible repeaters. For Michael Haley, who landed in Boston and entered the Tewksbury state almshouse since he had no family members, they wrote, "To Ire[land], if he is found again." The officials similarly decided to send to Ireland Jane Riley, who had entered the same almshouse twice already, "if she comes again."[27]

These cases suggest the general patterns of removal, but the criteria used for selecting deportation destinations were never absolute. In many ways, officers' subjective judgment determined the fate of paupers. Some officers simply thought immigrant paupers belonged to their land of birth, while others supposed they belonged to the American or Canadian port that had landed them. The commissioners' agents also often decided destinations based on the immediate availability of ships and railroads, completely ignoring the immigrants' migration histories and personal situations. Numerous Irish immigrant paupers shared similar backgrounds—initially landing in Canada or New York and coming to Massachusetts afterward. Yet depending on the perception of the officials and the expediency of removal, they could be sent to New York or Canada by railroad, deported to Europe by ship, or allowed to stay at the almshouses until the time of discharge.

The Know-Nothing movement stimulated the advocacy of pauper deportation in New York and the active enforcement of removal policy in Massachusetts. The most crucial implication of intense nativism for state-level immigration control in this period, however, lay not in the formal discussion and proceedings of state policy but in the unauthorized practice of removal by public officials. The Know-Nothings' aggressive language and policy against foreigners radicalized immigration regulation in the two states. In New York, nativist sentiment among residents in New York

City drove municipal authorities, who had become impatient with the lack of deportation law in the state, to execute the forcible return of foreigners at their discretion. Massachusetts officials, while enforcing deportation policy on an extended scale, facilitated removal through unlawful actions by banishing Irish paupers without required court warrants and by expelling even those who had American citizenship. The fundamental significance of Know-Nothingism for immigration control in antebellum America was the movement's influence on the manner, as well as the scale, of its execution.

In New York City, signs of radical nativism appeared in the form of city residents' vehement opposition to state policy for admitted immigrants. In May 1855, the New York Commissioners of Emigration leased an old fort in lower Manhattan known as Castle Garden to build an immigrant landing station where the commissioners alone could supervise the landing process. By prohibiting the entry of unauthorized persons into the depot, the commissioners sought to prevent fraudsters from approaching naïve newcomers upon arrival. The construction of the Castle Garden depot provoked fiery protests from residents and businessmen in lower Manhattan. New Yorkers believed that Castle Garden would become "a pest house" and draw poverty-stricken foreigners who would "spread pestilential diseases of every kind among us." Fearing that such a contaminated institution would cause a decline in property values in the city's First Ward, wealthy New Yorkers and businessmen also opposed the depot.[28]

The high level of anti-immigrant sentiment among residents of New York City eclipsed the weakness of political nativism in the city, propelling municipal officials to restrict immigration on their own. By 1855 municipal officials, including the Democrats who would otherwise sympathize with immigrants, had become utterly frustrated with the state immigration policy's incapability of reducing foreign pauperism. Democratic Mayor Fernando Wood represented city authorities' antipathy to assisted emigrants when he was reported to have stated that "if it be necessary to call out the forces within the power of the city government to fire on and sink every emigrant vessel coming into this harbor with pauper and criminal emigrants, I shall do so."[29] When a group of Belgian immigrants landed in New York City, officials arrested and detained twelve of them at the Tombs, a city jail in lower Manhattan, on an unfounded suspicion that they were assisted paupers and criminals sent by the Belgian government. New York law did not permit the deportation of foreign paupers. Also, although the New York legislature had passed a law to fine and imprison shipmasters for bringing foreign criminals to the state in 1833, the law did not expressly ban their landing itself. Nor did it provide for

Figure 4.1: "Newly-Landed Emigrants at Castle Garden, New York City," *Harper's Weekly*, September 2, 1865. Over 8 million immigrants landed in the United States through Castle Garden between 1855 and 1890. At the depot, the New York Commissioners of Emigration helped newcomers meet their friends and families, obtain fair-priced railroad tickets to their final destinations, and arrange employment with labor contractors.
Courtesy of Butler Library, Columbia University in the City of New York.

the expulsion of those already in the state. Nevertheless, the mayor fully intended to deport the twelve Belgians back to Antwerp. Newspapers quickly attributed their detention and prospect of forcible return to "the prevalence of the Know Nothing feeling." The *New York Citizen* remarked that "in these times of Know-Nothing ascendancy, any treatment is good enough for those who have the misfortune to be 'foreigners.'"[30]

Mayor Wood's plan to deport the detained Belgians, however, collapsed when the State Supreme Court intervened. News of the detention caught the attention of the Belgian Consul. In February 1855, trying to discharge the migrants from the jail, the consul petitioned the State Supreme Court for a writ of habeas corpus for them. A writ of habeas corpus requires the person under arrest to be brought before a court. It allows the court to assess whether the government has a valid reason for imprisoning or detaining the person, which can lead to his or her release from unlawful detention. At their trial, Justice James Roosevelt denied the migrants' status as paupers and criminals and, stating that their imprisonment by New York City officials was "gross oppression," ordered their immediate release. The decision infuriated the mayor, who believed that the court order would "nullify my efforts" to prevent the landing of assisted emigrants.[31]

The State Supreme Court's ruling did not diminish Wood's determination to pursue immigrant deportation. No provision in New York state law allowed for deportation, but the mayor vowed after the trial that if an immigrant was found destitute in the city, "he is immediately ordered back—and, if necessary, transferred forcibly back."[32] In September 1855, when city authorities discovered that passengers arriving on the *Deutschland* from Hamburg included four criminals who had been shipped from a prison in Germany, the mayor ordered their detention. Pledging to "return all such forthwith, in every case known to me, by the same vessel," Wood ordered the deportation of the four men to Hamburg in October.[33] Their criminal status might have been the decisive reason for their compulsory return. Yet Wood's earlier bellicose wish to sink vessels carrying paupers and criminals transported from Europe implies that assisted paupers might be subjected to similar treatment, as equal threats to public morality and as a similar kind of financial burden on the city for their inability to hold gainful employment. The *New York Evening Express*'s description of the *Deutschland* case as one of "a series of like imports from the *Prison and Pauper Houses* of the old World to the shores of the new" illuminates the almost identical status of assisted paupers and criminals in the public discourse on immigration control.[34]

Fernando Wood was not the only public official in New York who conducted the unauthorized deportation of foreigners from the state. Officials at charitable institutions practiced it as well. In an article titled "The Humanity of the Great Republic," the Irish newspaper *Galway Vindicator* reported on the arrival of two Irish pauper women with mental illness on the vessel *Circassian* from New York City. According to the ship's doctor, who discovered their insanity during the voyage, the two Irish women had lived in the United States for twenty years and had been inmates at an unspecified lunatic asylum in the state of New York. A few days before the embarkation of the vessel, the asylum's governor brought them to New York City and placed them on board the ship for Galway. Given the women's inability to communicate, the governor must have shipped them without their consent in violation of New York state law. The newspaper criticized the deportation of the pauper women as an act of "heartless barbarity."[35] In New York, the Commissioners of Emigration lamented their lack of power to deport destitute immigrants, but foreigners were expelled from the state by local officials. As an Ohio newspaper listed Massachusetts deportation law and unlawful removal in New York altogether as the same persecution of poor foreigners "under the patronage of the 'American' party," New York in practical terms became a deportation state similar to Massachusetts during the Know-Nothing period.[36]

The practice of pauper removal by local authorities in New York reinforced the concept of police power as the ideological backbone of American immigration control. In *City of New York v. Miln* (1837), the United States Supreme Court upheld state exclusion policies as an exercise of internal police power to protect citizens from outside physical and moral threats. Though invalidating state policies for taxing foreign passengers, the court affirmed states' right to exclude and deport aliens of undesirable character in the *Passenger Cases* (1849). During the Know-Nothing movement, New York officials vociferously promoted the concept of police power by way of justifying their aggressive policy toward foreign paupers. Fernando Wood asserted that "the inherent right of every community to protect itself from dangers arising from such [pauper] immigration, cannot be questioned." The mayor viewed immigration control and wartime national defense as equivalent. In January 1855, requesting federal assistance in preventing pauper immigration, Wood wrote to President Franklin Pierce that as the national government had a "duty to protect us from foreign aggression, with ball and cannon, so it is its duty to protect us against an enemy more insidious and destructive, though coming in another form."[37] New York immigration law changed little in the Know-Nothing years. Through the practice of deportation and the combative language that sought to legitimize it, however, New York authorities enhanced the concept of police power, setting precedents for its use to justify American officials' unrestrained action against objectionable aliens. Social realities at the site of immigration control, in conjunction with laws and court decisions, formed the principles of American immigration policy.

In Massachusetts, the Know-Nothing legislature's anti–Catholic Irish stance radicalized the implementation of state immigration policy. Massachusetts deportation law, which allowed officials to exert considerable control over individuals' lives, deeply worried people who considered Know-Nothing nativism unjust bigotry. The law of removal, they noted, empowered any justice of the peace "to send any man whom he may adjudge to be a State pauper out of the country, and to any other country where he may decide the man belongs, and he may deliver him up for that purpose to any constable or 'any other person.'" And the justice could order removal whether the pauper consented to leave or not. Given the deportation law's virtually unrestricted power over paupers, the critics warned, "a neglect or violation of this law may lead to the greatest abuses."[38] A member of the legislature from Salem plainly denounced deportation law as "a violation of humanity and human rights."[39] The radicalism of the Know-Nothings intensified these people's apprehension about state immigration policy.

Critics' concern was soon confirmed by the disclosure of the practice of illegal deportation by the Know-Nothings in February 1855. Shortly after the inauguration of Gardner, a report made by one member of the Alien Commissioners shook the Know-Nothing government. Peleg W. Chandler, who had spent a year as a Whig member of the commissioners, inserted his indictment of deportation policy into the commissioners' annual report for 1854. State law required the Superintendent of Alien Passengers, a chief figure in the commissioners, to bring paupers before a justice of the peace and procure an order for their removal. Chandler claimed that past superintendents had been sending paupers abroad illegally without putting them on trial and obtaining court warrants. Especially since the beginning of 1855, helpless paupers at a lunatic hospital had been "sent over the sea to their alleged homes" in this way. Chandler completely dismissed nativists' contention that "these people *consented* to go." "*The consent of lunatics!*" Chandler resented, "when it is one of the wisest and most humane maxims of the law that a lunatic can give no consent to anything."[40]

Chandler's disapproval of deportation law also came from the Know-Nothings' seemingly contradictory policy regarding personal liberty. As the center of the anti-slavery movement, Massachusetts had been a leading critic of the federal fugitive slave law that protected slaveholders' right to the return of their slaves who escaped into free states. When the Compromise of 1850 created a new fugitive slave act, which required northern states to cooperate with federal commissioners in capturing runaway slaves and rendering them to their masters, Bostonians fervently opposed the act as a threat to liberty in Massachusetts and organized a Vigilance Committee to protect fugitive blacks from "slave catchers" and "kidnappers." The rendition to the South of Anthony Burns, a fugitive from Virginia who was arrested in Boston in May 1854, even drove some abolitionists to break into the courthouse in an attempt to rescue Burns.[41] In Massachusetts, the Know-Nothing Party emerged as an anti-slavery party that included former Free Soilers, who opposed the extension of slavery, and abolitionists who were determined to destroy the institution of slavery itself. The Massachusetts Know-Nothings' anti-slavery stance was clearly presented in 1855 when they passed the so-called Personal Liberty Law to significantly strengthen the civil liberties of fugitive slaves. The law made it illegal for any state official to assist in the capture of fugitives, prohibited their detention without the right to habeas corpus, and established heavy fines and terms of imprisonment for kidnapping fugitives in Massachusetts.[42] Irish immigrants' tendency to endorse the fugitive slave law, including Irish Catholic militias' participation in the rendition of Burns, exacerbated the anti-Irish sentiment of the Know-Nothings and their anti-slavery supporters.[43]

Regardless of Irish immigrants' position on runaway slaves, Chandler found it hypocritical that the Know-Nothings deported, sometimes even illegally, Irish paupers to Ireland while they protected fugitive blacks from "deportation" to the South. "There has been in this Commonwealth unexampled excitement on account of the Fugitive Slave Act of 1850, which is generally regarded as unjust in principle, unnecessarily harsh in its details, and cruel in its practical operation," Chandler argued, yet "every one of the objections to this law applies to our own [deportation law]."[44] Edward Everett Hale, a well-known writer and nephew of the former Massachusetts governor, shared a similar view with Chandler. People in Massachusetts "writhe and struggle, really with one heart" to prevent the return of fugitives to southern slavery. When it came to Irish "fugitives" from British tyranny, Hale wrote, "we tax them first and neglect them afterwards, and provide by statute, and take care, in fact, to send back to Ireland."[45] The Boston Evening Telegraph reproached a judge, who had earlier distinguished himself as a Free Soiler by "making speeches against the Fugitive Slave Law," for so actively issuing warrants for the deportation of destitute immigrants.[46]

Sensing that Chandler's report could hurt the party's reputation, the Know-Nothing government quickly moved to suppress the document before it became available for people outside the legislature. On February 20, Governor Gardner corresponded with the house of representatives about the annual report of the Alien Commissioners and pressured it to print only "such parts of the same as seem advisable."[47] Two days later, members in the house discussed whether they should publish the report or not. The Know-Nothings controlled the house, but some of them hesitated to see their party becoming so proscriptive as to suppress a legislative document. After a heated hour-long debate, the house agreed on the publication of the entire document.[48]

The spread of the news on Chandler's report and the Know-Nothings' attempt to suppress it forced nativists to defend their party and deportation policy. In April, a legislative committee appointed by the Know-Nothings issued a report on state immigration policy, entirely defending deportation as an economic necessity to "obtain permanent relief from the burden of a case of established pauperism" and rejecting Chandler's charges as "groundless." Far from being inhumane, removals had been conducted with the utmost caution: "This power has been hitherto exercised with all proper humanity and discretion.... there is no room for the operation of any improper motives or unreasonable severity."[49] Governor Gardner insisted, "Nearly every one of those shipped to Liverpool went with their own consent."[50] The Alien Commissioners joined the governor by describing deportation policy as "just, expedient and humane."[51] Lunatic paupers were "returned to the places of their nativity, properly provided with all the comforts that were necessary," and "an attendant was provided to take charge of them on the passage."[52] Nativists repeatedly maintained that no pauper was forcibly deported and that state officials returned them home with appropriate care and protection.

Disappointed by the slim prospects for economic mobility and by the hostile environment, many immigrants did choose to return home during the Know-Nothing era. Nevertheless, the Massachusetts Know-Nothings' contention of consensual and humane removal ultimately proved untenable when the *Boston Daily Advertiser* published a report on a deportation case titled "An Infamous Case of Extradition." On the morning of May 15, 1855, thirty-five paupers were deported to Liverpool on the *Daniel Webster*. Among the deportees was an Irish-born woman, Mary Williams. As it turned out, she was "deceived" in Ireland and had emigrated to New York with her aunt a few months before "to conceal her shame." At some point after her arrival, she gave birth to a child and became destitute in Massachusetts. Williams and her daughter consequently entered the Monson state almshouse, from which she was taken for deportation. According to the *Advertiser*, she was sent away "against her own free will, constrained by force of the civil authorities of the State." No record for the warrant for her removal was ever found. The *Boston Daily Courier* added, "Paupers have been sent away by the score in this indecent and reckless manner by irresponsible magistrates." The newspaper rebuked state officials for forcibly sending human beings across the Atlantic "with less of recorded and documentary evidence—than goes to the sending of a tub of butter, or a barrel of apples, from Fitchburg to Boston," an indication of how lightly officials thought of the lives of deportees. Opponents of the Know-Nothings criticized the Williams deportation as "know-nothing intolerance."[53]

The case became even more sensational when newspapers publicized that Williams's American-born infant daughter Bridget was also sent to Liverpool with her mother. The *Advertiser* wrote that Bridget had to be deported because of poverty, "a crime which Massachusetts punishes as no other crime is punished in America, by banishment—banishment from one's native land."[54] The *Boston Post* asked "when, where, and how, have the people of Massachusetts obliged themselves to do such deeds as sending *natives* of her own soil to the honors of old world poverty."[55] The act of deporting "a native born citizen of Massachusetts" to Europe appeared so atrocious and so deviated from the concept of democratic freedom that the *New York Irish-American* declared: "If New Englanders are considered and presented as fair specimens or representatives of American citizens . . . then we grieve to say the grand experiment of the superiority of self-government has failed in the ancient Commonwealth of Massachusetts."[56]

The deportation of Mary and Bridget Williams also revived the point Chandler had made—the double standard for the personal liberty of fugitive slaves and Irish paupers. Contrasting the Williams deportation with the public excitement during the Anthony Burns rendition in 1854, the *Boston Daily Courier* lamented Bostonians' relative silence: "The echoes of Faneuil Hall were silent. . . . Our stock of sympathy is all taken up by the slave: we have none to spare for paupers."[57] The *Advertiser* resorted to racism and gender sensibility to criticize the deportation of Williams. The newspaper wrote that the forcible banishment of a delicate white woman was much more barbarous and cruel than the rendition of a robust black man who could "bear misfortune and hardship should they fall upon him." The *Advertiser* emphasized that, after all, Burns was "negro, 'a man and a brother,'" ridiculing abolitionists' phrase that underscored slaves' humanity. Williams, by contrast, was "only a white woman; a woman and a mother"—"with an infant a few weeks old, demanding all her care, and with nobody to protect or assist her."[58] Joining the *Advertiser*, another newspaper highlighted the anticipated misery of Williams in Liverpool by predicting that "in her desperation and urgent need," she would need to "join that heart-breaking assemblage of wretched women that haunt the large cities of Great Britain"—namely, prostitutes.[59]

Before the upheaval over Mary Williams receded, an additional fact about the *Daniel Webster* deportation exasperated Irish immigrants and inflamed the anti–Know-Nothing press. One of the *Daniel Webster* deportees was an Irish immigrant named Hugh Carr. He had lived in the United States for thirteen years and had already filed his declaration of intent to naturalize. Carr was living in East Cambridge, Massachusetts, with his six sisters and had regularly paid his taxes. Sometime in 1854, he developed symptoms of insanity and the family sent him to an insane asylum in East Cambridge. Finding his family members' frequent visits to him inconvenient, the officials directed them to stop the practice, promising to inform them of any change in Carr's condition. The next update Carr's sisters received about their brother was that he had been sent to Liverpool on the *Daniel Webster* as a foreign pauper eight days before. It was reported that state officials transferred Carr from the East Cambridge lunatic asylum to the state hospital on Rainsford Island. Immediately afterward, the officials put Carr on board the *Daniel Webster*, where he spent that night, and the ship departed for Liverpool the next morning. To the *Advertiser*'s inquiry about the situation of Carr's transfer from the East Cambridge lunatic hospital, an officer at the institution answered: "No valid, nor sufficient reason was given for sending an insane person into the streets, to go at large without any provision for his care," indicating that officials nearly kidnapped Carr from the hospital without considering the patient's physical and mental conditions. "We shall, perhaps, be told that this lunatic consented to his exile," the *Advertiser* derided the Know-Nothing legislature, which was "so profuse in its pretended love of personal liberty."[60]

Carr's deportation added fuel to the confrontation between Irish immigrants and the Know-Nothings. Carr's brother-in-law threatened to take legal action in the matter. In response, according to the *Advertiser*, "our State authorities have undertaken to effect his return to America," but no newspaper in subsequent months confirmed Carr's actual return.[61] The *Boston Pilot*, an organ of the Catholic Irish in Boston, condemned the arbitrary practice of deportation by the Know-Nothings. "If such an infamous law was abused under governments which were not particularly unfavorable to Catholics," the newspaper asked, "how much more will it be abused under this vile tyranny which decrees that poverty, Irishism and Catholicity are crimes, and to be punished as such?"[62] Irish immigrants' words, however, did not affect nativists' belief in deportation law as a "good law" that reduced the burden of "an ignorant and vicious Irish Catholic population."[63] Foreign paupers were "leeches upon our tax payers," the Know-Nothings asserted, and "the more vigorously this law is executed the better it will be."[64] Apparently, the *Daniel Webster* scandal did not discourage the Know-Nothings from expelling Irish paupers.

After the *Daniel Webster* incident, the *Boston Pilot* once again reminded its readers of the importance of immediate naturalization. In the face of the deportation of Williams and Carr, the press was convinced that "If these things do not cause a general rush for naturalization papers, we do not know what will."[65] The *Pilot*'s call for naturalization was theoretically an effective strategy to counter the threat of deportation because the lack of citizenship denied immigrants access to settlement and therefore made them removable. Yet the deportation of Bridget Williams, who few nineteenth-century Americans would doubt was an American citizen by birth, demonstrated that even citizenship would not safeguard the Irish against overseas deportation in the era of radical nativism.

Various sources reveal that nativists deported other minor citizens, boys and girls, besides Bridget Williams. Margaret and Henry Davis,

American-born children of Catherine Davis, were deported to Ireland by the Alien Commissioners with their mother from the Monson state almshouse, which they entered after Catherine was deserted by her Philadelphia-born husband.[66] After being discharged in Ireland, some deportees from Massachusetts entered local workhouses in search of immediate food and shelter. The admission registers of the North Dublin Union Workhouse reveal that two Irish women from Counties Limerick and Roscommon, who had been deported from America, entered the institution on January 29, 1859 with their American-born children.[67] While indicating that deportees included American-born minor citizens, these cases and that of Mary Williams should be interpreted as the reflection of officials' particular motivation to expel women with children because of high costs of supporting them compared to single men and women, a consideration inherited from the time of warning out in the colonial period.

The deportation of Hugh Carr, a "half-naturalized" citizen who had filed his declaration of intent to naturalize, also displayed the defenselessness of naturalized citizenship against overseas banishment. Whether Carr's brother ultimately succeeded in having him sent back from Liverpool was less important than Carr's initial removal. It is also crucial to note that the distinction between citizens and people whom legal scholar Hiroshi Motomura calls "intending citizens"—immigrants who filed their declaration of intent—was not always clear in the nineteenth century. Motomura argues that "intending citizens were not actually citizens, but they were treated like citizens for many purposes." They enjoyed "a favored status, something close to citizenship itself." Intending citizens voted in elections in the antebellum western states. In 1853 the federal government extended diplomatic protection to Martin Koszta, a Hungarian political refugee who was captured by Austrian authorities in Turkey after having filed his declaration of intent in the United States, on the grounds that he was "clothed with an American nationality."[68] In the 1850s, the declaration of intent even served as proof of the bearer's American citizenship, an alternative to a passport.[69]

Some evidence suggests that Massachusetts officials regarded fully naturalized citizens as deportable. After landing in Quebec in the 1830s, Irish immigrant Thomas Purcell came to Massachusetts and naturalized as a citizen in Boston in 1844. Becoming destitute without work and property, he entered the Bridgewater state almshouse twice. Upon his third admission, an almshouse official decided to deport him to Ireland, "if found here again," which indicates that Purcell's naturalized citizenship status did not exempt him from possible deportation to Ireland.[70] A more definite case came when the *New York Irish-American* disclosed that Hugh

Carroll, an Irish-born naturalized citizen, was expelled from Fitchburg, Massachusetts, "across the seas for the crime of *being poor*." Carroll was "a citizen and entitled to the protection of the law," the newspaper noted, "which he did not receive."[71] British sources also show that deportees included naturalized immigrant widows. When the vessel *Resolute* arrived in Liverpool from Boston with thirty-five passengers who were "sent over by the United States authorities in a state of destitution," a local official noticed that one of the pauper passengers was a woman who had emigrated to the United States and married an American. The husband had died and she was sent back to Liverpool with her three American-born children.[72] By naturalization law, this widow was an American citizen, while the children were citizens by birth. Congress passed a law in February 1855 that naturalized any alien woman upon marrying a citizen of the United States, as long as she met the other essential qualification that she was a "free white person."[73] Clearly, American citizenship meant little in the implementation of deportation law in Know-Nothing Massachusetts.

The *Daniel Webster* incident exposes the coercive nature of the Know-Nothings' deportation policy, but it also provides insights into the meaning of citizenship in antebellum America. Evidently, Bridget Williams and Hugh Carr were not the only citizen deportees. The Massachusetts Alien Commissioners periodically deported pauper citizens of Irish ancestry to Ireland and Britain. The nativism that had earlier made citizenship status central to Massachusetts deportation law now seems to have rendered Irish ethnicity a marker of potential deportability. If citizenship did not save Irish American paupers from overseas expulsion, what would shield them against banishment from their country of birth or adoption? How was deportation law operating in relation to cultural prejudice, economics, and citizenship in Massachusetts ruled by nativists?

Any inquiry into the deportation of Irish American paupers must start by acknowledging that American citizenship was not clearly defined for almost a century after independence. During the debates over the Constitution after the American Revolution, the founders failed to establish what comprised American citizenship and the relationship between states and the central government concerning the rights and privileges of citizens. The United States Constitution did not explicitly address birthright citizenship until the ratification in 1868 of the Fourteenth Amendment, which declared that all persons born or naturalized in the United States were citizens of the nation. Before that, the status of birthright citizenship was uncertain, though Americans vaguely assumed that birth within the national territory conferred the status and rights of citizenship, both state and federal. In March 1854, a notary public sent a letter to Secretary of State William L. Marcy to ask for his opinion on the citizenship status of an American-born person of foreign parentage, since the official could "find no law of Congress" on the subject. Admitting that the case under query was "not embraced by any law of the United States," Marcy replied, "I am under the impression that every person born in the United States must be considered a citizen," regardless of the status of parents.[74] Marcy's phrase "under the impression" might sound like a remarkably vague response by the Secretary of State to a question concerning the nation's rule for citizenship. This vagueness, however, suggests the fundamental uncertainty of antebellum American citizenship.

The uncertainty over citizenship was particularly noticeable in two parts in the Constitution. One was the naturalization authority articulated in Article 1, Section 8. This section gave Congress the power to "establish a uniform Rule of Naturalization," but it did not clarify whether Congress had the exclusive power over admission to citizenship. As a result, the states could virtually administer naturalization with their own criteria as long as they followed minimum congressional guidelines.[75] To acquire American citizenship, immigrants in the mid-nineteenth century had to make petitions for naturalization at a court of record such as a district or circuit court of a state or the United States after filing their declaration of intent (first paper). The judges of the court where immigrants made final petitions determined which applicants could become American citizens, based on a provision in the 1790 naturalization act that an applicant needed to prove his "good character" and residence "to the satisfaction of such court." This allowed the judges to exert individual discretion as to whether they admitted or rejected the petitions.[76] In 1852, the *Boston Pilot* noted that the first papers filed in lower courts such as police courts were less likely to be accepted by judges in Massachusetts as sufficient evidence to meet the requirement for naturalization at the time of final petition than in New York and other states, where lower courts were "proper to appear before." Warning that "it is not safe to apply to any of our police or justices' courts in this commonwealth," the writer of the article urged "all foreigners residing in Massachusetts to make application before the United States Circuit or District Courts if possible."[77] This illustrates some regional variation in the standards for naturalization.

The Constitution also addressed the rights of citizens in Section 2 of Article 4. The section provided that "the Citizens of each State shall be entitled to all Privileges and Immunities of Citizens in the several States."[78] The founders created this clause to foster national unity by ensuring that citizens of one state should not be treated as aliens in other states. But this clause was more confusing than self-evident. It was never clear whether citizens of each state were the same as citizens of the United States and whether each state was required to treat citizens from other states as its own citizens. The clause also did not clarify what exactly these privileges and immunities meant. The vagueness of the clause failed to bind the states under one overarching authority regarding the treatment of citizens of individual states.[79] Consequently, the rights and disabilities of citizens were defined on a state basis in the antebellum period. In pre–Civil War America, state citizenship, rather than national citizenship, was a primary marker of people's rights.

The states' assertion of their own principles over the rights of citizens came from the weakness of the antebellum federal government as well as the vagueness of the Constitution. In the words of political scientist Rogers Smith, "the Jacksonian story was one of minimizing the importance of national as opposed to state citizenship." After a brief moment in the late eighteenth century, when the Federalists advocated a strong national government and government-led commercial growth, limited government became the central doctrine in national politics. Regarding the federal government as a threat to an American liberty based on fair competition free from outside intervention, Jacksonian Democrats promoted the elimination of governmental regulations like federal tariffs. The Democrats' belief in limited central government was also rooted in their support of states' rights in defense of slavery in the South, which stood as a Democratic stronghold. In the case of *Barron v. Baltimore* (1833), the Supreme Court ruled that all the Constitutional amendments in the Bill of Rights, including the Fifth Amendment, which protected individuals' rights to life, liberty, or property, were meant to check the action of the federal government. By implying that state governments were not necessarily restricted by the Constitutional amendments, this ruling enhanced the states' control over the rights of citizens, even allowing the states to establish policies that would be regarded as violating the Bill of Rights had they been installed by the federal government. The limited presence of the federal government and the resultant weakness of national citizenship further obscured the conception of what rights American citizenship guaranteed.[80]

The *Dred Scott* decision of 1857 did not bring concrete definition to citizenship. Chief Justice Roger B. Taney argued that while some states recognized African Americans as citizens of their states, the state citizens thereby recognized were not necessarily citizens of the United States. As he put it, "we must not confound the rights of citizenship which a State may confer within its own limits and the rights of citizenship as a member of the Union." Individual states had the right to extend citizenship to an immigrant or a free black, but "the rights which he would acquire would be restricted to the State which gave them." Only the federal government could confer national citizenship on the citizens of states, and no state could "introduce a new member into the political community created by the Constitution of the United States." According to Taney, national citizenship was given only to those people, and their descendants, who were citizens at the time of the Constitution's ratification and to immigrants who naturalized under federal naturalization laws. Taney concluded that African Americans belonged to neither of these two categories and thus remained outside of national citizenry. This ruling settled for the moment the relationship between state and national citizenship. But it still did not clarify exactly what rights were secured for national citizens and it did not affect individual states' authority over the rights of state citizens, leaving the substance of American citizenship undefined.[81]

The ambiguity in definition and substance resulted in the relative insignificance of citizenship and its attendant rights in antebellum American public life. According to legal historian William Novak, before the Fourteenth Amendment made all persons born or naturalized in the United States national citizens and established the superiority of national citizenship to all other sorts of status and membership, American citizenship was never "a unified, universal, and unidirectional marker of the line between freedom and unfreedom, rights and servitudes, inclusion and exclusion." Some states drew only a fine distinction in legal status between citizens and intending citizens over political participation, taxation, and property ownership. Aliens and particular citizens such as women and free blacks in many states shared the same disabilities to vote and hold public office. In light of these overlaps between citizens and aliens in public life, Novak elaborates, personal privileges and immunities did not depend on "a single determination of whether one was a citizen." Legal statuses—master and servant, husband and wife, guardian and ward—were more critical than citizenship, as was membership of local associations such as private corporations and religious societies.[82]

The implications for the status and treatment of paupers were clear. With the weak presence of citizenship, paupers' rights were determined beyond issues of citizenship. The social status of paupers drastically declined over the first half of the nineteenth century. Although Americans despised pauperism as the antithesis of American independence, they generally assumed that paupers could be reformed into productive citizens through rehabilitation and education up to the early nineteenth century. As pauperism enormously expanded as a result of urbanization and industrialization, however, Americans had rejected this optimistic view of the poor by midcentury. Paupers appeared to be a separate, hostile, and morally depraved class of people who willfully exploited public relief and were a source of significant social problems such as crime and insanity. Accordingly, poor laws were modified from reformative to repressive by the 1850s, stigmatizing paupers as social outcasts and approving the denial of rights of paupers.[83] A New Jersey legislator stated in the 1840s that when a man became an inmate of a poorhouse, "he voluntarily surrenders his rights. . . . he parts with his liberty."[84]

One example of repressive pauper regulation is found in state laws that permitted the Overseers of the Poor to punish beggars by placing them in workhouses without judicial proceedings. In the antebellum period, local police regulation over moral issues such as begging and prostitution customarily overrode individual due process, and alleged moral offenders could be punished without solid evidence of criminal acts and trials.[85] In 1856, the Maine Supreme Court upheld the action of the Portland Overseers of the Poor to send a destitute unemployed woman and her daughter to a workhouse with no judicial process and solely on the overseers' judgment that they were "living a dissolute, vagrant life." The opinion of one dissenting justice in the case encapsulated what being a pauper meant in antebellum America, highlighting the unfree status of paupers. The pauper was deprived of "the control of his own person." "The pauper may be transported from town to town, and place to place, against his will," claimed the judge. "He may himself be sent to the work-house, or made the subject of a five years [labor] contract, without being personally consulted." In short, "the adjudged pauper is subordinated to the will of others, and reduced to a condition but little removed from that of chattel slavery."[86] A Maine lawyer had previously questioned the state poor law's infringement of due process provided in the state constitution, calling the law a violation of "absolute and natural rights," but the state supreme court turned down his challenge.[87]

The deterioration of paupers' status during the Know-Nothing period was part and parcel of the period's ethnic stereotypes of the Irish. In the mid-nineteenth century there was a burgeoning view of Irish pauperism as the result of Irish people's innate character, part of their ethnicity, rather than a condition into which they happened to fall due to external forces. Nativists began to think that Irish immigrants became paupers because they were Irish.[88] The nativist *Boston Daily Bee* declared the pauperism of the Irish to be "their normal condition."[89] Theodore Parker, a leading abolitionist and an outspoken nativist in Boston, wrote that the Irish were foreign in "ethnological disposition" and had "vices of their condition, wretchedness, beggary, drunkenness, deceit, lying, violence, treachery, malice, superstition." "All these Irishmen" were therefore "hostile to temperance, to education, to cleanliness."[90] Specialists in mental illness also argued that people of Irish extraction were inherently more likely to fall into insanity than those of other ethnic groups. Edward Jarvis, an established physician in Massachusetts, explained the cause of Irish insanity in 1855: "The Irish laborers have less sensibility.... They have also a greater irritability; they are more readily disturbed when they find themselves at variance with the circumstances about them, and less easily reconciled to difficulties they cannot overcome."[91] The idea that being Irish predisposed one to pauperism and insanity drew widespread acceptance by the 1850s.

IRISH BEGGAR *to generous Young Lady.* "Thank'ee, Miss; but I niver takes country money.

Figure 4.2: Untitled, *Harper's Weekly*, November 7, 1857. An Irish beggar rejects the offer of charity from a young woman, as he distrusts the value of "country money" during the Panic of 1857, when many currencies issued by local banks became worthless paper. The image reflects deep concerns about the financial situation of the nation as well as the immediate social chaos and poverty brought about by the Panic, with the Irish beggar standing as a potent symbol for both. Cartoons of this kind naturalized the connection between the Irish and pauperism in Americans' mind by presenting the Irish as quintessential beggars.
Courtesy of Butler Library, Columbia University in the City of New York.

The bias against Irish pauperism did not signify that Anglo Americans were blind to the poverty of other immigrant groups and African Americans, but they found Irish pauperism particularly vicious and troublesome. At almshouses, non-Irish inmates left a better impression than the Irish. Commenting on the inmates at the Tewksbury state alms- house, the *Lowell News* wrote that French Canadians were poor but clean, "exhibiting a marked contrast with the generality of the Irish paupers."[92] In a letter to an acquaintance, Theodore Parker explicated what he called "ethnology of pauperism." According to Parker, Anglo Saxon, American, English, or Scottish pauperism could be "easily disposed of." So was black pauperism. German pauperism, Parker predicted, "will give us little trou- ble," and Jewish was "quite inconsiderable." The pauperism of the Irish, however, was fundamentally different. Parker insisted, "Celtic pauperism is our stone of stumbling. The Irishman has three bad things—bad habits, bad religion, and worse of all, a bad nature." Parker characterized Irish pauperism with three maxims: "1 The Irishman will always lie, if it is for his momentary interest. 2 He will not work while he can exist by beg- ging. 3 He will steal when he can get chance, and preferentially from his benefactor."[93] Irish ethnicity was thus thought to foster an exceptionally obnoxious form of pauperism.

All of these ethnic biases fit well into the existing contexts of poverty discourse and free labor ideology. The New York Association for Improving the Condition of the Poor generally categorized the Irish as the undeserv- ing poor, whose poverty stemmed from individual moral failing, whereas the association thought that "natives and Germans" belonged to the class of the deserving poor for being "willing and anxious to earn their living." Some Germans could be as poor as the Irish, but they stood at "the oppo- site [end] of the Irish, being generally a self-reliant, sober, frugal, thrifty people." The Irish, by contrast, "are but little disposed to change their thriftless habits with a change of country." Convinced of the alleged lazi- ness of the Irish, charity officials remarked that "here, as in their own land, many of them evince too little force and energy to be the arbiters of their own destiny."[94] Antebellum white Americans viewed the dependency of paupers as a menace to their free republican society, which supposedly consisted of independent productive workers. The repressive poor law that stripped basic liberties from paupers, as legal scholar James W. Fox Jr. argues, further cultivated the notion that paupers were "anti-citizens" or "strangers in a nation of working-citizens."[95] By presenting dependency as the character of the Irish, nativists propagated the labeling of the Irish as anti-citizens and their particular unfitness for American society.

From the standpoint of the anti-slavery Know-Nothings in Massachusetts, their policies for Irish paupers and black fugitives were hardly contradictory but rather consistent under the framework of free labor ideology. At the center of pauper removal and fugitive protection stood the Know-Nothings' belief in the value of economic self-sufficiency and upward social mobility. Many anti-slavery Bostonians thought that black slaves in the South deserved their sympathy because slavery made it impossible for them to become self-sufficient workers. The Know-Nothings thus protected fugitive slaves in order to save them from the denial of self-ownership under slavery and give them a chance to support and advance themselves through free labor. By contrast, the Know-Nothings thought that by living a dependent and unproductive life despite being in free society which technically guaranteed freedom and upward mobility for everyone, Irish paupers threatened to destabilize the integrity of free northern society. Anti-slavery nativists saw no necessity to respect the personal liberty of Irish paupers, who violated American free labor ideology. They therefore aggressively seized and banished them.

The inchoate nature of antebellum citizenship, the degraded status of paupers, and prejudice against the Irish made paupers of Irish descent most vulnerable to deportation policy in Know-Nothing Massachusetts. By the mid-nineteenth century, the law had made it clear that overseas removal was reserved for noncitizens. The Massachusetts statutes of the 1850s stipulated that a nonsettled pauper would be sent to "any other state, or, if not a citizen of the United States, to any place beyond sea where he belongs."[96] At the site of law enforcement, however, nativist officials easily disregarded the citizenship of Irish American paupers, who they believed belonged to Ireland rather than the United States. At a time when the rights and privileges of American citizenship remained undefined and fragile, and citizenship was subordinate to other legal statuses, paupers' rights were routinely subjected to repression by local regulatory power. In these circumstances, nativists felt little bound to follow the formal guidelines for removal. It was easy for enforcing officers to deport from the nation pauper citizens, just like alien paupers. The Massachusetts Alien Commissioners sent non-Irish foreigners and Americans back to their places of origin. Yet the commissioners never displayed the same level of intolerance, including the expulsion from the nation of those who held American citizenship, to these groups as they did to Irish Americans. In antebellum Massachusetts, nativist hostility to Irish poverty outweighed the citizenship of Irish American paupers in the practical operation of deportation law.

The pace of the Know-Nothing Party's decline was as striking as the swiftness of its rise to power. Unable to reach a consensus over slavery, the national American Party was divided between northern and southern members and declined precipitously after the 1856 presidential election. In Massachusetts, Nathaniel P. Banks was elected governor in 1858 as a Know-Nothing candidate. Yet nativism occupied much smaller space in his political agenda than it did in Gardner's, and support for Banks came largely from the Republicans, who replaced the Know-Nothings as an anti-slavery party. In 1859 the Republican-controlled legislature enacted a law originally sponsored by the Know-Nothings in 1855, which required immigrant citizens to wait for two years after naturalization to vote or hold office, but nativism never regained the strength it had once enjoyed in state politics.[97]

The retreat of political nativism, however, did not ameliorate enmity against destitute immigrants or quell enthusiasm for pauper deportation. In New York, residents of Staten Island, alarmed by the potential spread of contagious diseases from sick immigrants at the marine hospital on the island, had since 1855 repeatedly asked the legislature to remove the institution. Staten Islanders became increasingly aggressive, and state officials received threats to destroy the institution. On the night of September 1, 1858, the tension over the hospital culminated in a mob of a thousand angry residents and property holders burning the institution to the ground.[98]

In Massachusetts, the new legislature reorganized the Commissioners of Alien Passengers and Foreign Paupers in 1858 with new officials. Upon starting their operation, the new commissioners resolved to uncompromisingly execute the deportation law.[99] The new Alien Commissioners' devotion to their duties resulted in a significant expansion of pauper removal. In the single year of 1858, the commissioners banished 3,369 paupers from Massachusetts. The scale of removal in that year appears striking, given that the number of people expelled during the three years between 1855 and 1857 combined was 4,028. The Panic of 1857, which had created massive poverty and unemployment in the nation's financial centers such as New York City and Boston, must have contributed to the active implementation of deportation in 1858. Yet the deeper cause for the extended removal lay in the new officials' conviction that the policy was "not *duly* executed" even under the Know-Nothing government, requiring far more rigorous enforcement. In 1859, the legislature finally empowered the Alien Commissioners to deport foreign inmates in state charitable institutions directly to "any state or place where they belong," *without* putting them on trial first. By the time a new state agency succeeded them in

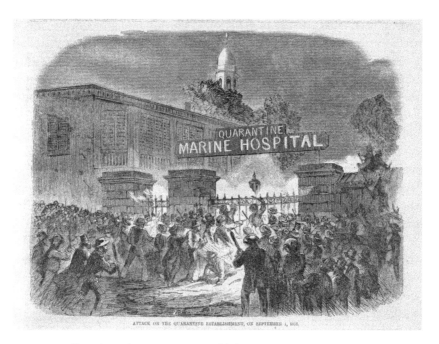

Figure 4.3: "Attack on the Quarantine Establishment, on September 1, 1858," *Harper's Weekly*, September 11, 1858.
Courtesy of Butler Library, Columbia University in the City of New York.

1863, the Massachusetts Alien Commissioners had removed more than 15,000 people from the state in their thirteen-year operation.[100]

The new commissioners maintained that they sent back paupers humanely and only upon their own requests, but skepticism about the manner of removal remained.[101] In September 1858, the scenes of paupers' arrival in Liverpool from Massachusetts made one local official suspect that "they had been almost forced on board the vessel."[102] In 1860, the *Boston Pilot* reported on a case that raised questions about the way the Alien Commissioners conducted deportation. The newspaper announced the prospect of a lawsuit against the officials by an Irish man for abducting his pauper wife, Catherine McGovern, who was "mysteriously lost" during her deportation from the Tewksbury state almshouse to Ireland, a case reminiscent of Hugh Carr's banishment in 1855.[103]

Radical nativism fomented by the Know-Nothings thus outlived the party. Historians have long considered the Know-Nothings' nativist achievements inconsequential because of the party's short life and its ultimate failure to accomplish some of its chief national-level goals, notably the twenty-one-year probation for naturalization. The enforcement of state immigration law by the Massachusetts Know-Nothings, however, proved their solid success in physically reducing foreign elements in the state as government policy. In New York, the Know-Nothings were not as successful in state politics as Bay State nativists, but the extreme anti-immigrant atmosphere created by Know-Nothingism stimulated the unlawful removal of destitute foreigners by local authorities. If the framework of state-level immigration control was established between 1847 and 1854, it was the Know-Nothings who brought it into full bloom with coercive elements that endured beyond the demise of the political movement. The Know-Nothings' determination to expel foreign paupers from the nation continued to shape state-level immigration control through the Civil War and Reconstruction, directly affecting the emergence of national immigration legislation in the 1880s.

The most significant consequence of the Know-Nothing movement for the history of American immigration control is that it established precedents for immigration officials' assertion of unlimited power over objectionable aliens. As seen in New York authorities' apparent dismissal of the undeportability of foreigners under state law and the Massachusetts commissioners' expulsion of Irish American citizens, state officials developed—and acted on—the conviction that they could practically do anything with aliens, or people whom the officials deemed aliens, if their action was the exercise of police power to protect Americans from economic, moral, and public health threats. The political situation of the 1850s that fostered the rise of the Know-Nothings, the low social and legal status of the poor, the fragility of antebellum citizenship, and most crucially intense anti-Irish sentiment contributed to the formation of that notion. While the concept of police power served as the foundation for the legal development of state and eventually national immigration policy, this notion also profoundly affected the ways American officials implemented immigrant exclusion and deportation thereafter, leaving the lasting mark of the Know-Nothing movement on the nation's immigration policy.

CHAPTER 5

A New Birth of Poverty

*Pauper Policy in the Age of the Civil War
and Reconstruction*

In the late 1860s, when the treatment of former slaves and Confederates occupied much of the public discourse in the United States, domestic pauperism stirred heated debate in Britain. While some advocated the overseas compulsory emigration of paupers as a solution to the social, economic, and moral problem of pauperism, others were more skeptical of the effectiveness of banishment. In January 1869, the *Pall Mall Gazette*, a London newspaper, fully endorsed the idea of compulsory pauper emigration. Emigration, according to the newspaper, was a "mild sentence" compared to various other kinds of punishment for paupers, such as forced labor at workhouses, as they could start a better and more independent life in new places. Also, host countries would appreciate paupers as a workforce. It was not anticipated, the *Pall Mall Gazette* wrote, that "either the United States or any of our own colonial possessions would object to receive such an importation."[1]

The *Pall Mall Gazette*'s characterization of America's reaction to pauper immigration proved utterly wrong. During the Civil War, the Abraham Lincoln administration welcomed immigration to the United States for the want of manpower to wage the war against the Confederacy. A democratic mindset brought about by slave emancipation empowered naturalized citizens through the Fourteenth Amendment and the Expatriation

Act of 1868, which affirmed the equality of birthright and naturalized citizenship. Massachusetts, the vanguard of nativism in antebellum America, also reformed its poor law, making unnaturalized foreigners eligible for settlement in the state and local relief—a firm recognition of their membership in the community of Massachusetts. This inclusive stance, however, did not apply to those who were paupers. Instead of shrinking with the decline of the Know-Nothing movement, hostility to indigent immigrants even grew stronger during wartime and the aftermath of emancipation.

This chapter explores immigration control in New York and Massachusetts in the era of the Civil War and Reconstruction. In the 1860s, the burgeoning presence of transient beggars, or vagrants, occupied the attention of northern charity officials. Able-bodied but unwilling to work, vagrants unquestionably represented the "undeserving" poor in their eyes. The concept of undeserving poverty was nothing new. Yet at the moment the Republicans and reformers were promoting the virtue of self-sufficiency based on contract wage labor as the foundation of a new American society purged of slave labor, vagrants who voluntarily withdrew from contract obligations appeared particularly disturbing. In northeastern states, vagrancy became a problem explicitly connected to immigration, as foreigners, especially the Irish, accounted for a large portion of street beggars. Immigrant vagrancy buttressed existing antipathy to assisted paupers, who seemed to represent another group of the undeserving poor. When an economic depression in the early 1870s exacerbated the already alarming state of vagrancy and pauperism in New York City, the state legislature sought to reduce the number of destitute foreigners by authorizing the state charity board to regulate immigration along with the Commissioners of Emigration. Massachusetts also expanded state policy for the deportation of the foreign poor by making immigrant vagrants removable, just like paupers and lunatics. While New York and Massachusetts advanced their systems of immigration restriction, other coastal states either failed to establish sustainable regulatory mechanisms or moved toward open-port policies. New York and Massachusetts officials' uninterrupted determination to exclude and deport destitute foreigners during Reconstruction eventually triggered the introduction of national immigration legislation in the early 1880s.

The federal government encouraged immigration and assumed an active role in protecting the rights of citizens during the Civil War and Reconstruction. State legislatures followed this trend of big government

by centralizing the administration of various state policies for social welfare to a single agency. In Massachusetts, the federal government's egalitarian policies for immigration and citizenship inspired the legislature to
modify the state laws of settlement and removal that had long discriminated against foreigners.

The outbreak of the Civil War disrupted immigration to the United
States, but the strategic necessity of manpower for the Union army and
for agricultural labor pressured the Lincoln administration to devise
mechanisms to boost immigration.[2] The Homestead Act of 1862, which
would grant 160 acres of public land in the West to a settler if he or she
improved the land for five years, partly aimed to attract immigrant farmers from Europe.[3] The federal government adopted a more direct approach
to facilitate emigration from Europe to the United States in 1864. In his
annual message in December 1863, President Lincoln urged Congress
to consider "the expediency of establishing a system for the encouragement of immigration" to fill "a great deficiency of laborers in every field of
industry."[4] Congress responded to Lincoln's request in July 1864 by passing the Act to Encourage Immigration, which would assist European emigrants who could not afford passage money to the United States through
the system of labor contract supervised by the federal Commissioner of
Immigration. The act provided that workers in Europe would make contracts with American companies, which would finance their emigration
to the United States. In return, the workers pledged to repay their passage with the wages they would earn in America. Contracted laborers were
exempted from military service for the war.[5]

The federal government's interests in profiting from international
trade and securing a labor force led to the continuation of favorable policies for immigration after the Civil War. In 1868 the United States signed
the Burlingame Treaty with China, ensuring unrestricted immigration
to the United States for Chinese nationals for the purpose of fostering
commerce between the two nations.[6] In the same year, Congress received
various bills for the establishment of emigration agencies in European
countries. These agencies would work under the direction of the Secretary
of State to accelerate emigrants' departure by disseminating information
on the United States such as travel routes, rates of wages, and ways to
acquire land. In his message to Congress in December 1871, President
Ulysses S. Grant called for congressional action to better protect newcomers from fraudulent practices such as the sale of fake railroad tickets. In the following congressional session, the House discussed a bill "to
promote immigration to the United States and for the protection of emigrants" and two similar ones.[7] Neither the presidential recommendation

nor the congressional bills were realized. Nevertheless, they reflected the generally positive sentiment toward immigration during Reconstruction.

The federal government also moved to improve the status of immigrants after the war. By way of securing civil rights and citizenship for freedpeople, the Radical Republicans passed the Fourteenth Amendment, which was ratified in 1868. Declaring that all persons born or naturalized in the United States were citizens of the nation, Section 1 of the amendment offered the first constitutional definition of who was an American citizen at the national level. In addition to overturning the *Dred Scott* decision and including African Americans in the American citizenry, this clause confirmed the legal equality of native-born and naturalized Americans as national citizens.[8] Congress addressed naturalized immigrants' citizenship rights with another piece of legislation. Shortly after the war, repeated arrests by the British government of naturalized Irish Americans who joined anti-British nationalist activities in Ireland stirred outrage in the United States as an insult to American citizenship. In 1868 Congress showed its sympathy with naturalized Irish Americans by passing the Expatriation Act, which provided that naturalized citizens outside the United States would receive from the American government the same protection as native-born citizens would receive under similar circumstances. In case any citizen, native-born or naturalized, was "unjustly deprived of his liberty by or under the authority of any foreign government," the president had a duty to resort to all necessary and proper means to effect the person's release. The Fourteenth Amendment had established the doctrine of equality between birthright and naturalized citizenship, but the Expatriation Act solidified this equality by specifically guaranteeing the American government's diplomatic protection of naturalized citizens abroad.[9]

The active involvement of the federal government in public affairs during and after the war stimulated the centralization of authority at the state level. Starting in Massachusetts, this pattern emerged most noticeably in the sphere of social welfare, due to the necessity of efficient charity policies to deal with the massive demand for relief caused by the war.[10] In Massachusetts, the Commissioners of Alien Passengers and Foreign Paupers (Alien Commissioners) had deported destitute immigrants from public charitable institutions such as almshouses and lunatic hospitals since 1851, but the maintenance and supervision of these institutions belonged to the officials of each establishment. Convinced that the merger of the Alien Commissioners and the administrative offices of charitable institutions into a single agency would create a more functional charity system and reduce overall operational expenses, the Massachusetts legislature decided to abolish the Alien Commissioners and establish a new bureau called the Board of State Charities in April 1863. The first comprehensive state welfare agency in the United States, the board was authorized to "investigate and supervise the whole system of the public charitable and correctional institutions of the Commonwealth." At the same time, the General Agent of the board, who would act as the Superintendent of Alien Passengers for the city of Boston, inherited the Alien Commissioners' duties over immigration control.[11] Thus in addition to supervising public welfare, the Board of State Charities would regulate immigration by excluding destitute foreign passengers who were not bonded by shipowners upon arrival and by deporting immigrant paupers and lunatics in charitable institutions to other American states, Canada, or Europe.

Soon after the creation of the Massachusetts Board of State Charities, other states followed suit in establishing state agencies to administer charitable and reformatory institutions. New York and Ohio created their state boards of charities in 1867, and Pennsylvania, Rhode Island, Illinois, and North Carolina in 1869. By the end of the nineteenth century, eleven more states had taken the same step. While serving as a model for charity boards in other states, the Massachusetts Board of State Charities differed from them with immigration control as its unique feature. The primary duty of other boards was the administration of public charity, and it usually did not include passenger regulation. In New York, the Commissioners of Emigration remained the enforcers of state passenger laws. In other coastal states, municipal officials continued to collect head money and bonds from shipmasters.[12]

Although Massachusetts had been a hotbed of nativism in the antebellum period, the greater acceptance of European immigrants at the national level in this period brought about a critical change in the state's policy toward foreigners. In Massachusetts, only those who had settlement in a given town or city could apply for local poor relief and the state law had limited settlement only to citizens, leaving foreigners deportable as nonsettled paupers when they became destitute, however long they had lived in the state and whatever forms of contribution they had made to their communities. As the Civil War came to the end, the Board of State Charities began to question the discrimination against foreigners over settlement. In the annual report of the board for 1865, General Agent H. B. Wheelwright presented a hypothetical case of an immigrant family:

> He might have resided in the town, upon his own real estate, for thirty years; all his children might have been born and reared there; he might have been a

good neighbor and a public benefactor, adding largely by his enterprise and business talent to the wealth of the municipality; and yet if adversity or disability should overtake him, no pittance from the abundance he had created could be legally claimed for his support.... Can it be excused? These people belong to the human brotherhood. They have well fulfilled, in their better days, their obligations to society.[13]

The board advocated reform, believing that the right to public relief should be shared by all the people who performed public duties like tax payment "without limitations of race or color, sex or citizenship."[14] Republican governors of Massachusetts agreed with the charity board. John A. Andrew contended in January 1865 that "aliens, having fulfilled all the conditions of settlement except the oath of naturalization, should enjoy the same privileges in this regard as the native born."[15] Alexander H. Bullock upheld his predecessor's position three years later. "In her justice and her charity," Massachusetts "should recognize no frontiers but those of humanity itself."[16]

The suggestions of the charity board and governors resulted in the legislature's pivotal decision to modify the old settlement law. Passed in July 1868, the new law provided that any male person, either citizen or foreigner, over the age of twenty-one years would be eligible for settlement in the state if the person met other qualifications, such as property ownership, sound tax payment records, and ten-year residency.[17] Despite the fundamental discrimination against women, this represented a monumental breakthrough in the treatment of immigrants in Massachusetts. It not only entitled settled immigrants to relief from their town or city of settlement in time of distress but also made them immune from deportation. The new legislation, as the board put it, would provide care for destitute people based on "actual and present settlement, rather than that of the merely technical one."[18] Pragmatic understanding of residents' tie to the community prevailed over the artificial detachment of foreigners from settlement through the legal distinction of citizens and noncitizens. By raising foreigners to the same level as the native-born in terms of access to settlement and public charity, Massachusetts recognized their social citizenship in the community, if they were self-supporting, industrious people. The Bay State thus joined the national reform impetus of the period to incorporate formerly neglected people into American society.[19]

Although the Civil War era introduced some progressive changes to people's rights, this period was also characterized by an economic ideology that was severely hostile to certain groups of the poor. The economic ideals of the Republicans, charity officials, and the business elite, which prized the wage contract as an emblem of American freedom and independence after the abolition of slavery, demonized transient beggars for their voluntary refusal to support themselves through wage labor. The fact that foreigners made up a large portion of beggars multiplied their social undesirability. Additionally, the rise of the idea of hereditary pauperism in the 1870s augmented existing anti-Irish prejudice in the discourse of poverty. The correlation of postbellum economic ideology and renewed nativist sentiment generated powerful forces for the expansion of state immigration policy in New York and Massachusetts.

The contrast of two kinds of poverty became a dominant theme in American social welfare. On the one hand, the realities of industrialization and the destructive effects of the Civil War created a class of paupers who charity officials believed happened to be destitute and disabled because of uncontrollable misfortune. Calling their destitution "honest poverty," officials sympathized with their plight.[20] Such paupers, the Massachusetts Board of State Charities admitted, had the "native vigor and capacity" for self-support. Pauperism for this class was "not inherent, but accidental, and may be only temporary." The board members thus believed that "the differences between them and us are seen to be accidental, while the essentials of humanity remain the same."[21] This conception of the "deserving" poor had certainly existed prior to the Civil War, but the increased number of people dependent on public charity because of the war and the inclusive atmosphere of the period consolidated the favorable recognition of the deserving poor.

At the same time, charity officials noticed the growing presence of indigent people whom they categorized as the undeserving poor. The poverty of this class allegedly stemmed from their own laziness, drunkenness, and lack of moral strength. They were "helpless, dependent, idle consumers, and destructives," and they would simply burden society without giving anything back to it, as if "the leeches are always drawing blood."[22] For charity officials, the increase of vagrants, or "tramps," represented the problem of undeserving poverty in the postwar years. Having no steady means to support themselves, vagrants depended on external assistance. But instead of entering charitable institutions as paupers, they sought to survive through street begging. Physically capable of conducting labor but unmotivated to sweat to earn their bread, vagrants perfectly symbolized the undeserving class of the poor.

The critique of vagrancy was not simply a continuation of the earlier discourse on pauperism but founded on a new understanding of idleness that emerged with the elimination of slave labor. The antebellum hostility to pauperism in the northern states owed part of its ideological basis to the institution of slavery in the South, as paupers' slave-like dependent and degraded status appeared to threaten northern free republican society. When the Civil War abolished slavery, the regulation of undeserving poverty needed an alternative ideological source. According to historian Amy Dru Stanley, that source was contract wage labor. Contract wage labor, which technically allowed employees to start and quit the relationship with their employers at their will, became a postwar symbol of freedom and independence and a path to wealth accumulation. All free Americans were expected to find employment, and vagrants who placed themselves outside the contract relation were viewed as a menace to the integrity of postslavery American society. For beggars, Stanley argues, "to subsist outside the matrix of contract obligations had become a crime." Legal scholar James W. Fox Jr. adds that "Reconstruction was simultaneously defining citizenship as universal (though implicitly male) and yet was enforcing a capitalist model of labor citizenship which increasingly sought to criminalize 'willful' poverty."[23] The industrial order in the postbellum period made voluntary idleness even more obnoxious than it appeared prior to the Civil War.

This economic ideology, shared widely among Republicans, capitalist entrepreneurs including Democratic merchants and bankers, and charity officials, was rooted in an idealistic understanding of wage labor. Many Republicans and most business leaders believed that employers and employees shared the same interests in wage labor. While employers benefited from their employees' labor, workers could accumulate wealth through wages and eventually rise to the point where they could hire employees of their own. Wage labor, therefore, would allow everyone to benefit from increased production in the end. It was a temporary status for workers and a source of wealth and mobility for all. This view of wage relationship between employers and employees, however, was harshly criticized by workers and Democratic labor leaders. Rather than harmony, they maintained, constant conflict characterized their relationship with employers. Workers realized that their economic conditions continued to deteriorate under capitalism and they would be trapped in a permanent proletarian class, instead of climbing the social and economic ladder with their wages. Contrasting ideas of political economy therefore existed in tension in the North during Reconstruction. Nevertheless, Republicans'— and capitalists'—understanding of wage labor proved most dominant in postwar welfare discourse, deeply influencing northern charity officials, many of whom shared similar worldviews with these groups of people. Revealingly, some state boards of charities, including those in New York and Massachusetts, were organized by state governments in which Radical Republicans enjoyed substantial power.[24] Adherents to their wage labor ideal regarded workers critical of it as disaffected, dangerous, unreliable, and finally lazy people who almost equaled vagrants or the undeserving poor.[25]

No clear-cut line between the deserving poor and the undeserving poor existed in reality. Believing that wage contracts always guaranteed self-sufficiency, charity officials saw no reason for workers to beg unless their own moral depravity urged them to do so. In practice, however, labor contracts remained so unstable and wages could be so low that workers frequently had to resort to begging to avoid starvation. Under the settings of harsh industrial capitalism, workers' subsistence depended on a combination of wages and alms. Beggars, labor leader Ira Steward explained, consisted of a "large class" that included wage workers who "must either sell days works, or live upon charity, or starve to death." In other words, the deserving poor, who possessed willingness to work and support themselves if the situation permitted, joined the begging population. Failing to recognize this reality in the world of contract wage labor, charity officials instead categorized all able-bodied beggars as undeserving vagrants who voluntarily chose to live on alms because of their indolence.[26]

The disproportionate representation of foreigners, especially the Irish, in the vagrant population provoked the ire of charity officials. Already in 1864, the Massachusetts Board of State Charities noticed that vagrants in the state were "in large proportion, foreigners."[27] The frequent arrival of bands of Irish vagrants who sought temporary shelter annoyed almshouse officials. One night in January 1874, for example, a "squad of tramps" composed of eight Irish men appeared at the Tewksbury state almshouse "for lodging."[28] Claiming that foreigners and their children accounted for two-thirds of tramps in Massachusetts, Franklin B. Sanborn, secretary of the charity board, remarked that "the two movements, as they show themselves in America—immigration and tramping—are but varieties of the same species."[29] Foreign-born tramps outnumbered American tramps in New York as well. By 1880 foreigners had come to account for about half the tramps in New York State, and half of them were born in Ireland. The New York Association for Improving the Condition of the Poor identified vagrancy as a formidable evil "to which immigration especially subjects the city of New York." The association thought that immigrant vagrancy epitomized "the deteriorating effects of foreign immigration on the social and moral condition of this commercial emporium," stressing the incompatibility of foreign beggars with American capitalist society where people engaged in production and trade.[30]

Vagrancy was not the only source of undeserving foreign poverty. Assisted pauper immigration from Europe continued throughout the Civil War and Reconstruction. Between 1862 and 1864, the Lansdowne estate in County Kerry, Ireland, sponsored the passage of its 668 impoverished tenants to New York.[31] The Massachusetts Board of State Charities noted that "many paupers from foreign countries are unquestionably sent to America as paupers, and in order to be rid of them."[32] The New York Commissioners of Emigration similarly complained about the assisted emigration of paupers with mental illness: "Idiots and imbeciles are systematically sent to this country from Europe, by relatives or local authorities, in order to shift on this Commission the burden of their support."[33] The admission of assisted paupers enlarged the already substantial size of the immigrant inmate population at charitable institutions. One Massachusetts official went so far as to remark that "nearly every inmate" of the Tewksbury state almshouse "is of foreign birth or parentage—largely Irish."[34] Since the antebellum period, Americans detested assisted paupers as the undeserving poor for their lack of self-sufficiency that had existed even before their emigration to the United States and their seemingly predestined unlikelihood to become ideal American citizens as productive workers. The criticism of vagrancy intensified Americans' loathing of assisted paupers who, just like vagrants, would undermine postslavery American freedom and independence with their dependent status and inability to support themselves through contract wage labor. And the Irish remained the chief target of this nativist sentiment after the Civil War.

In addition to the postbellum ideology of poverty and sustained assisted emigration, the increasingly influential scientific approach to the problem of pauperism worked against the Irish in distinct ways. In an effort to scientifically analyze the causes of poverty, reformers and charity officials began to adopt the concept of hereditary pauperism in the 1870s. Children of pauper parents were thought to be biologically predestined to become paupers like their parents. Vices such as idleness, improvidence, and drunkenness, New York charity officials noted, grew as a "result of tendencies which are to a greater or less degree hereditary." A Protestant minister in Boston warned that "pauperism was contagious as well as hereditary, and a score of beggars would soon produce a hundred."[35] The notion that people of Irish ancestry developed pauperism as their innate character had emerged earlier, yet the intellectual trend in social welfare after the Civil War tightened the supposed biological link between the Irish and pauperism.[36]

Anti-Irish cartoons helped legitimize the prejudiced association of the Irish with undeserving poverty in popular consciousness. In a cartoon titled "The King of A Shantee" in *Puck*, an illustrated humor magazine, Frederick Opper described an Irishman smoking a pipe and sitting on a piece of a broken barrel outside his poorly built house, apparently without willingness to engage in any form of labor.[37] By exaggerating the alleged laziness of the Irish, cartoons like this reinforced the notion that Irish immigrants by nature preferred to have an idle life and place themselves outside the world of contract obligations. Contrasting Irish and German immigrants, the New York Association for Improving the Condition of the Poor remarked in 1869 that "the Celt does very little to elevate himself, either socially or morally" but "the Saxon (German) is the reverse of this." "He may be a Roman Catholic," the organization stressed, "but thinks independently, and acts for himself."[38] The biological understanding of poverty, which entered into the mainstream of American social welfare during Reconstruction, perpetuated the view that Irish vagrants and paupers represented the quintessential undeserving poor, who would remain permanently unfit for American

PUCK'S GALLERY OF CELEBRITIES.

THE KING OF A-SHANTEE.

Figure 5.1: "The King of A Shantee," *Puck*, February 15, 1882.
Courtesy of Butler Library, Columbia University in the City of New York.

republican society due to their innate predisposition to idleness and chronic dependency.

The problems of undeserving poverty during Reconstruction had profound implications for immigration policy in New York and Massachusetts. The conspicuous presence of foreigners in the vagrant and pauper population induced these states to revise their policies for sending destitute foreigners back to Europe. In New York, the state government empowered additional officials to implement the policy for returning those who expressed their wish to go home. In Massachusetts the legislature, in an effort to better restrict street begging, added vagrants to the category of deportable people in state immigration law. The discussion of undeserving poverty in the postbellum period was not confined to the sphere of social welfare, but brought about significant developments in state-level immigration control as well.

In New York, when the worst economic collapse Americans had yet experienced deteriorated destitution and vagrancy in 1873, the legislature decided to reform the state's charity—and consequently immigration—policies. The Panic of 1873 hit New York City particularly hard as the center of the nation's economy, forcing a quarter of the city's laborers into unemployment. Since 1867, the New York Board of State Commissioners of Public Charities had administered poor relief in the state. To better handle mounting poverty and homelessness caused by the panic, the legislature reorganized the state's public charity system in 1873, renaming the board the State Board of Charities and extending the number of officials from eight to eleven.[39]

One of the powers the New York State Board of Charities acquired in 1873 was the authority for assisting destitute immigrants' voluntary return to Europe. In June, legislators passed a law providing that if any almshouse inmate expressed "a preference to be sent" to any state or country where he had original residence or sources of support, the secretary of the charity board could "cause the removal of such pauper to such state or country."[40] This power had hitherto been vested in the New York Commissioners of Emigration. The commissioners had no legal power to forcibly deport foreigners already in the state abroad, but the officials had tried to minimize the number of foreign paupers by financially aiding their voluntary return to Europe. In order to facilitate the removal of destitute immigrants, the New York legislature extended the authority for this policy to the State Board of Charities.

The 1873 act's removal provision aimed to supplement New York passenger policy's long-standing emphasis on the restriction of assisted pauper immigration. In discussing poverty in New York, Martin B. Anderson, a member of the State Board of Charities, identified assisted paupers, including "the redundancy of population of Ireland" shipped by the British government, as the major group of people who should be removed from the state through the new act. Many foreign paupers, Anderson admitted, "have been detected and sent back by the vigilance of the Emigration Commission in New York."[41] But the commissioners' effort had proven insufficient. Instead two state agencies were removing immigrant inmates from almshouses. Excited by the potential effectiveness of the act, board president John V. L. Pruyn proclaimed that "its faithful execution will largely benefit society, and result beneficially to the state."[42] Anderson upheld the act more aggressively by asserting that the people of the United States "are not willing to support that class of indolent and hereditary paupers which have been smuggled into our country."[43] The legislature retained its reluctance to make state immigration policy as rigid as that of Massachusetts by introducing mandatory deportation. Nevertheless, New York significantly scaled up immigration control with the empowerment of welfare officials to return immigrants to Europe.

Massachusetts immigration policy developed in direct response to the problem of vagrancy. From its inception in 1863, the Massachusetts Board of State Charities regarded the reduction and prevention of vagrancy, especially that of immigrants, as one of its principal goals. The most popular proposal to achieve that goal was to punish vagrants with forced labor at workhouses. Originally built for the accommodation of paupers who had no settlement in the state, Massachusetts state almshouses had housed a diverse population, including both "the unfortunate and well-deserving poor" who received relief from the state for excusable reasons and vagrants who used the institutions as free temporary shelters. Finding this coexistence of the deserving and undeserving poor unhealthy, the charity board called for the establishment of a separate state workhouse for the purpose of "punishing, and thereby preventing, the outrageous abuse of public charity" by vagrants. General Agent H. B. Wheelwright expected that "the meritorious poor [would] be relieved from most disgusting associations" by relocating vagrants to the workhouse. The fear of forced labor, he anticipated, would also deflect "the tide of vagabonds and paupers which for years has been flowing into Massachusetts."[44]

The charity board's arguments persuaded the legislature to pass in the spring of 1866 an act to change parts of the state almshouse in Bridgewater into a state workhouse for vagrants who had no settlement in Massachusetts. Under the act, any inmate of a state almshouse or the Rainsford Island hospital who was convicted as a vagrant by a local court would be transferred to the Bridgewater workhouse for a term between six months and three years to engage in compulsory labor—usually farm labor for male inmates and domestic labor such as sewing for female inmates.[45] Michael Doyle, a seventeen-year-old Irish-born inmate at the Tewksbury state almshouse, was one such immigrant vagrant. Before entering the almshouse, he had been sentenced to the State Reform School for some criminal act. Judging that he was "ugly tempered" and "will be a public charge most of [his] life," a board official sent Doyle to the state workhouse in Bridgewater.[46] Given that inmates at state almshouses and the Rainsford Island hospital were mostly immigrants, the foremost purpose in establishing the state workhouse lay in the restriction of immigrant vagrancy.

Important implications of the development of vagrancy restriction in Massachusetts emerge when placed in the context of Reconstruction. Shortly after the Civil War, southern states enacted a series of laws discriminatory against freed blacks, known as the Black Codes, in order to preserve white supremacy over blacks and bring former slaves back to plantation labor. The Black Codes included provisions that required blacks to enter into wage contracts and punished those without employment as vagrants. Under Mississippi law, for example, all blacks had to provide written evidence of "lawful employment or business" each January. Freedpeople vehemently resisted working under the supervision of former slaveholders, but they were compelled to make labor contracts with them. Those who left work could be arrested as vagrants and hired out to white employers to perform involuntary labor. In the face of the Black Codes, freedpeople in Mississippi petitioned the governor to ask for clarification: "Mississippi has abolished slavery. Does she mean it or is it a policy for the present?" In 1866, Radical Republicans in Congress voided the Black Codes with the Civil Rights Act, which guaranteed civil rights and legal equality for African Americans and laid the groundwork for the Fourteenth Amendment. The Massachusetts legislature enacted the state workhouse act only a few weeks after the passage of the Civil Rights Act.[47]

What may strike modern observers about the construction of the state workhouse in Massachusetts is its timing. Any comparison of chattel slavery with forced labor for vagrants might sound inadequate. It is nonetheless noteworthy that at a time when the nation was extremely sensitive to involuntary servitude, Massachusetts, the center of abolitionism, developed a system of compulsory labor. The workhouse itself was hardly a new institution, yet the fact that the legislature instituted a state-run workhouse at this moment in Reconstruction testified to the intensity of repugnance to the undeserving poor, especially foreign vagrants. Following

Massachusetts, many other northern and midwestern states also adopted various harsh measures to punish vagrants, including imprisonment at penitentiaries.[48]

The enhancement of vagrancy restriction invigorated immigration control in Massachusetts. Since immigration after the Civil War was bringing "a large percentage of defectives," the Board of State Charities anticipated that the expense of foreign pauperism would inevitably increase, "unless checked by the most watchful system of examination and removal." Inheriting the Alien Commissioners' view of pauper immigration restriction as an exercise of police power against external economic and moral threats, General Agent Wheelwright avowed that "any increase of the present burden would be intolerable; and hence the seaboard States must, in self-defense, maintain their existing regulations, and even make them more stringent."[49] The board also bolstered its justification of removal with the legal concept of belonging, which sat at the core of Massachusetts deportation policy since the colonial period. General Agent Wheelwright argued that by deporting foreign paupers, the board was only insisting on "the proper support of every dependent person in and by his own community."[50] The board's duty, officials believed, was to guard the state from the expense of "supporting pauper lunatics and others, who do not properly belong to her."[51]

The charity board's interrelated motivation for vagrancy restriction and immigration control resulted in an expansion of the state's deportation policy. The state workhouse had previously admitted only those transferred from state almshouses, but in 1869, the state legislature empowered the Overseers of the Poor to send any person who was sentenced as a vagrant by a local court to the Bridgewater State Workhouse. More critically, it also authorized the Board of State Charities to deport any vagrant inmate at the Bridgewater workhouse without settlement in Massachusetts to "the state or place where he belongs, or whence he came."[52] If enforced correctly, the board believed, this policy would "rid the Commonwealth of tramps and vagrants, by saying to them, kindly but firmly, 'If ye will not work, neither shall ye eat.'"[53] The reform in 1869 thus made a greater number of destitute foreigners subject to potential expulsion.

Meanwhile, the Board of State Charities energetically deported foreign inmates in almshouses and lunatic hospitals. In the 1870s, the board enforced removal with a particular focus on paupers with mental illness, or "lunatic paupers." Between 1856 and 1863, the Alien Commissioners removed 269 inmates from the Taunton State Lunatic Hospital. Over the next eight years, the Board of State Charities expelled twice as many inmates from the same institution as its predecessors.[54] Even after the board started its activities, lunatic pauper removal continued to grow. In the 1860s, with the exception of 1869, the number of lunatic paupers removed from the state per year never exceeded one hundred. Between 1870 and 1878, however, that figure was over two hundred.[55] An Irish deportee from the Worcester State Lunatic Hospital had entered the institution for "violent" temperament after jumping out of the third-story window of his boarding house and striking a local public officer. Once in the hospital, he talked continuously of "placing himself under the protection of the Queen of England and of going home to his wife and four little children." The board eventually shipped him to Ireland.[56] Like the Alien Commissioners, the Board of State Charities also tended to expel immigrants who entered charitable institutions multiple times to Europe, rather than other American states. Patrick Reynolds, an immigrant from County Leitrim, Ireland, entered the Tewksbury alms-house four times. During his third stay, he escaped from the institution. Upon his fourth admission to the same almshouse, the board deported Reynolds to Ireland.[57]

The consequence of the fifteen-year endeavor to remove the foreign poor from the state seemed satisfactory to the members of the Massachusetts Board of State Charities. In 1875, the board concurred, "By constant activity in removals, the General Agent has prevented any *apparent* accumulation of state paupers."[58] Between 1864 and 1878, the board shipped 2,489 persons to "transatlantic ports" and Canada. It also removed 2,891 lunatic paupers to other American states or from the United States. Numerous others were returned to either Canada or other American states by railroad. Taken together, the annual reports of the Board of State Charities indicate that the board in its fifteen-year operation expelled 32,672 paupers from Massachusetts, about twice as many as were deported by the Alien Commissioners between 1851 and 1863.[59] In 1878, General Agent S. C. Wrightington praised the accomplishments of the board as "surprisingly great."[60] Despite its diverse duties, including the administration of public charity in the state, the Board of State Charities was an indisputable heir of the Alien Commissioners as the gatekeeper of Massachusetts.

With the opening of settlement eligibility for immigrants, including women and Civil War veterans, by 1874, Massachusetts arguably became a better place for foreigners in general, but not for ones unable to support themselves. Foreign-born inmates in charitable institutions remained ineligible for the privilege of settlement.[61] Destitute foreigners were denied membership in the community, excluded from settlement, and therefore subjected to forcible expulsion. The Board of State Charities also enforced deportation even more vigorously than the Alien Commissioners. Massachusetts had historically developed a dual pattern of progressive reform and exclusiveness, as seen in the state's role as the center of abolitionism and nativism in the mid-nineteenth century. The state's parallel settlement and removal policies symbolized this dualism in the age of the Civil War and Reconstruction.

A comparison with the situations in other coastal states illuminates the leading role of New York and Massachusetts in immigration control in postbellum America. In Pennsylvania, except for a small modification of language in the bonding provision made in response to the invalidation of state head money in the *Passenger Cases* (1849), state immigration policy changed little in the 1860s and 1870s, operating under an arrangement introduced in 1828. The state never developed any system of state-led immigration regulation, and the Philadelphia Board of Guardians of the Poor loosely continued to implement the exclusion of unbonded destitute immigrants upon arrival.[62]

In California, where nearly all state-level anti-Chinese measures failed before the Civil War, restrictionists in the legislature attempted to prevent Chinese immigration once again, even after the Burlingame Treaty of 1868 secured the free entry of Chinese nationals to the United States. In 1870, convinced of the ubiquity of prostitution among Chinese women and their deleterious influence on American society, California legislators passed a law banning the admission of any "Mongolian, Chinese or Japanese females" without proof of their "correct habits and good character."[63] Presumably realizing that the court would strike down such sweeping legislation, as it had voided the 1858 act that plainly excluded any persons of the "Chinese or Mongolian races," the state government modified its immigration law in 1874. The new law reintroduced the exclusion provision of the 1852 passenger act, which prohibited the landing without bonds of certain groups of foreign passengers such as paupers and lunatics, and added "lewd or debauched" women to the list of excludable immigrants. Although the bonding provision sounded broad, the 1874 law clearly aimed to exclude Chinese women suspected of prostitution by pressuring shipmasters to bring them back to China instead of preparing large bonds for them.[64]

But the policy for requiring money for the admission of foreigners able to support themselves, however immoral the officials found them, was doomed almost from the beginning. In 1876, the United States Supreme Court struck down California's law as a form of taxation on passengers which infringed upon federal authority over foreign commerce, just as the state supreme court had earlier invalidated a series of anti-Chinese state legislation. The Supreme Court also annulled parts of New York's passenger law on the same day, but New York had developed and implemented an array of immigration policies by that point.[65] In contrast, California's three-decade effort to restrict Chinese immigration was a story of recurrent failures.

The impact of the Civil War reinforced southern states' hesitation to restrict immigration for the purpose of securing white European settlers. Postwar Louisiana's immigration policy exemplified this trend. The war disrupted European immigration to southern ports in general, but New Orleans, the second busiest port after New York in the antebellum period, suffered most. After the Civil War, New Orleans was surpassed by Boston, San Francisco, and Baltimore in the number of immigrants who annually arrived in the port. The war, state officials worried, reduced New Orleans' significance in immigration to the extent that Europeans could no longer tell "whether Louisiana is in New Orleans, or New Orleans in Louisiana."[66] Furthermore, the intellectual and policy trend in the postbellum South, which emphasized the necessity of foreign workers for the region's industrial development, augmented the sense that Louisiana should attract immigrants to the state more aggressively than before.[67] The Louisiana legislature established the Board of Commissioners of Emigration in 1869, which like the New York Commissioners of Emigration and the Massachusetts Board of State Charities was a state agency devoted to issues of immigration, but the regulation of immigration occupied little space on its agenda. Upon the organization of the board, the commissioners identified the invitation of "population and capital" to Louisiana "from Europe, and especially from France, Germany, Great Britain and the Scandinavian countries" as its principal task. The Louisiana commissioners thus followed the federal government's policy for the encouragement of immigration.[68]

The Civil War also affected immigration policy in the South in a different way. Southern states' Negro Seamen laws for banning the admission of free black sailors had already begun to collapse on the eve of the Civil War due to diplomatic pressure from Britain. The abolition of slavery deprived southern states of the necessity to adhere to these laws, which had originally been created to preserve the institution. Southern states practically retreated from immigration control and instead concentrated on the recruitment of immigrants through open-port policy.[69] Throughout the Civil War and Reconstruction, as in the antebellum period, no state was more committed to immigration control or more successful in implementing regulatory policies than New York and Massachusetts.

In both New York and Massachusetts, militant nativism during the Know-Nothing movement in the 1850s radicalized immigration control. State officials insisted that they executed removal humanely and with paupers' consent. In reality, they forcibly and illegally deported paupers against their will. The development of immigration laws in postbellum New York and Massachusetts exhibits the enduring strength of nativist sentiment, and hostility to destitute immigrants clearly seemed to have become even stronger with the related problem of vagrancy. Under the influence of this renewed antagonism toward foreign poverty, the implementation of state immigration policy retained its harsh aspects.

One of the crucial premises for the examination of immigration law enforcement during Reconstruction is the highly discretionary nature of vagrancy restriction in this period. Two weeks after the decision to build a state workhouse in Bridgewater in 1866, the Massachusetts legislature passed a new vagrancy law. It authorized local police officers to arrest any person suspected of vagrancy based on "the request of *any person* or upon *their own information or belief.*"[70] This provision is striking for how loose and informal the rationale for arrest could be, as well as the seemingly limitless authority local officials could consequently exert in arresting somebody as a vagrant. Enormous discretion fell to police authorities. For people in postbellum America, according to historian Linda Kerber, it was essential not to be *perceived* as idle. Kerber argues that "vagrancy is a status offense; the crime is not what the person has done but what the person *appears* to be."[71]

Local authorities easily took advantage of the discretionary nature of vagrancy laws to abuse their power. Racist assumptions that African Americans should engage in visible manual labor all the time and that they would indulge in laziness without white supervision made freed-people in the South particularly vulnerable to vagrancy provisions in the Black Codes. After the Civil War, many former slaves left their plantations and took the opportunity to enjoy the freedom of movement and to travel in search of work and missing family members. White southerners quickly charged these "lazy, worthless negroes" for loitering without work and arrested them as vagrants.[72] But poor white workers in the North also found themselves caught in the clutch of abusive officials. Police officers in New York City sometimes assaulted and arrested workers whom they deemed vagrants simply upon seeing them standing on the streets. On one occasion, one laboring man testified, a police officer "came up and said, 'What are you tramps doing here insulting respectable people?'" and struck him "several violent blows on the head with his baton and kicked him."[73]

Vagrancy regulation was also gendered in both the North and the South. Following nineteenth-century gender norms, police officers tended to view women in public unescorted by men as disorderly prostitutes and arrest them under vagrancy law, a charge reserved uniquely for women. As historian Patricia Cline Cohen has put it, "vagrancy proved an elastic concept, most elastic in the moment of encounter on the street between an officer and a woman of doubtful character."[74] While racism made freed black women in the postwar South easy prey for the vagrancy charge, the gendered operation of vagrancy regulation also had serious consequences for immigrant women in the North, especially Massachusetts. Poor-looking immigrant women walking on the street could be easily arrested and placed in the Bridgewater workhouse. And admission into the state workhouse automatically made them deportable foreign vagrants. Women had already been more exposed than men to the threat of deportation due to their particularly precarious economic situations. Widowhood, abandonment, and the temporary absence of husbands who had gone in search of jobs often forced immigrant women to enter almshouses, from which they could be expelled as foreign paupers. The combination of discretion and gender bias in the enforcement of vagrancy law made immigrant women even more vulnerable to deportation policy.

With the disproportionate representation of foreigners among the undeserving poor, the features of vagrancy restriction directly affected state-level immigration control, intensifying its discretionary and inhumane aspects. Since 1847, the New York Commissioners of Emigration had prohibited the landing of destitute foreign passengers for whom shipmasters refused to provide bonds upon arrival. After the Civil War, the commissioners regulated the landing of pauper passengers in an even more restrictive way. Technically, shipmasters could still land pauper passengers with the payment of bonds for them. Starting in the postbellum years, however, the officials routinely compelled shipmasters to bring destitute passengers back to the other side of the ocean without giving them the option for bonds. Paupers or criminals, the commissioners wrote, were to be detained on arrival so that "measures may be taken to cause their return to the port of embarkation." In June 1873, when the commissioners found a destitute Swiss man named August Cruger among arriving passengers on the *Batavia* and confirmed his assisted pauper status, the commissioners "required the steamship company to return him to his home in Switzerland."[75] In this way, the practical operation of entry regulation in New York increasingly became subject to officials' discretion. The hospitable aspects of New York immigration policy were fading away as well. This tendency became clear in January 1872, when some members of the legislature attempted to dismiss from the commissioners the presidents of the Irish Emigrant Society and the German Society, who had worked for the protection of admitted immigrants as ex officio members since the agency's foundation.[76]

In Massachusetts, the Board of State Charities took pains after the Civil War to revise negative images attached to deportation policy stemming from infamous cases in the Know-Nothing years. Fully aware of the charge made in 1855 against the Alien Commissioners and the Know-Nothings over the deportation to Liverpool of Irish immigrant Mary Williams and her American-born child Bridget, General Agent H. B. Wheelwright stressed, "None are now sent against their will, and women with children born in the country are never sent, except at their own desire, because of the issue of a noted case of this kind some years ago."[77] In 1860, the legislature had authorized the Alien Commissioners to send destitute people before their admission into state almshouses to "whence they came" upon their request. The board annually assisted the return of 200 to 600 persons to their homes within the United States and abroad under this policy.[78] The board also emphasized the humane nature of deportation by establishing a principle that the general agent "must not only see that such paupers and lunatics are removed to the places where they belong, or whence they came, but must attend personally to the removal of all feeble persons and the dangerous insane."[79]

Law enforcement in Massachusetts, however, was never as consensual and humane as charity officials claimed. To begin with, the legal culture of vagrancy restriction reinforced the fundamentally arbitrary nature of immigration control in the Bay State. The assertion by state officials of indefinite power over foreigners had long characterized the implementation of Massachusetts deportation policies. Inspecting officers' subjective decision of where paupers belonged—whether other American states, Canada, or Europe—dictated the selection of destinations for removal. And nativist officials routinely banished paupers without court warrants and expelled abroad those with American citizenship, all of which violated state immigration law. Given the direct connection between immigration and vagrancy laws in Massachusetts, discretionary power granted to vagrancy restriction created substantial space for nativist officials' abuse of their deportation authority. Especially in the case of foreign-born vagrants, the Board of State Charities viewed their removal simply as an extension of their arrest, which could be done with minimal, informal evidence. Finally, board members permitted the use of coercion if law enforcement required it. General Agent Wheelwright acknowledged that border control and deportation could cause cases of "hardship" for immigrants. Yet such possibility, he maintained, should not invite "a lax execution of the laws on the part of the Alien officers."[80]

In 1868, Merrick Bemis, the Superintendent of the Worcester State Lunatic Hospital, filed a revealing report on the treatment of lunatic pauper immigrants. He regretfully stated that "there cannot be a fair understanding and an equitable arrangement between the authorities of different countries ... for the purpose of facilitating and rendering such transfers humane and desirable." When the Board of State Charities deported lunatic paupers abroad, the destination was often Liverpool, "where it not unfrequently [sic] happens that all trace of them is lost." The board maintained that it provided deportees with necessary care in the process of removal, but enforcing officers had actually been abandoning deportees, including lunatics, in Liverpool without making arrangements to protect their immediate safety. The same criticism also applied to inter-state removal. After being conveyed to his alleged state of settlement, a lunatic pauper, "unable to provide for himself, is let loose on the public streets, to take his chance of what Providence may do for him." Bemis went so far as to imply the board's practice of illegal banishment. Some lunatic paupers, Bemis declared, had been "very injudiciously removed" from the hospital without any provision for care and "have consequently been readmitted in a much more hopeless condition than when they were taken away."[81] Bemis's indictment suggests that contrary to the charity board's claims, the nature of immigration control in Massachusetts had improved little since the era of the Know-Nothings.

An extensive interaction between Massachusetts and New York officials over the treatment of the transient poor in the late 1870s validated Bemis's concerns about the manner of deportation in the Bay State. Since the days of the Alien Commissioners, charity officials in New York had accused Massachusetts of sending to New York immigrant paupers who had first landed in that state, but New York officials became more vocal in their opposition to Massachusetts policy in the late 1870s. What annoyed New York officials most was that destitute foreigners sent from Massachusetts included people who seemingly had no connection with New York, such as those who came from other American states or Canada. Furthermore, Massachusetts officials sent away these paupers to New York without minimum provisions for self-support. As a result, they became public charges immediately upon their entry. In November 1877, believing that New York should no longer tolerate pauper dumping by Massachusetts, Charles S. Hoyt, secretary of the New York State Board of Charities, sent a letter to the Massachusetts Board of State Charities asking it to discontinue the practice.[82]

Within a month Nathan Allen, chairman of the Massachusetts board, responded to Hoyt by entirely defending his state's removal policy. Allen affirmed Massachusetts law's central principle that "paupers should be sent to the places where they belong or whence they came."[83] After the further fruitless exchanges of correspondence, the New York State Board of Charities managed to set up a conference with Massachusetts officials in November 1879 in New York City. The conference opened with the New York officials' complaint that Massachusetts imposed "a grievous burden" of over 7,000 paupers upon New York between 1870 and 1879.[84]

The conference almost undermined Massachusetts officials' justification for their policy. Massachusetts delegate Charles F. Donnelly sought to rationalize pauper removal by stating that "persons who have come to us from New York can rightfully be returned to New York." When asked about the practice of sending to New York paupers from other American states or Canada, Donnelly unhesitatingly denied this happening. The New York board then presented the case of Henry Morrisett, who came to Boston with his family from Quebec, his birthplace. When he became destitute and applied for public charity in Boston in November 1873, Massachusetts officials rejected his request and sent Morrisett and his family "without means" to Albany, even though he had never been to New York. Confronted with Morrisett's case, Donnelly had no choice but to helplessly deny that "it has the sanction of the Massachusetts authorities."[85]

James Fanning, assistant secretary of the New York charity board, continued the charge against Massachusetts with another case. Henry Peblow, an immigrant who first landed in New York, went to Boston after losing his job in Chicago, where he lived for four years. Finding no employment in Boston, Peblow requested relief from the Massachusetts Board of State Charities for himself, his wife, and his two-year-old child. In response the board sent the family to Albany, dismissing Peblow's objection and the fact that the family had never been to the city. Once in Albany, the family was left with "no money or means of support whatever." Peblow testified that his wife had to sell her shoes to procure a meal for the family.[86] The practice of dropping in New York paupers who belonged elsewhere was outrageous enough, but New York delegates found it even more immoral that Massachusetts "has been utterly negligent of the welfare of the individual" by forcibly expelling the poor to unfamiliar places and deserting them in merciless ways. At this point, Donnelly had to step back from the Massachusetts board's earlier claims of consensual removal and admitted that in deporting a pauper, Massachusetts officials "would not in such a case consult his volition, but send him on."[87]

The conference closed without any agreement being reached between the two charity boards, but it exposed crucial aspects of deportation by the Massachusetts Board of State Charities. First, it confirmed the apprehension of Superintendent Bemis about the neglect of deportees' welfare. The board officials removed immigrant paupers from the state and subsequently forsook them without basic supplies for survival. Second, the accusation of the New York State Board of Charities disclosed that the Massachusetts board forcibly expelled persons to places they had never been. Despite the state's long-term adherence to the principle of legal settlement in its removal policy, enforcing officers found dumping paupers in neighboring states quicker and more convenient than making sure that they were returned to their places of settlement. In short, paupers could be sent even to places where they did *not* belong. The Massachusetts Board of State Charities generally succeeded in distancing itself from much of the public criticism the Alien Commissioners had suffered, but the Worcester Superintendent's report and the New York board's charges revealed that deportation policy in Massachusetts retained coercive and ruthless nature in the 1860s and 1870s.

Immigration control in New York and Massachusetts during the Civil War and Reconstruction reveals the lingering strength of anti-immigrant sentiment after the pinnacle of nativism in the 1850s. While many historians assume that no significant organized nativism against immigrants from northern and western Europe developed in the era of the Civil War and Reconstruction, their relative silence about old nativism in this period by no means indicates its disappearance after the 1850s.[88] The words and actions of officials in postbellum New York and Massachusetts demonstrate that they certainly inherited their antebellum predecessors' determination to reduce foreign pauperism through the unyielding execution of state immigration policy, and the regulatory policies in the two states expanded after the Civil War. Old nativism continued to operate in the form of concrete social policy, profoundly affecting the lives of destitute European immigrants, especially those from Ireland.

Immigration control in New York and Massachusetts was driven by the issues of political economy that were simultaneously national concerns. The period's prevailing economic ideal prized self-sufficiency based on contract wage labor. Those who depended on assistance from others and subsisted without earning wages were regarded as the undeserving poor. Ultimately, these notions plagued Reconstruction. Besides racism against freed blacks, repulsion for dependency on public relief turned white northerners against the taxes that financed federal welfare programs for former slaves. This opposition eventually led to the federal government's retreat from Reconstruction in the South. Adherents of the postemancipation free labor ideology believed that by attempting to obtain land, social services, and civil rights through governmental assistance, freedpeople, or the undeserving poor, were subverting the American way.[89] Propagating this idea with racism, a Pennsylvania Democratic poster criticized the Freedmen's Bureau as "an agency to keep the Negro in idleness at the expense of the white man." At the center of the poster lies a lazy black man wondering, "Whar is de use for me to work as long as dey make dese appropriations." The poster illustrates hard-working white men next to the black man with the label "The white man must work to keep his children and pay his taxes."[90] The restriction of pauper immigration in the North and the abandonment of postwar reform in the South took place under the same atmosphere of the fear among respectable classes of Americans that idleness would undermine the core principles of American free labor society.

A deep skepticism about the aptitude of Irish immigrants, as well as freed blacks, for American self-government also remained throughout the Reconstruction period. Approximately 150,000 Irish and Irish Americans fought for the Union during the Civil War. Their contribution to Union war efforts resulted in the advancement of the legal status of immigrants in that postwar projects of the Republicans, such as the Fourteenth Amendment and the Expatriation Act of 1868, affirmed the equality of birthright and naturalized citizenship.[91] Social and economic progress, by contrast, came more slowly. The Irish-born continued to account for a disproportionate share, often over 50 percent, of inmate populations in charitable institutions in northern cities. Shortly after the end of Reconstruction, 20 percent of the Irish in New York City earned wages as unskilled laborers, compared to 4 percent for nativeborn Americans. Respectability proved to be the hardest thing to come by for the Irish. The brutal violence Irish immigrants demonstrated during the Draft Riots of 1863 and Orange Riots of 1870 and 1871, both in New York City, reinforced the stereotype of the Irish as violent and ignorant people lacking the capacity for rational judgment, an indispensable quality for citizens in participatory democracy.[92] Thomas Nast's 1876 cartoon in *Harper's Weekly*, titled "The Ignorant Vote—Honors Are Easy," reflected this stereotype by placing an Irish immigrant on the one side and an African American on the other side, both depicted in derogatory ways, on balanced scales of civic virtue. The cartoon ridiculed the two groups as equally incapable of American republican democracy and equal threats to it.[93]

Figure 5.2: "The Ignorant Vote—Honors Are Easy," *Harper's Weekly*, December 9, 1876.
Courtesy of the American Antiquarian Society.

Such a view originated from cultural prejudice and racism against the intellectual capacity of the Irish and blacks, but the economic consideration—their undeserving poverty as the antithesis of American freedom and independence—also contributed to doubts about their fitness for the American polity. Reconstruction's incorporation of previously neglected people into American citizenry remained in many ways contingent on their ability to support themselves and their commitment to wage contract obligations. State immigration policy played its part in the exclusion of unqualified people, such as foreign-born paupers and vagrants, by literally removing them from the nation, and New York and Massachusetts pursued this policy more intensively than any other state.

State-level immigration control faced a formidable challenge to its constitutionality from the United States Supreme Court, which invalidated state exclusion laws in 1876. This prompted New York and Massachusetts officials to campaign for federal immigration legislation. Their leadership in the process hardly appears random, given the record of immigration control that the two states had built. New York and Massachusetts officials' ongoing struggle with pauper immigration provided decisive momentum to this move toward federal immigration regulation.

CHAPTER 6

✧

The Journey Continued

Postdeportation Lives in Britain and Ireland

Little is known about Ann Gray's early life. She was born in County Galway, Ireland, around 1821. After surviving Connacht's devastating famine years, she decided to emigrate to the United States in 1860. A few days after landing in Boston on the *Hibernia*, Gray went to Portland, Maine, where she spent four or five months before moving to Island Pond, Vermont. After living in Vermont for five years, she returned to Portland, where her sisters had settled. Sometime during her stay there, she became destitute and entered an almshouse in Portland. When Gray developed symptoms of insanity, the institution sent her to one of the Massachusetts state almshouses, in Tewksbury, in June 1867. Gray's two-year residence at Tewksbury did not cure her insanity, and the Massachusetts Board of State Charities decided to deport her to Ireland in the spring of 1869, along with three other lunatic Irish women. In late April, the board sent them to New York, where they were placed on a ship to Cork. Upon arrival in Cork, Gray and the three women were dropped on the street without money, food, or shelter. Luckily, they were found by a local officer and admitted to the workhouse in Cork. Yet the atmosphere of the workhouse was far from welcoming, as the officials thought that they "ought not to come at all." Deported from Massachusetts as foreign paupers who did not belong to that state, the four women were regarded as outsiders who did not belong in Cork either. Thus, after having gone through two transatlantic voyages, Gray became a social outcast in her land of birth.[1]

The story of American immigration control did not end when American officials shipped foreign paupers from the port of Boston or New York. If officials in Massachusetts and New York, whether legally or illegally, deported immigrant paupers to Europe, what happened to them after being discharged from the ship? This chapter examines their postdeportation experiences in Britain and Ireland. Since Liverpool received the largest portion of Irish deportees from the United States, the chapter first explores the situation there and then shifts its focus to Ireland. The use of force, illegal removal, and detention characterized the ways Massachusetts and New York officials implemented state immigration policy. The paupers' postdeportation experiences provide vivid portrayals of the policy's other harsh aspects, including the utter neglect of the deportees' welfare during the cross-ocean voyage and the practice of deserting deportees without basic means to support themselves. Stories presented in this chapter demonstrate that how deportation affected the lives of people far beyond the moment of expulsion from the nation.

This chapter also uncovers transnational dimensions of American deportation policy. Liverpool officials sent some of the Irish deportees from the United States to Ireland under the British poor law, which allowed for the removal of Irish paupers in Britain to Ireland. In Ireland, local officials protested against American and British removal policies, insisting that the paupers from the United States and Britain did not belong to their communities, just as American nativists and Liverpool authorities did. At the center of the deportees' expulsion from the United States and Britain and their social marginalization in Ireland lay the legal principles of settlement and removal, which American, British, and Irish officials shared. Deportation from the United States was a product of American nativism, but this policy unfolded within a transatlantic legal culture of excluding the poor from societies.

Nineteenth-century Liverpool was a town of the Irish poor. Located within the nearest reach of Dublin, Liverpool drew so large a number of Irish migrants that it came to be known as the capital of Ireland in England.[2] As one of the major European gateways to North America, Liverpool had a sizable population of poor migrants, but the Irish were noticeably poorer than other migrant groups. Some groups, such as the Mormons from Scandinavia and Jews, were able to establish their own organizations to protect themselves from unscrupulous boarding-house keepers and fraudsters. Yet poverty prevented Irish migrants from forming effective ethnic societies, leaving them vulnerable to exploitation and vicious practices. At the height of the famine, with the Irish making up 88 percent of the sick people who received care from Liverpool's health authorities, British officials dubbed Liverpool "the hospital and cemetery of Ireland." At the bottom of both the labor market and the social hierarchy, the Irish who settled in Liverpool lived in overcrowded and filthy working-class sectors of the town close to the docks and consistently occupied a substantial portion in the town's vagrant, pauper, and criminal populations.[3] In addition to those who settled in slums of the town as permanent residents and migrants who just sojourned in the town on their way to the New World, deportees who came back from it also contributed to the poverty of the Irish in Liverpool.

Once in Liverpool, the deportees followed one of the three possible courses. Some of them immediately left the town and moved to other parts of Britain or to Ireland in search of better living conditions. The deportees also became street beggars in Liverpool, living on private and public outdoor relief such as food and clothes. During the famine, begging by the Irish in Liverpool became so rife that local officials believed that "the Irish are more addicted to begging than the English and there are more impostors among the Irish than the people of any other country."[4] Finally, many deportees entered the local workhouse to secure both immediate and long-term shelter. Besides those who voluntarily entered the workhouse, there were also deportees with mental illness found wandering on the streets and taken there by local officers. If admitted paupers displayed symptoms of insanity, the Liverpool Workhouse often transferred such inmates to the Rainhill Asylum, a lunatic hospital a few miles outside Liverpool. Biddy Biglan, a twenty-six-year-old Protestant Irish woman, for example, entered the Liverpool workhouse in August 1858 and was sent to the Rainhill Asylum two months later for "chronic mania." The examining doctor discovered that she was "sent from America from an Asylum in Boston" and noted the "impossibility of getting her to speak or answer questions." Biglan spent the rest of her life without her health improving at the asylum until she died of "phthisis," or tuberculosis, in February 1861.[5]

In a sense, the poor relief officers of Liverpool were prepared for the admission of the deportees into the workhouse and lunatic asylum, though not eager for it. Since the Irish famine, the British press and government had kept track of anti-Irish nativism in the United States. In 1850, when the Massachusetts legislature authorized the Superintendent of Alien Passengers to initiate the deportation of immigrant paupers, Edmund A. Grattan, British consul for Boston, reported to London that "it will in future become the practice to send back at the public expense to the country they came from, all aliens being, or who may hereafter become, a public charge within the State as paupers."[6] In June 1855, when anti-immigrant sentiment in America intensified with the rise of Know-Nothingism, the London *Morning Chronicle* pointed out that "the practice of reshipping to England emigrants from the United Kingdom who may happen to fall into poverty or sickness, after years of residence in the United States, was exciting considerable comment," and it reported the deportation of Mary Williams, her daughter Bridget, and Hugh Carr to Liverpool.[7] Even though "what is most wanted [in the United States] is labour" of immigrants, the *Liverpool Daily Post* wrote, "the foolish Know-nothings would now turn them back."[8] Thus the Liverpool officials predicted that some measures would be taken in the United States to send back migrant paupers.

The problem for the Liverpool authorities in receiving Irish paupers from the United States was that the town had already suffered a considerable influx of Irish paupers from Ireland during the famine. In 1847, the worst year of the famine, Liverpool accepted twice the number of migrants than Glasgow, which was the second major British port for famine migrants, and nearly 40 percent of the Liverpool passengers were categorized as paupers. The workhouse quickly became a house of famine refugees. Approximately 30 percent of the persons admitted to the workhouse in the year ending in March 1848 were Irish, and the Irish accounted for half the inmate population at the peak.[9] The growth of Irish poverty in Liverpool seemed so fast that within twelve hours of disembarkation, a town official thought, Irish migrants would be "found in one of three classes—paupers, vagrants, or thieves."[10] In 1847, the Select Vestry of the Parish of Liverpool, which supervised poor relief in the town, petitioned the British Home Department for banning the emigration of the poor from Irish ports to Liverpool. Irish people should not be allowed to land in Liverpool, the petitioners demanded, unless they had "probable or reasonable means of support."[11] Two years later Edward Rushton, Stipendiary Magistrate of Liverpool, appealed to the Home Department to stop the "unchecked immigration of the miserable of the Irish people."[12]

Given the existing antagonism to imported pauperism, it is not surprising that the Liverpool officials frowned at the admission to the workhouse of non-British paupers sent from the United States. In October 1855, after being informed of the arrival of fifty-four non-British paupers "in a state of great destitution," the Workhouse Committee, a division within the Select Vestry, resolved that the Vestry Clerk write to the British Foreign Office "in the hope that some remedy may be provided against the recurrence of so great an evil."[13] As a result of investigation conducted by the British consul in New York, the Foreign Office later discovered that these destitute people, who included the disabled, were sent to Liverpool by the

New York Commissioners of Emigration. Their arrival in Liverpool was most likely a consequence of the commissioners' policy for assisting the voluntary return to Europe of indigent foreigners in the state. While calling the commissioners' practice to "get rid of these paupers" an "unjust system" for Britain, the consul admitted that "it would be difficult to control the New York Commissioners of Emigration" and anticipated the continuation of the practice.[14]

As this case suggests, destitute persons who arrived in Liverpool from the United States included diverse groups of people. In addition to deportees banished by Massachusetts officials, Liverpool received voluntary returnees sent by the New York Commissioners of Emigration. Also, destitute migrants who had been denied landing at Boston, New York, and other American port cities by local immigration officials were usually sent back to their place of embarkation, often Liverpool. Finally, although the New York Commissioners of Emigration did not implement deportation, local authorities in New York expelled destitute and insane foreigners to Europe at their discretion. The Liverpool officials, however, uniformly classified all of these returnees as an external burden imposed by a foreign government, precisely as Americans protested against the assisted emigration of paupers from Europe.

The arrival of paupers returned from the United States provoked heated reaction by the Liverpool officials in 1858. In a meeting in June, reporting on the recent admission to the workhouse of two women and one man, "who had been sent over from America as of unsound mind," the chairman of the Workhouse Committee wondered that "it was questionable what right the parties had to send them there."[15] When a group of thirty-five paupers (29 Irish, 3 English, and 3 Germans) arrived from Boston on the *Resolute* in August, the frustrated chairman predicted that "we might, doubtless, expect many more."[16] The chairman proved correct. Within two weeks, Liverpool received a batch of thirty-four destitute persons, this time from New York on the *Cultivator*. Most of these sixty-nine returnees, as a Liverpool newspaper revealed, entered the town's workhouse and were "idiots and imbeciles, most of them hopelessly insane." In a subsequent meeting, one committee member called for the attention of the Select Vestry to "the importation of paupers from America."[17] These arrivals received extensive newspaper coverage. One report called the returnees "forcibly-returned emigrants," implying that they had been expelled against their will, or at least without their consent, by American officials. The condition of the returnees, including many lunatics who "apparently cannot speak at all," convinced newspaper correspondents of the cruelty of the "wholesale deportation of this unhappy class of being."[18]

One aspect of pauper deportation that received extensive attention among the British press was American officials' lack of care for lunatic deportees during the voyage. In September 1858, a correspondent of the *Liverpool Northern Whig* published a report on what he witnessed on his trip from New York to Liverpool, which other newspapers cited as a testimony to the inhumanity of American immigration policy. As his ship embarked from New York, the correspondent noticed a group of sixteen lunatics among the passengers. They had earlier emigrated to the United States, but "some Yankee asylum had disgorged its unhappy inmates." What troubled the reporter most was that no person attended to the deportees. These people were left "to wander unguarded among the other passengers," roaming through the ship in quest of food. The correspondent added that during the passage "acts too odious even to contemplate" were committed among the lunatics and seamen, clearly implying sexual coercion against some of the deportees. Another Liverpool newspaper provided a similar observation later when a group of paupers were shipped from a lunatic asylum near Boston to Liverpool, with "no one being appointed in charge of them." Condemning American officials' neglect of protecting helpless deportees, the *Northern Whig* reporter claimed that if the United States "is to return its lunatics," it should not "mix them unprotected among sane people."[19]

British observers also accused American officials of their practice of leaving deportees without minimal provisions for self-support in Liverpool. Those who witnessed deportees' arrival described the scene as "a woeful sight." They did not fail to notice "hunger stamped upon them" as a result of the neglect during the voyage. The deportees were then left helpless without basic things to support themselves such as money, food, and clothes, once they disembarked. As a consequence of these policies of American officials, returned paupers sought admission to the Liverpool workhouse "in a condition of extreme wretchedness."[20] Massachusetts deportation policy, therefore, was extremely harsh not simply because of the forcible nature of removal but also because officials provided little care to deportees, including those with insanity, through the process and abandoned them in the end. In this respect, the policy of the New York Commissioners of Emigration for assisting the voluntary return of indigent foreigners was no less harsh than deportation from Massachusetts. The commissioners might have sent immigrants back to Europe with their consent, but officials in both states shared the habit of dumping returned paupers on the street of Liverpool without immediate means of self-support.

One deportation case in the fall of 1858 caused Liverpool officials, who had been increasingly frustrated by the arrival of paupers from the

United States, to investigate the situation on the other side of the ocean. In November, a group of thirteen paupers, who had been sent from Boston on the *Manhattan*, entered the Liverpool workhouse. Among the destitute persons, the workhouse officials found a black man who had no legs. The person claimed that he was a British subject and had been sailing on American ships for three and half years. To obtain further information about his arrival in Liverpool, the Liverpool Workhouse Committee summoned him. According to his testimony, his name was Williams and he was born in Demerara, a British colony in the northern part of South America. He had spent ten years sailing between Liverpool, Bristol, and the United States. During the previous winter, he was frostbitten in Boston and taken to sailors' hospital where a doctor amputated his legs. Five months later, he was transferred to a hospital about eight miles from Boston. At the hospital, he was asked "where he belonged." Upon confessing his British subjectship, he was told that he could not remain at the hospital. Finding no ship to Demerara, the officials, apparently the Massachusetts Alien Commissioners, sent him against his will to Liverpool.[21]

Williams's testimony was one of the very few pieces of evidence provided by the deportees themselves about the process of removal. Above all, Williams's statement verified the practice of forced banishment by the Alien Commissioners. His removal to Liverpool, instead of Demerara, suggests that immigration officials' priority lay in the expediency of removal over deportees' lives. Williams stated that about forty persons were deported to Liverpool on the same vessel, and some of them had spent fourteen years in the United States. The group also included eight persons "out of their senses." These deportees with insanity were allowed to walk on the deck freely but they received no extra care. In concluding the testimony, the Workhouse Committee decided to record the number of paupers who had been sent from the United States for a year up to November 1858.[22]

The Liverpool Workhouse Committee summarized the information on returned paupers in a week. Over the preceding twelve months, the workhouse had admitted 108 paupers sent from the United States, with 90 Irish, 6 English and Welsh, 8 Scottish, and 1 from each of Germany, Demerara, St. Domingo, and Newfoundland. Of these 108 persons, seventeen were "lunatics and epileptics," and "the great majority [were] broken down and sickly men and women."[23] Referring to the large presence of the Irish—90 out of 108—one committee member complained, "why should not the Irish be sent at once to their own country instead of Liverpool." The workhouse officials also found deeply annoying the fact that many of the returnees lived in the United States for years and they included women who became naturalized American citizens through marriage to Americans and had American-born children. For the officials, such return-ees belonged to the United States, rather than the United Kingdom.[24]

Realizing that it could do little to stop deportation from the United States, the Liverpool Workhouse Committee attempted to reduce "imported" Irish pauperism by transferring the deportees to Ireland instead of continuing to pay for their maintenance. A Dublin newspaper in March 1855 reported that the authorities in Liverpool sent to Dublin a group of lunatic Irish women who had been deported from Boston to Liverpool.[25] When the thirty-five paupers on the *Resolute* from Boston entered the workhouse in 1858, a committee member named Denton proposed to "send home the Irish portion."[26] In September 1859, when sixteen Irish paupers sent from Boston on the *Harvest Queen* entered the workhouse "in a state of extreme destitution," the chairman of the committee remarked: "I was here when they came, and I never saw a more miserable lot of people." The paupers' testimony amazed the workhouse officials. It turned out that the average age of five particularly old-looking paupers among the sixteen was seventy-one. To the officials' inquiry, the five elderly persons answered that it was wrong that "after being 40 years there they should be sent back here." Within a week of the *Harvest Queen*'s arrival, the workhouse officials for-warded eleven of them to Ireland and showed an intention of sending the rest shortly.[27]

The *Harvest Queen* deportation finally induced Parliamentary action. On October 10, 1859, the Liverpool Select Vestry wrote a letter to Lord John Russell, the Foreign Secretary, on the admission into the Liverpool workhouse of the paupers and lunatics who were "originally emigrants from Gt. Britain" but "becoming destitute had been sent back to England by the Authorities of the U.S." The letter also referred to the latest case of deportation on the *Harvest Queen* from Boston and the aged deport-ees. Upon receiving the letter from Liverpool, Russell directed British Consulates in major American cities such as Baltimore, Boston, Charleston, Chicago, New Orleans, New York, Philadelphia, Portland, Richmond, San Francisco, Savannah, and Washington, DC to file a report on each state's poor law and its immigration policy.[28]

Between November 1859 and January 1860, British consuls in the United States responded to Russell's inquiry. Most consuls denied the existence of removal policy within their knowledge, and only Francis Lousada for Boston and Edward M. Archibald for New York specifically addressed the practice of sending paupers to Britain from their states. In his report, Lousada in Boston stated that paupers were sent home based on their request. From "verbal enquiry," he understood that "the applicants sent home are chosen from those who apply personally, or by their friends. There seems to be no fixed rule as to the selection." Lousada apparently failed to acknowledge the Massachusetts removal law, which provided for the compulsory deportation of foreign paupers. His report nevertheless confirmed Massachusetts officials' practice of dumping deportees on the street. Upon discharge in Liverpool, Lousada wrote, "all action on the part of the Boston Authorities ceases and determines indeed they consider themselves freed from liability from the time of shipping." Lousada continued, "It does not appear that any provision however slight—either of subsistence for a few days, or pecuniary aid to help them to return to their friends is afforded."[29]

New York consul Archibald reported on the Empire State's policy for assisting the return of migrants to Europe, but he denied both the pauper status of the returnees and the involuntary nature of their departure. Archibald claimed that people who returned had friends and relatives in either England or Ireland, and the majority of them had some means to reach their final destination from Liverpool or London. As to the possibility of unconsented removal of foreigners by the Commissioners of Emigration, Archibald asserted, "I am assured that no such case has occurred with reference to any emigrant landed at this port since the creation of the Commission in 1847." Archibald might have been correct about the absence of deportation law in New York, but the British consul missed the fact that those returning to Liverpool with assistance from the New York commissioners were predominantly destitute people unable to support themselves in the United States.[30]

The result of the Parliamentary investigation disappointed the Liverpool officials. George Cornewall Lewis, the Secretary of the Home Office, advised the Foreign Office that "it can hardly be admitted that the Liverpool Authorities have any valid ground of complaint." In his understanding, the vast majority of the migrants from the United Kingdom to the United States were able-bodied healthy laborers. If the migrants were returned to Britain at the expense of the United States after becoming destitute in America, Lewis believed that "no reasonable objection to such a course can be made by this country." Also, if paupers were returning voluntarily as Francis Lousada of Boston wrote, Lewis thought that "the blame, if blame there be, must attach to the British Subjects sent home, or their friends, rather than to the Authorities of Boston." Finally, as individual states, not the federal government, ran the reported pauper policies, he doubted that the British consuls could exert any diplomatic influence on these policies. Lewis concluded that he "does not see that any thing more can be done in the matter."[31] The level of Lewis's influence on the

Foreign Office's decision remains unknown, but the Foreign Office ultimately took no action on American state policies for sending Irish paupers
to Britain.

Although Liverpool remained the most popular destination for deportation from the United States in the era of state-level immigration control,
Massachusetts and New York immigration officials sent some of the Irish
paupers directly to Ireland. Some deportees were also transferred from
Liverpool to Ireland by the Liverpool Workhouse Committee. What sorts
of lives awaited the Irish paupers who finally returned to their land of
origin after going through migration experiences in the United States
and often Britain and Canada as well?

In general, the paupers sent to Ireland followed paths similar to those
available in Liverpool. The workhouse, whether it was for a temporary or
permanent stay, was the most immediate option. In late January 1855,
for example, eight female Irish paupers were deported from the Worcester
Lunatic Hospital to Liverpool by the Massachusetts Alien Commissioners.[32]
On March 4 six of them arrived in the port of Dublin on the *Trafalgar*,
which implies the death of two women during the deportation voyage. The
Freeman's Journal reported that one of the lunatic women "had in a great
degree recovered her sanity upon the voyage across the Atlantic." She told
the newspaper correspondent that when they arrived in Liverpool, the
port's authorities put them on board the *Trafalgar* to Dublin. Five of the
arriving six—Anne Arbuthnot, Mary Shiel, Hannah Irvine, Anne Taggart,
and Mary Sheeby—were found by a local constable "wandering about the
quay, not knowing what to do or where to go," and were taken to the North
Union Dublin Workhouse. Of the five, Irvine and Shiel left the workhouse
within six months. Taggart, originally from County Antrim, spent nearly
twenty years at the workhouse and in 1874 was transferred to a lunatic asylum, where she presumably spent the rest of her life. Arbuthnot,
a Protestant from Antrim, and Sheeby from County Kerry stayed at the
workhouse until their deaths in 1858 and 1877, respectively.[33]

The available information is too fragmented to draw any solid general-
izations on the deportees' lives beyond workhouses, but some observations
can be made. As to the woman on the *Trafalgar* who regained her sanity,
she took the first train to "join her friends" in Killarney, Kerry.[34] If the
deportee was physically robust and was fortunate enough to secure transportation and still have acquaintances in his or her native place, there was
a slim possibility for reunion, but this would have been a rare occurrence.
One newspaper article on the migrants who voluntarily returned from
the United States to Ireland pictures a possible scenario for the deportees

who successfully reached their homes. According to the report, "on coming to their native sod they find the old homesteads levelled, and sheep
browsing where the plough once subdued the soil."[35] Given that eviction
and the commercialization of land were prevalent in nineteenth-century
Ireland (after all, these were often the reasons for the decision to emigrate), it would be difficult for even the most fortunate deportees to see
their homes standing in original places.

Liverpool officials usually forwarded the deportees to Dublin, but other
Irish ports also received Irish paupers sent from the United States. In
the second half of the nineteenth century, Queenstown in County Cork
acquired a stronger position in the transatlantic passenger trade than
during earlier periods. As the railroad system developed and cheap transportation became available for poor migrants in the postfamine period,
more people chose to go to Cork to take the transatlantic passage departing from Queenstown, though the option of taking the railroad to Dublin
for further migration to Liverpool and North America remained popular.
When two British steamship companies launched services at Queenstown
in 1859, Liverpool still enjoyed its prominent status in the passenger
trade. After 1870, however, Queenstown (and Moville near Londonderry)
surpassed Liverpool as the ports of North America–bound embarkation
for Irish migrants.[36] With the growing presence in the passenger business,
Cork emerged as a major destination for American deportation policy.

Cork had received paupers sent from the United States sporadically, but
the arrival of those with insanity became a recurring issue for local officials in the late 1860s. In October 1867, officials found among the arriving
passengers from New York seventy persons who had been "sent back to
this country by the American Government." Fifteen of them, including
one "violent lunatic," were "in a sick and imbecile state."[37] In December
1868, five Irish lunatic paupers landed in Queenstown from a ship run
by the National Steamer, one of the companies operating between
Queenstown and New York. Upon finding them, the ship agent brought
them to the Cork workhouse "out of charity."[38] Of the five, three appeared
on the workhouse admission register, while the fates of the other two have
been lost to history. All three were single, either laborer or servant, and
described as "from America" and "Insane of Mind." Two of the three died
within three years at the workhouse, and the remaining one was transferred to a lunatic asylum in Cork in 1873.[39]

The admission of returning Irish paupers into the Cork workhouse indicates that the pattern of postdeportation experiences seen in Liverpool
also appeared in Ireland, but the Cork officials' reaction illustrates a further parallel. In short, like the Liverpool authorities, Cork officials regarded

the deportees as an uninvited drain on their treasury. The Irish Poor Law Act of 1838 divided Ireland into 130 regional administrative units, called poor law unions, and poor relief in each district was overseen by a Board of Guardians, who consisted of local magistrates, often local landlords, and the elected representatives of the taxpayers in the union.[40] When the five deportees entered the workhouse in December 1868, the Cork Board of Guardians called them "Irish-American lunatics" who "ought not to come at all."[41] They must have used the adjective "Irish-American" in more of a metaphorical than a legal sense to underscore the outsider status of the returning Irish paupers for the board. The poor relief fund collected from taxpayers in the Cork Poor Law Union should be spent, the officials believed, only on the local poor and not on those coming from outside their union in Ireland, let alone the United States.

In the following weeks, the Cork Board of Guardians inquired into the American practice of sending Irish migrants to Cork, in an attempt to prevent further entry of "Irish-American" paupers. In a December 16 meeting, a board member named D. Cahill revealed that nineteen lunatic paupers arrived in Cork from the United States in 1867 and stated, by explaining American exclusion policy for paupers and lunatics, that it was "very great hardship that this country should be made a place for the reception of lunatics from America." He proposed to issue a protest against the National Steamer Company, which brought the five lunatics to Cork earlier in the month.[42] He ironically ridiculed the National Steamer Company, an Irish shipping firm, by pointing out that "there was nothing 'national' in bringing lunatic paupers to Ireland to be a burthen upon the country." The Board of Guardians resolved to request that the National Steamer Company not bring any more lunatic paupers from the United States.[43] A week later, the board officers demanded an explanation from the National Steamer Company on the returning paupers.[44] The steamship firm responded that it was "at a loss to know why they [lunatic paupers] were brought over in their steamers" and had given strict instruction to the company's agent in New York to "refuse all such passengers."[45]

The Cork board's instruction to the National Steamer Company might have had some influence on the company's selection of passengers in New York, but that did not deter the arrival of paupers on other companies' vessels. In January 1869, the local police brought to the Cork workhouse three lunatic Irish women—thirty-year-old Mary Driscoll from Skibbereen, Cork, who had emigrated to America about five or six years earlier; Mary Conway from County Galway, who was twenty-five years of age and had left Ireland roughly in the same period as Driscoll; and forty-nine-year-old Mary Cunagh from County Fermanagh in Ulster.

These women left New York on the *Siberia*, one of the Cunard steamers, on January 7, landing in Queenstown eleven days later. Driscoll was first seen at the Queenstown Post Office "talking incoherently." She then appeared at a railway station in Cork with Conway and Cunagh, "wandering about the roads." When the stationmaster found out that they had no ticket, he handed them over to a local policeman. He stated that the women were "half furnished" and "scarcely able to give any account of themselves" when he met them. As the Cork guardians investigated the case of these women, they easily realized that no one attended the migrants with insanity upon discharge from the ship, noting their misery for being left "at distance from their former homes, unprotected, friendless, and in a condition of social and mental destitution." The fact that Conway died six months later indicates her fragile condition at the time of her admission to the workhouse.[46]

Provided that the New York Commissioners of Emigration adhered to state law which prohibited the unconsented deportation of foreigners, the repeated arrival in Cork of lunatic paupers from New York who could not communicate must have been a consequence of Massachusetts deportation policy. Depending on the availability of ships for removal in Boston, Massachusetts officials sent foreign paupers to New York for overseas deportation. Irish officials demanded shipping companies not bring lunatics and paupers from the United States to Ireland. Shippers, however, found the screening of passengers practically unenforceable. William Inman, the representative of the Inman Steamer company, revealed the difficulty of detecting lunatic passengers before embarkation in New York. In general, somebody purchased their tickets on their behalf. The vigilance of the company's ticket agent did little to help him exclude lunatics in advance, as "no information is given as to there being anything wrong with the passenger" upon the sale of tickets. Also, if the passenger appeared to be sane on boarding, the vessel embarked with the person and "it is not in general discovered until after the voyage has been commenced that he is a lunatic."[47] Massachusetts officials could easily evade the agents' vigilance and place insane deportees on board ships.

Ample evidence suggests that as seen in the attempt of deportation of Eliza Sullivan from Boston to Liverpool through New York in 1851, Massachusetts officials had been routinely conducting step-deportation— sending paupers to Europe through New York. In June 1859, the British Colonial Office in London received a letter from the Governor of Newfoundland stating that the Galway-bound steamer *Argo* wrecked on the coast of Newfoundland en route from New York, and surviving passengers included four lunatic Irish women. The information collected from various New York officials based on the Colonial Office's request for investigation established that the Irish women were neither in charitable institutions of New York nor in the record of the Commissioners of Emigration, and one Emigration Commissioner suspected that "they were sent from Boston or some other place East."[48] In the winter of 1868, in examining a case of lunatic paupers returned from New York, one Cork official commented that "all the man who was before me could say was 'Boston, Boston.'"[49]

The arrival of four insane Irish women in Cork in May 1869 further verifies the practice of shipping lunatic paupers from Boston through New York to Ireland orchestrated by Massachusetts officials. Four middle-aged insane women—Abbey Butler, Ann Gray, Mary Cullen, and Esther Daly—landed in Queenstown from New York on the *City of Antwerp* of the Inman Line. All of them except Butler had originally come from Irish counties other than Cork, but they all entered the Cork workhouse. After their landing in Queenstown, one guardian found two of them "sheltering at a hall door on the beach" and the police found the other two wandering about on the street in Cork. None of them had any money or provisions for self-support. The Cork officials initially thought that the paupers "had been in an Asylum in New York." The subsequent investigation, however, ascertained that they had been inmates of "the Tewksbury Lunatic Asylum" in Massachusetts.[50]

The headache for the Cork Board of Guardians lingered after the arrival of the women from Tewksbury. Within a week after the *City of Antwerp*'s arrival, the Cork workhouse admitted two more returned lunatics from Counties Donegal and Cavan. Then just two days later, the workhouse received two new "fresh arrivals." About a month before, the *City of Baltimore*, another ship of the Inman Steamer Company, brought six female lunatic paupers to Queenstown on its way to Liverpool from New York. After the Queenstown officials refused to let the vessel land the paupers, the *City of Baltimore* proceeded to Liverpool, where the local authorities told the shipowner to bring the paupers back to New York. Fearing that such an action would lead to a lawsuit against the company, which had already violated its responsibility by not discharging the paupers at Queenstown, the shipowner brought them back and landed them in the Irish port with the intention of sending them to their native places. The company forwarded four of them to their homes, but the remaining two, one from County Waterford and the other from County Kildare, appeared "so mad" that they could not be sent home and were brought to the Cork workhouse.[51] Upon hearing that the *City of Baltimore* discharged the lunatics at Queenstown, a guardian regretted that "it was a pity the people were not dropped at Liverpool instead of at Queenstown."[52] "When landed here," another guardian lamented, "there was nothing for them but the workhouse."[53] From the perspectives of the Cork guardians, the entry into the workhouse of returned paupers was nothing but a financial imposition on their union, a problem exacerbated by British authorities' refusal to receive those Irish paupers.

Irish officials' perception of American pauper deportation was part of a longer history of tensions between Britain and Ireland over the treatment of Irish paupers within the context of British colonialism. Since the late sixteenth century, Ireland had been subject to British rule. Britain could not have sustained its rule over Ireland without the cooperation and participation of local allies, including the Protestant Irish (known as the Ascendancy) and the wealthy Catholic Irish, but these Irish allies were never the political equals of the British. One hundred Irish men sat in Parliament, for example, but their participation occurred only through the abolition of an independent Irish Parliament with the Act of Union in 1801.[54]

Poor law administration in Ireland fit into this colonial relationship. When the Irish Poor Law Act of 1838 established a system of poor relief based on the existing British poor law, the activities of Boards of Guardians were placed under centralized supervision by the British Poor Law Commissioners. In 1847, by way of imposing the responsibility for famine relief on the shoulders of Irish taxpayers, the British government created a separate poor law commission in Ireland. This Irish Poor Law Commission did not alter Irish guardians' ultimately subordinate status; they had to conform to the provisions of the British poor law even if these came into conflict with the interests of their unions. Since the famine period, Irish Boards of Guardians had complained about the asymmetrical arrangement whereby the British poor law allowed British unions to deport their Irish paupers to Ireland, but Irish unions could not transfer their British paupers to Britain. In such a situation Irish officials viewed the arrivals of paupers from the United States, including those coming via Liverpool, through the lens of Irish nationalism.

On the eve of the Irish famine, poor relief in Britain was guided by the Settlement Act of 1662 and the Poor Law Amendment Act of 1834. These laws bound each poor law union to provide relief and medical treatment to poor people who had the status of "being settled" in the parish within the union, which could be obtained usually either through inheritance from the father or by birth in the parish. If one claimed relief outside one's settlement, the person would be forced to return to the parish of settlement where he or she belonged. Thus if Irish migrants without settlement in Britain claimed relief in British unions, the unions had no legal obligation to support them and could forcibly remove the migrants back to Ireland.[55]

In Liverpool, with its large Irish pauper population, the impulse for removal was naturally strong. In January 1847, the Churchwardens and the Overseers of the Parish of Liverpool resolved that "the removal of the destitute Irish immigrants back to their own country, was a proper and necessary proceeding to be adopted."[56] Liverpudlians in a public meeting proclaimed with loud cheers "the Irish poor ought to be maintained by Irish landlords and Irish property."[57] In addition to afflicting townsmen with the expense of supporting the famine Irish, who occupied the workhouse, the migrants threatened the town's public health and morality. A satirical local newspaper derided the arrival of "Irish Pauper, Esq. and family, attended by his suite, including Messrs. Fever, Starvation, Taxes, Impudence and Knavery, etc."[58]

The high demand for the banishment of Irish paupers in Liverpool resulted in the passage of the Poor Removal Act in June 1847. The act facilitated the expulsion of Irish paupers by simplifying legal proceedings for removal and enabling union officers to deport Irish paupers to Ireland on the exact day when the pauper claimed relief, upon confirming that the person was born in Ireland and had no settlement in the parish. In 1847 alone, approximately 15,000 Irish men and women were sent back to Ireland from Liverpool.[59] The fervor for deporting Irish paupers did not wane in Liverpool after the passage of the 1847 act. In 1849 Edward Rushton, Stipendiary Magistrate of Liverpool, requested that the Home Office expand the removal law to deport not just those who claimed parochial relief but also "all who are found begging" on the street, in order to guard Liverpool against "the great danger, moral as well as physical."[60] Between 1846 and 1853 Liverpool shipped 62,781 Irish paupers to various parts of Ireland, chiefly Dublin but also Belfast, Cork, Drogheda, Dundalk, Newry, and Waterford.[61] In 1854, Liverpudlians remained firmly convinced of the absolute necessity of removal policy to reduce the "calamitous results" that had arisen from "relief to Irish paupers" for the town's treasury and public health.[62]

The British deportation of Irish paupers was extremely unpopular in Ireland and among Irish Americans in the United States. In the first place, the practice appeared cruel and inhumane. Like the deportees from the United States, those from Britain received only minimal provisions, usually some bread and a shilling on leaving Britain, and were abandoned upon discharge at Irish ports. For those who had lived for a long time in Britain, deportation to Ireland was essentially banishment to a foreign land where they had no family or acquaintance.[63] A young girl named Mary Hart was deported to Dublin from the Manchester workhouse she entered after her mother's death and her father's enlistment in the army. Hart was born in County Mayo but was brought to Manchester by her Irish parents when she was a few weeks old. In Dublin, she was "abandoned without a friend to apply to or the slightest knowledge of where she was."[64] The deportees from Britain included British-born Irish paupers. Sixteen-year-old John Driscoll was born and grew up in Britain and spoke "with a thorough English accent." When he entered a workhouse in London, the officials put him on board a ship to Cork "against his will" just because his parents were natives of Cork, though he had never lived there.[65]

Illegality made British deportation policy even more notorious among the Irish. In fact, certain groups of the Irish—such as persons who resided in the parish for five years without interruption, widows within twelve months of their husband's death, and persons applying for relief on account of temporary sickness and accident—were technically exempted from deportation under the Five Years Residence Act of 1846.[66] The administration of pauper removal, however, proved so sloppy that British officials often deported to Ireland the so-called irremovable Irish, who had resided in the same parish for more than five years. In June 1856, for instance, the North Dublin Union received a ninety-year-old woman who had lived in Britain for sixty-eight years, twenty-two of them in Oldham, Lancashire. The newspaper reporting the case wrote that "she has no friend or relative left in Ireland, and consequently was, when landed here, ten times more helpless and dependent than she would have been had she remained at home."[67] Unlawful removal sometimes caused forcible family disruption. An Irish woman was deported to Cork with her three children from a London workhouse after having lived in London for nearly sixteen years. When she requested discharge from the workhouse to avoid removal, the officers of the house "altogether refused" her request. They then immediately and forcibly sent her to the port for deportation without giving her a chance to see two of her sons, who were employed in London.[68] Illegal deportation continued to be practiced to the extent that the British government admitted in 1861 that the law's provisions "have not been rigidly observed in England as affecting removals to Ireland."[69]

Irish and Irish American newspapers repeatedly reported cases of deportation from Britain in ways that highlighted the cruelty of the removal law. The *Galway Vindicator* indicted British deportation policy in harsh language: "The cruelties practiced under this poor removal system were as revolting to humanity as they were repugnant to every notion of our vaunted civil and British liberty." The Irish laborer in England was "*forcibly* shut up, in a free country, *forcibly* carried on board ship, and *forcibly* and *starvingly* thrust forth from the scene of his labours, under the sanction of English law and by the brutality of English officials!"[70] Despite the irremovability provision, the Dublin *Freeman's Journal* declared, British officials illegally deported Irish paupers to Ireland "in the most inhumane manner on the decks of vessels, just as if they were horses and dogs" after a residence of thirty or forty years.[71] The *Boston Pilot* cited an Ulster newspaper which bemoaned Irish deportees' lack of supporters like abolitionists: "Tears and sympathy for the negro slave—a dog's death for the worn out Irish beggar."[72]

Workhouse officials in Irish port cities particularly resented British unions' tendency to ship paupers who were originally from various parts of Ireland to Irish ports without making further arrangements to forward them to their native places. As a result, the inmate population at these workhouses continued to expand with paupers from outside their unions. The *Belfast News-Letter* commented on what the Belfast workhouse officials considered the "great grievance": "No matter what part of Ireland is the native place of the individuals, the English and Scotch authorities ship them to Belfast, where . . . they would probably remain if they were not forwarded to the places of their birth."[73]

Most exasperating for Irish guardians was the asymmetrical nature of pauper law within the British Empire. The British unions were legally authorized to deport Irish paupers to Ireland, based on the law of settlement. Yet the Irish poor law did not include provisions on settlement. This meant that a pauper could obtain relief in any Irish poor law union and enter any workhouse as long as it had space, and Irish workhouses had no legal right to send back their British inmates to Britain.[74] The Cork Board of Guardians found the deportation law "unjust, the power to be conferred by it to be unfair towards the Irish rate payer, as well as harsh and apprehensive towards the Irish poor."[75] Since the British population in mid-nineteenth-century Ireland was tiny—less than 5 percent of Dublin's population in 1851, for example—supporting British paupers must have cost little for Irish poor law unions. But the inequality in principle considerably irritated Irish guardians.[76] From the standpoint of Irish poor law boards, if "the English born poor are entitled to and receive relief in Ireland, without being subject to removal," the Irish poor should be allowed to claim relief in England.[77] Otherwise the law of settlement, as North Dublin workhouse officials demanded, should apply to Ireland so that they had the means of "sending English and Scotch Paupers of whom there are a few sizable numbers in this House back to their own country."[78] Irish officials thus claimed their right to deport British paupers in Ireland to Britain, where they belonged, just as Americans and the British adopted the legal concept of belonging in their own deportation policies.

Irish officials were determined to resist the uneven system of poor relief between Britain and Ireland. In 1855, the Cork Board of Guardians resolved that "the Irish pauper in England should be placed precisely on the same footing as regards removal with the English pauper in Ireland, or the English pauper in England." The difference in the policies for Irish and British paupers, the Cork board declared, "must be regarded as unfair, unjust, and impolitic." Seeing the asymmetry as "a national wrong, a national crime, and a national dishonor," Boards of Guardians in Ireland attempted to correct the inequality through collective action.[79] Beginning in 1855, Irish officials in several counties, including Antrim, Cork, Dublin, Galway, and Kerry, exchanged correspondence and repeatedly sent petitions to Parliament to repeal the laws of settlement and removal.[80] The efforts of the Irish Boards of Guardians, however, failed to instigate any actual change. In April 1860, the North Dublin Union Workhouse was still receiving deportees from Britain and protesting against "the injustice inflicted on this country by the deportation of Irish paupers."[81] Nine years later, the *Tralee Chronicle* lamented that "the 'patent of injustice' is still in full operation." The *Belfast News-Letter* repeated the Irish claim that "what we insist upon is absolute reciprocity. If Irish poor may be deported from England, let us have the right to banish Saxon paupers from our shores."[82]

Given Irish workhouse officials' attitudes toward British deportation policy, it is not difficult to imagine how they interpreted deportation from the United States. Precisely when Irish officials were struggling with the pauperism imposed by Britain, Americans were sending the poor to Ireland in a markedly similar manner. In examining the "vast increase of paupers" in the workhouse as a result of the British removal law, Dublin officials found those sent "from America" contributed to the expanded inmate population.[83] A section of the *Belfast News-Letter* reporting on the "Deportation of Paupers" between December 1857 and January 1858 listed the admission of a young woman "who was sent here by the parochial authorities of Boston, in America," along with the cases of paupers deported from Scotland.[84] Guardian Lyons of Cork complained, "This city is the receptacle for every poor person who comes from America or England."[85] The Massachusetts and New York policies for returning Irish paupers to Ireland enhanced the sense of injustice felt by Irish officials. The *Freeman's Journal* bitterly criticized American state governments for "outraging Irish feeling by playing the part of English Board of Guardians in sending back used-up Irish labour."[86] In Irish eyes, Americans joined the British government's scheme to compel Ireland to support paupers who had lost tangible connections to Ireland other than by birth.

The paupers returned from the United States through Liverpool posed an especially frustrating problem to Irish officials. Legally these deportees, upon landing in Liverpool, entered into the same category as Irish paupers who were removable from Britain under the British poor law. One Cork official wondered, "Are those people Irish-born subjects, or are they Americans?" "If they are Americans, you might remonstrate," he suspected, "but if they are not, I fear there would be some difficulty." The problem was, he continued, "that supposing those persons (being Irish-born) are landed in England, they will, under the present law, become removable to Ireland, and there will be no redress."[87] Another Cork guardian Julian regretted that British authorities "could send each individual to his own union from Liverpool, which the Cork Board of Guardians had not the power to do."[88] In the face of British law, Irish officials could not raise any effective argument against deportees coming through Liverpool.

Irish guardians believed that they were enduring the worst part of the entire system of pauper removal. In addition to Irish deportees from Britain, over whom they had no control under the colonial legal structure, Irish workhouses accepted paupers sent from the United States. The remonstration of Liverpool and Irish officials against American states' immigration policy through the 1850s and 1860s never led to Parliamentary action to stop it. Liverpool officials grumbled about the paupers from America, but they could ultimately transfer them to Ireland. When the Liverpool Workhouse Committee was criticizing American deportation policy in 1859, the chairman of the committee accurately pointed out that "we do the same thing to Ireland," which made his colleagues laugh.[89] Thus Irish officials had no choice but to accept all the Irish paupers returning to Ireland, whatever trajectory they might have taken in arriving there. In discussing the admission of returning lunatic paupers into the Cork workhouses in 1869, one official suggested, "Could we send any of our paupers to America," only to be told by others, "If you send the lame, the blind, or the mad there, they will be returned to you."[90] Irish workhouses had to assume a disproportionate share of responsibility for the Irish poor.

Irish officials found themselves powerless against the British pauper removal law, yet they did not feel entirely powerless against American deportation policy. Even though Irish guardians acknowledged that destitute foreign passengers would be excluded at American ports, they considered shipping Irish paupers deported from the United States back to America. Clearly, Irish officials did not implement redeportation from

Ireland to the United States routinely, but one possible case is found in the late summer of 1859. That September two Irish lunatic paupers, Bridget M'Gilroy and Anne Murphy, arrived in Galway after having been sent from New York. The newspaper reported that M'Gilroy "will be shipped to America," while Murphy would be sent to Fermanagh to join her friends.[91] Whether or not Galway authorities sent M'Gilroy back to New York in the end, the idea of redeportation serves as a grim reminder of the low status of Irish deportees in guardians' minds. All parties involved in their removal—American nativists, Liverpool officials, and Irish guardians— treated them as unwanted burdens on their communities. Irish migrant paupers were not welcome anywhere, including in Ireland. To borrow the title of John Higham's definitive work on American nativism, returned Irish paupers were indeed "strangers in the land."[92]

The postdeportation experience of expelled paupers, and the British and Irish reaction to American deportation, is not a mere footnote to the story of American nativism, even though the deportees' profiles and postremoval lives were rarely recorded by US officials. The British and Irish officials' investigations and some deportees' own testimonies offer additional perspectives on the problems with state immigration policy. Contrary to their claims of consensual and humane removal, Massachusetts officials forcibly banished immigrants, neglected them during deportation, and dropped them off at quays in Europe without means to support themselves. The neglect of returnees also applied to the assisted return policy of the New York Commissioners of Emigration. Far from benevolent and humane in its practical operation, it was a policy propelled by nativist calculation to reduce the cost of maintaining destitute foreigners in New York whom the officials would have happily deported without their consent had state law allowed it. Once the paupers left American soil, the New York commissioners rejected any further commitment to them. These American policies resulted in the entry of helpless returnees into British or Irish workhouses. Debilitated by the removal process, some paupers died soon after admission. The full significance of immigration law cannot be measured without including their postdeportation lives.

Returned paupers' situations in Britain and Ireland highlight the transnational dimensions of American deportation policy. Like the American policy, the British poor law made all Irish paupers without settlement in Britain subject to removal, and British officials conducted unlawful deportation, expelling even those who had acquired irremovability. In both American and British deportation, migrant paupers were banished regardless of the length of their residence in the host land or family

connections. Irish paupers shipped to Liverpool under American deportation policy thus entered into a society where a very similar removal policy
was in operation, and some of these paupers were further deported to
Ireland under this policy.

Even though Irish workhouse officials had no legal authority to execute deportation, they certainly took part in forming the world in which
Irish migrant paupers were thrown out. One thing that American nativists, Liverpool workhouse officials, and Irish guardians shared was an
opposition to receiving Irish migrant paupers, which was founded on the
concept of belonging. Transplanted in America, the British law of settlement developed into deportation law to return foreign paupers back to the
place where they were judged to belong. The British law of settlement, in
turn, provided for the removal to Ireland of Irish deportees sent from the
United States to Liverpool. In Ireland, driven by the nationalist motive
to correct the unequal relationship between Ireland and Britain in the
sphere of poor law, guardians invoked the law of settlement, which would
allow them to expel English paupers in Ireland as well as Irish paupers
who did not belong to their unions.

In reality, the settlement law was integrated into the activities of Irish
Boards of Guardians. Despite the lack of legal right to refuse relief to the
transient poor, as historian Virginia Crossman has noted, the guardians
removed at least Irish paupers who had residence in other poor law unions
within Ireland "to their place of origin." Poor law guardians, Crossman
argues, sought to limit relief to "local residents, regarding applicants who
came from outside the union with suspicion and, in some cases, hostility."[93]
Irish workhouse officials therefore not only demanded the settlement law
but also actually exercised it to send Irish paupers back to the union where
they belonged in a practical sense. The very concept that the needy should
be cared for in places whey they belonged directly influenced the way
Irish officials responded to deportees from the United States, who hardly
seemed to belong to Ireland as a result of their emigration, and led to the
consideration of their redeportation to America. The deportation of Irish
paupers in the United States stemmed from American nativism, but their
longer return trip, from embarkation at American ports to unfriendly
reception at workhouses in Ireland, was shaped by a wider conception of
belonging shared by American, British, and Irish officials alike.

Additionally, the postdeportation story reveals a critical intersection
of American and British lawmakers' responses to the consequences of
nineteenth-century industrialization. In the United States, as industrialization substantially lowered native-born workers' economic standing,
fear of further impoverishment as a result of competition for jobs with

indigent foreigners willing to work for extremely low wages contributed to the growth of restrictive immigration policy. For the same reason, the influx of destitute unskilled Irish laborers during the famine greatly disturbed working-class people in Britain, whose lives had increasingly become precarious due to the rise of industrial capitalism. "Raw and unskilled labourers" from Ireland were daily pouring into Liverpool, the London *Morning Chronicle* warned, "at the imminent risk of pauperizing of thousands of men who have hitherto managed to earn a decent subsistence."[94] Paupers in workhouses and unskilled migrant laborers who earned wages belonged to different categories, but American and British workers conflated the two. Lawmakers in the United States and Britain used the removal of Irish paupers as a safety valve to reduce native-born workers' anxiety about employment and deteriorating economic conditions, thereby appeasing their criticism against governments for insufficiently handling the detrimental effects of industrialization.

British and Irish officials' reaction to returned Irish paupers also illuminates a transatlantic convergence in the ideology of poverty during the age of industrialization. In a milieu that prized productivity and wealth, middle-class Protestant Anglo Americans despised the alleged laziness of the "undeserving" poor, who remained dependent on relief despite their physical ability to work. These Americans' cultural prejudice against the Catholic Irish quickly placed indigent Irish migrants into this category, which helped develop pauper immigration restriction in Atlantic seaboard states. A similar ideology of poverty existed in nineteenth-century Britain. And given the British bias that considered poverty an innate character of the Irish, Irish paupers in Britain, whatever the cause for their poverty, easily fell into the category of the undeserving poor. The worst features of the Celtic character, the London *Times* asserted, were "its inertness, its dependence on others, its repulsion of whatever is clean, comfortable, and civilised."[95]

The concept of the undeserving poor also affected Irish workhouse officials' attitude toward deportees. In Ireland, where attachment to land and locality was especially cherished, the transient poor received much less sympathy from Boards of Guardians than the local poor. Guardians believed that transient paupers, including those returned from the United States or Britain, threatened the values and integrity of Irish settled society and were undeserving of relief. Industrial development in Ireland remained well behind the United States and Britain, but American and British officials' industrial ethos against idle poverty spread to Ireland, encouraging Irish officials to deny relief to those who were capable of working but refused to do so. This ethos undoubtedly reinforced Irish guardians' frustration with returned paupers, whom they deemed undeserving as lazy beggars.[96] Deeply connected with the law of settlement, the concept of the undeserving poor fostered antipathy to destitute Irish migrants, promoting the expulsion of Irish paupers in Britain and the social alienation of deportees in Ireland. American deportation policy, then, functioned as part of a larger legal culture of regulating the movement of the poor and excluding nonproducing members from societies in the nineteenth-century Atlantic world.

CHAPTER 7

⌀⌀⌀

The Moment of Transition

State Officials, the Federal Government, and the Formation of American Immigration Policy

Mary Clifford had been an inmate of a workhouse in Cahirciveen, a town in County Kerry, Ireland, for five years by the time she was twenty-five. In the spring of 1883 she heard that the workhouse would finance her emigration to the United States, giving her an opportunity to build a better life abroad. It was part of a British government decision the previous year to assist the emigration of impoverished Irish people by distributing funding to workhouses through the Local Government Board for Ireland. Clifford, her two children, and about three hundred other Irish emigrants who had received some form of government assistance arrived in New York City in June 1883, but none of them were allowed to disembark. The federal Immigration Act of 1882, passed three months after the enactment of the Chinese Exclusion Act, prohibited the entry into the United States of alien passengers whom immigration officials deemed unable to support themselves without becoming public charges. After detaining the passengers for a week at the Castle Garden landing depot for further examination, American port officials identified sixteen persons, including Clifford and her children, as excludable paupers and shipped them back to Ireland. Although their exclusion was based on a federal act, the actual process of their return was administered by the New York Commissioners of Emigration—state officials who had been charged with supervising immigration in New York since 1847. State authorities retained an active role in immigration regulation because Congress authorized existing state immigration agencies to execute the provisions of the 1882 law, making such officials the central figures in federal immigration control.[1]

The period between the 1870s and the 1880s has been acknowledged as pivotal in the history of American immigration policy. By the 1870s, white workers' animosity toward inexpensive Chinese labor led to the anti-Chinese movement. That rising sentiment resulted in the passage of the Page Act in 1875, prohibiting the entry of convicted criminals, Asian laborers brought involuntarily, and women imported for prostitution (a provision targeted chiefly against Chinese women). The movement then culminated in the Chinese Exclusion Act of 1882, which suspended the immigration of Chinese laborers for ten years. These two acts marked the federal government's first direct involvement in immigration restriction since the Alien and Sedition Acts of 1798.

Chinese exclusion was certainly one of the decisive events in American immigration history, but its place in the evolution of American immigration policy needs critical reappraisal. Most studies of American immigration policy start with Chinese exclusion, giving the impression that immigration control by the federal government emerged suddenly in response to Chinese immigration or that there was an abrupt shift of authority over immigration from states to the federal government with the passage of the Chinese exclusion laws.

This view fails to explain the significance of states' earlier roles in the development of immigration policy in the United States and simplifies the complicated relationship between states and the federal government in the formative period of national immigration control. In fact, Chinese exclusion recounts only half the story of the genesis of federal regulation in the 1880s. Shortly after the enactment of the Chinese Exclusion Act in May 1882, Congress passed another immigration act. It was largely a consequence of northeastern states' attempts to protect themselves from undesirable European immigrants. This piece of legislation, the Immigration Act of 1882, was the first general immigration law at the national level that applied to all aliens. It had an exclusion clause that prohibited the landing of paupers and criminals and provided for the deportation of criminals who escaped exclusion at the time of arrival. These provisions were modeled on the passenger laws of New York and Massachusetts, and the Immigration Act left the enforcement of its provisions to state officials. Before and after the implementation of that law, officials were firmly committed to restricting the immigration of the poor from Europe, especially Ireland. Thus the federalization of immigration control was a gradual and contingent process, building upon the practices of immigration regulation that had started at the state level long before and involving officials from those states through their participation in the 1882 federal act.[2]

This chapter explores the state-federal joint administration of immigration control in the United States during the 1880s. After tracing the creation of the 1882 Immigration Act, the chapter analyzes the local implementation of the federal legislation. When the British government sent groups of destitute Irish people to the United States in 1883, state officials were charged with implementing the act's exclusion provision against the paupers among the arriving assisted emigrants. The 1882 act limited the deportable class to criminals, but a close examination of state officials' activities reveals that they extended deportation to paupers as well. Despite their lack of legal authority over deportation, the Commissioners of Emigration in New York returned assisted Irish emigrants who had become public charges after landing. In Massachusetts, state officials deported assisted emigrant paupers under state removal policies, with funding from the federal government. The state agents enforcing federal immigration law thus included paupers in the deportable category and established the environment for the introduction in 1891 of a general deportation provision at the federal level that applied to paupers and people likely to become public charges.

The significance of state control in New York and Massachusetts extends beyond the determination of who was deportable under regulatory provisions in federal legislation. The manner of exclusion and deportation established by state officials profoundly affected the nature of federal immigration control. The act of 1882 was partly designed to provide charitable assistance to newcomers who were admitted to the United States, yet federal control from the late nineteenth century onward was characterized by almost unlimited official power in determining the excludability and deportability of aliens. An analysis of northeastern states' responses to assisted emigration in 1883 suggests that the roots of this severely restrictive aspect of federal immigration policy lay in the actions and motivations of state officials in New York and Massachusetts prior to the introduction of federal immigration law. The state-level treatment of undesirable foreigners became embedded in federal policy with the officials' administration of the 1882 act. Nativist sentiment against Irish poverty had catalyzed state-level immigration regulation and, in turn, shaped the nature of federal immigration control in the United States.

Passenger control in the coastal states faced crises in the 1870s. Steamship companies had long viewed the fee that shipmasters paid for the landing of every healthy passenger—the capitation tax or so-called head money—as an unnecessary burden on their business. Shippers presumed that without head money, which they usually included in the price of passage tickets, they could have increased their ticket sales. Shippers and merchants sought to repeal the capitation tax during Reconstruction. Hamilton A. Hill, secretary of the Boston Board of Trade, argued that "the channels of trade should everywhere be made as unobstructed and free as possible."[3] When officials of charity boards in various states held a joint conference on poverty and welfare in Detroit in 1875, the debate over head money occupied the floor at length. Hill, who participated in the convention, advocated the total abolition of state policies for collecting head money, criticizing it as "unworthy of any of the great commonwealths on the seaboards." Charity boards in coastal states, by contrast, emphasized the absolute necessity of head money, as the aggregate of the tax supported the administration of public charitable institutions which accommodated destitute and sick immigrants. To Hill's proposal for the repeal of head money, charity officials responded that "instead of relaxation more stringent protective laws are demanded" to shield their states' treasuries from the cost of maintaining foreign paupers.[4] Business interests called for free immigration, but charity officials in seaboard states never doubted the value and necessity of head money.

A turning point in the head money dispute occurred in July 1875. Two British men, John Henderson and Thomas Henderson of the Henderson Brothers steamship company running the vessel *Ethiopia* between Glasgow and New York, launched a suit against the mayor of New York City and the New York Commissioners of Emigration in the Circuit Court of the United States for the Southern District of New York. The Hendersons claimed that New York's passenger acts, including its head money of $1.50, violated the Constitution of the United States. After the Circuit Court upheld the New York laws, the Hendersons brought the case to the United States Supreme Court. The focal issue was clear: whether existing state policies of collecting head money for the landing of immigrant passengers under the guise of optional fee infringed upon congressional power over foreign commerce.[5] The constitutionality of state passenger laws had been discussed without definite answers from the Supreme Court since the 1840s. Anyone interested in the head money debate knew the significance of the court's decision on this case.

The Supreme Court's ruling in *Henderson v. Mayor of the City of New York* in March 1876 represented a decisive triumph for shippers. The court dismissed the theory that head money was not a mandatory tax but an option which shipowners chose to pay. Delivering the opinion of a unanimous court, Justice Samuel Miller argued: "In whatever language a statute may be framed, its purpose must be determined by its natural and reasonable effect." Requiring shipowners to pay an impossibly high amount of bonds with the alternative of a much smaller fee was equivalent to demanding the payment of head money, which had been declared unconstitutional in 1849. The passenger trade, as regulated by the capitation tax, affected foreign commerce and was therefore an international issue. The Constitution conferred power over international relations on the president and Congress, rather than state governments. Miller concluded that Congress, instead of state governments, could exercise passenger regulation "more appropriately and with more acceptance." Miller reversed the decision of the Circuit Court, invalidating passenger laws in New York and similar statutes in Louisiana. On the same day the Court also struck down in *Chy Lung v. Freeman* California's 1874 law, which required a bond for the landing of a passenger who was likely to become a public charge or a "lewd or debauched woman," a stricture designed against Chinese women suspected of prostitution.[6]

The decision in the *Henderson* case deeply alarmed state immigration officials. The Supreme Court judged that any form of the collection of passenger taxes by states was regulation of commerce in conflict with congressional power. State officials feared that the abolition of head money would reduce the prices of passage tickets, thereby encouraging the departure of poorer persons who could not otherwise emigrate. The ban on the capitation tax also signified the permanent loss of states' financial resources previously used for, among other related expenses, the care of foreign paupers and sick immigrants at charitable institutions. Soon after the decision New York Governor Samuel J. Tilden wrote to the New York Commissioners of Emigration, saying: "The effect of this decision is totally and instantly to destroy the whole income of the commission, by means of which their beneficent operations have been hitherto carried on."[7] Owners of vessels now refused to pay head money and bonds upon arrival, landing all their passengers including paupers. The *Henderson* decision shattered the entire system of deterring the admission of indigent foreigners and procuring funds for their maintenance in coastal states.

The *Henderson* decision had a catastrophic impact on state immigration policy, but from the ashes of state policy emerged a path to national-level immigration control. By endorsing Congress's authority over passenger regulation, the Supreme Court implicitly proposed the establishment of national immigration law that would replace state laws. Stephen C. Wrightington, General Agent of the Massachusetts Board of State Charities, realized that "in this exigency, there would seem to be a necessity for some Congressional legislation which should practically reenact the several State laws."[8] In New York, the state legislature instructed the Commissioners of Emigration to "impress upon Congress the necessity for speedy national legislation in regard thereto."[9] Immediately after the *Henderson* decision, immigration officials in Atlantic seaboard states campaigned to secure national immigration legislation as a substitute for state passenger laws.

The course of the campaign suggests that the essence of national immigration legislation came from state policies in New York and Massachusetts. Soon after the Supreme Court decision, Franklin Benjamin Sanborn, chairman of the Massachusetts Board of State Charities, went to Albany by invitation to collaborate with the New York Commissioners of Emigration as they crafted a national immigration bill.[10] Clearly modeled on immigration policies in these two states, the draft bill had a provision for head money payable to the United States treasury secretary and prohibited the entry of criminals, inmates of any lunatic asylum, poorhouse, or charitable institution, and immigrants unable to take care of themselves at the time of arrival. Each of such passengers would be kept on board and sent back "to the country from which he or she may have been brought" at the expense of the steamship company.[11] During the campaign, Sanborn explained to officials in other states that the bill was "an extension to the whole nation and under the authority of law, of the old state system of dealing with immigration" adopted in New York and Massachusetts. He confidently stated that the experience of these states over preceding decades "proves that much good can thus be done" to protect states from the burden of supporting destitute immigrants.[12]

After further consultation with the state boards of charities in Pennsylvania, Rhode Island, Michigan, Wisconsin, and Illinois, the New York officials sent the bill to Congress with a memorial. The memorial emphasized that the *Henderson* decision left all seaboard states open to undesirable immigration and that without adequate management of pauper immigration in the seaboard states, the midwestern states were also exposed to the influx of foreign paupers.[13] Franklin Sanborn then sent copies of the bill to officials in several states, asking them to "use such influence as you deem proper with the Senators and members of Congress from your State" to realize swift passage. He also went to Washington, DC to explain the merits of the bill to members of Congress in person.[14]

The mobilization efforts by New York and Massachusetts officials, however, did not invite the instant passage of the national immigration bill. Predictably, merchants vigorously opposed the idea of national head money. The Boston Board of Trade declared that "it cannot but protest in the most earnest manner now against this attempt to reimpose them [capitation taxes] under new sanctions." The trade board unanimously resolved to exert all its influence on Congress to kill the bill and garner assistance from every member of Congress from New England and the boards of trade and chamber of commerce in the country.[15] Steamship companies also pledged to use their connection with an international trade association titled the North Atlantic Steam Traffic Conference to lobby against the bill.[16]

Regional politics also worked against national legislation. Head money had allowed coastal states, where the tax was collected, to minimize the expense of supporting destitute immigrants. But in reality many immigrants became paupers after having moved from seaboard to interior states. From the perspectives of midwestern states, eastern states such as New York and Massachusetts were enjoying huge revenues out of head money, while they were bearing all the cost related to foreign pauperism.[17] Congressmen in the interior states thus distrusted the New York Commissioners' national immigration bill as their "scheme to support state institutions, run by state officials, at the expense of the national Treasury."[18] Midwestern politicians also had little interest in adopting policies that would impede the immigration of European settlers into their states. This western politics coincided with southern states' longstanding reluctance to develop immigration restriction due to their need for European immigrants to maintain white electoral dominance in the region. Furthermore, many national politicians, regardless of their partisan affiliation, feared that promoting a nativist federal policy would alienate immigrant voters. These distrusts and hesitations turned out to be more formidable to overcome than New York and Massachusetts officials had imagined. They could not advance congressional proceedings for the bill for six years after its initial introduction.[19]

Congress remained unmoved, but the tide gradually began to turn for the national immigration bill by the beginning of 1882 for several reasons. First, the prolonged influx into the United States of destitute immigrants, including assisted paupers, enhanced the necessity of the prompt installation of federal immigration control. The implementation of state-level deportation against foreign paupers already in the United States also helped increase national legislators' awareness of the problem of immigrant poverty. In Massachusetts the State Board of Health, Lunacy, and

Charity, which succeeded the Board of State Charities in 1879, kept deporting destitute aliens to Ireland, Britain, Canada, and other American states during the debate over national legislation. In 1880, the board removed more than 2,000 paupers from the state.[20]

It is crucial to note that the Supreme Court did not deny states the right to control immigration entirely in *Henderson v. Mayor of the City of New York*. The court confirmed that the whole subject of passenger taxation belonged to the domain of Congress's power over foreign commerce, but it did not dismiss the right of states to exercise police power to protect their people from external threats, a central principle of state-level immigration control since the court upheld it in *City of New York v. Miln* (1837). In the *Henderson* case, Justice Samuel Miller declared that "we do not decide" whether states could "protect themselves against actual paupers, vagrants, criminals, and diseased persons" from abroad.[21] In *Chy Lung v. Freeman*, Miller reconfirmed that the court would not "lay down the definite limit" of states' police power. The problem with the California law, the justice made it clear, was not its regulatory nature in itself but its "manifest purpose" to obtain money from passengers "far beyond" the appropriate application of police regulation, an invasion of congressional authority over foreign commerce.[22] Legal scholar Hiroshi Motomura has pointed out that the Supreme Court "did not repudiate the state police power" in these decisions and "continued to acknowledge" its exercise.[23] While states' exclusion policies for regulating entry through taxation were invalidated, the court did not deprive states of the right to deport undesirable aliens. The *Henderson* decision only partially endorsed federal superiority to states in the realm of immigration control, leaving space for sustained state involvement.

With state police power untouched by the Supreme Court, New York legislators introduced a long awaited reform to state immigration policy during the years of little progress for national immigration legislation. In New York the enactment of the 1873 act, which expanded state policy for assisting destitute foreigners' voluntary return to Europe, had galvanized calls for deportation. While acknowledging the importance of the new law in reducing foreign pauperism in the state, Martin B. Anderson, a member of the state charity board, advocated a further step, namely the compulsory removal of immigrant paupers, especially those transported to the United States by foreign authorities: "Should we not be justified in sending back to Europe to be cared for by their own people, these *unnaturalized* paupers and convicts, who have been surreptitiously introduced into our country and made a burden to the tax payers of New York?"[24] Every "blind, idiotic, crippled, epileptic, lunatic, or other infirm foreign pauper, designedly thrust upon us," declared the New York charity board, "should immediately be sent back to the place whence he or she came."[25]

Yet the state still lacked a deportation law. In February 1879, the Commissioners of Emigration accommodated three "almost entirely penniless" Swiss immigrants who had been sent to New York by the local authorities in the Canton of Aargau, Switzerland. The *New York Times* lamented: "There is no law which empowers the Commissioners to send such persons back."[26] Six months later, when another group of assisted paupers arrived, the commissioners regretted that "the law, as now in force, does not give power to compel the return of any pauper, lunatic or criminal that may be brought to this country."[27] After the *Henderson* decision, deportation began to appear as a more indispensable measure than ever in New York. If the state could not secure money to support foreigners dependent on public charity through taxation, the remaining means of protecting the state's treasury was their removal.

The combination of the continual arrival of assisted paupers, the four-year absence of the head money revenue, and the sluggish progress of national immigration legislation convinced the New York legislature, which had been reluctant to resume pauper removal since its abolition in 1824, to introduce a new deportation law in 1880. In June, legislators authorized the New York State Board of Charities to return to their countries of origin "any crippled, blind, lunatic, or other infirm alien paupers" in any charitable institutions in the state, who had been sent by foreign governments, private organizations, or landlords.[28] Unlike deportation policy in Massachusetts, which made all destitute foreigners dependent on public charity deportable, New York's 1880 law was limited to assisted paupers. It did not apply to those who crossed the Atlantic on their own, exempting most foreign inmates from forcible removal. The implementation of the law was modest at best. During 1881, for example, forty-five paupers were banished from New York under the 1880 act.[29] Furthermore, the law vested removal authority only in the charity board, and the Commissioners of Emigration still lacked legal power to deport foreigners abroad. Nevertheless, the 1880 act resurrected pauper removal in New York nearly half a century after its abolition. Even more critically, the enforcement of deportation by Massachusetts and New York during the early 1880s reminded national politicians of the ongoing problem of foreign pauperism and the necessity of a federal law as a more fundamental and far-reaching remedy for it.

Besides state-level activism, realistic and humanitarian considerations moved shippers toward a compromise and urged lawmakers to support the immigration bill. Frustrated with steamship companies' stubborn opposition to national legislation, especially the idea of national head money, the New York Commissioners of Emigration threatened to close Castle Garden in 1881.[30] Fearing the possible disturbance and chaos the closure would bring, the steamship companies finally consented to pay fifty-cent head money for each passenger. One steamship agent reportedly stated that "I don't want to take the responsibility of dumping a lot of ignorant foreigners on the wharf and leaving them to the tender mercies of City sharps and ruffians."[31] Some congressmen and immigrant societies also raised humanitarian concerns about the absence of a fixed policy to provide aid to admitted immigrants. Wisconsin representative Richard W. Guenther, even though he would be "perfectly willing" to let New York pay immigrant-related expenses, supported the bill on the grounds that "none would have greater reason to deplore the failure of this bill than the immigrant himself."[32]

Perhaps the exclusion sentiment of 1882 pushed the national immigration bill forward most decisively. The growing presence of Chinese workers, who had come to account for a quarter of the wage-earning labor force in California during the 1870s, led white workers to launch the anti-Chinese movement under the banner "The Chinese Must Go."[33] Nativist state legislators sponsored resolutions to pressure Congress to rescind the Burlingame Treaty and to discourage the further entry of people from China. Asians, restrictionists repeatedly claimed, were "incapable of assimilation with our own race." Also, cheap Chinese labor was "offensive to the exalted American idea of the dignity of labor" as well as "detrimental to the prosperity and happiness of our own laboring classes."[34] In 1880, the California legislature went so far as to authorize cities and towns in the state to pass any acts and ordinances for the expulsion of the Chinese from the city or town.[35] In May 1882 restrictionist impetus forced President Chester A. Arthur to sign the Chinese Exclusion Act, prohibiting the landing of Chinese laborers for ten years.[36] The national immigration bill undoubtedly benefited from the political culture of Chinese exclusion as Congress backed up the idea of closing American borders.

In many ways, the Chinese Exclusion Act owed its passage to earlier state-level passenger regulation on the East Coast. Atlantic seaboard states' policies for preventing pauper immigration from Europe provided direct rationale for restricting Chinese immigration. During the anti-Chinese movement in the 1870s, opponents of Chinese immigration demanded its suspension by acknowledging that "any immigration that is hurtful ... has theretofore always been shut out, and paupers and criminals are sent back to their original homes."[37] The ongoing campaign by New York and Massachusetts officials for national immigration legislation also molded the context of the debate over Chinese exclusion in Congress. The state of New York, one restrictionist pointed out, was seeking to re-enact under national authority a system "once in force under State authority for a period of thirty years" to regulate pauper immigration from Europe. For him, the idea to suspend Chinese immigration "is of the same class, in principle, with this general legislation sought by New York." Congress should act to prevent any further increase of objectionable people, "whether pauper, criminal, cooly."[38]

The concept of internal police power, which had served as the basis of state immigration policy, also became the backbone of Chinese exclusion. Just as state officials had defended their constitutional right to protect citizens from the alleged economic, moral, and sanitary menace of European paupers, anti-Chinese restrictionists contended that Chinese immigrants were destabilizing American society with their "low standard of living and morality," stressing Americans' "right in self-defense to exclude such a crowd from access to our shores."[39] John F. Miller, a senator from California, advocated the right of a nation to reject "any class of immigrants or invaders whom it may regard as either dangerous to its peace and happiness or undesirable from any other cause." "Self-preservation," asserted Miller, "is the foundation principle of the constitution of nations."[40] San Francisco lawyer H. N. Clement, a more radical restrictionist, even claimed that a "nation has a right to do *everything* that can secure it from threatening danger."[41]

Again, opponents of Chinese immigration used earlier state-level discourse against European paupers as a precedent for the application of police power to immigration control. In 1855 New York City Mayor Fernando Wood wrote to President Franklin Pierce, asking for federal aid in checking the assisted emigration of paupers from Europe. Wood argued that "the inherent right of every community to protect itself from dangers arising from such immigration cannot be questioned." The disease and pauperism brought by destitute aliens was "of itself a sufficient evil." As the national government must "protect us from foreign aggression with ball and cannon," Wood stressed the necessity of federal intervention, "so it is its duty to protect us against an enemy more insidious and destructive, though coming in anther form." Quoting Wood's letter to President Pierce at length, advocates of Chinese exclusion in Congress proclaimed in 1880 that they "fully indorse the opinions and statements set forth" in the mayor's letter and recommended that "the Golden Gate be closed" for the protection against the Chinese of "an outraged people" on the Pacific coast.[42] Chinese exclusion is crucial for the explicit integration of racism into federal immigration policy. Nevertheless, its chief principle—an exercise of internal police power against outside threats—was derived from preexisting measures and ideas that had developed on the Atlantic seaboard. State-level policy on the East Coast and federal Chinese exclusion were directly connected and part of a single story of immigration control in the United States.

The influx of destitute immigrants after the *Henderson* decision, state-level activism, the humanitarian necessity of national policy, and finally the enactment of the Chinese Exclusion Act all contributed to the passage of the federal Immigration Act in August 1882. In supporting the final version of the immigration bill that he introduced in Congress, John Van Voorhis, a Republican representative from New York, elaborated on the United States' sovereign right to decide members of the nation: "One of the most important matters of internal concern of a nation is the control over the people who inhabit its territory." "As it must exclusively govern its own population," he argued, "so it must exclusively determine who shall be admitted within its territory to become a part of that population." Van Voorhis then built upon this idea to defend a nation's power to deport immigrants who the nation judged were not qualified for membership: "If we have the right to prohibit the immigration of such persons [paupers, idiots, lunatics, and criminals] we have also a right . . . to return them to the place whence they came."[43]

The federal Immigration Act of 1882 consisted of four sections, with immigrant exclusion and deportation at its core. The first section established a federal capitation tax of fifty cents on each immigrant to be paid to the United States Treasury as the "Immigrant Fund." The money would be expended for the administration of the act and the care for admitted immigrants. Section 2 prohibited the entry into the United States of "any convict, lunatic, idiot, or any person unable to take care of himself or herself without becoming a public charge." Deriving from precedents in state-level exclusion, this policy returned those passengers denied landing to their places of embarkation at the expense of the owners of the vessels that brought them. The exclusion policy sought not only to regulate immigrants' admission to the United States but also to screen prospective emigrants while they were in Europe. The possibility of paying for return passages would discourage shipping companies from accepting potentially excludable passengers on US-bound packets. During the campaign for the national immigration bill, Franklin Sanborn claimed that the return policy would make "it more and more difficult for the unworthy and undesirable elements of the European populations to flow this way." Continuing their long-time criticism of assisted pauper immigration, the New York Commissioners of Emigration also regarded this exclusion policy as "an absolute necessity" to check the shipment of paupers from Europe. The third section of the 1882 law authorized the secretary of the treasury to establish whatever regulations he regarded as necessary for the enforcement of the act.[44]

Section 4 of the act requires particular attention to explain the overall intentions of the legislation. The section stipulated that foreign criminals "shall be sent back to the nations to which they belong and from whence they came." This wording does not make entirely clear whether the provision was designed for exclusion upon arrival or deportation after initial landing. Historians have often seen it simply as an exclusion clause, yet John Van Voorhis revealed during floor debate in Congress that "the object of the fourth section was to reach paupers, lunatics, criminals, &c., who *got into the country* . . . by eluding the vigilance of the officials."[45] The phrases "to which they belong" and "from whence they came" found in the clause were the generic terms that had been used in American legal and public discourse since the eighteenth century for the banishment of people from a territory. A notable example is a 1794 Massachusetts act that provided for the deportation of any destitute alien to "any place beyond [the] sea, where he belongs."[46] Congress decided not to make the 1882 act extensive enough to cover paupers and lunatics in the final version. Even so, Section 4 was clearly a deportation provision aimed at criminals who escaped exclusion under Section 2, though it did not establish a concrete enforcing apparatus. As the first federal act to regulate general immigration, the Immigration Act of 1882, together with the Chinese Exclusion Act, set the groundwork for subsequent federal immigration policies.

The enactment of the Immigration Act in 1882 was a monumental departure from earlier state policies, but it by no means disconnected the states from immigration control. The act authorized the secretary of the treasury to "enter into contracts with such State commission, board, or officers as may be designated for that purpose by the governor of any State" to administer federal immigration policy. In other words, though federal in scope, the Immigration Act of 1882 relied on state officials to enforce its provisions, such as collecting head money, inspecting the condition of arriving passengers, and excluding paupers and criminals. The federal government, unlike the already-established state agencies, had neither the administrative capacity nor the experience in passenger control to implement the act.[47] That the provisions of the national act were modeled on state laws demonstrates the significance of earlier state experiences. The gradual transfer of authority and the enduring involvement of state agencies further illuminate the essential importance of state policies in the evolution of immigration control in the United States. In New York and Massachusetts, the Commissioners of Emigration and the State Board of Health, Lunacy, and Charity respectively signed a contract with United States Treasury Secretary Charles F. Folger to administer the act.

The first major test of the state-federal joint administration of immigration control came when the British government sent impoverished Irish men and women to the United States in 1883. Despite the catastrophe of the famine in the 1840s, the population of Ireland increased in the post-famine years. Starvation and destitution, however, once again engulfed the west of the country when an economic depression and the failure of the potato crop hit Ireland in the late 1870s. With growing pauperism and reports on misery and distress reminiscent of the 1840s, philanthropic Englishmen called for assisted emigration by the government. Some of them privately sponsored their own emigration schemes between 1880 and 1882, with the conviction that "there was no hope but in emigration" in western Ireland. Yet realizing the limitations of private enterprise, proponents of state-aided emigration persuaded Parliament to finance the transatlantic passage of destitute Irish people. In 1883 and 1884 a total of 23,536 persons were sent from Ireland to North America with the government's sponsorship. The largest portion of them went to New York, but at least 7,459 people embarked for Massachusetts. Pennsylvania also became the destination for 294 emigrants in 1883.[48]

As groups of assisted emigrants arrived in American ports during the spring and summer of 1883, their poverty immediately drew public attention. In reporting the April 15 arrival in Boston of 650 passengers (mostly assisted Irish emigrants) aboard the *Nestoria*, the *New York Times* noted that they had "brought little with them in the way of money or household goods." A physician for the port of Boston reported that many of the assisted emigrants he had examined were "scantily clothed" as well as "too feeble by reason of age or other infirmities for self-support, and must be aided by private and public charities." Those who arrived in Philadelphia shocked American observers for "a pitiable picture of distress," carrying "all their worldly effects in a sack or bundle."[49] More than any earlier cases of assisted pauper immigration from Europe, the British government's large-scale scheme in 1883 infuriated Americans, who believed that the Old World was imposing its surplus population on the United States. "England ought not," Massachusetts governor Benjamin Butler wrote to Treasury Secretary Charles J. Folger, "to be permitted to empty her alms-houses into the United States." The Massachusetts legislature condemned the action of the British government as "an insult to the people of the United States." "Honest, intelligent, and industrious immigrants from all parts of the globe are always welcome," *Harper's Weekly* claimed, "but this country should not be made the dumping ground of European crime, pauperism, and idleness."[50]

The federal government's response to the British scheme reflected the states' centrality in the implementation of federal immigration legislation. In June 1883, President Arthur expressed his opinion of assisted emigrants that "if it should be found that anyone is unable to take care of himself without becoming a pubic charge he will not be permitted to land" under the 1882 Immigration Act and that "the law will be strictly enforced."[51] In actuality, Arthur's promise of law enforcement relied on

THE BALANCE OF TRADE WITH GREAT BRITAIN SEEMS TO BE STILL AGAINST US.
650 Paupers arrived at Boston in the Steamship *Nestoria*, April 15th, from Galway, Ireland, shipped by the British Government.

Figure 7.1: "The Balance of Trade with Great Britain Seems to Be Still Against Us," *Harper's Weekly*, April 28, 1883. The assisted emigration scheme by the British government created the impression among Americans that Britain was imposing the burden of maintaining workhouses in Ireland on the United States.
Courtesy of Butler Library, Columbia University in the City of New York.

state officials. Later that month, Treasury Secretary Folger instructed the federal collector for the port of New York to cooperate with the New York Commissioners of Emigration to prevent the landing of immigrants who were regarded as paupers. Folger declared that New York officials should "exercise a 'preliminary supervision'" and "determine before any immigrants land from a vessel who are legally entitled to that privilege and who are not." "This duty is incumbent upon them," he wrote, "and is not imposed upon the officers of the United States." On the commissioners' side, they resolved to work with the federal port collector and later confirmed that they attained "the hearty co-operation of the Collector of the Port."[52]

The exclusion of assisted Irish paupers, however, proved difficult. It was clear to American officials, from the appearance of the emigrants, that a significant portion of them had been excludable paupers before being sent to the United States. The New York commissioners even procured affidavits from several emigrants stating that they had been workhouse inmates in Ireland.[53] To evade the exclusion provision, agents of the British government supplied the assisted emigrants with some cash and clothes at the time of arrival. When state port officers inspected the assisted passengers, the British agents accompanying them insisted that a person "who is possessed of £5 cannot be classed as a pauper." Massachusetts officials also noticed that the British government had required assisted emigrants to obtain advance letters from their acquaintances in America as proof of their sources of support, even if they were "not well to do, and have scarcely the wherewith to support themselves and families." A Boston newspaper showed its frustration with the British tricks: "They were paupers when they left Ireland, but not when landed in Boston!"[54]

Despite the problems in enforcing the law, American officials were determined to prohibit pauper passengers from landing and to return them to Ireland. Prior to 1882 the New York commissioners routinely detained pauper and criminal passengers at Castle Garden to expedite their exclusion. Following this practice, the New York officials in June 1883 placed all emigrants who "have been sent here by funds furnished by the British government" at the landing depot. Responding to assisted emigrants detained at Castle Garden, the *New York Times* asserted that "the laws of the Republic . . . forbid the landing in this country of any convict, lunatic, idiot, or any person not competent of taking care of himself." If the assisted passengers were destined to become public charges, wrote the newspaper, "they may be returned to their home port." Later the same month, the federal government decided to return the assisted emigrants

ASSISTED IMMIGRANT FROM KERRY WORKHOUSE.
"Who says I'm a pauper, or will be a burden upon the country?"

Figure 7.2: "Assisted Immigrant from Kerry Workhouse," *Harper's Weekly*, July 7, 1883. The barefooted boy sent from a workhouse in County Kerry, with a railroad ticket to the interior and a bag, claims that "Who says I'm a pauper, or will be a burden upon the country?" representing the British attempt to evade the pauper exclusion provision in American immigration law.
Courtesy of Butler Library, Columbia University in the City of New York.

at Castle Garden. Treasury Secretary Folger authorized Collector of the Port of New York William H. Robertson to notify the New York agents of the steamship companies that carried the assisted emigrants that they must take back to Ireland all detained passengers verified as "persons likely to become public charges." Two days later the commissioners started returning assisted paupers.[55]

Statements by the people who witnessed the scene at New York and reports in Irish newspapers provide insight into how the New York commissioners treated the assisted emigrants. In a meeting of the Guardians of the Poor in Tralee, County Kerry, Ireland, a representative of the Anchor Line Steamship Company, which brought back some of the returnees, stated: "As far as I can see from the proceedings in New York these people were coerced altogether against their own will to come back." Mary Brennan, who had been an inmate in a workhouse in County Kerry for thirty years prior to her emigration to the United States, was reported to have "implored not to be sent back, if for nothing but the shame of it." Her request was ignored. One returnee found his entire experience with the New York officials to be so bitter that he confessed, "To tell God's truth I could not have been worse treated in any gaol in the country than I was at Castle Gardens."[56]

Personal accounts of those who were returned to County Cork, published by the *Cork Examiner*, reveal further details of the activities of the New York commissioners. As the enforcing agents of the Immigration Act of 1882, the New York Commissioners of Emigration were authorized to prohibit the landing of foreign paupers, but no law permitted them to deport those who had once managed to pass through Castle Garden. In other words, immigrants could be excluded but not be deported for poverty under the 1882 federal act. The New York state law of 1880 permitted the deportation of assisted paupers from charitable institutions, but this authority was vested in the State Board of Charities, not the Commissioners of Emigration. Nevertheless the experiences of returned emigrants suggest that the New York commissioners conducted deportation as well as exclusion. John McCarthy, one of the returnees, had migrated from the town of Tralee to the United States and was a naturalized US citizen. During the Civil War he enlisted in the Union army and voted for George B. McClellan in the presidential election of 1864. After the war, he suffered from poor health and returned to his hometown in Ireland. In late May 1883 McCarthy and his wife were sent by Tralee officials to New York with £2, two blankets, clothes, and some cooking utensils, and they passed through landing inspection. Within three weeks, McCarthy and his wife had lost all their money and belongings and went to Castle Garden to apply for relief. The New York commissioners told them that his wife, who was then blind, should go back to Ireland; presumably the officials feared that she would become a public charge if she remained. McCarthy tried to claim public relief for himself and his wife on the basis of his American citizenship, but the commissioners ultimately sent both of them back to Ireland.[57]

New York immigration officials' decisions on deportation extended to minors who earned wages through employment or had someone who could take care of them. Ellen Sullivan was assisted in emigrating to New York with her three children. Her oldest daughter was married and had an infant. The fourteen-year-old second daughter secured employment as a domestic servant, and Sullivan's uncle agreed to take care of the youngest daughter, who was thirteen years of age. When Sullivan and her oldest daughter decided to return to Ireland voluntarily due to their inability to obtain employment and went to Castle Garden, one of the emigration commissioners insisted that "the entire family should return from whence they came." Sullivan argued that her second daughter's steady employment and the presence of the uncle guaranteed the self-sufficiency of the two daughters, but all three daughters were compelled to return to Ireland with their mother.[58] The Immigration Act of 1882 technically limited deportation to criminal aliens. In practical terms, however, state officials' discretion dictated who could enter and stay in the nation and who would be removed. In New York, the introduction of the federal act in 1882 did not disrupt the charity board's implementation of the 1880 state deportation law, which officials could justify as an expression of state police power. As long as another state agency was deporting foreign paupers to Europe, the Commissioners of Emigration might have found it easy, or even natural, to do the same, especially in a period when the coexistence of state and federal immigration policies blurred boundaries among various offices committed to immigration regulation.

The working of immigration control in Massachusetts reveals a unique relationship between state and federal authorities. The notable difference between Massachusetts and other states, including New York, was that in the Bay State, immigration officials had formally deported alien paupers as state policy throughout the nineteenth century. Officials in the Board of Health, Lunacy, and Charity continued pauper removal after they became the enforcers of the federal Immigration Act of 1882. The state board acknowledged its "special duty" over immigration, under which it performed "by an arrangement with the United States government" *and* "in conformity with long established State policy."[59] Massachusetts immigration officials therefore assumed the responsibility for both exclusion under the national immigration act and deportation under state law.

The dual mode of immigration control guided the Massachusetts board's responses to assisted Irish emigrants. In accordance with the 1882 act, Massachusetts officials prevented the landing of those classified as paupers upon arrival. Yet as they did elsewhere, some passengers entered the state with money and clothes provided by the British government. If such assisted emigrants sought public relief afterward, the Massachusetts board shipped them back to Ireland under the state's deportation law. Cornelius Flahavan, a thirty-year-old native of Talbert in County Kerry and a "deaf-mute" inmate of a workhouse in County Limerick, was one of the assisted Irish emigrants who were deported from Massachusetts. In July 1883 he was assisted by the Limerick authorities to join his mother in New York City. He arrived in Boston on the *Austrian* to proceed to

New York. With "a considerable sum of money" in his pocket (presumably provided either by the British government through the Limerick officials or by his mother via remittances) and a written statement that proved his mother's presence in New York City, he was permitted to land in Boston. Within a few weeks, he had spent all his money and had become a homeless vagrant. Flahavan was soon arrested in Worcester and sent to a state workhouse in Bridgewater. The Massachusetts board eventually deported him from the workhouse to Ireland.[60]

In addition to individuals like Flahavan, Massachusetts officials deported assisted emigrants in families. Michael and Ellen Maloney and their five children landed in New York on the *Belgravia* as assisted emigrants from a workhouse in Cahirciveen. Having no friends in the United States, they went to Worcester with another emigrant who had a cousin in Massachusetts. With Michael unable to work because of "a withered arm" and sick children, the family appealed to the Overseers of the Poor in Worcester "for full support as paupers." The overseers transferred them to the Tewksbury state almshouse. The newspaper covering the case noted that "the State authorities are expected to send them back to Ireland." The Massachusetts Board of Health, Lunacy, and Charity later stated that during 1883, it shipped back assisted emigrant families whose "head thereof, the bread-winner, had been killed by sun-stroke during the month of July."[61]

Perhaps even more important than the coexistence of federal exclusion and state deportation policies in Massachusetts was the federal government's involvement in state policies. The Massachusetts State Board of Health, Lunacy, and Charity reported in 1884 that "the Act of Congress regulating Immigration" reimbursed the board for its expenses in removing immigrant paupers from the state. Between August 3, 1882, and October 1, 1883, the board received $1,848.30 "for the removal of lunatics and paupers landing at the port of Boston," though the 1882 Immigration Act only defined criminal aliens as deportable.[62] When asked by Minnesota officials if they could deport destitute foreigners already in the nation to Europe on another occasion, the Secretary of the Treasury replied that the 1882 Immigration Act gave him no authority to "arrest and return" immigrants who had "passed the examination [upon arrival]" and "been permitted to land."[63] Not until 1891 did Congress officially introduce a general deportation policy that made all excludable aliens, including paupers and people likely to become public charges, deportable. Yet even before 1891 the federal government was already engaged in general deportation by financing Massachusetts policies for expelling immigrant paupers to their countries of origin.

The record of Massachusetts immigration officials hints that deportees from the Bay State had worse experiences than those returned from
New York. Nativism against the Irish had been particularly intense
in Massachusetts partly due to the state's exceptionally strong Anglo
Protestant cultural tradition. Since midcentury, Massachusetts had cultivated a notorious reputation among steamship companies for its stringent exclusion policy. Compared to New York authorities, officials in
Massachusetts were far more likely to declare an immigrant to be a pauper
in need of a bond for landing. Also, while the existence of a deportation
policy reflected the state's tough attitude toward unwanted foreigners,
the policy's arbitrary nature, which gave immigration officials complete
power in determining where the person in question belonged, and the
abuse of defenseless deportees by enforcing officers, provoked criticism
on humanitarian grounds. Opponents of removal policies had constantly
denounced nativist state officials for their seizure of Irish paupers and
illegal banishment with force, including the overseas removal of citizens.
Furthermore, Bay State officials showed little concern for the welfare of
deportees, routinely discharging them from railroads or ships without
provisions for immediate self-support. Consequently helpless deportees,
including those with insanity, often ended up roaming on the streets of
Albany, Liverpool, or Irish port cities in search of food and shelter. The
manner of deportation remained the same in 1883. Reporting on the
arrival of Mary Flaherty, one of the assisted emigrants expelled from
Massachusetts, the *Cork Examiner* noted that she was sent back "without
any probable means of support."[64] Immigration control in Massachusetts
thus had been particularly harsh and operated in a way that diminished
the protection of deportable aliens. State officials preserved their relent-
less approach to immigration control after they became the agents of the
federal immigration act.

The assisted emigration of Irish paupers to North America lasted after
1883, but the British government gradually abandoned the scheme
by the end of the 1880s. While the United States remained critical of
assisted emigration, opposition also came from Canada. Partly to evade
American immigration law, British officials sent Irish emigrants to
Canada. Canadians, however, believed that the British government was
using Canada as a dumping ground for Irish paupers and vehemently
protested assisted emigration. Throughout the 1880s the Canadian
authorities maintained that they would not accept Irish emigrants who
were sent by British officials or from workhouses in Ireland. In 1884 the
Local Government Board for Ireland retained the funds appropriated by

the British government for assisted emigration, but it did not exhaust its resources due to the opposition from Americans and Canadians.[65]

The activities of officials in New York and Massachusetts during 1883 hold crucial implications for understanding the legislative development of federal immigration control. Under the Immigration Act of 1882, state agencies retained a significant level of involvement in immigration regulation. During the period of an embryonic system of national control, state officials exercised substantial influence on the lives of aliens, sometimes beyond their legal authority, as seen in the deportation of Irish paupers by the New York Commissioners of Emigration. In the meantime, the New York State Board of Charities kept enforcing the 1880 state law for the deportation of assisted paupers, considering the federal Immigration Act of 1882 "supplementary."[66] In Massachusetts, destitute foreigners had been expelled under state deportation law since the eighteenth century, and state officials maintained the law after 1882, implementing it with funding from the federal government. The 1882 act provided only for the exclusion of paupers, but paupers were not simply excluded from the United States; they were also deported under the de facto general deportation regime. The federalization of immigration control was therefore a gradual process at best, and the actions of officials in the northeastern states set the conditions for the introduction of general deportation by the federal government in 1891.

The nationalization of immigration regulation technically reached completion in 1891. Responding to the inefficiency of state-federal joint administration at Castle Garden revealed in legislative investigations, Congress passed a new immigration act in March 1891. The act placed issues of immigration under the control of the federal superintendent of immigration in the Treasury Department and appointed federal commissioners of immigration at major ports, replacing state enforcers with federal employees. The passage of the act was followed by the construction of the federally operated Ellis Island landing station.[67] The 1891 law also expanded the excludable category to cover people with mental defects and insanity, paupers and people "likely to become a public charge," people with contagious diseases, people convicted of a felony or other crime involving "moral turpitude," polygamists, and assisted emigrants—making all of them deportable.[68]

The introduction of general deportation in 1891 was partly a response to pleas from states for a stricter federal policy against undesirable immigrants. In 1885, the Pennsylvania Commissioners of Public Charities demanded new legislation to deport any excludable foreigner who "escapes detention upon arrival and does land."[69] Three years later,

Massachusetts Governor Oliver Ames requested in a special message to Congress the modification of federal immigration law to better prevent the landing of assisted emigrants, by reminding national lawmakers of the British government' scheme to send Irish paupers to the United States in 1883. The *Baltimore Sun* commended the Massachusetts governor's action as "a good example to other States."[70] These pressures from states critically influenced Congress's decision to start general deportation. Yet this decision's context cannot be fully understood without realizing that state officials' activities in New York and Massachusetts had already made general deportation a practical reality in the implementation of federal immigration law by 1891.

The complete federalization of administrative authority over immigration control does not necessarily signify the end of state officials' participation in federal policy. During the construction of Ellis Island, the Treasury Department, having no trained staff of its own, ended up hiring former New York state officials from Castle Garden, many of whom continued to serve at Ellis Island. The staff of the first federal Commission of Immigration for New York consisted almost entirely of former Castle Garden workers.[71] In Massachusetts, state officials stubbornly defied the idea of complete federal control. When the Treasury Department suggested to the Massachusetts Board of Lunacy and Charity the abrogation of the contract with it for the purpose of enhancing federal administrative authority, the board solicited the intervention of congressional representatives from the state to overturn the plan.[72] Massachusetts officials' resistance forced Treasury Secretary Charles Foster to appoint board member Stephen C. Wrightington, who had served on the state immigration board since the 1860s, as the federal commissioner of immigration. Other board members were also employed as US immigration officers. In December 1892 the Massachusetts board concluded that the formal transfer of authority had resulted in "no practical change of administration."[73] The Treasury Department itself admitted in 1891 that federal officers, whether formerly state officials or not, were expected to maintain "amicable cooperation" with existing state boards and that a state board "has authority to decide all questions as to the exclusion of immigrants."[74]

State officials' involvement helped shape some of the critical features of federal regulation that had a profound and lasting influence on immigrants to the United States in the following decades. Many newcomers found their experience of temporary detention and medical inspection at Ellis Island and Angel Island severely traumatic and depressing. American officials' hostility toward Mexicans also characterized border control in the Southwest in the early twentieth century.[75] Of these harsh aspects of federal control, one that stood out for its direct impact on immigrants' presence in the United States was immigration officers' virtually unqualified power over the decision on exclusion and deportation. The introduction into federal immigration law in 1891 of the "likely to become a public charge (LPC)" clause, which originated from state passenger laws, made the *seeming* incapability of self-support—due to poverty, physical and mental defects, or disease—a principal ground for exclusion. As the term "likely" implies, the LPC clause was open to varying interpretations by officers at points of entry who oversaw the admission of immigrants.[76] Federal immigration inspectors in the early twentieth century, as a contemporary scholar observed, abused the provision by extensively and arbitrarily applying it as "a kind of miscellaneous file" for cases "where the officers think the alien ought not to enter, but the facts do not come within any specific requirements of the statutes."[77]

The power of immigration officers represented in the LPC clause also appeared in the form of a legal doctrine. The Supreme Court's rulings between 1889 and 1893 on Asian immigrants' challenges to restriction laws established what immigration scholars call the plenary power doctrine, which assumed that Congress possessed absolute power over the control of the nation's borders and that its immigration policy was not subject to judicial scrutiny for constitutionality. Immigration scholars often refer specifically to a clause in the 1891 act declaring that inspection officers' decisions regarding admission "shall be final" (the so-called finality clause). This interpretation of Congress's authority allowed immigration officers to determine aliens' excludability and deportability in a way that was not restricted by judicial oversight, minimizing constitutional protections such as due process.[78]

The origins of these developments in federal immigration policy clearly lie in state-level immigration control in New York and Massachusetts. Throughout the nineteenth century, the landing of immigrants in these states depended on state officials' subjective judgment on their conditions at the time of arrival. One task of the New York Commissioners of Emigration was to protect newcomers from fraudsters. Yet the commissioners treated destitute passengers whom they judged excludable with an unyielding determination to prevent their entry, as seen in the detention and forcible return of assisted Irish emigrants in 1883. The cases of the McCarthy and Sullivan families reveal that immigrants who had once been admitted to New York could be compelled to return to Europe solely at the commissioners' discretion. New York officials sometimes even excluded apparently self-sufficient immigrants as paupers. In May 1889, a Commissioner of Emigration refused to land an Irish family from County

Tipperary—Patrick Murnane, his wife, and their eight children. Despite the proof of Murnane's payment for their own passage and possession of one hundred dollars in cash, the *New York Irish-American* reported, the commissioner denied them admission, "stigmatising them as 'paupers.'" The newspaper suspected that the nativist official viewed the family of ten as "too large an addition to the Irish-American population."[79]

The history of pauper deportation in Massachusetts illuminates the powerlessness of immigrants in the face of removal. Deportation decisions were made regardless of the length of the pauper's residency in the United States, his or her connection to the community, or even citizenship status. Since the antebellum period critics of removal policy continuously pointed out the unchecked power of state officials over foreigners, as well as the absence of consideration for deportees' welfare. While denying the states' right to collect head money, however, the courts never questioned their right to exclude and deport undesirable aliens or the manner in which they did so.

Herein lies the fundamental contribution of New York and Massachusetts officials to the evolution of American immigration control. The approach to undesirable aliens developed in these states, where immigration restriction had been pursued most systematically and rigorously prior to the 1880s, was integrated into national policy through the 1882 Immigration Act's state-federal joint administration and state officials' continuous presence after the passage of the 1891 Immigration Act. The finality clause in the 1891 act, which affirmed inspection officers' judgment on immigrant exclusion as unchallengeable, did not attract any attention in Congress during floor debate. Legal historian Lucy Salyer insightfully argues that certain successes by the Chinese in using the courts to circumvent the restriction laws during the early years of Chinese exclusion drove Congress to introduce this clause, which would prevent other immigrants from resorting to the same means to enter the United States.[80] But congressmen's knowledge of immigration control in 1891 derived mainly from the work of officials in New York and Massachusetts, who had long exercised unrestricted power over immigrants. In making federal immigration law more comprehensive, policymakers simply codified what had become the norm in the actual enforcement of immigrant exclusion and deportation. Chinese exclusion undoubtedly facilitated the consolidation of plenary power, but that power built upon practices and mindsets that had emerged from the Atlantic seaboard states' treatment of destitute European—especially Irish—immigrants through the antebellum, Civil War, and Reconstruction periods.

Conclusion

In 1883 Emma Lazarus, a Jewish American poet in New York City, composed a sonnet which she titled "The New Colossus." She contributed it to a fundraising auction for the construction of a pedestal in New York harbor, on which a Statue of Liberty, a gift from France to the United States as a symbol of friendship between the two nations, would be erected. Inspired by the recent arrival in New York of refugees fleeing the persecution of Jews in Russia, Lazarus dedicated the poem to the motif of America as a haven for the oppressed and the poor. America, or "Mother of Exiles," proclaims to the Old World: "Give me your tired, your poor, Your huddled masses yearning to breathe free" as well as the "wretched refuse of your teeming shore." Lazarus's cry, however, did not reflect prevailing sentiment about immigration in American society at that time. By the 1880s alarm about the "huddled masses" of penniless and diseased immigrants from Europe, as well as seemingly unassimilable people from Asia, had overshadowed the sense of asylum mission in American immigration policy, increasingly directing it toward restriction rather than reception. "The New Colossus" drew little attention from the American public upon its publication, and when Lazarus died in 1887, obituaries did not mention the sonnet. Reviewers of her collected works, which appeared after her death, hardly referred to it.[1] Yet nothing reveals the distance between Lazarus's tone and the reality of American immigration policy more strikingly than the intensive implementation of the 1882 Immigration Act by New York and Massachusetts officials to send destitute Irish migrants back to Ireland in 1883, the same year as Lazarus wrote the poem.

The history of immigration control in the United States up to the time of Emma Lazarus can be read as a story of American state development. The influx of impoverished people from Ireland over the first half of the nineteenth century kindled intense anti-Irish nativism in New York and Massachusetts. Building upon colonial poor laws for regulating the movement of the poor, these states developed policies for excluding and deporting destitute foreigners. Policies of this kind had long been implemented on a local basis by town or city officers, but mounting calls for the tighter restriction of pauper immigration from Ireland induced a shift of responsibility for immigration from towns and cities to the state in midcentury. Under the direction of state immigration agencies established as a result, New York and Massachusetts regulated immigration throughout the antebellum, Civil War, and Reconstruction periods, while constantly broadening the category of excludable and deportable foreigners. After the United States Supreme Court declared state passenger law unconstitutional in 1876, New York and Massachusetts officials' effort to continue the restriction of pauper immigration led to the introduction of federal immigration legislation in 1882. The federalization of immigration control proceeded only at a gradual pace, with state officials deeply involved in designing and implementing federal policy. Nevertheless, the direction was firmly set toward the national supervision of immigration control by the final decade of the nineteenth century. *Expelling the Poor* has narrated a story of American state development by demonstrating how governmental policy for regulating membership in American society on an economic basis evolved from the local, to the state, and eventually to the national levels under the influence of anti-Irish nativism.

Anti-Irish nativism not only stimulated the legal development of immigration policy but also considerably affected the manner of its enforcement. Contrary to state officials' claims of humane and consensual removal, the expansion of their authority over immigration fostered coercive and illegal expulsion, with some paupers virtually kidnapped from charitable institutions and some citizens banished abroad. Driven by anti-Irish sentiment, state-level immigration control operated in ways that allowed officials to exert tremendous power over objectionable foreigners and disregard their basic rights and protection in the execution of laws. Through their treatment of Irish paupers, New York and Massachusetts officials cultivated the notion that any action against undesirable aliens would be permissible if it was an exercise of internal police power. This notion, as well as state officials' ruthless approaches to destitute foreigners, was inherited by federal immigration policy with the officials' involvement in the Immigration Act of 1882, setting the stage for the rise of the plenary power doctrine in the late nineteenth century.

Indeed, the period between 1882 and 1891 displays how the features of immigration control in New York and Massachusetts became normative for national immigration policy. In 1885 the Treasury Department formalized the practice of immigrant detention exercised by the New York Commissioners of Emigration, officially authorizing them to detain all excludable foreigners "either on shipboard or elsewhere" until shipping companies brought them back to their places of departure. The department later extended this power to other states. The California Commissioner of Immigration, for example, obtained the same detention authority "as that conferred on the Commissioner of Emigration at the port of New York" in June 1888.[2] The styles of immigration control in the two Atlantic seaboard states served as models for officials in other states with less experience in passenger regulation. The Pennsylvania Board of Immigration sent two officers to New York City and Boston in June 1889 to "examine the working of the immigration law" in these cities "with the view of promoting the efficiency of the service at Philadelphia."[3] State officials' harsh treatment of objectionable foreigners also seemed to be adopted as national policy. In June 1890, Treasury Secretary William Windom publicly allowed executors of federal immigration policy to use "all the force," if it became necessary to "secure obedience to the law."[4] The secretary further declared that federal action "cannot be controlled by humanitarian considerations, however strong they may be." He rejected a request from a sympathizer of immigrants for the appropriation of collected head money to provide more humane care to detained aliens.[5]

The history of state-level immigration control in New York and Massachusetts revises the ethnic history of immigration control in the United States. Antebellum nativism against European immigrants, especially the Irish, has drawn much scholarly attention, but anti-European nativism in the pre-1880s period is usually seen as a form of bigotry that did not fundamentally affect America's border policy. The Atlantic seaboard states, however, responded to widespread frustration with Irish pauperism by passing a series of laws for regulating immigration. And these states' policies shaped the framework of United States immigration policy and critically influenced the way it was implemented, even before the introduction of federal Chinese exclusion and the opening of Ellis Island. Far from simply a temporary regional hysteria in the antebellum period or a matter of cultural stereotyping, anti-Irish nativism in New York and Massachusetts produced lasting, tangible consequences in American immigration law and policy at initially state and ultimately national levels. At the turn of the twentieth century, opponents of immigration in Massachusetts formed the Immigration Restriction League, becoming the major promoters of immigration control in the nation.[6] The rise of this organization in Massachusetts was hardly random. It was founded upon the deep-seated nativist cultural and political tradition in the Bay State and, more critically, the state's exceptional record of excluding and deporting undesirable immigrants since the eighteenth century.

The development of restrictive state legislation underscores the centrality of economics in American immigration control. Prejudice against the Irish undoubtedly played a crucial role in the growth of regulatory state laws. Considering Irish immigrants culturally and biologically degraded people, Anglo Americans viewed Irish poverty as particularly odious compared to the poverty of other immigrant groups. But if anti-Irish prejudice served as a catalyst for state-level immigration control, the policies that emerged from it functioned largely on the basis of economics. Deriving from the colonial poor law, the foremost purpose of states' exclusion policies was to protect their treasuries from the cost of maintaining destitute foreigners. Some contemporaries advanced a humanitarian defense of the head money system, claiming that it would fund immigrant hospitals for needy foreigners. But the core principle of head money, which was usually included in the passage fare, was to make immigrants bear the expense of those institutions and to refuse admission to those who could not do so. The essential objective of Massachusetts deportation policy was to physically eliminate Irish paupers, the source of financial drain, from the state.

State control was also driven by antagonism to poor immigrants who appeared to erode the wages of native-born workers. "Would you prevent the NATIVE AMERICAN MECHANICS and LABORERS from becoming paupers," a nativist handbill in the 1840s appealed to American workers. Warning against the arrival of "trained pauper bands of Europe," the handbill urged Americans to support immigration restriction: "Are you content that the immense influx of needy foreigners shall remedilessly reduce your wages to the lowest pittance? Are you ready to sink to the degraded level of the laborers of enslaved Europe, and bid against the old world paupers for work?"[7] In 1885, antipathy to imported European contract workers from labor unions, such as the Knights of Labor, resulted in the passage of the federal Foran Act, which prohibited the entry of immigrants under labor contract.[8] This expansion of federal regulatory policy was in essence a continuation of the earlier state-level efforts to restrict the immigration of the poor, in that the rationale for the expansion lay in the protection of Americans from foreigners who would jeopardize their employment.

The economic impetus of state immigration policy had significant ideological dimensions. What lay behind aversion to Irish paupers and the aggressive enforcement of restrictive laws was the question of who deserved to be American in the nineteenth century. In the antebellum period, economic self-sufficiency based on free, independent labor defined the quality of ideal white American citizens, especially those in the North. The presence of racial slavery led them to assume that its antitheses, unfreedom and dependency, were conditions reserved for blacks. The dominant social thinking after the Civil War that all free Americans should earn their bread through contract wage labor—a supposed symbol of freedom and upward mobility in postbellum America—enhanced the virtue of self-support as an indispensable capacity for American citizens. The rising capitalist order in the late nineteenth century that prized productivity further reinforced this ideological trend. Entitled to the privilege of naturalized citizenship, Irish immigrants unquestionably belonged to the dominant racial group in American society throughout the nineteenth century in this fundamental sense. Nevertheless, dependent on public charity and living outside the world of contract wage labor, Irish paupers appeared to destabilize the integrity of American free labor ideology. Anti-Irish prejudice also critically strengthened their hopelessness as people who would not become productive citizens. Nativist officials therefore expelled them from the nation. Deeply entangled with the economic ideals of nineteenth-century America, state immigration policy functioned as a vanguard of these visions and determined who deserved to belong to America in the most literal sense by physically removing from the nation those deemed undeserving.[9]

A number of issues, including the alleged menace of the Chinese to American labor, morality, and public health, converged in the introduction of federal laws to restrict Chinese immigration in the late nineteenth century. But the words of anti-Chinese restrictionists made it clear that at the most critical level, Chinese exclusion was about race. Above all other related considerations, it was an attempt to minimize the presence in American society of nonwhite immigrants, or "Orientals." The racist dimension of American immigration policy laid by Chinese exclusion developed into broader Asian exclusion in the early twentieth century and culminated in the passage in 1924 of the Johnson-Reed Act, which banned the admission of aliens "ineligible to citizenship" and practically suspended all Asian immigration as a result.[10] If Chinese exclusion legitimized racism as federal immigration policy, the northeastern states' policies established the economic underpinning of federal restriction laws.

THE COMING MAN—JOHN CHINAMAN.
Uncle Sam introduces Eastern Barbarism to Western Civilization.

Figure C.1: "The Coming Man—John Chinaman: Uncle Sam introduces Eastern Barbarism to Western Civilization," *Harper's Weekly*, August 28, 1869. The image represents the two roots of American immigration policy: economic and cultural nativism against the Irish in Atlantic seaboard states and anti-Chinese racism arising from the West. Note that the Irishman on the left wears ragged clothes, reflecting the widespread stereotype that viewed poverty as an essential characteristic of the Irish.
Courtesy of Butler Library, Columbia University in the City of New York.

No less significant, the state-level deportation of Irish paupers unfolded in a transnational setting. In Liverpool, Irish paupers sent from the United States were treated in the same way as Irish paupers in Britain and subjected to deportation to Ireland under British pauper removal law. In Ireland, workhouse officials resisted the admission of Irish paupers sent from Britain and the United States altogether as burdens on their community. Physical expulsion and social marginalization, then, seemed to be the destiny of indigent Irish migrants in the United States, Britain, and Ireland. At the center of the efforts to exclude Irish migrant paupers in these locations stood public officials' shared hostility to them as the undeserving poor, a sentiment that intensified during nineteenth-century industrialization. State deportation law thus operated within a wider system of banishing and alienating nonproducing people that emerged in the Atlantic world as a transnational embodiment of the force of industrialization. If the manners of removal from New York and Massachusetts denote the rightless status of Irish migrant paupers in nineteenth-century

America, their postdeportation experience illuminates their statelessness in the north Atlantic world.

By the end of the nineteenth century, the principal target of immigration control in the United States had shifted from Irish paupers to immigrants from southern and eastern Europe as well as Asia. In the early decades of the twentieth century, the US–Mexico land border became the site of militant immigration regulation with the formation of the Border Patrol. Following the practices of entry inspection established at Ellis Island and their own racial presumptions about Mexicans, American officers at the border applied regulatory laws, including the "likely to become a public charge" clause, to Mexicans in humiliating and uncivil ways with the character of criminal pursuit.[11] These developments in federal immigration policy, though aiming at different targets, built upon the earlier experiences of New York and Massachusetts against destitute immigrants from western Europe, especially Ireland. Many of the issues seen in the time of state-level control—such as foreigners' alleged threat to Americans' jobs and the morality of American society, advocacy of the uncompromising implementation of deportation law, resultant family disruption, the rights and welfare of deportable immigrants and their American-born children, concerns about the aftermath of deportation, the manner and civility of law enforcement, and tensions between states and the federal government over immigration regulation—appear in remarkably similar ways in the United States today and shape present debates over immigration and the nation's policies on this matter.

As much as the United States has remained the world's major receiver of migrants, American immigration history can be characterized by persistent efforts to assert national sovereignty against undesirable foreigners. Nineteenth-century New York and Massachusetts shaped the way this effort could be pursued in their response to Irish immigration. Landing stations established after the 1880s and run under federal supervision, such as Ellis Island and Angel Island, have now come to symbolize the tradition of immigration control in the United States. Yet Atlantic seaboard states' earlier efforts to reduce foreign pauperism reveal that restriction was an integral part of the American immigration experience long before the building of these gateways to America.

APPENDIX A

Warning Out in Boston, 1745–1792

A.1. NUMBERS OF WARNING OUT

Year	Number Warned	Number Warned/1,000 Population
1745–1749	363	23.1
1750–1754	528	33.6
1755–1759	1,160	74.2
1760–1764	765	49.3
1765–1769	2,499	151.1
1770–1773	1,587	95.9
1791–1792	2,405	133.9

Source: Allan Kulikoff, "The Progress of Inequality in Revolutionary Boston," *William and Mary Quarterly* 28, no. 3 (July 1971): 400.

A.2. BIRTHPLACES OF PERSONS WARNED OUT FROM BOSTON, 1791

Foreign	237	Other States	62	Massachusetts	740
England	84	Philadelphia	28	Within 10 miles of Boston	341
Ireland	52	New York City	19	Southeast of Boston	181
Scotland	31	Carolina	4	North of Boston	143
Africa	29	Maryland	3	West of Boston	75
Germany	16	New Hampshire	3		
France	14	Albany	3		
Nova Scotia	3	Hartford	2		
West Indies	8				
Total	1,039				

Source: Allan Kulikoff, "The Progress of Inequality in Revolutionary Boston," *William and Mary Quarterly* 28, no. 3 (July 1971): 401.

APPENDIX B

Paupers Removed from Massachusetts and Costs of Removal, 1837–1845

Year	Number of Passengers			Amount of Money	
	Arrived	Sent back to Ireland	Sent out of the State	Received as Head Money	Expended in sending away
1837	2,594	8	80	$5,188	$346.00
1838	1,262	31	362	2,524	1,237.42
1839	2,039	29	236	4,078	750.04
1840	2,884	31	402	5,768	1,338.82
1841	3,649	46	605	7,298	1,853.95
1842	5,445	207	1,110	10,890	5,007.45
1843	2,411	90	605	4,822	2,888.75
1844	4,602	70	526	9,204	2,330.73
1845	8,550	203	780	17,100	4,410.07
Total	33,436	715	4,706	$66,872	$20,163.23

Source: Lemuel Shattuck, *Report to the Committee of the City Council Appointed to Obtain the Census of Boston for the Year 1845, Embracing Collateral Facts and Statistical Researches, Illustrating the History and Condition of the Population, and Their Means of Progress and Prosperity* (Boston: John H. Eastburn, 1846), 41.

APPENDIX C

Persons Removed from Massachusetts by the Commissioners of Alien Passengers and Foreign Paupers, 1851–1863

			C.1. TOTAL NUMBERS			
Year	Sent to Liverpool and Transatlantic Ports	Sent to Canada and Other US States	Removed under the Act of 1851*	Removed from Almshouses	Removed from Lunatic Hospitals	Total
1851			112			112
1852			132			132
1853			118			118
1854			187	118	14	319
1855	286	443	499	309	40	1,577
1856	193	483	363	319	28	1,386
1857	132	396	263	256	18	1,065
1858	342	1,074	827	1,024	102	3,369
1859	181	348	589	166	45	1,329
1860	208	502	624	96	21	1,451
1861	301	1,175	576		35	2,087
1862	123	788	374		31	1,316
1863	75	639	399		64	1,177
Total	1,841	5,848	5,063	2,288	398	15,438

Source: Annual Reports of the Commissioners of Alien Passengers and Foreign Paupers, 1851–1863.
* The Act of 1851 required railroad companies to bring their former passengers back to their places of origin or to pay for their maintenance, if they applied for public relief within one year of arrival.

C.2. PERSONS REMOVED UNDER THE ACT OF 1851
(RETURN OF RAILROAD PASSENGERS)

Year	Incoming Railroad Passengers	Immediately Removed	Removed after Treatment	Total	Destination		
					New York	Other US States	Canada
1851	6,675			112			
1852	12,788	120	12	132	105		27
1853	14,097	118		118			
1854	13,195	122	65	187	164	13	10
1855	10,836	453	46	499	460	29	10
1856	10,024	337	26	363	278	93	2
1857	5,501	240	23	263	226	27	10
1858	5,010	812	15	827	706	112	9
1859				589	419	170	
1860				624	444	153	27
1861				576	391	153	32
1862				374	244	112	18
1863				399	240	150	9
Total	78,126	2,264	238	5,063	3,677	1,012	154

Source: Annual Reports of the Commissioners of Alien Passengers and Foreign Paupers, 1851–1863.

APPENDIX D

Persons Removed from Massachusetts by the Board of State Charities, 1864–1878

Year	Sent to Transatlantic Ports and British Provinces	Sent to Canada	Sent to Other US States	Removed under the Act of 1851	Removed from Lunatic Hospitals	Total
1864	86	16	458	640	73	1,273
1865	75	53	623	775	35	1,561
1866	111	29	745	758	25	1,668
1867	99	75	717	824	53	1,768
1868	99	39	768	835	52	1,793
1869	198	26	911	657	169	1,961
1870	168	66	1,387	654	202	2,477
1871	129	64	1,179	494	210	2,076
1872	102	87	1,025	406	242	1,862
1873	141	52	1,066	415	260	1,934
1874	214	49	1,411	669	209	2,552
1875	281	61	1,693	780	353	3,168
1876	329	88	1,559	559	326	2,861
1877	207	60	1,650	594	327	2,838
1878	250	39	1,567	669	355	2,880
Total	2,489	804	16,759	9,729	2,891	32,672

Source: Annual Reports of the Board of State Charities, 1864–1878.

APPENDIX E

Persons Assisted to Return, Removed, or Excluded from New York by the Commissioners of Emigration and the State Board of Charities, 1850–1890

Year	Returned by NYCE	Returned by NYSBC under the 1873 NY Act	Deported by NYSBC under the 1880 NY Act	Excluded by NYCE under the 1882 Federal Act
1850	53			
1851	311			
1852	433			
1853	271			
1854	444			
1855	570			
1856	54			
1857	64			
1858	170			
1859	68			
1860	67			
1861	326			
1862	53			
1863	65			
1864	101			
1865	94			
1866	156			

1867	136		
1868	241		
1869	237		
1870	210		
1871	240		
1872	–		
1873	–		
1874	297	354	
1875	465	384	
1876	1,480	313	
1877	1,841	565	
1878	1,408	684	
1879	2,292	1,043	
1880	624	670	30	
1881	913	745	45	
1882	1,253	778	43	157
1883	1,056	784	69	294
1884	781	1,246	114	363
1885	850	1,208	152	422
1886	554	1,025	175	443
1887	495	1,097	216	289
1888	569	1,137	323	501
1889	432	1,174	229	422
1890	176	983	165	82
Total	19,850	14,190	1,561	2,973

Source: Annual Reports of the Commissioners of Emigration of the State of New York, 1850–1890; Annual Reports of the New York State Board of Charities, 1874–1890.

NOTES

INTRODUCTION

1. *Trimountain*, September 18, 1850, Roll 2, Item 4, and *Chariot of Fame*, December 4, 1854, Roll 3, Item 4, Registers of Passengers Arriving in Mass. Port, 1848–1891, Massachusetts Archives; Case Histories, Volume 1, Bridgewater State Almshouse Records, Massachusetts Archives.
2. David J. Rothman, *The Discovery of the Asylum: Social Order and Disorder in the New Republic*, rev. ed. (New Brunswick, NJ: Aldine Transaction, 2002); Gerald N. Grob, *Mental Institutions in America: Social Policy to 1875* (New York: Free Press, 1973); Douglas C. Baynton, "Defectives in the Land: Disability and American Immigration Policy, 1882–1924," *Journal of American Ethnic History* 24, no. 3 (Spring 2005): 31–44.
3. For the plenary power doctrine, see T. Alexander Aleinikoff, *Semblances of Sovereignty: The Constitution, the State, and American Citizenship* (Cambridge, MA: Harvard University Press, 2002), 11–38; Hiroshi Motomura, *Americans in Waiting: The Lost Story of Immigration and Citizenship in the United States* (New York: Oxford University Press, 2006), 15–37.
4. On the political culture of Massachusetts, see Ronald P. Formisano, *The Transformation of Political Culture: Massachusetts Parties, 1790s–1840s* (New York: Oxford University Press, 1983); Dale Baum, *The Civil War Party System: The Case of Massachusetts, 1848–1876* (Chapel Hill: University of North Carolina Press, 1984); Bruce Laurie, *Beyond Garrison: Antislavery and Social Reform* (New York: Cambridge University Press, 2005).
5. Daniel J. Tichenor, *Dividing Lines: The Politics of Immigration Control in America* (Princeton, NJ: Princeton University Press, 2002).
6. On the poverty of women in nineteenth-century America, see Hasia R. Diner, *Erin's Daughters in America: Irish Immigrant Women in the Nineteenth Century* (Baltimore: Johns Hopkins University Press, 1983), 106–119; Christine Stansell, *City of Women: Sex and Class in New York, 1789–1860* (Urbana: University of Illinois Press, 1987), 3–37.
7. For classic works on nativism, see Ray Allen Billington, *The Protestant Crusade, 1800–1860: A Study of the Origins of American Nativism* (1938; Chicago: Quadrangle Books, 1964); John Higham, *Strangers in the Land: Patterns of American Nativism, 1860–1925* (1955; New York: Atheneum, 1970); Oscar Handlin, *Boston's Immigrants: A Study in Acculturation*, rev. ed. (New York: Atheneum, 1968). For a representative work on anti-Irish sentiment, see Dale T. Knobel, *Paddy and the Republic: Ethnicity and Nationality in Antebellum America* (Middletown,

CT: Wesleyan University Press, 1986). The proliferation of "whiteness" studies in the 1990s reinforced this trend by focusing on verbal epithets, anti-Irish cartoons, and other forms of cultural representation. On Irish whiteness, see David R. Roediger, *The Wages of Whiteness: Race and the Making of the American Working Class*, rev. ed. (New York: Verso, 1999); Matthew Frye Jacobson, *Whiteness of a Different Color: European Immigrants and the Alchemy of Race* (Cambridge, MA: Harvard University Press, 1998).

8. For the Know-Nothing movement, see John R. Mulkern, *The Know-Nothing Party in Massachusetts: The Rise and Fall of A People's Movement* (Boston: Northeastern University Press, 1990); Tyler Anbinder, *Nativism & Slavery: The Northern Know Nothings & the Politics of the 1850s* (New York: Oxford University Press, 1992).

9. Gerald L. Neuman, *Strangers to the Constitution: Immigrants, Borders, and Fundamental Law* (Princeton, NJ: Princeton University Press, 1996), 19. The Alien and Sedition Acts of 1798, passed by the Federalists in the midst of escalating diplomatic tension with France, contained a provision that allowed the president to arrest and deport any alien threatening the nation's peace and safety. But President John Adams never implemented his deportation power, and the provision silently expired a few years after its enactment. Marilyn C. Baseler, *"Asylum for Mankind": America, 1607–1800* (Ithaca, NY: Cornell University Press, 1998), 243–309; Terri Diane Halperin, *The Alien and Sedition Acts of 1798: Testing the Constitution* (Baltimore: Johns Hopkins University Press, 2016).

10. For Chinese exclusion, see Alexander Saxton, *The Indispensable Enemy: Labor and the Anti-Chinese Movement in California* (Berkeley: University of California Press, 1971); Charles J. McClain, *In Search of Equality: The Chinese Struggle Against Discrimination in Nineteenth-Century America* (Berkeley: University of California Press, 1994); Lucy E. Salyer, *Laws Harsh as Tigers: Chinese Immigrants and the Shaping of Modern Immigration Law* (Chapel Hill: University of North Carolina Press, 1995); Andrew Gyory, *Closing the Gate: Race, Politics, and the Chinese Exclusion Act* (Chapel Hill: University of North Carolina Press, 1998); Erika Lee, *At America's Gates: Chinese Immigration during the Exclusion Era, 1882–1943* (Chapel Hill: University of North Carolina Press, 2003); Erika Lee and Judy Yung, *Angel Island: Immigrant Gateway to America* (New York: Oxford University Press, 2010).

11. *Chinese Immigration*, 46th Cong, 2d sess., House, Report No. 572, 25, 28–29.

12. For the history of federal immigration policy, see Roger Daniels, *Guarding the Golden Door: American Immigration Policy and Immigrants Since 1882* (New York: Hill and Wang, 2004); Erika Lee, "A Nation of Immigrants and a Gatekeeping Nation: American Immigration Law and Policy," in *A Companion to American Immigration*, ed. Reed Ueda (Malden, MA: Blackwell, 2006), 5–35; Deirdre M. Moloney, *National Insecurities: Immigrants and U.S. Deportation Policy Since 1882* (Chapel Hill: University of North Carolina Press, 2012). On Ellis Island, see Amy L. Fairchild, *Science at the Borders: Immigrant Medical Inspection and the Shaping of the Modern Industrial Labor Force* (Baltimore: Johns Hopkins University Press, 2003); Anna Pegler-Gordon, *In Sight of America: Photography and the Development of U.S. Immigration Policy* (Berkeley: University of California Press, 2009); Vincent J. Cannato, *American Passage: The History of Ellis Island* (New York: HarperCollins, 2009); Ronald H. Bayor, *Encountering Ellis Island: How European Immigrants Entered America* (Baltimore: Johns Hopkins University Press, 2014).

13. *Sacramento Weekly Union*, May 1, 1852.

14. *Philadelphia Public Ledger*, August 8, 1870; *Congressional Record*, 45th Cong., 3d sess., volume 8, p. 797.

15. John Cummings, "Poor-Laws of Massachusetts and New York: With Appendices Containing the United States Immigration and Contract-Labor Laws," *Publications of the American Economic Association* 10, no. 4 (July 1895): 15–135; Roy L. Garis, *Immigration Restriction: A Study of the Opposition to and Regulation of Immigration into the United States* (New York: Macmillan, 1927); Richard J. Purcell, "The New York Commissioners of Emigration and Irish Immigrants: 1847–1860," *Studies: An Irish Quarterly Review* 37, no. 145 (March 1948): 29–42; Benjamin J. Klebaner, "State and Local Immigration Regulation in the United States Before 1882," *International Review of Social History* 3, no. 2 (1958): 269–295; Neuman, *Strangers to the Constitution*; Kunal M. Parker, "State, Citizenship, and Territory: The Legal Construction of Immigrants in Antebellum Massachusetts," *Law and History Review* 19, no. 3 (Autumn 2001): 583–643; Aristide R. Zolberg, *A Nation by Design: Immigration Policy in the Fashioning of America* (Cambridge, MA: Harvard University Press, 2006); Daniel Kanstroom, *Deportation Nation: Outsiders in American History* (Cambridge, MA: Harvard University Press, 2007); Anna O. Law, "Lunatics, Idiots, Paupers, and Negro Seamen—Immigration Federalism and the Early American State," *Studies in American Political Development* 28 (October 2014): 107–128. For the most recent work on state-level immigration control, see Brendan P. O'Malley, "Protecting the Stranger: The Origins of U.S. Immigration Regulation in Nineteenth-Century New York" (PhD diss., City University of New York, 2015). Some northern states, such as Illinois, Indiana, and Oregon, had laws for barring the entry of African Americans. Leon F. Litwack, *North of Slavery: The Negro in the Free States, 1790–1860* (Chicago: University of Chicago Press, 1961). For an overview of legal scholarship on immigration law, see Allison Brownell Tirres, "Who Belongs? Immigration and the Law in American History," in *A Companion to American Legal History*, ed. Sally E. Hadden and Alfred L. Brophy (Malden, MA: Blackwell, 2013), 228–246.

16. For representative works on the relationship between citizenship and immigration laws, see James H. Kettner, *The Development of American Citizenship, 1608–1870* (Chapel Hill: University of North Carolina Press, 1978); Rogers M. Smith, *Civic Ideals: Conflicting Visions of Citizenship in U.S. History* (New Haven, CT: Yale University Press, 1997); Mae M. Ngai, *Impossible Subjects: Illegal Aliens and the Making of Modern America* (Princeton, NJ: Princeton University Press, 2004); Martha Gardner, *The Qualities of a Citizen: Women, Immigration, and Citizenship, 1870–1965* (Princeton, NJ: Princeton University Press, 2005); Motomura, *Americans in Waiting*; Kunal M. Parker, *Making Foreigners: Immigration and Citizenship Law in America, 1600–2000* (New York: Cambridge University Press, 2015).

17. Scholars are increasingly challenging this trend by analyzing how Asian exclusion unfolded on a hemispheric scale in the Americas. Erika Lee, "The 'Yellow Peril' and Asian Exclusion in the Americas," *Pacific Historical Review* 76, no. 4 (November 2007): 537–562; Adam M. McKeown, *Melancholy Order: Asian Migration and the Globalization of Borders* (New York: Columbia University Press, 2008); Kornel Chang, *Pacific Connections: The Making of the U.S.–Canadian Borderlands* (Berkeley: University of California Press, 2012); David Scott Fitzgerald and David Cook-Martín, *Culling the Masses: The Democratic Origins of Racist Immigration Policy in the Americas* (Cambridge, MA: Harvard University

Press, 2014); Elliott Young, *Alien Nation: Chinese Migration in the Americas from the Coolie Era Through World War II* (Chapel Hill: University of North Carolina Press, 2014).

18. Some historians have provided valuable studies on return migration, though a sustained study on Irish return migration has yet to be written. Theodore Saloutos, *They Remember America: The Story of the Repatriated Greek-Americans* (Berkeley: University of California Press, 1956); A. William Hoglund, *Finnish Immigrants in America, 1880–1920* (Madison: University of Wisconsin Press, 1960); Wilbur S. Shepperson, *Emigration & Disenchantment: Portraits of Englishmen Repatriated from the United States* (Norman: University of Oklahoma Press, 1965); Mark Wyman, *Round-Trip America: The Immigrants Return to Europe, 1880–1930* (Ithaca, NY: Cornell University Press, 1996).

19. For major works on the transnational history of Irish migration and Irish Americans, see Kerby A. Miller, *Emigrants and Exiles: Ireland and the Irish Exodus to North America* (New York: Oxford University Press, 1985); Robert James Scally, *The End of Hidden Ireland: Rebellion, Famine, and Emigration* (New York: Oxford University Press, 1995); Kevin Kenny, *Making Sense of the Molly Maguires* (New York: Oxford University Press, 1998); Deirdre M. Moloney, *American Catholic Lay Groups and Transnational Social Reform in the Progressive Era* (Chapel Hill: University of North Carolina Press, 2002); Angela F. Murphy, *American Slavery, Irish Freedom: Abolition, Immigrant Citizenship, and the Transatlantic Movement for Irish Repeal* (Baton Rouge: Louisiana State University Press, 2010); Cian T. McMahon, *The Global Dimensions of Irish Identity: Race, Nation, and the Popular Press, 1840–1880* (Chapel Hill: University of North Carolina Press, 2015); Ely M. Janis, *A Greater Ireland: The Land League and Transatlantic Nationalism in Gilded Age America* (Madison: University of Wisconsin Press, 2015); David Brundage, *Irish Nationalists in America: The Politics of Exile, 1798–1998* (New York: Oxford University Press, 2016).

20. For the problems of present American immigration policy, see Daniel Kanstroom, *Aftermath: Deportation Law and the New American Diaspora* (New York: Oxford University Press, 2012); Tanya Maria Golash-Boza, *Deported: Immigrant Policing, Disposable Labor, and Global Capitalism* (New York: New York University Press, 2015).

21. Herman Melville, *Redburn: His First Voyage* (1849; New York: Penguin Books, 1986), 382.

CHAPTER 1

1. John Crowley, William J. Smyth, and Mike Murphy, eds., *Atlas of the Great Irish Famine* (New York: New York University Press, 2012), 372.

2. June 14 and 21, 1854, June 20, 1855, Board of Guardians Minute Book, BG69/A18, Records of the Cork Poor Law Union, Cork City and County Archives; April 27, 1855, Galway Poor Law Union Minute Book, Galway County Archives.

3. Kevin Kenny, *The American Irish: A History* (New York: Longman, 2000), 100; Gerard Moran, *Sending Out Ireland's Poor: Assisted Emigration to North America in the Nineteenth Century* (Dublin: Four Court Press, 2004), 36.

4. Kenny, *The American Irish*, 7–44; Kerby A. Miller, *Emigrants and Exiles: Ireland and the Irish Exodus to North America* (New York: Oxford University Press, 1985), 137–192; Timothy Meagher, *The Columbia Guide to Irish American History* (New York: Columbia University Press, 2005), 19–59; Maurice J. Bric, *Ireland, Philadelphia and the Re-invention of America, 1760–1800* (Dublin: Four Courts Press, 2008),

1–45; Jay P. Dolan, *The Irish Americans: A History* (New York: Bloomsbury Press, 2008), 3–29.

5. Kenny, *The American Irish*, 23; Dolan, *The Irish Americans*, 19; Miller, *Emigrants and Exiles*, 162–164; Thomas H. O'Connor, *The Boston Irish: A Political History* (Boston: Northeastern University Press, 1995), 9–10.

6. Kenny, *The American Irish*, 23–25; O'Connor, *The Boston Irish*, 11–13. For Ulster migration, see also James G. Leyburn, *The Scotch-Irish: A Social History* (Chapel Hill: University of North Carolina Press, 1962); R. J. Dickson, *Ulster Emigration to Colonial America, 1718–1775* (London: Routledge and Kegan Paul, 1966); Patrick Griffin, *The People with No Name: Ireland's Ulster Scots, America's Scots Irish, and the Creation of a British Atlantic World, 1689–1764* (Princeton, NJ: Princeton University Press, 2001); Kevin Kenny, *Peaceable Kingdom Lost: The Paxton Boys and the Destruction of William Penn's Holy Experiment* (New York: Oxford University Press, 2009); Warren R. Hofstra, ed., *Ulster to America: The Scots-Irish Migration Experience, 1680–1830* (Knoxville: University of Tennessee Press, 2012).

7. Kenny, *The American Irish*, 46; James S. Donnelly Jr., *The Great Irish Potato Famine* (Phoenix Mill, UK: Sutton Publishing, 2001), 3–6.

8. Kenny, *The American Irish*, 46–50; Miller, *Emigrants and Exiles*, 1–25. For land use in nineteenth-century Ireland, see Peter Gray, *Famine, Land and Politics: British Government and Irish Society, 1843–1850* (Dublin: Irish Academic Press, 1999).

9. Kenny, *The American Irish*, 51–53; Miller, *Emigrants and Exiles*, 26–101 (quotation on 32), 201–223.

10. Kenny, *The American Irish*, 45–46; Miller, *Emigrants and Exiles*, 198.

11. Gustave de Beaumont, *Ireland: Social, Political and Religious* (1839), in Peter Gray, *The Irish Famine* (New York: Harry N. Abrams, 1995), 136–137; John M'Gregor, *British America* (Edinburgh, 1833), in Edith Abbott, *Historical Aspects of the Immigration Problem* (Chicago: University of Chicago Press, 1926), 82.

12. Miller, *Emigrants and Exiles*, 200. Emphasis in original.

13. Philip Hone, *The Diary of Philip Hone, 1828–1851*, ed. Allan Nevins (1927; New York: Kraus Reprint, 1969), 209.

14. Kenny, *The American Irish*, 57–59; Miller, *Emigrants and Exiles*, 254–263.

15. Miller, *Emigrants and Exiles*, 54.

16. Henry Inglis, *A Journey throughout Ireland* (1845), in Gray, *The Irish Famine*, 133.

17. Kenny, *The American Irish*, 90–91; Donnelly, *The Great Irish Potato Famine*, 1–3, 6–11. For the social and economic situation of Ireland on the eve of the famine, see Oliver MacDonagh, "The Economy and Society, 1830–45," in *A New History of Ireland V, Ireland Under the Union, I, 1801–70*, ed. W. E. Vaughan (Oxford: Clarendon Press, 1989), 218–241.

18. Kenny, *The American Irish*, 89, 91; Miller, *Emigrants and Exiles*, 281–282; Cormac Ó Gráda, *Black '47 and Beyond: The Great Irish Famine in History, Economy, and Memory* (Princeton, NJ: Princeton University Press, 1999), 13–24, 84–104.

19. Kenny, *The American Irish*, 93–97; Miller, *Emigrants and Exiles*, 282–284, 286–291, 306–307; Donnelly, *The Great Irish Potato Famine*, 41–168; Gray, *Famine, Land and Politics*, 95–338; Ó Gráda, *Black '47*, 47–83; Cecil Woodham-Smith, *Great Hunger: Ireland, 1845–1849* (New York: Harper and Row, 1962), 15–93, 103–205, 285–413; John Mitchel, *The Last Conquest of Ireland (Perhaps)* (Glasgow: R. & T. Washbourne, [1861]), 219.

20. James H. Tuke, *A Visit to Connaught in the Autumn of 1847. A Letter Addressed to the Central Relief Committee of the Society of Friends, Dublin*, 2nd ed. (London: Charles Gilpin, 1848), 23, 26–27. Emphasis in original.

21. *Liberator* (Boston), March 27, 1846.
22. Charles Northend, ed., *Elihu Burritt; A Memorial Volume Containing a Sketch of His Life and Labors, with Selections from His Writings and Lectures, and Extracts from His Private Journals in Europe and America* (New York: D. Appleton, 1879), 52.
23. February 27, March 30, and April 21, 1847, RG. I. 05. 01: John Bernard Fitzpatrick Papers, Archdiocese of Boston Archives. For the famine relief, see Christine Kinealy, *Charity and the Great Hunger in Ireland* (New York: Bloomsbury, 2013).
24. Kenny, *The American Irish*, 97–99; Miller, *Emigrants and Exiles*, 291, 293–298; Ó Gráda, *Black '47*, 104–114.
25. "The Irish Crisis," *Edinburgh Review*, LXXXVII (January 1848), in Abbott, *Historical Aspects of the Immigration Problem*, 112.
26. Robert James Scally, *The End of Hidden Ireland: Rebellion, Famine, and Emigration* (New York: Oxford University Press, 1995), 166–168, 172; Oliver MacDonagh, "The Irish Famine Emigration to the United States," *Perspectives in American History* 10 (1976): 396–397.
27. Kenny, *The American Irish*, 56–57, 100–101; Miller, *Emigrants and Exiles*, 194–199, 252–253; Scally, *The End of Hidden Ireland*, 176–183; Deirdre M. Mageean, "Emigration from Irish Ports," *Journal of American Ethnic History* 13, no. 1 (Fall 1993): 13–19.
28. Miller, *Emigrants and Exiles*, 253. For the nineteenth-century transatlantic passenger business, see also Robert Scally, "Liverpool Ships and Irish Emigrants in the Age of Sail," *Journal of Social History* 17, no. 1 (Autumn 1983): 5–30; Gordon Read, "Liverpool—The Flood-Gate of the Old World: A Study in Ethnic Attitudes," *Journal of American Ethnic History* 13, no. 1 (Fall 1993): 31–47.
29. Kenny, *The American Irish*, 101–102; Miller, *Emigrants and Exiles*, 253–254; Scally, *The End of Hidden Ireland*, 184–216; Woodham-Smith, *Great Hunger*, 270–284.
30. David Hollett, *Passage to the New World: Packet Ships and Irish Famine Emigrants, 1845–1851* (Abergavanny, UK: P.M. Heaton, 1995), 68–69.
31. Herman Melville, *Redburn: His First Voyage* (1849; New York: Penguin, 1986), 276–277.
32. Quotation in Scally, *The End of Hidden Ireland*, 200.
33. MacDonagh, "The Irish Famine Emigration to the United States," 403.
34. Kenny, *The American Irish*, 102–104; Miller, *Emigrants and Exiles*, 292–293, 316; Donnelly, *The Great Irish Potato Famine*, 178–186; Scally, *The End of Hidden Ireland*, 217–229; Donald MacKay, *Flight from Famine: The Coming of the Irish to Canada* (Toronto: McClelland & Stewart, 1992), 260–309; Woodham-Smith, *Great Hunger*, 206–238; Aristide R. Zolberg, *A Nation by Design: Immigration Policy in the Fashioning of America* (Cambridge, MA: Harvard University Press, 2006), 145–147.
35. Massachusetts, *Annual Report of the Superintendent of Alien Passengers for the Port of Boston*, 1850, Senate Doc. 14, 3. Emphasis in original.
36. *Spectator* (London), October 18, 1851, in Abbott, *Historical Aspects of the Immigration Problem*, 127.
37. Scally, *The End of Hidden Ireland*, 220.
38. Case Histories, Volume 1, Bridgewater State Almshouse Records, Massachusetts Archives.
39. *New York Commercial Advertiser*, January 15, 1845.
40. Moran, *Sending Out Ireland's Poor*, 17–34. For Irish assisted emigration, see also Patrick J. Duffy, ed., *To and From Ireland: Planned Migration Schemes c. 1600–2000* (Dublin: Geography Publications, 2004).

41. Moran, *Sending Out Ireland's Poor*, 70–90; Eilish Ellis, *Emigrants from Ireland, 1847–1852: State-Aided Emigration Schemes from Crown Estates in Ireland* (1960; Baltimore: Genealogical Publishing, 1993), 22–59; Sandra Flaherty and Catherine Lavelle, "The State-Aided Emigration from the Crown Estates of Boughill and Irvilloughter, 1848–1849," *Galway Roots: Journal of the Galway Family History Society* 3, Famine Edition (1995): 77–86. In addition to these crown estates, at least eighty-five tenants on the estate of Castlemaine in County Kerry and fifty-six tenants from the Kilconcouse crown estate in King's County were sent to New York via Liverpool between 1848 and 1851.

42. Ellis, *Emigrants from Ireland, 1847–1852*, 10–21. For the Ballykilcline rebellion and assisted emigration, see Scally, *The End of Hidden Ireland*, 82–129, 159–229; Mary Lee Dunn, *Ballykilcline Rising: From Famine Ireland to Immigrant America* (Amherst: University of Massachusetts Press, 2008).

43. Moran, *Sending Out Ireland's Poor*, 35–50; Miller, *Emigrants and Exiles*, 200, 244; Kenny, *The American Irish*, 55–56. For an overview of estate-sponsored emigration, see Patrick J. Duffy, "'Disencumbering Our Crowded Places': Theory and Practice of Estate Emigration Schemes in Mid-Nineteenth Century Ireland," in *To and From Ireland*, 79–104.

44. Petitions of Pat Dullard, dated January 25, 1842, and Patt Henesy, dated January 30, 1842, Applications to Emigrate, Ms. 35524 (1), Prior-Wandesforde Papers, National Library of Ireland.

45. Duffy, "'Disencumbering Our Crowded Places,'" 91–93.

46. Passenger Contract Ticket, D4131/H/8, Miscellaneous letters and papers of Sir Robert Gore-Booth, Lissadell Papers, Public Record Office of Northern Ireland.

47. Emigration Ticket, D3531/P/1, Shirley Papers, Public Record Office of Northern Ireland.

48. Miller, *Emigrants and Exiles*, 296; Moran, *Sending Out Ireland's Poor*, 36.

49. Moran, *Sending Out Ireland's Poor*, 58–64.

50. Donnelly, *The Great Irish Potato Famine*, 96, 138.

51. Tyler Anbinder, "Lord Palmerston and the Irish Famine Emigration," *Historical Journal* 44, no. 2 (2001): 456. For assisted emigration from Palmerston's estate, see also Thomas Power, "The Palmerston Estate in County Sligo: Improvement and Assisted Emigration Before 1850," in *To and From Ireland*, 105–135.

52. Woodham-Smith, *Great Hunger*, 230.

53. Gerard Moran, *Sir Robert Gore Booth and His Landed Estates in County Sligo, 1814–1876: Land, Famine, Emigration and Politics* (Dublin: Four Court Press, 2006), 35.

54. Patrick J. Duffy, "Assisted Emigration from the Shirley Estate, 1843–1854," *Clogher Record* 14, no. 2 (1992): 7, 17.

55. Tyler Anbinder, "From Famine to Five Points: Lord Lansdowne's Irish Tenants Encounter North America's Most Notorious Slum," *American Historical Review* 107, no. 2 (April 2002): 351. For the Lansdowne estate, see also Gerard J. Lyne, *The Lansdowne Estate in Kerry Under the Agency of William Steuart Trench, 1849–1872* (Dublin: Geography Publications, 2001).

56. W. Steuart Trench, *Realities of Irish Life* (London: Longmans, Green, 1869), 113.

57. Trench, *Realities of Irish Life*, 115.

58. Trench, *Realities of Irish Life*, 123–125.

59. Lyne, *The Lansdowne Estate in Kerry Under the Agency of William Steuart Trench*, 43.

60. Trench, *Realities of Irish Life*, 132.

61. Trench, *Realities of Irish Life*, 126.

62. Moran, *Sir Robert Gore Booth and His Landed Estates in County Sligo*, 36.

63. Lyne, *The Lansdowne Estate in Kerry Under the Agency of William Steuart Trench*, 40–41.
64. For samples of the petitions, see Duffy, "Assisted Emigration from the Shirley Estate," 31–45, Appendix 2.
65. Donnelly, *The Great Irish Potato Famine*, 144.
66. Moran, *Sending Out Ireland's Poor*, 60; Kenny, *The American Irish*, 103.
67. Moran, *Sending Out Ireland's Poor*, 61.
68. John O'Connor, *The Workhouses of Ireland: The Fate of Ireland's Poor* (Dublin: Anvil Books, 1995), 161; Emigration Book, p. 10, Ms. 4975, Fitzwilliam Estate Papers, National Library of Ireland. For assisted emigration from the Fitzwilliam estate, see also Jim Rees, *Surplus People: The Fitzwilliam Clearances, 1847–1856* (Cork: Collins Press, 2000).
69. David Fitzpatrick, "Emigration, 1801–70," in *A New History of Ireland V, Ireland Under the Union, I, 1801–70*, 595; Donnelly, *The Great Irish Potato Famine*, 115.
70. David Fitzpatrick, *Irish Emigration, 1801–1921* (Dundalk, Ireland: Economic and Social History Society of Ireland, 1984), 19–20; Moran, *Sending Out Ireland's Poor*, 66–67; Lyne, *The Lansdowne Estate in Kerry Under the Agency of William Steuart Trench*, 71–72.
71. Lyne, *The Lansdowne Estate in Kerry Under the Agency of William Steuart Trench*, 69.
72. Woodham-Smith, *Great Hunger*, 230.
73. Scally, *The End of Hidden Ireland*, 39; Moran, *Sending Out Ireland's Poor*, 95. Private philanthropists conducted assisted emigration as well. Their schemes were generally more organized than those of the government and landlords. For assisted emigration by philanthropists, see Ruth-Ann M. Harris, "'Where the Poor Man Is Not Crushed Down to Exalt the Aristocrat': Vere Foster's Programmes of Assisted Emigration in the Aftermath of the Irish Famine," in *The Meaning of the Famine* (Irish World Wide Vol. 6), ed. Patrick O'Sullivan (London: Leicester University Press, 1997), 172–194.
74. Cited in *New York Herald*, November 10, 1847.
75. Anbinder, "Lord Palmerston and the Irish Famine Emigration," 462; Woodham-Smith, *Great Hunger*, 227–230.
76. Letter from the Colonial Land and Emigration Office to Gore-Booth, November 20, 1847, D4131/H/8, Miscellaneous letters and papers of Sir Robert Gore-Booth, Lissadell Papers; Moran, *Sir Robert Gore Booth and His Landed Estates in County Sligo*, 39; Peter D. Murphy, *Poor Ignorant Children: Irish Famine Orphans in St John, New Brunswick* (Halifax: Saint Mary's University, 1999), 11.
77. Lyne, *The Lansdowne Estate in Kerry Under the Agency of William Steuart Trench*, 72.
78. Letter from the Colonial Land and Emigration Office to Gore-Booth, November 20, 1847, D4131/H/8, Miscellaneous letters and papers of Sir Robert Gore-Booth, Lissadell Papers.
79. Moran, *Sir Robert Gore Booth and His Landed Estates in County Sligo*, 46.
80. Power, "The Palmerston Estate in County Sligo," 132; Moran, *Sir Robert Gore Booth and His Landed Estates in County Sligo*, 45–46.
81. Rees, *Surplus People*, 111–112.
82. Virginia Crossman, *The Poor Law in Ireland, 1838–1948* (Dublin: Dundalgan Press, 2006), 3–18. For the Irish poor law, see also Peter Gray, *The Making of the Irish Poor Law, 1815–1843* (Manchester: Manchester University Press, 2009); Virginia Crossman, *Poverty and the Poor Law in Ireland, 1850–1914* (Liverpool: Liverpool University Press, 2013); Moran, *Sending Out Ireland's Poor*, 123–127. For assisted

emigration from workhouses, see also O'Connor, *The Workhouses of Ireland*, 155–176.

83. Between May 1848 and April 1850, with financial assistance from the Australian authorities, Irish workhouses sent 4,175 orphan girls from 118 unions to Australia. Moran, *Sending Out Ireland's Poor*, 127–136; Kenny, *The American Irish*, 100; Virginia Crossman, *Local Government in Nineteenth-Century Ireland* (Belfast: The Queen's University of Belfast for the Ulster Society of Irish Historical Studies, 1994), 48.

84. Moran, *Sending Out Ireland's Poor*, 136–148; Crossman, *The Poor Law in Ireland*, 29–32; Christine Kinealy, *This Great Calamity: The Irish Famine, 1845–52* (Boulder, CO: Roberts Rinehart, 1995), 309–315.

85. S. C. O'Mahony, "Emigration from the Limerick Workhouse, 1848–1860," *Irish Ancestor* 14, no. 2 (1982): 84.

86. March 3, 1854, Mountbellow Poor Law Union Minute Book, Galway County Archives.

87. April 11, 1855, Board of Guardians Minute Book, BG69/A19, Records of the Cork Poor Law Union.

88. April 27, 1855, Galway Poor Law Union Minute Book; Kenny, *The American Irish*, 100.

89. Admission Registers, Book B, 1847–1852, Saint John Alms House Records, Provincial Archives of New Brunswick.

90. Anbinder, "From Famine to Five Points," 381–385; Tyler Anbinder, "Moving Beyond 'Rags to Riches': New York's Irish Famine Immigrants and Their Surprising Savings Accounts," *Journal of American History* 99, no. 3 (December 2012): 741–770.

91. Moran, *Sending Out Ireland's Poor*, 148–149.

92. O'Mahony, "Emigration from the Limerick Workhouse," 93.

93. See for example *Boston Herald*, April 29, 1851; *Boston Daily Bee*, April 9, 1855.

94. *Boston Daily Bee*, April 19, 1851.

95. For non-Irish assisted emigration, see Benjamin J. Klebaner, "The Myth of Foreign Pauper Dumping in the United States," *Social Service Review* 35, no. 3 (September 1961): 302–309; H. J. M. Johnson, *British Emigration Policy, 1815–1830: 'Shovelling out Paupers'* (Oxford: Oxford University Press, 1972); Katharine Mary Grigsby Franzen, "Free to Leave: Government Assisted Emigration Under the 1834 Poor Law" (PhD diss., University of Virginia, 1996); Wolfgang Helbich and Walter D. Kamphoefner, "The Hour of Your Liberation is Getting Closer and Closer . . .," *Studia Migracyjne—Przeglad Polonijny* 35, no. 3 (2009): 43–58.

CHAPTER 2

1. Walter Harding and Carl Bode, eds., *The Correspondence of Henry David Thoreau* (New York: New York University Press, 1958), 128.

2. *New York Commercial Advertiser*, January 15, 1845.

3. Robert W. Kelso, *The History of Public Poor Relief in Massachusetts 1620–1920* (Boston: Houghton Mifflin Company, 1922), 3–29.

4. On the transition from poor law to immigration law, see Kunal M. Parker, "From Poor Law to Immigration Law: Changing Visions of Territorial Community in Antebellum Massachusetts," *Historical Geography* 28 (2000): 61–85.

5. Kelso, *The History of Public Poor Relief in Massachusetts*, 92; John Cummings, "Poor-Laws of Massachusetts and New York: With Appendices Containing the United States Immigration and Contract-Labor Laws," *Publications of the*

American Economic Association 10, no. 4 (1895): 22–24; Kunal M. Parker, "State, Citizenship, and Territory: The Legal Construction of Immigrants in Antebellum Massachusetts," *Law and History Review* 19, no. 3 (Autumn 2001): 588–590.

6. Acts Relating to the Poor, *The Charters and General Laws of the Colony and Province of Massachusetts Bay*, chapter LXXV (Boston: T. B. Wait, 1814), 173; Cummings, "Poor-Laws of Massachusetts and New York," 21–22.

7. David M. Schneider, *The History of Public Welfare in New York State, 1609–1866* (Chicago: University of Chicago Press, 1938), 47.

8. Schneider, *The History of Public Welfare in New York State*, 51.

9. Josiah Henry Benton, *Warning Out in New England, 1656–1817* (Boston: W. B. Clarke Company, 1911); Benjamin J. Klebaner, "Public Poor Relief in America, 1790–1860" (PhD diss., Columbia University, 1952), 500–506; Elna C. Green, *This Business of Relief: Confronting Poverty in a Southern City, 1740–1940* (Athens: University of Georgia Press, 2003), 9–21.

10. Benton, *Warning Out in New England*, 96. For warning out, see also Allan Kulikoff, "The Progress of Inequality in Revolutionary Boston," *William and Mary Quarterly* 28, no. 3 (1971): 375–412; Douglas Lamar Jones, "The Strolling Poor: Transiency in Eighteenth-Century Massachusetts," *Journal of Social History* 8, no. 3 (Spring 1975): 28–54; Ruth Wallis Herndon, *Unwelcome Americans: Living on the Margin in Early New England* (Philadelphia: University of Pennsylvania Press, 2001); Cornelia H. Dayton and Sharon V. Salinger, *Robert Love's Warnings: Searching for Strangers in Colonial Boston* (Philadelphia: University of Pennsylvania Press, 2014).

11. Herndon, *Unwelcome Americans*, 16–18.

12. Herndon, *Unwelcome Americans*, 5–6; Daniel Kanstroom, *Deportation Nation: Outsiders in American History* (Cambridge, MA: Harvard University Press, 2007), 33–39.

13. Herndon, *Unwelcome Americans*, 14.

14. Martha Branscombe, *The Courts and the Poor Laws in New York State, 1784–1929* (Chicago: University of Chicago Press, 1943), 18, 26–36; Schneider, *The History of Public Welfare in New York State*, 211–230; Raymond A. Mohl, *Poverty in New York, 1783–1825* (New York: Oxford University Press, 1971), 58, 62–65.

15. An Act Ascertaining What Shall Constitute a Legal Settlement of Any Person in Any Town or District within This Commonwealth, so as to Entitle Him to Support therein, in Case He Becomes Poor and Stands in Need of Relief; and for Repealing All Laws heretofore Made Respecting Such Settlement (February 11, 1794), *Acts and Laws of the Commonwealth of Massachusetts*, 1793, chapter 34 (Boston: Wright and Potter, 1895), 439–442; Parker, "State, Citizenship, and Territory," 595–601.

16. An Act Providing for the Relief and Support, Employment and Removal of the Poor, and for Repealing All Former Laws Made for Those Purposes (February 26, 1794), *Acts and Laws of the Commonwealth of Massachusetts*, 1793, chapter 59 (Boston: Wright and Potter, 1895), 491. For the Overseers of the Poor in Boston, see Eric Nellis and Anne Decker Cecere, eds., *The Eighteenth-Century Records of the Boston Overseers of the Poor* (Charlottesville: University of Virginia Press, 2007).

17. Kulikoff, "The Progress of Inequality in Revolutionary Boston," 400–401. The remaining sixty-two were from other American cities such as New York City and Philadelphia. On poverty in eighteenth-century Boston, see also Jared Ross Hardesty, *Unfreedom: Slavery and Dependence in Eighteenth-Century Boston* (New York: New York University Press, 2016).

18. Parker, "State, Citizenship, and Territory," 601–602.
19. An Act Directing the Admission of Town Inhabitants (March 14, 1701), *The Acts and Resolves, Public and Private, of the Province of the Massachusetts Bay*, chapter 23, 1: 452; Cummings, "Poor-Laws of Massachusetts and New York," 30; F. B. Sanborn, "The Poor-Laws of New England," *North American Review* 106, no. 2 (1868): 491.
20. An Act to Prevent the Introduction of Paupers, from Foreign Ports or Places (February 25, 1820), *The General Law of Massachusetts, from the Adoption of the Constitution, to February, 1822*, Vol. II, 1819, chapter 165 (Boston: Wells & Lilly and Cummings & Hilliard, 1823), 531.
21. An Act in Addition to an Act, Entitled, "An Act to Prevent the Introduction of Paupers from Foreign Ports or Places" (March 19, 1831), *The General Laws of Massachusetts. From June 1822, to June 1831*, 1831, chapter 150 (Boston: Hilliard, Gray, Little, and Wilkins, 1832), 381–382.
22. Schneider, *The History of Public Welfare in New York State*, 55; An Act for the Better Settlement and Relief of the Poor (March 7, 1788), in Edith Abbott, *Immigration: Select Documents and Case Records* (Chicago: University of Chicago Press, 1924), 104–105; Gerald L. Neuman, *Strangers to the Constitution: Immigrants, Borders, and Fundamental Law* (Princeton, NJ: Princeton University Press, 1996), 27–28; Benjamin J. Klebaner, "State and Local Immigration Regulation in the United States Before 1882," *International Review of Social History* 3, no. 2 (1958): 272–273; An Act Concerning Passengers in Vessels Coming to the Port of New York (February 11, 1824), in *Immigration: Select Documents and Case Records*, 107; Friedrich Kapp, *Immigration and the Commissioners of Emigration of the State of New York* (New York: The Nation Press, 1870), 45–46.
23. An Act Imposing a Duty on Persons Convicted of Heinous Crimes and to Prevent Poor and Impotent Persons Being Imported, *Laws of the State of Delaware, 1700–1797*, 1740, Vol. 1., chapter lxvi, in Edith Abbott, *Historical Aspects of the Immigration Problem* (Chicago: University of Chicago Press, 1926), 547; *Rules for the Government of the Board of Guardians of the Poor in the City of Philadelphia, Adopted May, 1851* (Philadelphia: King and Baird, 1851), 102; US Senate, *Reports of the Immigration Commission: Immigration Legislation*, 61st Cong., 3d sess., Document No. 758 (Washington, DC: US Government Printing Office, 1911), 603. For colonial and early state immigration legislation, see also Emberson Edward Proper, *Colonial Immigration Laws: A Study of the Regulation of Immigration by the English Colonies in America* (New York: Columbia University Press, 1900); Roy L. Garis, *Immigration Restriction: A Study of the Opposition to and Regulation of Immigration into the United States* (New York: Macmillan, 1927), 1–21.
24. Parker, "State, Citizenship, and Territory," 609; Kapp, *Immigration and the Commissioners of Emigration*, 45.
25. Nicholas P. Canny, "The Ideology of English Colonization: From Ireland to America," *William and Mary Quarterly* 30, no. 4 (October 1973): 575–598, quotation on 587.
26. Thomas H. O'Connor, *The Boston Irish: A Political History* (Boston: Northeastern University Press, 1995), 14.
27. Thomas Colley Grattan, *Civilized America* (London: Bradbury and Evans, 1859), 1: 30; Sven Beckert, *The Monied Metropolis: New York City and the Consolidation of the American Bourgeoisies, 1850–1896* (New York: Cambridge University Press, 2001), 65.
28. O'Connor, *The Boston Irish*, xv–xvi, 61–62.

29. Kevin Kenny, *The American Irish: A History* (New York: Longman, 2000), 40–41; Jay P. Dolan, *The Irish Americans: A History* (New York: Bloomsbury Press, 2008), 32; Joseph A. Conforti, *Imagining New England: Explorations of Regional Identity from the Pilgrims to the Mid-Twentieth Century* (Chapel Hill: University of North Carolina Press, 2001), 121; O'Connor, *The Boston Irish*, 57. On Irish immigrant radicals, see David A. Wilson, *United Irishmen, United States: Immigrant Radicals in the Early Republic* (Ithaca, NY: Cornell University Press, 1998).

30. Dolan, *The Irish Americans*, 55–57; Robert H. Lord, John E. Sexton, and Edward T. Harrington, *History of the Archdiocese of Boston: In the Various Stage of Its Development, 1604 to 1943* (New York: Sheed and Ward, 1944), 2: 126.

31. O'Connor, *The Boston Irish*, 46–49.

32. David H. Bennett, *The Party of Fear: The American Far Right from Nativism to the Militia Movement*, revised and updated ed. (New York: Vintage Books, 1995), 39; Dolan, *The Irish Americans*, 60.

33. For anti-Catholicism in antebellum America, see Ray Allen Billington, *The Protestant Crusade 1800–1860: A Study of the Origins of American Nativism* (1938; Chicago: Quadrangle Books, 1964); Jenny Franchot, *Roads to Rome: The Antebellum Protestant Encounter with Catholicism* (Berkeley: University of California Press, 1994).

34. Oscar Handlin, *Boston's Immigrants: A Study of Acculturation*, rev. ed. (New York: Atheneum, 1968), 91–101, 109–123; Tyler Anbinder, *Five Points: The 19th-Century New York City Neighborhood That Invented Tap Dance, Stole Elections, and Became the World's Most Notorious Slum* (New York: Plume, 2002). For charity and poverty in antebellum cities, see also Robert H. Bremner, *The Discovery of Poverty in the United States* (New York: New York University Press, 1956); Paul Boyer, *Urban Masses and Moral Order in America, 1820–1920* (Cambridge, MA: Harvard University Press, 1978); Maureen Fitzgerald, *Habits of Compassion: Irish Catholic Nuns and the Origins of New York's Welfare System, 1830–1920* (Urbana: University of Illinois Press, 2006); Gunja SenGupta, *From Slavery to Poverty: The Racial Origins of Welfare in New York, 1840–1918* (New York: New York University Press, 2009).

35. Thomas W. Page, "Some Economic Aspects of Immigration Before 1870: I," *Journal of Political Economy* 20, no. 10 (December 1912): 1012.

36. Kenny, *The American Irish*, 60.

37. *Boston Daily Bee*, January 26, 1856.

38. Garis, *Immigration Restriction*, 38.

39. Schneider, *The History of Public Welfare in New York State*, 299.

40. Eric Foner, *Free Soil, Free Labor, Free Men: The Ideology of the Republican Party Before the Civil War* (1970; New York: Oxford University Press, 1995), ix–xxxix, 23–29, 231–232. For the concept of the deserving and undeserving poor, see Michael B. Katz, *The Undeserving Poor: America's Enduring Confrontation with Poverty*, 2nd ed. (New York: Oxford University Press, 2013).

41. Jonathan A. Glickstein, *Concepts of Free Labor in Antebellum America* (New Haven, CT: Yale University Press, 1991), 11–16; Jonathan A. Glickstein, *American Exceptionalism, American Anxiety: Wages, Competition, and Degraded Labor in the Antebellum United States* (Charlottesville: University of Virginia Press, 2002). For the nineteenth-century ideology of labor and productivity, see also Robert J. Steinfeld, *Coercion, Contract, and Free Labor in the Nineteenth Century* (New York: Cambridge University Press, 2001); Andrew Lyndon Knighton,

Idle Threats: Men and the Limits of Productivity in Nineteenth Century America (New York: New York University Press, 2012).

42. Foner, *Free Soil, Free Labor, Free Men*, xvii–xx; Bruce Laurie, *Artisans into Workers: Labor in Nineteenth-Century America* (New York: Hill and Wang, 1989).

43. Massachusetts, *Report of the Joint Special Committee on Alien Passengers*, 1847, Senate Doc. 109, 4–6; Rose May Pirraglia, "The Context of Urban Pauperism: Foreign Immigration and American Economic Growth, 1815–1855" (PhD diss., Columbia University, 1984); Glickstein, *American Exceptionalism, American Anxiety*, 183–210.

44. Massachusetts, *Report of the Select Committee to Whom Was Referred the Subject of the Practicality of Preventing the Introduction of Foreign Paupers into the State*, 1835, House Doc. 60, 15.

45. Massachusetts, *Report of the Select Committee*, 15.

46. Max Berger, "The Irish Emigrant and American Nativism as Seen by British Visitors, 1836–1860," *Pennsylvania Magazine of History and Biography* 70, no. 2 (April 1946): 147.

47. *Baltimore Sun*, September 3, 1839.

48. *Gibbons v. Ogden*, 22 US 1 (1824). In *Gibbons v. Ogden*, the Supreme Court did not entirely deny states' rights to regulate the admission of foreigners. The court admitted, for example, that state quarantine laws constituted part of an "immense mass of legislation" that operated as an exercise of state police power, an authority that was "not surrendered to the General Government." On the case, see Thomas H. Cox, *Gibbons v. Ogden, Law, and Society in the Early Republic* (Athens: Ohio University Press, 2009); Herbert A. Johnson, *Gibbons v. Ogden: John Marshall, Steamboats, and the Commerce Clause* (Lawrence: University Press of Kansas, 2010).

49. *City of New York v. Miln*, 36 US 102 (1837). For the *Miln* case, see Mary Sarah Bilder, "The Struggle Over Immigration: Indentured Servants, Slaves, and Articles of Commerce," *Missouri Law Review* 61, no. 4 (Fall 1996): 799–807; Aristide R. Zolberg, *A Nation by Design: Immigration Policy in the Fashioning of America* (Cambridge, MA: Harvard University Press, 2006), 140–145; Tony Allan Freyer, *The Passenger Cases and the Commerce Clause: Immigrants, Blacks, and States' Rights in Antebellum America* (Lawrence: University Press of Kansas, 2014), 31–41.

50. Edward Bartlett Rugemer, *The Problem of Emancipation: The Caribbean Roots of the American Civil War* (Baton Rouge: Louisiana State University Press, 2008).

51. Neuman, *Strangers to the Constitution*, 34–40. On the Negro Seamen law, see also Michael Alan Schoeppner, "Navigating the Dangerous Atlantic: Racial Quarantines, Black Sailors and United States Constitutionalism" (PhD diss., University of Florida, 2010).

52. Anna O. Law, "Lunatics, Idiots, Paupers, and Negro Seamen—Immigration Federalism and the Early American State," *Studies in American Political Development* 28 (October 2014): 122–124.

53. Rogers M. Smith, *Civic Ideals: Conflicting Visions of Citizenship in U.S. History* (New Haven, CT: Yale University Press, 1997), 226–227.

54. An Act Relating to Alien Passengers (April 20, 1837), *Laws of the Commonwealth of Massachusetts, Passed by the General Court, in the Year 1837 and 1838*, 1837, chapter 238 (Boston: Dutton and Wentworth, 1839), 270–271.

55. Parker, "State, Citizenship, and Territory," 611–612.

56. Lemuel Shattuck, *Report to the Committee of the City Council Appointed to Obtain the Census of Boston for the Year 1845, Embracing Collateral Facts and Statistical*

Researches, Illustrating the History and Condition of the Population, and Their Means of Progress and Prosperity (Boston: John H. Eastburn, 1846), 41.

57. Letters from Anthony Barclay to the Foreign Office, September 19, 1843 and December 30, 1843, HO45/478, Registered Papers, Records of the Home Office, National Archives (UK).

58. Schneider, *The History of Public Welfare in New York State*, 298; E. P. Hutchinson, *Legislative History of American Immigration Policy, 1798–1965* (Philadelphia: University of Pennsylvania Press, 1981), 27.

59. *Foreign Paupers and Naturalization Laws*, 25th Cong., 2d sess., 1838, H. Rep. 1040, 1–2. Emphasis in original; Hutchinson, *Legislative History of American Immigration Policy*, 28–29.

60. *Foreign Paupers and Naturalization Laws*, 20, 34, 35.

61. Dolan, *The Irish Americans*, 61; Bennett, *Party of Fear*, 56–58; Kenneth W. Milano, *The Philadelphia Nativist Riots: Irish Kensington Erupts* (Charleston, SC: History Press, 2013).

62. Tyler Anbinder, *Nativism & Slavery: The Northern Know Nothings & the Politics of the 1850s* (New York: Oxford University Press, 1992), 11–13; Bennett, *Party of Fear*, 53–60.

63. J. D. B. DeBow, *Statistical View of the United States* (Washington, DC: Beverley Tucker, 1854), 117.

64. J. D. B. DeBow, *The Seventh Census, of the United States: 1850* (Washington, DC: Robert Armstrong, 1853), 53, 111; Raymond L. Cohn, *Mass Migration Under Sail: European Immigration to the Antebellum United States* (New York: Cambridge University Press, 2009), 170, 172.

65. Handlin, *Boston's Immigrants*, 240, 256.

66. Massachusetts, *Report of the Joint Special Committee on Alien Passengers and Paupers*, 1848, Senate Doc. 46, 9–10.

67. Shattuck, *Report to the Committee of the City Council Appointed to Obtain the Census of Boston for the Year 1845*, 110.

68. Robert Ernst, *Immigrant Life in New York City, 1825–1863* (1949; Syracuse: Syracuse University Press, 1994), 200–201.

69. Massachusetts, *Report of the Joint Special Committee on Alien Passengers and Paupers*, 6.

70. Anonymous correspondence on foreign paupers, May 12, 1847, Folder 2, Box 2, Boston City Council Joint Committee on Alien Passengers Records, City of Boston Archives.

71. Massachusetts, *Report of the Joint Special Committee on Alien Passengers and Paupers*, 5

72. *New York Commercial Advertiser*, January 15, 1845.

73. *Boston Daily Bee*, February 3, 1847.

74. *Boston Pilot*, April 10, 1847.

75. *Boston Pilot*, May 29 and June 5, 1847. Emphasis in original.

76. *Baltimore Sun*, June 12, 1847.

77. Petitions May–June 1847, Folder 3, Box 2, Boston City Council Joint Committee on Alien Passengers Records.

78. *National Era* (Washington, DC), October 14, 1847. Emphasis in original.

79. *Newburyport Herald*, July 17, 1846.

80. *Boston Pilot*, July 3, 1847.

81. Form of Certificates of Port Physicians, Folder 8, Box 2, Boston City Council Joint Committee on Alien Passengers Records.

82. John Duffy, *A History of Public Health in New York City 1625–1866* (New York: Russell Sage, 1968), 330–332.

83. Neuman, *Strangers to the Constitution*, 42. For state quarantine laws, see Neuman, *Strangers to the Constitution*, 31–34; William J. Novak, *The People's Welfare: Law and Regulation in Nineteenth-Century America* (Chapel Hill: University of North Carolina Press, 1996), 204–217; Law, "Lunatics, Idiots, Paupers, and Negro Seamen," 118–119.

84. *Saint John Morning News*, May 28, 1847; *Halifax Christian Messenger*, June 4, 1847.

85. Letter of Consul William Elliott, June 30, 1847, FO5/473, Consul at Boston, 1847, Records of the Foreign Office, National Archives (UK); Thomas H. O'Connor, *Fitzpatrick's Boston, 1846–1866: John Bernard Fitzpatrick, Third Bishop of Boston* (Boston: Northeastern University Press, 1984), 82–83.

86. Massachusetts, *Report of the Joint Special Committee on Alien Passengers and Paupers*, 8.

87. Kapp, *Immigration and the Commissioners of Emigration*, 45, 50–84.

88. Kapp, *Immigration and the Commissioners of Emigration*, 85–93.

89. Kapp, *Immigration and the Commissioners of Emigration*, 45–50.

90. Freyer, *The Passenger Cases and the Commerce Clause*, 19–20.

91. Massachusetts, *Report of the Joint Special Committee on Alien Passengers*, 8–9.

92. Memorial on Foreign Paupers, Folder 1, Box 2, Boston City Council Joint Committee on Alien Passengers Records.

93. *Boston Daily Advertiser*, May 6, 1847.

94. *Boston Daily Bee*, June 4, 1847; June 14, 1847, Board of Aldermen Summary Minutes with Index, Vol. 25, 1847, City of Boston Archives.

95. Massachusetts, *Report of the Joint Special Committee on Alien Passengers and Paupers*, 3, 14.

96. Hidetaka Hirota, "'The Great Entrepot for Mendicants': Foreign Poverty and Immigration Control in New York State to 1882," *Journal of American Ethnic History* 33, no. 2 (Winter 2014): 11. For the Commissioners of Emigration, see Richard J. Purcell, "The New York Commissioners of Emigration and Irish Immigrants: 1847–1860," *Studies: An Irish Quarterly Review* 37, no. 145 (March 1948): 29–42; John H. Fahey, "James Irwin: Irish Emigrant Agent, New York City, 1846–1858," *New York History* 93, no. 3 (Summer 2012): 219–245; Brendan P. O'Malley, "Protecting the Stranger: The Origins of U.S. Immigration Regulation in Nineteenth-Century New York" (PhD diss., City University of New York, 2015).

97. *Annual Reports of the Commissioners of Emigration of the State of New York: From the Organization of Commission, May 5, 1847, to 1860, Inclusive* (New York: John F. Trow, 1861), Appendix, 2.

98. Kapp, *Immigration and the Commissioners of Emigration*, 125–127; Schneider, *The History of Public Welfare in New York State*, 313; *Annual Reports of the Commissioners of Emigration of the State of New York*, Appendix, 3.

99. Saturday, January 15, 1848, Journals of House of Representatives of the Commonwealth of Massachusetts, State Library of Massachusetts.

100. An Act Concerning Alien Passengers (May 10, 1848), *Acts and Resolves passed by the General Court of Massachusetts in the Year 1848*, 1848, chapter 313 (Boston: Dutton and Wentworth, 1848), 796–799; Cummings, "Poor-Laws of Massachusetts and New York," 40.

101. An Act Concerning Alien Passengers (May 10, 1848), 797–798.

102. Hutchinson, *Legislative History of American Immigration Policy*, 400, 403–404.
103. An Act Concerning Alien Passengers (May 10, 1848), 798.

CHAPTER 3

1. *Boston Daily Bee*, May 18, 1848; May 13, 1848, Item 1, Roll 1, Registers of Passengers arriving in Mass. Port, 1848–1891, Massachusetts Archives.
2. Massachusetts, *Annual Report of the Superintendent of Alien Passengers for the Port of Boston*, 1850, Senate Doc. 14, 3. Emphasis in original.
3. *Boston Daily Bee*, November 7, 1848.
4. *Annual Reports of the Commissioners of Emigration of the State of New York: From the Organization of Commission, May 5, 1847, to 1860, Inclusive* (New York: John F. Trow, 1861), 106.
5. *Passenger Cases*, 48 US 283 (1849).
6. *Passenger Cases*, 48 US 283 (1849).
7. *Passenger Cases*, 48 US 283 (1849). On the *Passenger Cases*, see Mary Sarah Bilder, "The Struggle over Immigration: Indentured Servants, Slaves, and Articles of Commerce," *Missouri Law Review* 61, no. 4 (Fall 1996): 812–819; Rogers M. Smith, *Civic Ideals: Conflicting Visions of Citizenship in U.S. History* (New Haven, CT: Yale University Press, 1997), 226–228; Aristide R. Zolberg, *A Nation by Design: Immigration Policy in the Fashioning of America* (Cambridge, MA: Harvard University Press, 2006), 147–150; Tony Allan Freyer, *The Passenger Cases and the Commerce Clause: Immigrants, Blacks, and States' Rights in Antebellum America* (Lawrence: University Press of Kansas, 2014).
8. *Boston Herald*, January 7, 1850.
9. *Acts and Resolves Passed by the General Court of Massachusetts, in the Years 1849, 1850, 1851* (Boston: Dutton and Wentworth, 1851), 266.
10. Caleb S. Woodhull, 7, Box 1202, Records of the Office of the Mayor, New York Municipal Archives.
11. *The Eighth Annual Report of the New York Association for Improving the Condition of the Poor, for the Year 1851* (New York: John F. Trow, 1851), 24.
12. Robert Ernst, *Immigrant Life in New York City, 1825–1863* (1949; Syracuse: Syracuse University Press, 1994), 201.
13. Tyler Anbinder, "From Famine to Five Points: Lord Lansdowne's Irish Tenants Encounter North America's Most Notorious Slum," *American Historical Review* 107, no. 2 (April 2002): 356–365.
14. Anbinder, "From Famine to Five Points," 368–370; *Boston Daily Advertiser*, April 2, 1851.
15. *Boston Daily Bee*, May 9, 1851.
16. *Boston Daily Bee*, June 11, 1851.
17. An Act to Amend Certain Acts Concerning Passengers Coming to the City of New York (April 11, 1849), *Laws of the State of New York, Passed at the Seventy Second Session of the Legislature*, chapter 350 (Troy: Albert W. Scribner and Albert West, 1849), 505–506; An Act Relating to Alien Passengers (March 20, 1850), *Acts and Resolves Passed by the General Court of Massachusetts, in the Years 1849, 1850, 1851*, chapter 105, 338–339.
18. Gerald L. Neuman, *Strangers to the Constitution: Immigrants, Borders, and Fundamental Law* (Princeton, NJ: Princeton University Press, 1996), 26, 28; Kunal M. Parker, "State, Citizenship, and Territory: The Legal Construction of Immigrants in Antebellum Massachusetts," *Law and History Review* 19, no. 3 (Autumn 2001): 624–625.

19. An Act to Amend Certain Acts Concerning Passengers Coming to the City of New York (April 11, 1849), *Laws of the State of New York, Passed at the Seventy Second Session of the Legislature*, chapter 350, 506. Emphasis added.

20. An Act to Amend . . . Acts Concerning Passengers Coming to the City of New York, and the Public Health (July 11, 1851), *Laws of the State of New York, Passed at the Seventy Fourth Session of the Legislature*, chapter 523 (Albany: Charles Van Benthuysen, 1851), 971–972.

21. Anbinder, "From Famine to Five Points," 366; Gerard Moran, *Sending Out Ireland's Poor: Assisted Emigration to North America in the Nineteenth Century* (Dublin: Four Court Press, 2004), 139.

22. *Annual Reports of the Commissioners of Emigration*, 105.

23. *Annual Reports of the Commissioners of Emigration*, 135, 157, 397; Raymond L. Cohn, *Mass Migration under Sail: European Immigration to the Antebellum United States* (New York: Cambridge University Press, 2009), 163–165.

24. *Annual Reports of the Commissioners of Emigration*, 156.

25. Cited in *Charleston Mercury*, October 3, 1854.

26. *The Revised Statutes of the Commonwealth of Massachusetts, Passed November 4, 1835*, chapter 46, (Boston: Dutton and Wentworth, 1836), 371–372.

27. An Act Relating to Alien Passengers (March 20, 1850), *Acts and Resolves Passed by the General Court of Massachusetts, in the Years 1849, 1850, 1851*, chapter 105, 339; Parker, "State, Citizenship, and Territory," 625.

28. *Boston Herald*, September 13, 1851; *Boston Daily Bee*, September 15, 1851.

29. *Boston Evening Transcript*, September 8, 1851; *New York Irish-American*, November 1, 1851.

30. Massachusetts, *Report of the Superintendent of Alien Passengers for the Port of Boston*, 1851, Senate Doc. 10, 5; *Boston Daily Advertiser*, May 20, 1851.

31. From William Elliott to John Bidwell, June 30, 1847, FO5/473, Letters of Consuls, 1847, Records of the Foreign Office, National Archives (UK).

32. An Act to Appoint a Board of Commissioners in Relation to Alien Passengers and State Paupers (May 24, 1851), *Acts and Resolves Passed by the General Court of Massachusetts, in the Years 1849, 1850, 1851*, chapter 342, 848.

33. An Act to Appoint a Board of Commissioners in Relation to Alien Passengers and State Paupers (May 24, 1851), *Acts and Resolves Passed by the General Court of Massachusetts, in the Years 1849, 1850, 1851*, chapter 342, 847.

34. Massachusetts, *Annual Report of the Superintendent of Alien Passengers for the Port of Boston*, 1852, 6.

35. *Boston Evening Transcript*, July 1, 1851.

36. *Boston Daily Bee*, September 14, 1852.

37. Massachusetts, *Annual Report of the Commissioners of Alien Passengers and Foreign Paupers*, 1852, 5–6; Parker, "State, Citizenship, and Territory," 625–626.

38. An Act in Relation to Paupers Having No Settlement in This Commonwealth (May 20, 1852), *Acts and Resolves Passed by the General Court of Massachusetts, in the Years 1852*, chapter 275 (Boston: White and Potter, 1852), 190–193. On the history of almshouses in Massachusetts, see David Wagner, *The Poorhouse: America's Forgotten Institution* (Lanham, MD: Rowman & Littlefield, 2005); Heli Meltsner, *The Poorhouses of Massachusetts: A Cultural and Architectural History* (Jefferson, NC: McFarland, 2012).

39. City of Boston, *Report of the Board of Visitors of the Boston Lunatic Hospital*, 1851, City Doc. 72, 11.

40. Massachusetts, *Twenty-First Annual Report of the Trustees of the State Lunatic Hospital, at Worcester*, 1854, Senate Doc. 1, 7; Massachusetts, *Annual Report of the Commissioners of Alien Passengers and Foreign Paupers*, 1854, Senate Doc. 158, 12.

41. An Act Concerning Lunatic State Paupers, and Admission to the State Pauper Establishments (April 29, 1854), *Acts and Resolves Passed by the General Court of Massachusetts, in the Years 1854*, chapter 437 (Boston: William White, 1854), 344–345.

42. David J. Rothman, *The Discovery of the Asylum: Social Order and Disorder in the New Republic*, rev. ed. (New Brunswick, NJ: Aldine Transaction, 2002), 122; Gerald N. Grob, *Mental Institutions in America: Social Policy to 1875* (New York: Free Press, 1973), 221–256; Hasia R. Diner, *Erin's Daughters in America: Irish Immigrant Women in the Nineteenth Century* (Baltimore: Johns Hopkins University Press, 1983), 109.

43. Zolberg, *A Nation by Design*, 110–113, 145–147, 156–158. Congress passed another passenger law in 1855.

44. *Passenger Cases*, 48 US 283 (1849).

45. For the history of major American port cities, see M. Mark Stolarik, ed., *Forgotten Doors: The Other Ports of Entry to the United States* (Cranbury, NJ: Associated University Presses, 1988).

46. *Rules for the Government of the Board of Guardians of the Poor Adopted May, 1851* (Philadelphia: King and Baird, 1851), 18, 100–101, 103–104; *Rules Adopted by Board*, 1844, 14, Records of the Guardians of the Poor, Philadelphia City Archives; August 20, 1849, Minutes, Records of the Guardians of the Poor; Priscilla Ferguson Clement, *Welfare and the Poor in the Nineteenth-Century City: Philadelphia, 1800–1854* (Cranbury, NJ: Associated University Presses, 1985), 55.

47. See for example, February 19, 1849, February 26, 1849, Minutes, Records of the Guardians of the Poor.

48. January 21, 1856, Minutes, Records of the Guardians of the Poor. For Irish poverty in antebellum Philadelphia, see J. Matthew Gallman, *Receiving Erin's Children: Philadelphia, Liverpool, and the Irish Famine Migration, 1845–1855* (Chapel Hill: University of North Carolina Press, 2000), 48–85; Dennis Clark, *The Irish in Philadelphia: Ten Generations of Urban Experience* (Philadelphia: Temple University Press, 1973), 24–60.

49. *Foreign Pauperism in Philadelphia: A Memorial to the Legislature of Pennsylvania, Exhibiting Reasons for the Amendment of Certain Laws in Relation to the Poor and to Foreign Emigrants, with the Bill Annexed* (Philadelphia, 1851), 7; *Philadelphia Public Inquirer*, December 3, 1851.

50. *Foreign Pauperism in Philadelphia*, 5.

51. *Report of the Delegation Appointed by the Philadelphia Emigrant Society of the Emigration Laws in the State of New York: Together with a Memorial to the Legislature of Pennsylvania Praying That Honorable Body to Enact Similar Laws* (Philadelphia: Merrihew and Thompson, 1854), 2, 10, 11; Gallman, *Receiving Erin's Children*, 42–45.

52. *Report of the Executive Committee to the Board of Directors of the Emigrant's Friend Society, Established, April, 1848; Foreign Pauperism in Philadelphia*, 3, 5, 9; Gallman, *Receiving Erin's Children*, 37–40.

53. Tyler Anbinder, *Nativism & Slavery: The Northern Know Nothings & the Politics of the 1850s* (New York: Oxford University Press, 1992), 66–68, 127–128, 150–157. On antebellum Pennsylvania politics, see also John F. Coleman, *The Disruption*

of the Pennsylvania Democracy, 1848–1860 (Harrisburg: Pennsylvania Historical and Museum Commission, 1975).

54. For a summary of passenger laws in Pennsylvania, see Frank F. Brightly, *A Digest of the Laws and Ordinances of the City of Philadelphia* (Philadelphia: Kay & Brothers, 1887), 453–456.

55. W. Darrell Overdyke, *The Know-Nothing Party in the South* (Baton Rouge: Louisiana State University Press, 1950); Jean H. Baker, *Ambivalent Americans: The Know-Nothing Party in Maryland* (Baltimore: Johns Hopkins University Press, 1977); Randall M. Miller, "The Enemy Within: Some Effects of Foreign Immigrants on Antebellum Southern Cities," *Southern Studies* 24, no. 1 (1985): 30–53.

56. David T. Gleeson, *The Irish in the South, 1815–1877* (Chapel Hill: University of North Carolina Press, 2001), 94–120. For the southern view of immigration, see also Rowland T. Berthoff, "Southern Attitudes Toward Immigration, 1865–1914," *Journal of Southern History* 17, no. 3 (August 1951): 328–360. The necessity of white settlers similarly prevented the growth of border control policy in the Midwest. Interior states without ocean ports, such as Illinois and Ohio, received a large number of immigrants, including indigent ones, who came from port cities via canals and railroads. Although immigrant poverty became a social and public health problem, the region's extensive reliance on the labor of newcomers for its economic and physical growth made business and political leaders in the interior states little interested in disrupting the inflow of settlers by developing regulatory immigration policy. Nativism emerged in antebellum midwestern cities with a heavy concentration of immigrants, but nativists there usually pursued issues other than border control, such as temperance. David H. Bennett, *The Party of Fear: The American Far Right from Nativism to the Militia Movement*, revised and updated ed. (New York: Vintage Books, 1995), 135–141; Mimi Cowan, "Immigrants, Nativists, and the Making of Chicago, 1835–1893" (PhD diss., Boston College, 2015), 11–46.

57. Marcus Lee Hansen, *The Atlantic Migration 1607–1860: A History of the Continuing Settlement of the United States* (New York: Harper and Brothers, 1961), 258; *Baltimore Sun*, January 24, 1844; *Baltimore Sun*, February 9, 1850.

58. The 1833 act also allowed two ethnic societies, the German Society of Maryland and the Hibernian Society of Baltimore, to use portions of collected head money for the care of newcomers. An Act Relating to the Importation of Passengers (March 22, 1833), *Maryland State Laws*, 1833, chapter 303, in US Senate, *Reports of the Immigration Commission: Immigration Legislation*, 61st Cong., 3d sess., Document No. 758, 683–684.

59. Cohn, *Mass Migration Under Sail*, 156–159.

60. J. D. B. DeBow, *Statistical View of the United States* (Washington, DC: Beverley Tucker, 1854), 46.

61. Benjamin J. Klebaner, "State and Local Immigration Regulation in the United States Before 1882," *International Review of Social History* 3, no. 2 (1958): 280, 293–294; Hansen, *The Atlantic Migration*, 259.

62. Joseph Logsdon, "Immigration through the Port of New Orleans," in *Forgotten Doors*, 109–110; Randall M. Miller, "'Immigration through the Port of New Orleans': A Comment," in *Forgotten Doors*, 133–135.

63. Neuman, *Strangers to the Constitution*, 37–39, 214; Michael Alan Schoeppner, "Navigating the Dangerous Atlantic: Racial Quarantines, Black Sailors and United States Constitutionalism" (PhD diss., University of Florida, 2010), 264–297.

64. *San Francisco Bulletin*, March 2, 1863.
65. An Act Concerning Passengers Arriving in the Ports of the State of California (May 3, 1852), *The Statutes of California, Passed at the Third Session of the Legislature*, chapter 36 (San Francisco: G. K. Fitch & Co., and V. E. Geiger & Co., 1852), 78–82.
66. Lucy E. Salyer, *Laws Harsh as Tigers: Chinese Immigrants and the Shaping of Modern Immigration Law* (Chapel Hill: University of North Carolina Press, 1995), 7–8; Charles J. McClain, *In Search of Equality: The Chinese Struggle Against Discrimination in Nineteenth-Century America* (Berkeley: University of California Press, 1994), 9–10; Jean Pfaelzer, *Driven Out: The Forgotten War Against Chinese Americans* (New York: Random House, 2007), 36; Mae M. Ngai, "Chinese Gold Miners and the 'Chinese Question' in Nineteenth-Century California and Victoria," *Journal of American History* 101, no. 4 (March 2015): 1084.
67. *Sacramento Weekly Union*, May 1, 1852. On anti-Chinese sentiment in California, see also Alexander Saxton, *The Indispensable Enemy: Labor and the Anti-Chinese Movement in California* (Berkeley: University of California Press, 1971); Scott Zesch, *The Chinatown War: Chinese Los Angeles and the Massacre of 1871* (New York: Oxford University Press, 2012).
68. *Journal of the Seventh Session of the Legislature of the State of California* (Sacramento: James Allen, 1856), 39–40; *Journal of the Proceedings of the Assembly*, April 26, 1852, p. 667.
69. An Act to Discourage the Immigration to This State of Persons who Cannot Become Citizens Thereof (April 28, 1855), *The Statutes of California, Passed at the Sixth Session of the Legislature*, chapter 153 (Sacramento: B. B. Redding, 1855), 194.
70. An Act Amendatory of "An Act to Provide for the Protection of Foreigners, and to Define Their Liabilities and Privileges" (May 13, 1854), *The Statutes of California, Passed at the Fifth Session of the Legislature*, chapter 49 (Sacramento: B. B. Redding, 1854), 55; Pfaelzer, *Driven Out*, 3–46. For anti-Chinese legislation in antebellum California, see also McClain, *In Search of Equality*, 12–30; Mark Kanazawa, "Immigration, Exclusion, and Taxation: Anti-Chinese Legislation in Gold Rush California," *Journal of Economic History* 65, no. 3 (September 2005): 779–805; Stacey L. Smith, *Freedom's Frontier: California and the Struggle over Unfree Labor, Emancipation, and Reconstruction* (Chapel Hill: University of North Carolina Press, 2013), 80–108.
71. McClain, *In Search of Equality*, 18.
72. An Act to Prevent the Further Immigration of Chinese or Mongolians to This State (April 26, 1858), *The Statute of California, Passed at the Ninth Session of the Legislature*, chapter 313 (Sacramento: John O'Meara, 1858), 295–296.
73. *Journal of the House of Assembly of California at the Tenth Session of the Legislature* (Sacramento: John O'Meara, 1859), 467; McClain, *In Search of Equality*, 18.
74. *Journal of the House of Assembly of California at the Tenth Session of the Legislature*, 467–468.
75. McClain, *In Search of Equality*, 24–31; Salyer, *Laws Harsh as Tigers*, 8–9.
76. *New York Irish-American*, January 18, 1851.
77. *New York Irish-American*, January 20, 1850.
78. *Boston Pilot*, March 23, 1850.
79. *New York Irish-American*, January 20, 1850.
80. *New York Citizen*, March 15, 1856.
81. *New York Irish-American*, January 27, 1850.

82. *American Celt* (Boston), September 21, 1850.
83. *Boston Pilot*, April 19, 1851.
84. *Boston Pilot*, May 3, 1851.
85. *New York Irish-American*, April 26, 1851; *Boston Pilot*, May 3, 1851; *Boston Pilot*, June 7, 1851.
86. *New York Irish-American*, April 26, 1851.
87. *Boson Pilot*, May 17, 1851. Emphasis in original.
88. *Boson Pilot*, May 17, 1851. Emphasis in original.
89. *Boston Evening Transcript*, October 8, 1851.
90. *Boston Evening Transcript*, September 25, 1851; *Boston Evening Transcript*, October 8, 1851.
91. Anbinder, *Nativism & Slavery*, 3; Alexander Keyssar, *The Right to Vote: The Contested History of Democracy in the United States* (New York: Basic Books, 2000), 82.
92. Anbinder, *Nativism & Slavery*, 43–52.
93. Oscar Handlin, *Boston's Immigrants: A Study in Acculturation*, rev. ed. (New York: Atheneum, 1968), 200–201; John R. Mulkern, *The Know-Nothing Party in Massachusetts: The Rise and Fall of A People's Movement* (Boston: Northeastern University Press, 1990), 68–69; Bruce Laurie, *Beyond Garrison: Antislavery and Social Reform* (New York: Cambridge University Press, 2005), 272–296.
94. *Boston Daily Bee*, September 19, 1854, September 20, 1854, October 6, 1854.
95. *Know-Nothing and American Crusader* (Boston), June 3, 1854.
96. *Boston Daily Bee*, October 5, November 10, 1854.
97. *Boston Daily Bee*, September 26, September 27, 1854.
98. *Boston Daily Bee*, October 16, 1854. Emphasis in original.
99. Martin Duberman, *Charles Francis Adams, 1807–1886* (Stanford: Stanford University Press, 1960), 194.
100. Cohn, *Mass Migration Under Sail*, 156.
101. Daniel J. Tichenor, *Dividing Lines: The Politics of Immigration Control in America* (Princeton, NJ: Princeton University Press, 2002), 59.
102. Ernst, *Immigrant Life in New York City*, 162.
103. O'Connor, *The Boston Irish*, 70.
104. Thomas H. O'Connor, *Fitzpatrick's Boston, 1846–1866: John Bernard Fitzpatrick, Third Bishop of Boston* (Boston: Northeastern University Press, 1984), 96.
105. Laurie, *Beyond Garrison*, 8–14, 102–104, 177–178, 273–275.

CHAPTER 4

1. T. McIntyre, August 27, 1855, T2722/1, Sample Family Emigrant Papers, Public Record Office of Northern Ireland; *Boston Daily Bee*, August 28, 1855.
2. John R. Mulkern, *The Know-Nothing Party in Massachusetts: The Rise and Fall of A People's Movement* (Boston: Northeastern University Press, 1990), 61–86; Tyler Anbinder, *Nativism & Slavery: The Northern Know Nothings & the Politics of the 1850s* (New York: Oxford University Press, 1992), ix, 52–102, 127–128; Thomas H. O'Connor, *The Boston Irish: A Political History* (Boston: Northeastern University Press, 1995), 76.
3. Anbinder, *Nativism & Slavery*, 104–106.
4. Ray Allen Billington, *The Protestant Crusade, 1800–1860: A Study of the Origins of American Nativism* (1938; Chicago: Quadrangle Books, 1964), 412–415; Anbinder, *Nativism & Slavery*, 135–142; O'Connor, *The Boston Irish*, 76–77; Mulkern, *The Know-Nothing Party in Massachusetts*, 102–103.

5. See for example *New York Herald*, December 31, 1854; *New York Evening Express*, January 23, 1855; *Boston Daily Bee*, April 5, 1855; *New Orleans Picayune*, September 11, 1855.

6. Erastus Brooks, *American Citizenship and the Progress of American Civilization: An Oration Delivered before the Order of United Americans, at the Academy of Music, February 22d, 1858* (New York: C. E. Gildersleve, 1858), 17.

7. Thomas R. Whitney, *A Defence of the American Policy, as Opposed to the Encroachments of Foreign Influence, and Especially to the Interference of the Papacy in the Political Interests and Affairs of the United States* (New York: DeWitt & Davenport, 1856), 180, 185. On Whitney, see Bruce Levine, "Conservatism, Nativism, and Slavery: Thomas R. Whitney and the Origins of the Know-Nothing Party," *Journal of American History* 88, no. 2 (September 2001): 455–488.

8. *A Bill to Prevent the Introduction into the United States of Foreign Criminals and Paupers*, HR 124, 34th Cong., 1st sess., 1856; *Congressional Globe*, 33rd Cong., 2d sess., 1855, 1182. The consular inspection of immigrants was formally included in federal immigration law in 1924.

9. *The Know Nothing Almanac and True Americans' Manual, for 1856* (New York: DeWitt & Davenport, 1855), 20; *The Know Nothing Almanac and True Americans' Manual, for 1855* (New York: DeWitt & Davenport, 1854), 23. Emphasis in original.

10. *New York Times*, July 23, 1857.

11. Robert Ernst, *Immigrant Life in New York City, 1825–1863* (1949; Syracuse: Syracuse University Press, 1994), 54, 194, 200, 201; Josiah Curtis, *Report of the Joint Special Committee of the Census of Boston, May, 1855, Including the Report of the Censors, with Analytical and Sanitary Observations* (Boston: Moore & Crosby, 1856), 3; Oscar Handlin, *Boston's Immigrants: A Study in Acculturation*, rev. ed. (New York: Atheneum, 1968), 256.

12. *Census of the State of New York, for 1855; Taken in Pursuance of Article Third of the Constitution of the State, and of Chapter Sixty-Four for the Laws of 1855* (Albany: Charles Van Benthuysen, 1857), xl. For the Know-Nothings in New York, see Thomas Joseph Curran, "Know Nothings of New York" (PhD diss., Columbia University, 1963).

13. *New York Evening Express*, January 10, 1855.

14. *Philadelphia Public Ledger*, August 10, 1855.

15. New York, *Reports of County Superintendents of the Poor*, 1856, Assembly Doc. 214, in Edith Abbott, *Immigration: Select Documents and Case Records* (Chicago: University of Chicago Press, 1924), 163.

16. Massachusetts, *Address of His Excellency Henry J. Gardner, to the Two Branches of the Legislature of Massachusetts, January 9, 1855*, 1855, Senate Doc. 3, 15–16, 24–25; Kunal M. Parker, "State, Citizenship, and Territory: The Legal Construction of Immigrants in Antebellum Massachusetts," *Law and History Review* 19, no. 3 (Autumn 2001): 630.

17. Massachusetts, *Address of His Excellency Henry J. Gardner, to the Two Branches of the Legislature of Massachusetts, January 9, 1855*, 17–19, 22.

18. Massachusetts, *Annual Report of the Commissioners of Alien Passengers and Foreign Paupers*, 1856, House Doc. 41, 29.

19. See appendix C, this volume.

20. Massachusetts, *Annual Report of the Commissioners of Alien Passengers and Foreign Paupers*, 1854, Senate Doc. 158, 5–6; Admission Registers, Volume 8, Monson Almshouse Records, Massachusetts Archives.

21. See appendix C, this volume.

22. Massachusetts, *Third Annual Report of the Inspectors of the State Almshouse, at Tewksbury*, 1857, Senate Doc. 6, 9.

23. Histories of Alien Residents of Almshouses and Other Institutions, 1852–1857, Massachusetts Archives, 193.

24. Case Histories, Volume 1, Bridgewater State Almshouse Records, Massachusetts Archives.

25. Massachusetts, *Sixth Annual Report of the Inspectors of the State Almshouse, at Bridgewater*, 1859, Public Doc. 28, 9.

26. Case Histories, Volume 1, Monson State Almshouse Records; Admission Registers, Volume 8, Monson Almshouse Records.

27. Inmate Case Histories, Reel 1, Volume 1, Tewksbury State Almshouse Records, Massachusetts Archives.

28. *New York Evening Express*, May 15, 1855; Friedrich Kapp, *Immigration and the Commissioners of Emigration of the State of New York* (New York: The Nation Press, 1870), 105–111; Vincent J. Cannato, *American Passage: The History of Ellis Island* (New York: HarperCollins, 2009), 30–36. For Castle Garden, see also George J. Svejda, *Castle Garden as an Immigrant Depot, 1855–1890* (Washington, DC: National Park Service, 1968). For nativist perceptions of the sanitary threat of immigrants, see Alan M. Kraut, *Silent Travelers: Germs, Genes, and the "Immigrant Menace"* (Baltimore: Johns Hopkins University Press, 1995).

29. *New York Herald*, February 16, 1855. On Fernando Wood, see Jerome Mushkat, *Fernando Wood: A Political Biography* (Kent, OH: Kent State University Press, 1990).

30. *New York Herald*, December 24, 1854; *New York Citizen*, December 30, 1854; *New York Evening Express*, February 13 and 27, 1855; An Act to Prevent the Introduction of Foreign Convicts (April 25, 1833), *Laws of the State of New York, Passed at the Fifty-Sixth Session of the Legislature*, chapter 230 (Albany: E. Croswell, 1833), 313–314. On state legislation for foreign criminals, see Gerald L. Neuman, *Strangers to the Constitution: Immigrants, Borders, and Fundamental Law* (Princeton, NJ: Princeton University Press, 1996), 21–23.

31. *New York Evening Express*, February 27, 1855; *Boston Daily Advertiser*, March 7, 1855. In the late nineteenth century, Chinese immigrants used habeas corpus to challenge federal Chinese exclusion policy and to secure admission into the United States. For the use of habeas corpus by the Chinese, see Lucy E. Salyer, *Laws Harsh as Tigers: Chinese Immigrants and the Shaping of Modern Immigration Law* (Chapel Hill: University of North Carolina Press, 1995).

32. *New York Evening Express*, February 27, 1855.

33. *New York Evening Express*, October 16, 1855.

34. *New York Evening Express*, October 17, 1855. Emphasis added. For the antebellum views of paupers and criminals, see David J. Rothman, *The Discovery of the Asylum: Social Order and Disorder in the New Republic*, rev. ed. (New Brunswick, NJ: Aldine Transaction, 2002).

35. Cited in *London Morning Chronicle*, September 7, 1859.

36. Cited in *National Era* (Washington, DC), March 22, 1855.

37. US Congress, *Foreign Criminals and Paupers*, 137.

38. Massachusetts, *Annual Report of the Commissioners of Alien Passengers and Foreign Paupers*, 1855, House Doc. 123, 46.

39. Massachusetts Constitutional Convention, *Official Report of the Debates and Proceedings in the State Convention, Assembled May 4th, 1853, to Revise and Amend*

the Constitution of the Commonwealth of Massachusetts (Boston: White & Potter, 1853), 3: 461.

40. Massachusetts, *Annual Report of the Commissioners of Alien Passengers and Foreign Paupers*, 1855, 45–46. Emphasis in original. Parker, "State, Citizenship, and Territory," 630.

41. For the rendition of Anthony Burns, see Albert J. von Frank, *The Trial of Anthony Burns: Freedom and Slavery in Emerson's Boston* (Cambridge, MA: Harvard University Press, 1998); Earl M. Maltz, *Fugitive Slave on Trial: The Anthony Burns Case and Abolitionist Outrage* (Lawrence: University of Kansas Press, 2010). On fugitive slave law, see also Eric Foner, *Gateway to Freedom: The Hidden History of the Underground Railroad* (New York: Norton, 2015).

42. An Act to Protect the Rights and Liberties of the People of the Commonwealth of Massachusetts (May 21, 1855), *Acts and Resolves Passed by the General Court of Massachusetts, in the Year 1855*, chapter 489 (Boston: William White, 1855), 924–929; Mulkern, *The Know-Nothing Party in Massachusetts*, 104–105; Anbinder, *Nativism & Slavery*, 155–157; Bruce Laurie, *Beyond Garrison: Antislavery and Social Reform* (New York: Cambridge University Press, 2005), 275–282.

43. O'Connor, *The Boston Irish*, 83–84; von Frank, *The Trial of Anthony Burns*, 248.

44. Massachusetts, *Annual Report of the Commissioners of Alien Passengers and Foreign Paupers*, 1855, 47.

45. Edward Everett Hale, *Letters on Irish Emigration* (Boston: Phillips, Sampson, 1852), 52–53.

46. Cited in *Worcester National Aegis*, November 8, 1854.

47. February 20, 1855, Journal of the House of Representatives of the Commonwealth of Massachusetts, State Library of Massachusetts.

48. February 22, 1855, Journal of the House of Representatives of the Commonwealth of Massachusetts; *Boston Daily Advertiser*, February 23, 1855; *Boston Post*, February 23, 1855.

49. Massachusetts, *Report on Pauper Immigration*, 1855, House Doc. 255, 18–19.

50. Massachusetts, *Address of His Excellency Henry J. Gardner, to the Two Branches of the Legislature of Massachusetts, January 3, 1856*, 1856, Senate Doc. 3, 20–21.

51. Massachusetts, *Annual Report of the Commissioners of Alien Passengers and Foreign Paupers*, 1856, House Doc. 41, 22.

52. Massachusetts, *Annual Report of the Commissioners of Alien Passengers and Foreign Paupers*, 1856, 31; Massachusetts, *Annual Report of the Commissioners of Alien Passengers and Foreign Paupers*, 1857, 31.

53. *Boston Daily Advertiser*, May 16, 1855; *Boston Post*, May 18, 1855; *Boston Atlas*, May 23, 1855; *Boston Daily Courier*, May 29, 1855; *Boston Pilot*, May 26, 1855; *New York Irish-American*, May 26, 1855.

54. *Boston Daily Advertiser*, May 16, 1855.

55. *Boston Post*, May 18, 1855. Emphasis in original.

56. *Boston Pilot*, June 16, 1855; *New York Irish-American*, May 26, 1855.

57. *Boston Daily Courier*, May 29, 1855.

58. *Boston Daily Advertiser*, May 16, 1855.

59. *Boston Daily Courier*, May 29, 1855.

60. *Boston Daily Advertiser*, May 31 and June 7, 1855; *Boston Evening Transcript*, June 1, 1855.

61. *Boston Daily Advertiser*, May 31, 1855; *Freeman's Journal* (Dublin), June 19, 1855.

62. *Boston Pilot*, June 16, 1855.

63. *Boston Daily Bee*, May 28, 1855.
64. *Boston Daily Bee*, December 19, 1855; *Know-Nothing and American Crusader* (Boston), June 9, 1855. Emphasis in original.
65. *Boston Pilot*, June 16, 1855.
66. Case Histories, Volume 1, Monson State Almshouse Records; Admission Registers, Volume 8, Monson Almshouse Records.
67. January 29, 1859, Admission and Discharge, BG78/G18, North Dublin Poor Law Union Records, National Archives of Ireland.
68. Hiroshi Motomura, *Americans in Waiting: The Lost Story of Immigration and Citizenship in the United States* (New York: Oxford University Press, 2006), 115–119.
69. Craig Robertson, *The Passport in America: The History of A Document* (New York: Oxford University Press, 2010), 129–130. For the history of the passport, see also John Torpey, *The Invention of the Passport: Surveillance, Citizenship, and the State* (New York: Cambridge University Press, 2000).
70. Case Histories, Volume 1, Bridgewater State Almshouse Records.
71. *New York Irish-American*, January 21, 1860. Emphasis in original.
72. *Liverpool Daily Post*, August 20, 1858; *Liverpool Mercury*, September 15, 1858.
73. Her citizenship status remained valid after the dissolution of marriage due to divorce or the husband's death, if she continued to reside in the United States. For the citizenship status of immigrant women and the 1855 act, see Candice Lewis Bredbenner, *A Nationality of Her Own: Women, Marriage, and the Law of Citizenship* (Berkeley: University of California Press, 1998), 15–44.
74. *New York Citizen*, March 25, 1854.
75. US Const. art. I, sec. 8; James H. Kettner, *The Development of American Citizenship, 1608–1870* (Chapel Hill: University of North Carolina Press, 1978), 213–247; Rogers M. Smith, *Civic Ideals: Conflicting Visions of Citizenship in U.S. History* (New Haven, CT: Yale University Press, 1997), 119–120; David M. Ricci, *Good Citizenship in America* (New York: Cambridge University Press, 2004), 70.
76. Marilyn C. Baseler, *"Asylum for Mankind": America, 1607–1800* (Ithaca, NY: Cornell University Press, 1998), 302–309; Dorothee Schneider, *Crossing Borders: Migration and Citizenship in the Twentieth-Century United States* (Cambridge, MA: Harvard University Press, 2011), 196.
77. *Boston Pilot*, July 10, 1852.
78. US Const. art. IV, sec. 2.
79. Kettner, *The Development of American Citizenship*, 231, 254–267; Smith, *Civic Ideals*, 125–127; Austin Allen, *Origins of the* Dred Scott *Case: Jacksonian Jurisprudence and the Supreme Court, 1837–1857* (Athens: University of Georgia Press, 2006), 116–132.
80. Smith, *Civic Ideals*, 220–221; William J. Novak, "The Legal Transformation of Citizenship in Nineteenth-Century America," in *The Democratic Experiment: New Directions in American Political History*, ed. Meg Jacobs, William J. Novak, and Julian E. Zelizer (Princeton, NJ: Princeton University Press, 2003), 106–107.
81. *Dred Scott v. Sandford*, 60 US 393 (1857); Kettner, *The Development of American Citizenship*, 324–333; Smith, *Civic Ideals*, 253–271; Allen, *Origins of the* Dred Scott *Case*, 160–177; Don E. Fehrenbacher, *The Dred Scott Case: Its Significance in American Law and Politics* (New York: Oxford University Press, 1978), 335–364.
82. Novak, "The Legal Transformation of Citizenship in Nineteenth-Century America," in *The Democratic Experiment*, 90–91, 94–112.
83. Rothman, *The Discovery of the Asylum*, 1–56, 155–179.

84. Robert J. Steinfeld, "Property and Suffrage in the Early Republic," *Stanford Law Review* 41, no. 2 (January 1989): 363.

85. William J. Novak, *The People's Welfare: Law and Regulation in Nineteenth-Century America* (Chapel Hill: University of North Carolina Press, 1996), 169.

86. *Portland v. Bangor*, 42 Me. 403, in Novak, *The People's Welfare*, 168, 320n122.

87. James W. Fox Jr., "Citizenship, Poverty, and Federalism: 1787–1882," *University of Pittsburgh Law Review* 60, no. 2 (Winter 1999): 462–463.

88. Dale T. Knobel, *Paddy and the Republic: Ethnicity and Nationality in Antebellum America* (Middletown, CT: Wesleyan University Press, 1986), 63–67, 86–90. For ethnic stereotypes of the Irish, see also Matthew Frye Jacobson, *Whiteness of a Different Color: European Immigrants and the Alchemy of Race* (Cambridge, MA: Harvard University Press, 1998).

89. *Boston Daily Bee*, May 28, 1855.

90. Theodore Parker, *The Material Condition of the People of Massachusetts* (Boston: Geo. C. Rand & Avery, 1860), 43; From Theodore Parker to Francis Jackson, August 21, 1859, Theodore Parker Papers, Roll 1, Volume 3, Massachusetts Historical Society.

91. Massachusetts, *Report on Insanity and Idiocy in Massachusetts*, 1855, House Doc. 144, 61–62.

92. Cited in *Boston Daily Bee*, July 10, 1857.

93. John Weiss, ed., *Life and Correspondence of Theodore Parker, Minister of the Twenty-Eighth Congregational Society, Boston* (New York: D. Appleton, 1864), 1: 397.

94. *The Fifteenth Annual Report of the New York Association for Improving the Condition of the Poor, for the Year 1858* (New York: John F. Trow, 1858), 37; *The Seventeenth Annual Report of the New York Association for Improving the Condition of the Poor, for the Year 1860* (New York: John F. Trow, 1860), 51.

95. Fox, "Citizenship, Poverty, and Federalism," 462–463.

96. Massachusetts, *The General Statutes of the Commonwealth of Massachusetts: Revised by Commissioners Appointed under a Resolve of February 16, 1855, Amended by the Legislature and Passed December 28, 1859*, chapter 71, Section 52 (Boston: Wright and Potter, 1860), 403.

97. Anbinder, *Nativism & Slavery*, 247–253; Laurie, *Beyond Garrison*, 284–287; Mulkern, *The Know-Nothing Party in Massachusetts*, 155–173.

98. Kathryn Stephenson, "The Quarantine War: The Burning of the New York Marine Hospital in 1858," *Public Health Reports* 119, no. 1 (2004): 82–90.

99. Massachusetts, *Annual Report of the Commissioners of Alien Passengers and Foreign Paupers*, 1858, Public Doc. 14, 6–7, 19–25. Emphasis in original.

100. Massachusetts, *Annual Report of the Commissioners of Alien Passengers and Foreign Paupers*, 1858, 6. Emphasis in original; An Act Concerning State Paupers (April 6, 1859), *Acts and Resolves Passed by the General Court of Massachusetts, in the Years 1858, '59*, chapter 255 (Boston: William White, 1860), 415; appendix C, this volume.

101. Massachusetts, *Annual Report of the Commissioners of Alien Passengers and Foreign Paupers*, 1859, Public Doc. 14, 6.

102. *Liverpool Mercury*, September 15, 1858.

103. *Boston Pilot*, September 18, 1860.

CHAPTER 5

1. *Pall Mall Gazette* (London), January 13, 1869.

2. Personally, Lincoln detested the Know-Nothing movement and had no interest in proscriptive policy against foreigners. For Lincoln's views of immigration, see

Bruce Levine, "'The Vital Element of the Republican Party': Antislavery, Nativism, and Abraham Lincoln," *Journal of the Civil War Era* 1, no. 4 (December 2011): 481–505; Jason H. Silverman, *Lincoln and the Immigrant* (Carbondale: Southern Illinois University Press, 2015); Kevin Kenny, "Immigration," in *A Companion to Abraham Lincoln*, ed. Michael Green (Malden, MA: Blackwell, forthcoming).

3. James M. McPherson, *Battle Cry of Freedom: The Civil War Era* (New York: Oxford University Press, 1988), 450–451; Heather Cox Richardson, *The Greatest Nation of the Earth: Republican Economic Policies during the Civil War* (Cambridge, MA: Harvard University Press, 1997), 139–149. In the same year, Congress passed an act to prohibit the importation into the United States of indentured Chinese laborers known as coolies, a product of Republican legislators' policy against involuntary servitude. Moon-Ho Jung, *Coolies and Cane: Race, Labor, and Sugar in the Age of Emancipation* (Baltimore: Johns Hopkins University Press, 2006), 36–38.

4. Roy P. Basler, ed., *The Collected Works of Abraham Lincoln* (New Brunswick, NJ: Rutgers University Press, 1953), 7: 40.

5. US Congress, *Reports of the Immigration Commission: Abstracts of Reports of the Immigration Commission*, Volume 2, 61st Cong., 3d sess., 1911, Senate Doc. 747, 565; E. P. Hutchinson, *Legislative History of American Immigration Policy, 1798–1965* (Philadelphia: University of Pennsylvania Press, 1981), 49; Richardson, *The Greatest Nation of the Earth*, 160–168.

6. Lucy E. Salyer, *Laws Harsh as Tigers: Chinese Immigrants and the Shaping of Modern Immigration Law* (Chapel Hill: University of North Carolina Press, 1995), 8–9.

7. Hutchinson, *Legislative History of American Immigration Policy*, 53–55, 60–66; *Congressional Record*, 43rd Cong., 1st sess., 1873, pt. 2: 66–68.

8. James H. Kettner, *The Development of American Citizenship, 1608–1870* (Chapel Hill: University of North Carolina Press, 1978), 340–343; Rogers M. Smith, *Civic Ideals: Conflicting Visions of Citizenship in U.S. History* (New Haven, CT: Yale University Press, 1997), 308–312.

9. Christian G. Samito, *Becoming American Under Fire: Irish Americans, African Americans, and the Politics of Citizenship During the Civil War Era* (Ithaca, NY: Cornell University Press, 2009), 194–216. For the Expatriation Act, see also Mitchell Snay, *Fenians, Freedmen, and Southern Whites: Race and Nationality in the Era of Reconstruction* (Baton Rouge: Louisiana State University Press, 2007); David Sim, *A Union Forever: The Irish Question and U.S. Foreign Relations in the Victorian Age* (Ithaca, NY: Cornell University Press, 2013). The expansion of naturalized citizenship during Reconstruction had a critical limitation. When the Naturalization Act of 1870 extended eligibility for naturalization to "aliens of African nativity" and "persons of African descent," Radical Republican Charles Sumner's proposal to make naturalization law completely free from racial terms was rejected by several members of Congress, who hesitated to give Asians the right to become American citizens. Smith, *Civic Ideals*, 310.

10. On welfare policy for Civil War veterans, see Robert H. Bremner, *The Public Good: Philanthropy and Welfare in the Civil War Era* (New York: Knopf, 1980); Theda Skocpol, *Protecting Soldiers and Mothers: The Political Origins of Social Policy in the United States* (Cambridge, MA: Harvard University Press, 1992); Patrick J. Kelly, *Creating a National Home: Building the Veterans' Welfare State, 1860–1900* (Cambridge, MA: Harvard University Press, 1997).

11. An Act in Relation to State Charitable and Correctional Institutions (April 29, 1863), *Acts and Resolves Passed by the General Court of Massachusetts, in the Year 1863*, chapter 240 (Boston: Wright and Potter, 1863), 540–541.

12. Michael B. Katz, *In the Shadow of the Poorhouse: A Social History of Welfare in America*, rev. ed. (New York: Basic Books, 1996), 88–89; Walter I. Trattner, *From Poor Law to Welfare State: A History of Social Welfare in America*, 6th ed. (New York: Free Press, 1999), 77–107; David M. Schneider and Albert Deutsch, *The History of Public Welfare in New York State, 1867–1940* (Chicago: University of Chicago Press, 1941), 13–34.

13. Massachusetts, *Second Annual Report of the Board of State Charities*, 1866, Public Doc. 19, 248–249.

14. Massachusetts, *Fourth Annual Report of the Board of State Charities*, 1868, Public Doc. 17, lxxxix–xc.

15. *Acts and Resolves Passed by the General Court of Massachusetts, in the Year 1865* (Boston: Wright and Potter, 1865), 722–723.

16. *Acts and Resolves Passed by the General Court of Massachusetts, in the Year 1868* (Boston: Wright and Potter, 1868), 310.

17. An Act in Relation to the Settlement of Paupers (June 9, 1868), *Acts and Resolves Passed by the General Court of Massachusetts, in the Year 1868*, chapter 328, 247–248.

18. Massachusetts, *Fifth Annual Report of the Board of State Charities of Massachusetts*, 1868, Public Doc. 17, 13.

19. Kunal M. Parker, "State, Citizenship, and Territory: The Legal Construction of Immigrants in Antebellum Massachusetts," *Law and History Review* 19, no. 3 (Autumn 2001): 636–637.

20. Massachusetts, *First Annual Report of the Board of State Charities*, 1864, 328.

21. Massachusetts, *Second Annual Report of the Board of State Charities*, 1866, Public Doc. 19, xxxiii–xxxiv.

22. Massachusetts, *Second Annual Report of the Board of State Charities*, 1866, xx, xxii. Emphasis in original.

23. Amy Dru Stanley, *From Bondage to Contract: Wage Labor, Marriage, and the Market in the Age of Slave Emancipation* (New York: Cambridge University Press, 1998), 98–137; James W. Fox Jr., "Citizenship, Poverty, and Federalism: 1787–1882," *University of Pittsburgh Law Review* 60, no. 2 (Winter 1999): 565–569; James D. Schmidt, *Free to Work: Labor Law, Emancipation, and Reconstruction, 1815–1880* (Athens: University of Georgia Press, 1998), 222–235.

24. Eric Foner, *Reconstruction: American's Unfinished Revolution, 1863–1877* (New York: Harper & Row, 1988), 469–470.

25. Eric Foner, *Free Soil, Free Labor, Free Men: The Ideology of the Republican Party Before the Civil War* (1970; New York: Oxford University Press, 1995), xiii–xxvii; Heather Cox Richardson, *The Death of Reconstruction: Race, Labor, and Politics in the Post-Civil War North, 1865–1901* (Cambridge, MA: Harvard University Press, 2001), 6–40; Sven Beckert, *The Monied Metropolis: New York City and the Consolidation of the American Bourgeoisies, 1850–1896* (New York: Cambridge University Press, 2001), 175–180, 210–218. For postbellum free labor ideology, see also David Montgomery, *Beyond Equality: Labor and the Radical Republicans, 1862–1872* (1967; Urbana: University of Illinois Press, 1981).

26. Stanley, *From Bondage to Contract*, 105–107. For the problem of unemployment in the postbellum period, see Alexander Keyssar, *Out of Work: The First Century of Unemployment in Massachusetts* (New York: Cambridge University Press, 1986), 9–76.

27. Massachusetts, *First Annual Report of the Board of State Charities*, 382; Massachusetts, *Eighth Annual Report of the Board of State Charities of Massachusetts*, 1871, Public Doc. 17, 21.

28. Inmate Case Histories, Reel 5, Volume 20, Tewksbury State Almshouse Records.

29. Jackson Lears, *Rebirth of a Nation: The Making of Modern America, 1877–1920* (New York: HarperCollins, 2009), 112.

30. Michael B. Katz, *Poverty and Policy in American History* (New York: Academic Press, 1983), 275; *The Twenty-First Annual Report of the New York Association for Improving the Condition of the Poor, for the Year 1864* (New York: John F. Trow, 1864), 45, 49.

31. Gerard Moran, *Sending Out Ireland's Poor: Assisted Emigration to North America in the Nineteenth Century* (Dublin: Four Court Press, 2004), 160.

32. Massachusetts, *Twelfth Annual Report of the Board of State Charities of Massachusetts*, 1876, Public Doc. 17, lxxxii.

33. *Annual Report of the Commissioners of Emigration, of the State of New York: For the Year Ending December 31, 1870* (New York: New York Printing Company, 1871), 34.

34. *Boston Pilot*, May 12, 1883.

35. *Atlantic Monthly*, June 1881, 756; *Boston Daily Advertiser*, February 15, 1875.

36. Matthew Frye Jacobson, *Barbarian Virtues: The United States Encounters Foreign Peoples at Home and Abroad, 1876–1917* (New York: Hill and Wang, 2000), 139–172; Brent Ruswick, *Almost Worthy: The Poor, Paupers, and the Science of Charity in America, 1877–1917* (Bloomington: Indiana University Press, 2013), 35–69.

37. *Puck*, February 15, 1882.

38. *The Twenty-Sixth Annual Report of the New York Association for Improving the Condition of the Poor, for the Year 1869* (New York: Troy & Smith Book Manufacturing Co., 1869), 27–28.

39. Schneider and Deutsch, *The History of Public Welfare in New York State*, 13–26, 39–59; Edwin G. Burrows and Mike Wallace, *Gotham: A History of New York City to 1898* (New York: Oxford University Press, 1999), 1020–1038. For New York City during Reconstruction, see David Quigley, *Second Founding: New York City, Reconstruction, and the Making of American Democracy* (New York: Hill and Wang, 2004); Beckert, *The Monied Metropolis*.

40. Montgomery H. Throop, ed., *The Revised Statutes of the State of New York* (Albany: Banks & Brothers, 1882), Volume 3: 1888–1891; Martha Branscombe, *The Courts and the Poor Laws in New York State, 1784–1929* (Chicago: University of Chicago Press, 1943), 145–151; Schneider and Deutsch, *The History of Public Welfare in New York State*, 109, 114–115.

41. *Eighth Annual Report of the State Board of Charities of the State of New York* (Albany: Weed, Parsons and Company, 1875), 135–139.

42. *Seventh Annual Report of the State Board of Charities of the State of New York* (Albany: Weed, Parsons and Company, 1874), 39.

43. *Eighth Annual Report of the State Board of Charities of the State of New York*, 139.

44. Massachusetts, *Second Annual Report of the Board of State Charities*, xcix, 254.

45. An Act to Establish a State Work-House (April 30, 1866), *Acts and Resolves Passed by the General Court of Massachusetts, in the Year 1866*, chapter 198 (Boston: Wright and Potter, 1866), 141–142.

46. Inmate Case Histories, Reel 3, Volume 9, Tewksbury State Almshouse Records, Massachusetts Archives.

47. Leon F. Litwack, *Been in the Storm So Long: The Aftermath of Slavery* (New York: Vintage Books, 1980), 316–322, 364–371; Foner, *Reconstruction*, 199–210; Linda K. Kerber, *No Constitutional Right to be Ladies: Women and the Obligations of Citizenship* (New York: Hill and Wang, 1998), 56–58; Stanley, *From*

Bondage to Contract, 122–128; Schmidt, *Free to Work*, 122–164. Freedpeople in Mississippi quoted in Litwack, *Been in the Storm So Long*, 369.

48. Stanley, *From Bondage to Contract*, 108–109; Schmidt, *Free to Work*, 209–215.

49. Massachusetts, *Fifth Annual Report of the Board of State Charities of Massachusetts*, 174, 235.

50. Massachusetts, *Second Annual Report of the Board of State Charities*, 261–262.

51. Massachusetts, *Eighth Annual Report of the Board of State Charities of Massachusetts*, 1871, Public Doc. 17, xix–xx.

52. An Act in Addition to an Act Establishing the State Work-House at Bridgewater (March 10, 1869), *Acts and Resolves Passed by the General Court of Massachusetts, in the Year 1869*, chapter 258 (Boston: Wright and Potter, 1869), 589.

53. Massachusetts, *Sixth Annual Report of the Board of State Charities of Massachusetts*, xxxvi.

54. Compiled from the *Annual Reports of the Trustees of the State Lunatic Hospital at Taunton*, 1856–1871. Information before 1855 and after 1872 is not available.

55. See appendix D, this volume.

56. Male Case Book, p. 3, Box 10, Volume 41, 1873–1876, Worcester Lunatic Hospital Records, Francis A. Countway Library of Medicine, Harvard University.

57. Inmate Case Histories, Reel 2, Volume 5, 8, Tewksbury State Almshouse Records.

58. Massachusetts, *Twelfth Annual Report of the Board of State Charities of Massachusetts*, lxxxiv. Emphasis in original.

59. See appendix D, this volume.

60. Massachusetts, *Fifteenth Annual Report of the Board of State Charities of Massachusetts*, 1879, Public Doc. 17, 24.

61. An Act for the More Efficient Relief of the Poor (May 28, 1874), *Acts and Resolves Passed by the General Court of Massachusetts, in the Year 1874*, chapter 274 (Boston: Wright and Potter, 1874), 187–188.

62. *Rules for the Government of the Board of Guardians of the Poor in the City of Philadelphia* (Philadelphia 1883), 63–67.

63. An Act to Prevent the Kidnapping and Importation of Mongolian, Chinese and Japanese Females, for Criminal or Demoralizing Purposes (March 18, 1870), *The Statutes of California, Passed at the Eighteenth Session of the Legislature*, chapter 230 (Sacramento: D. W. Gelwicks, 1870), 330–331.

64. An Act to Amend the Political Code (March 30, 1874), *Acts Amendatory of the Codes, Passed at the Twentieth Session of the Legislature, 1873–74*, Section 70 (Sacramento: G. H. Springer, 1874), 39–40.

65. *Chy Lung v. Freeman*, 92 US 275 (1875); *Henderson v. Mayor of the City of New York*, 92 US 259 (1875).

66. US Treasury Department, *Arrivals of Alien Passengers and Immigrants in the United States from 1820 to 1892* (Washington, DC: US Government Printing Office, 1893), 86; *Report of the Commissioners of Emigration to the General Assembly of Louisiana, January, 1870* (New Orleans: A. L. Lee, 1870), 21.

67. For the "New South" ideology, see C. Vann Woodward, *Origins of the New South, 1877–1913* (Baton Rouge: Louisiana State University Press, 1955); Edward L. Ayers, *The Promise of the New South: Life After Reconstruction* (New York: Oxford University Press, 1992).

68. *Report of the Commissioners of Emigration to the General Assembly of Louisiana*, 4–5. For Louisiana's immigration policy after the Civil War, see also E. Russ Williams Jr., "Louisiana's Public and Private Immigration Endeavors: 1866–1893," *Louisiana History* 15, no. 2 (Spring 1974): 153–173.

69. Anna O. Law, "Lunatics, Idiots, Paupers, and Negro Seamen—Immigration Federalism and the Early American State," *Studies in American Political Development* 28 (October 2014): 127.

70. An Act Concerning Vagrants and Vagabonds (May 15, 1866), *Acts and Resolves Passed by the General Court of Massachusetts, in the Year 1866*, chapter 235, 229–230. Emphasis added.

71. Kerber, *No Constitutional Right to be Ladies*, 50–55. Emphasis in original.

72. Kerber, *No Constitutional Right to be Ladies*, 58–59; Litwack, *Been in the Storm So Long*, 314.

73. Stanley, *From Bondage to Contract*, 117.

74. Patricia Cline Cohen, *The Murder of Helen Jewett: The Life and Death of a Prostitute in Nineteenth-Century New York* (New York: Vintage Books, 1999), 74.

75. *Annual Report of the Commissioners of Emigration, of the State of New York: For the Year Ending December 31, 1873* (New York: F. B. Fisher, 1874), 8, 72–73.

76. *New York Times*, January 31, 1872.

77. November 2, 1864, Volume 4, Records, Minutes, and Correspondence, Board of State Charities Records, Massachusetts Archives.

78. An Act Relating to the Removal of State Paupers (March 17, 1860), *Acts and Resolves Passed by the General Court of Massachusetts, in the Year 1860*, chapter 83 (Boston: William White, 1860), 64–65.

79. Massachusetts, *Eleventh Annual Report of the Board of State Charities of Massachusetts*, 1875, Public Doc. 17, 4.

80. Massachusetts, *Third Annual Report of the Board of State Charities of Massachusetts*, 239.

81. Massachusetts, *Thirty-Sixth Annual Report of the Trustees of the State Lunatic Hospital, at Worcester*, 1868, Public Doc. 23, 13–14.

82. New York State Board of Charities, Minutes of the Board's Meetings from July 11, 1867 to January 3, 1878, 145, New York State Library; Massachusetts, *Fourteenth Annual Report of the Board of State Charities of Massachusetts*, 1878, Public Doc. 17, 46.

83. Massachusetts, *Fourteenth Annual Report of the Board of State Charities of Massachusetts*, 47–48.

84. *Proceedings of a Conference Between Representatives of the Massachusetts State Board of Health, Lunacy and Charity, and the State Board of Charities of New York. Held in New York City, November 12, 1879* (Albany: Weed, Parsons, 1880), 7–8; Schneider and Deutsch, *The History of Public Welfare in New York State*, 109–111. By the time of the conference, the Massachusetts Board of State Charities had been renamed the State Board of Health, Lunacy, and Charity.

85. *Proceedings of a Conference*, 9–10.

86. *Proceedings of a Conference*, 11.

87. *Proceedings of a Conference*, 13.

88. There are some notable exceptions to this scholarly trend. On anti-European nativism during the Civil War and Reconstruction, see Dale T. Knobel, *"America for the Americans": The Nativist Movement in the United States* (New York: Twayne Publishers, 1996); Kevin Kenny, *Making Sense of the Molly Maguires* (New York: Oxford University Press, 1998).

89. For a representative work on this theme, see Richardson, *The Death of Reconstruction*.

90. The Freedman's Bureau, Broadside Collection, Rare Book and Special Collections Division, Library of Congress. For the opposition to the Freedmen's Bureau, see also Chad Alan Goldberg, *Citizens and Paupers: Relief, Rights, and Race,*

from the Freedmen's Bureau to Workfare (Chicago: University of Chicago Press, 2007), 31–75.

91. Samito, *Becoming American Under Fire*. For recent works on Irish Union soldiers, see also Susannah Ural Bruce, *The Harp and the Eagle: Irish-American Volunteers and the Union Army, 1861–1865* (New York: New York University Press, 2006); Ian Delahanty, "Immigrants in a Time of Civil War: The Irish, Slavery, and the Union, 1845–1865" (PhD diss., Boston College, 2013).

92. Kevin Kenny, *The American Irish: A History* (New York: Longman, 2000), 145–146; Jay P. Dolan, *The Irish Americans: A History* (New York: Bloomsbury Press, 2008), 100–104; Bruce, *The Harp and the Eagle*, 233–262.

93. *Harper's Weekly*, December 9, 1876; Matthew Frye Jacobson, *Whiteness of a Different Color: European Immigrants and the Alchemy of Race* (Cambridge, MA: Harvard University Press, 1998), 55. As the Irish gained increasing political power during Reconstruction, attempts were made to check it. In 1871, for example, the New Jersey legislature dominated by native-born Protestant Americans abolished the municipal government of Jersey City in order to minimize Irish influence on the city's politics. City governance was instead left to special commissions appointed by the legislature. Stephen P. Erie, *Rainbow's End: Irish-Americans and the Dilemmas of Urban Machine Politics, 1840–1985* (Berkeley: University of California Press, 1988), 35–38.

CHAPTER 6

1. Inmate Case Histories, Reel 2, Volume 6, Tewksbury State Almshouse Records, Massachusetts Archives; House of Commons, "Annual report of the commissioners for administering the laws for relief of the poor in Ireland, including the twenty-third report under the 10 & 11 Vic., c. 90, and the eighteenth report under the 14 & 15 Vic., c. 68; with appendices," 1870 (C.156), 74; *Cork Constitution*, December 10, 1868.

2. John Belchem, *Irish, Catholic and Scouse: The History of the Liverpool-Irish, 1800–1939* (Liverpool: Liverpool University Press, 2007), 1.

3. Belchem, *Irish, Catholic and Scouse*, 3–6, 56–60, 73–74. For the Irish in Liverpool and Britain, see also Robert Scally, "Liverpool Ships and Irish Emigrants in the Age of Sail," *Journal of Social History* 17, no. 1 (Autumn 1983): 5–30; Donald M. MacRaild, *The Irish Diaspora in Britain, 1750–1939* (New York: Palgrave Macmillan, 2011).

4. John Crowley, William J. Smyth, and Mike Murphy, eds., *Atlas of the Great Irish Famine* (New York: New York University Press, 2012), 506.

5. Admission and Discharge Register, 1857-9, 353SEL/19/10, Records of the Liverpool Board of Guardians, Liverpool Records Office; Female Patients Casebooks, 614RAI/8/3, Records of the Rainhill Hospital, Liverpool Records Office.

6. Letter from Edmund A. Grattan to the Foreign Office, April 15, 1850, FO5/516, Letters of Consuls, 1850, Records of the Foreign Office, National Archives (UK).

7. *Morning Chronicle* (London), June 18, 1855.

8. *Liverpool Daily Post*, August 22, 1855.

9. Frank Neal, *Black '47: Britain and the Famine Irish* (London: Newsham Press, 1998), 53, 61, 139, 249; J. Matthew Gallman, *Receiving Erin's Children: Philadelphia, Liverpool, and the Irish Famine Migration, 1845–1855* (Chapel Hill: University of North Carolina Press, 2000), 67.

10. Belchem, *Irish, Catholic and Scouse*, 34.

11. House of Commons, "Destitute Irish (Liverpool). Copies of, or extracts from, any correspondence addressed to the Secretary of State for the Home Department, relative to the recent immigration of destitute Irish into Liverpool," 1847 (193), 1. The Poor Law Amendment Act of 1834 integrated parishes into administrative units known as poor law unions to be responsible for poor relief in respective unions. In Liverpool, the parish was big enough to form itself a single union. Neal, *Black '47*, 217.

12. House of Commons, "Copy of a letter addressed to Her Majesty's Secretary of State for the Home Department, by Edward Rushton, Esquire, Stipendiary Magistrate of Liverpool, bearing date 21st April 1849," 1849 (266), 1–2.

13. October 11, 1855, Workhouse Committee Minute Book, 1855-57, 353SEL/10/4, Records of the Liverpool Board of Guardians, Liverpool Records Office; *Liverpool Mercury*, October 24, 1855.

14. From Anthony Barclay to the Foreign Office, November 26, 1855, FO5/625, Letters of Consuls, 1855, Records of the Foreign Office.

15. *Liverpool Daily Post*, June 4, 1858; *Liverpool Mercury*, June 4, September 15, 1858.

16. *Liverpool Daily Post*, August 20, 1858.

17. *Liverpool Mercury*, September 15, 18, 1858; *Freeman's Journal* (Dublin), September 27, 1858.

18. *Freeman's Journal* (Dublin), September 27, 1858.

19. *Freeman's Journal* (Dublin), September 27, 1858. The report of the *Liverpool Northern Whig* correspondent appeared in *Quebec Mercury*, October 18, 1858.

20. *Freeman's Journal* (Dublin), September 27, 1858; *Quebec Mercury*, October 18, 1858.

21. *Liverpool Mercury*, November 5, 1858.

22. *Liverpool Mercury*, November 5, 1858.

23. *Liverpool Mercury*, November 12, 1858.

24. *Liverpool Mercury*, November 12, 1858.

25. *Freeman's Journal* (Dublin), March 5, 1855.

26. *Liverpool Daily Post*, August 20, 1858.

27. *Liverpool Mercury*, September 30, 1859.

28. Letter from the Foreign Office to British Consuls in the United States, October 15, 1859, with an attached letter from the Liverpool Select Vestry to John Russell, October 10, 1859, HO45/6849, Registered Papers, Records of the Home Office, National Archives (UK).

29. Letter from Francis Lousada to the Home Office, November 19, 1859, HO45/6849, Registered Papers, Records of the Home Office.

30. Letter from Edward M. Archibald to the Home Office, December 8, 1859, HO45/6849, Registered Papers, Records of the Home Office.

31. Letter to Edmund Hammond (sender unknown), March 1860, HO45/6849, Registered Papers, Records of the Home Office.

32. *Boston Daily Advertiser*, June 7, 1855.

33. *Freeman's Journal* (Dublin), March 5, 1855; Admission and Discharge, BG78/13, Records of the North Dublin Poor Law Union, National Archives of Ireland.

34. *Freeman's Journal* (Dublin) March 5, 1855.

35. *New York Citizen*, October 28, 1854.

36. Deirdre M. Mageean, "Emigration from Irish Ports," *Journal of American Ethnic History* 13, no. 1 (Fall 1993): 24–26.

37. *Irish Times*, October 29, 1867.

38. December 9, 16, 1868, Board of Guardians Minute Book, BG69/A47, Records of the Cork Poor Law Union, Cork City and County Archives; *Cork Examiner*, December 24, 1868.

39. Indoor Relief Register, 1867-9, BG69/G14, Records of the Cork Poor Law Union.

40. Virginia Crossman, *Local Government in Nineteenth-Century Ireland* (Belfast: The Queen's University of Belfast for the Ulster Society of Irish Historical Studies, 1994), 48. For the administration of the poor law in Ireland, see also Virginia Crossman and Peter Gray, eds., *Poverty and Welfare in Ireland, 1838–1948* (Dublin: Irish Academic Press, 2011); Virginia Crossman, *Poverty and the Poor Law in Ireland, 1850–1914* (Liverpool: Liverpool University Press, 2013).

41. *Cork Constitution*, December 10, 1868.

42. *Cork Constitution*, December 17, 1868.

43. *Cork Examiner*, December 17, 1868.

44. *Cork Constitution*, December 24, 1868.

45. *Cork Examiner*, December 31, 1868.

46. January 20, 1869, Board of Guardians Minute Book, BG69/A47, Records of the Cork Poor Law Union; House of Commons, "Annual report of the commissioners for administering the laws for relief of the poor in Ireland," 71–72; *Cork Examiner*, January 21, 1869. Driscoll and Curragh were eventually transferred to the Cork Lunatic Asylum. Indoor Relief Register, 1867-9, BG69/G14, Records of the Cork Poor Law Union.

47. House of Commons, "Annual report of the commissioners for administering the laws for relief of the poor in Ireland," 77.

48. Letter from Edward M. Archibald to the Foreign Office, September 5, October 31, 1859, letter from I. B. Auld to Edward M. Archibald, September 23, 1859, letter from George Kellock to Daniel F. Tiemann, September 23, 1859, FO5/717, Letters of Consuls, 1859, Records of the Foreign Office.

49. *Cork Examiner*, December 24, 1868.

50. *Cork Constitution*, May 13, 1869; House of Commons, "Annual report of the commissioners for administering the laws for relief of the poor in Ireland," 74.

51. House of Commons, "Annual report of the commissioners for administering the laws for relief of the poor in Ireland," 75, 77; *Cork Constitution*, May 27, 1869.

52. *Cork Constitution*, May 27, 1869.

53. *Cork Examiner*, December 24, 1868.

54. For the relationship between Ireland and the British Empire, see Keith Jeffery, ed., *'An Irish Empire'? Aspects of Ireland and the British Empire* (Manchester: Manchester University Press, 1996); Kevin Kenny, ed., *Ireland and the British Empire* (Oxford: Oxford University Press, 2004).

55. For the British poor law, see Derek Fraser, ed., *The New Poor Law in the Nineteenth Century* (New York: St. Martin's, 1976); Michael E. Rose, ed., *The Poor and the City: The English Poor Law in Its Urban Context, 1834–1914* (New York: St. Martin's, 1985); Felix Driver, *Power and Pauperism: The Workhouse System, 1834–1884* (Cambridge: Cambridge University Press, 1993); K. D. M. Snell, *Parish and Belonging: Community, Identity and Welfare in England and Wales, 1700–1950* (Cambridge: Cambridge University Press, 2006); David R. Green, *Pauper Capital: London and the Poor Law, 1790–1870* (Burlington, VT: Ashgate, 2010).

56. Letter dated January 19, 1847, HO45/1080B, Registered Papers, Records of the Home Office.

57. *Liverpool Mercury*, May 14, 1847.

58. Belchem, *Irish, Catholic and Scouse*, 33.

59. Neal, *Black '47*, 220–221; Crowley, Smyth, and Murphy, eds., *Atlas of the Great Irish Famine*, 505.
60. House of Commons, "Copy of a letter addressed to Her Majesty's Secretary of State for the Home Department, by Edward Rushton, Esquire, Stipendiary Magistrate of Liverpool."
61. Neal, *Black '47*, 222, 227; *Freeman's Journal* (Dublin), July 14, 1847.
62. March 28, 1854, Select Vestry Board Minute Book, 1852-1855, 353SEL/1/1, Records of the Liverpool Board of Guardians.
63. Neal, *Black '47*, 221.
64. *New York Citizen*, August 25, 1855.
65. *New York Citizen*, March 28, 1857.
66. Neal, *Black '47*, 220.
67. *New York Citizen*, June 21, 1856.
68. *New York Citizen*, March 28, 1857.
69. Letter from Robert Peel to the Home Office, HO45/7253, Registered Papers, Records of the Home Office.
70. *Galway Vindicator*, June 23, 1855. Emphasis in original.
71. *Freeman's Journal* (Dublin), January 5, 1854.
72. *Ulsterman*, quoted in *Boston Pilot*, December 31, 1853. For a similar line of argument, see *New York Citizen*, January 21, 1857.
73. *Belfast News-Letter*, November 23, 1857.
74. Crossman, *The Poor Law in Ireland*, 10; Christine Kinealy, *This Great Calamity: The Irish Famine, 1845–52* (Boulder, CO: Roberts Rinehart, 1995), 25–26, 334–341.
75. April 16, 1856, Board of Guardians Minute Book, BG69/A22, Records of the Cork Poor Law Union.
76. Cormac Ó Gráda, *Black '47 and Beyond: The Great Irish Famine in History, Economy, and Memory* (Princeton, NJ: Princeton University Press, 1999), 174.
77. April 16, 1856, Board of Guardians Minute Book, BG69/A22, Records of the Cork Poor Law Union.
78. April 30, 1856, Board of Guardians Minute Book, Roll 347, Item 5, Records of the North Dublin Poor Law Union, National Archives of Ireland.
79. *Galway Vindicator*, February 3, 1855.
80. February 7, 1855, Board of Guardians Minute Book, BG69/A19, Records of the Cork Poor Law Union; March 23, 1855, Galway Poor Law Union Minute Book, Galway County Archives; May 2, 1856, Mountbellow Poor Law Union Minute Book, Galway County Archives; March 3, April 16, 1856, Belfast Board of Guardians Minute Book, BG7/A18, Public Record Office of Northern Ireland.
81. April 11, 1860, Board of Guardians Minute Book, Roll 348, Item 6, Records of the North Dublin Poor Law Union, National Archives of Ireland.
82. *Tralee Chronicle*, July 9, 1869; *Belfast News-Letter*, July 3, 1869.
83. *Freeman's Journal* (Dublin), January 5, 1854.
84. *Belfast News-Letter*, January 21, 1858.
85. *Cork Examiner*, December 24, 1868.
86. *Freeman's Journal* (Dublin), July 21, 1864.
87. *Cork Examiner*, December 24, 1868. Parentheses in original.
88. *Cork Constitution*, May 27, 1869.
89. *Liverpool Mercury*, September 30, 1859.
90. *Cork Examiner*, May 20, 1869.
91. *Galway Vindicator* quoted in *Morning Chronicle* (London), September 7, 1859.

92. John Higham, *Strangers in the Land: Patterns of American Nativism, 1860–1925* (1955; New York: Atheneum, 1970).

93. Crossman, *Poverty and the Poor Law in Ireland*, 114–115, 198.

94. Belchem, *Irish, Catholic and Scouse*, 35. For the economic condition of the working-class British in the nineteenth century, see David R. Green, *From Artisans to Paupers: Economic Change and Poverty in London, 1790–1870* (Aldershot: Scolar Press, 1995).

95. James S. Donnelly Jr., *The Great Irish Potato Famine* (Phoenix Mill, UK: Sutton Publishing, 2001), 130. For the British perceptions of the Irish, see L. Perry Curtis Jr., *Apes and Angels: The Irishman in Victorian Caricature*, rev. ed. (Washington, DC: Smithsonian Institution Press, 1997); Michael de Nie, *The Eternal Paddy: Irish Identity in the British Press, 1798–1882* (Madison: University of Wisconsin Press, 2004).

96. Crossman, *Poverty and the Poor Law in Ireland*, 12–32, 198–225.

CHAPTER 7

1. *Freeman's Journal* (Dublin), June 27, July 3, 1883; *Cork Examiner*, July 20, 1883.

2. On the federalization of immigration policy, see Matthew J. Lindsay, "Preserving the Exceptional Republic: Political Economy, Race, and the Federalization of American Immigration," *Yale Journal of Law and the Humanities* 17, no. 2 (Summer 2005): 181–251; Anna O. Law, "Lunatics, Idiots, Paupers, and Negro Seamen— Immigration Federalism and the Early American State," *Studies in American Political Development* 28 (October 2014): 107–128. Some historians have recently argued that the year 1882 is overrated in the history of Chinese exclusion. See Moon-Ho Jung, *Coolies and Cane: Race, Labor, and Sugar in the Age of Emancipation* (Baltimore: Johns Hopkins University Press, 2006); Beth Lew-Williams, "Before Restriction Became Exclusion: America's Experiment in Diplomatic Immigration Control," *Pacific Historical Review* 83, no. 1 (February 2014): 24–56.

3. Hamilton A. Hill, Thomas Russell, and E. H. Derby, *Arguments in Favor of the Freedom of Immigration at the Port of Boston, Addressed to the Committee on State Charities of the Massachusetts Legislature, April, 1871* (Boston: Wright & Porter, 1871), 6.

4. *Proceedings of the Conference of Charities, Held in Connection with the General Meeting of the American Social Science Association, Detroit, May, 1875* (Boston: Tolman & White, 1875), 93, 96.

5. *Annual Report of the Commissioners of Emigration of the State of New York, for the Year Ending December 31, 1875* (New York: Cherouny and Kienle, 1876), 20–21; *Henderson v. Mayor of the City of New York*, 92 US 259 (1875).

6. *Henderson v. Mayor of the City of New York*, 92 US 259 (1875); Tony Allan Freyer, *The Passenger Cases and the Commerce Clause: Immigrants, Blacks, and States' Rights in Antebellum America* (Lawrence: University Press of Kansas, 2014), 136–142; An Act to Amend the Political Code (March 30, 1874), *Acts Amendatory of the Codes, Passed at the Twentieth Session of the Legislature, 1873–74* (Sacramento: G. H. Springer, 1874), 39–41. On the 1874 California law, see Charles J. McClain, *In Search of Equality: The Chinese Struggle Against Discrimination in Nineteenth-Century America* (Berkeley: University of California Press, 1994), 54–63.

7. New York, *Communication from the Governor Relative to the Commissioners of Emigration*, 1876, Senate Doc. 69, 1.

8. Massachusetts, *Thirteenth Annual Report of the Board of State Charities of Massachusetts*, 1877, Public Doc. 17, xxxvii.

9. *Annual Report of the Commissioners of Emigration of the State of New York for the Year Ending December 31, 1876* (Albany: Jerome B. Parmenter, 1877), 8.
10. Letter from F. B. Sanborn to H. J. Jackson, May 4, 1876, letter from F. B. Sanborn to John S. Devlin, May 15, 1876, and letter from F. B. Sanborn to H. J. Jackson, May 24, 1876, F. B. Sanborn Confidential Letter Book, Volume 1, Board of Health, Lunacy, and Charity Records, Massachusetts Archives; State Board of Charities, *Minutes of the Board's Meetings from July 11, 1867, to January 3, 1878*, May 2, 1876, New York State Library.
11. *Annual Report of the Commissioners of Emigration of the State of New York for the Year Ending December 31, 1876*, 74–78.
12. *Proceedings of the Conference of Charities, Held in Connection with the General Meeting of the American Social Science Association, at Saratoga, September, 1876* (Albany: Joel Munsell, 1876), 166–168.
13. *New York Irish-American*, July 29, 1876; Massachusetts, *Thirteenth Annual Report of the Board of State Charities of Massachusetts*, xliii; *Annual Report of the Commissioners of Emigration of the State of New York for the Year Ending December 31, 1876*, 72.
14. Letter from F. B. Sanborn to H. J. Jackson, June 15, 1876, F. B. Sanborn Confidential Letter Book, Volume 1, Board of Health, Lunacy, and Charity Records; June 7, 1876, Minutes of Monthly Meetings, Board of State Charities Records.
15. Boston Board of Trade, *Report on Congressional Bill (H.R. 3853), Proposing to Levy a National Head-Money Tax, and Otherwise to Interfere with the Freedom of Immigration* (Boston, 1877), 4–8; *Boston Globe*, January 6, 1877.
16. Letter from H. J. Jackson to F. B. Sanborn, September 27, 1876, F. B. Sanborn Confidential Letter Book, Volume 1, Board of Health, Lunacy, and Charity Records.
17. New York, *Report of the Delegates to the Emigration Convention, Held at Indianapolis*, 1871, Assembly Doc. 25, 1–6.
18. Quoted in Edith Abbott, "Federal Immigration Policies, 1864–1924," *University Journal of Business* 2, no. 2 (March 1924): 141.
19. Daniel J. Tichenor, *Dividing Lines: The Politics of Immigration Control in America* (Princeton, NJ: Princeton University Press, 2002), 68–69.
20. Massachusetts, *Second Annual Report of the State Board of Health, Lunacy, and Charity of Massachusetts*, 1881, Public Doc. 17, lxxxiv–lxxxv.
21. *Henderson v. Mayor of the City of New York*, 92 US 259 (1875).
22. *Chy Lung v. Freeman*, 92 US 275 (1875).
23. Hiroshi Motomura, *Americans in Waiting: The Lost Story of Immigration and Citizenship in the United States* (New York: Oxford University Press, 2006), 24.
24. *Eighth Annual Report of the State Board of Charities of the State of New York* (Albany: Weed, Parsons and Company, 1875), 139. Emphasis in original.
25. *Thirteenth Annual Report of the State Board of Charities of the State of New York* (Albany: Weed, Parsons and Company, 1880), 42–43.
26. *New York Times*, February 9, 1879.
27. New York, *Annual Report of the Commissioners of Emigration, of the State of New York: For the Year Ending December 31, 1879*, 1880, Assembly Doc. 14, 30–32.
28. An Act Making Appropriations for Certain Expenses of Government and Supplying Deficiencies in Former Appropriations (June 7, 1880), *Laws of New York*, chapter 549 (Albany: Weed, Parsons and Company, 1880), 1: 795.
29. *Fifteenth Annual Report of the State Board of Charities* (Albany: Weed, Parson and Company, 1882), 35.

30. *New York Times*, June 15, 1882; Aristide R. Zolberg, *A Nation by Design: Immigration Policy in the Fashioning of America* (Cambridge, MA: Harvard University Press, 2006), 192.
31. *New York Times*, June 18, 1882.
32. *Congressional Record*, 47th Cong., 1st sess., June 19, 1882, p. 5113.
33. Alexander Saxton, *The Indispensable Enemy: Labor and the Anti-Chinese Movement in California* (Berkeley: University of California Press, 1971), 11.
34. *The Statute of California, Passed at the Nineteenth Session of the Legislature* (Sacramento: T. A. Springer, 1872), 970; *The Statute of California, Passed at the Twentieth Session of the Legislature* (Sacramento: T. A. Springer, 1874), 979.
35. An Act to Provide for the Removal of Chinese, Whose Presence Is Dangerous to the Well Being of Communities, Outside the Limits of Cities and Towns in the State of California (April 3, 1880), *The Statutes of California, Passed at the Twenty-Third Session of the Legislature*, chapter 29 (Sacramento: J. D. Young, 1880), 22.
36. E. P. Hutchinson, *Legislative History of American Immigration Policy, 1798–1965* (Philadelphia: University of Pennsylvania Press, 1981), 66–83; Erika Lee, *At America's Gates: Chinese Immigration during the Exclusion Era, 1882–1943* (Chapel Hill: University of North Carolina Press, 2003), 25–30.
37. *Philadelphia Public Ledger*, August 8, 1870.
38. *Congressional Record*, 45th Cong., 3d sess., volume 8, p. 797.
39. *The Statute of California, Passed at the Twentieth Session of the Legislature*, 979; *Congressional Record*, 45th Cong., 3d sess., volume 8, p. 1312.
40. *Congressional Record*, 47th Cong., 1st sess., volume 13, p. 1486.
41. Lee, *At America's Gates*, 29. Emphasis in original.
42. *Chinese Immigration*, 46th Cong., 2d sess., House, Report No. 572, 28–29.
43. *Congressional Record*, 47th Cong., 1st sess., 1882, 13, pt. 5: 5108–5113.
44. Immigration Act of 1882, 22 Stat. 214 (1882); *Proceedings of the Conference of Charities, Held in Connection with the General Meeting of the American Social Science Association, at Saratoga, September, 1876*, 166; New York, *Annual Report of the Commissioners of Emigration of the State of New York for the Year Ending December 31, 1877*, 1878, Senate Doc. 18, 25.
45. Immigration Act of 1882, 22 Stat. 214 (1882); *Congressional Record*, 47th Cong., 1st sess., 1882, 13, pt. 6: 5406. Emphasis added.
46. An Act Providing for the Relief and Support, Employment and Removal of the Poor, and for Repealing All Former Laws Made for Those Purposes (February 26, 1794), *Acts and Laws of the Commonwealth of Massachusetts*, 1793, chapter 59 (Boston: Wright and Potter, 1895), 491.
47. Immigration Act of 1882, 22 Stat. 214 (1882); Lucy E. Salyer, *Laws Harsh as Tigers: Chinese Immigrants and the Shaping of Modern Immigration Law* (Chapel Hill: University of North Carolina Press, 1995), 5–6; Tichenor, *Dividing Lines*, 69; Patricia Russell Evans, "'Likely to Become a Public Charge': Immigration in the Backwaters of Administrative Law, 1882–1933" (PhD diss., George Washington University, 1987), 89–94.
48. Gerard Moran, *Sending Out Ireland's Poor: Assisted Emigration to North America in the Nineteenth Century* (Dublin: Four Court Press, 2004), 161–181; Deirdre M. Moloney, *American Catholic Lay Groups and Transatlantic Social Reform in the Progressive Era* (Chapel Hill: University of North Carolina Press, 2002), 69–115; *Boston Pilot*, September 9, 1882; Massachusetts, *Sixth Annual Report of the State*

Board of Health, Lunacy, and Charity of Massachusetts, 1885, Public Doc. 17, 250; *Fourteenth Annual Report of the Board of Commissioners of Public Charities of the State of Pennsylvania* (Harrisburg: Lans S. Hart, 1884), ix.

49. *New York Times*, April 16, 1883; *New York Irish-American*, April 28, 1883; *New York Tribune*, June 30, 1883.

50. *New York Irish-American*, May 19, 1883; *Boston Herald*, June 29, 1883; *Harper's Weekly*, June 23, 1883, p. 387.

51. *Boston Herald*, June 24, 1883; *Irish Times*, June 25, 1883.

52. *Boston Herald*, June 28, 1883; *Annual Report of the Commissioners of Emigration of the State of New York: For the Year Ending December 31, 1883* (New York, 1884), 14.

53. *Boston Pilot*, June 30, 1883.

54. *Boston Globe*, June 28, 1883; *Boston Herald*, June 28, 1883; letter from Charles A. Colcord to S. C. Wrightington, July 6, 1883, Correspondence of the Board, Vol. 2, Board of Health, Lunacy, and Charity Records; *Boston Pilot*, May 19, 1883.

55. *Annual Report of the Commissioners of Emigration of the State of New York: For the Year Ending December 31, 1883*, 13; *New York Times*, June 25, 1883; *New York Irish-American*, July 7, 1883; *Freeman's Journal* (Dublin), July 3, 1883; *Cork Examiner*, July 11, July 20, 1883; *Irish Times*, July 5, 1883.

56. *Irish Times*, July 5, 1883; *Cork Examiner*, July 12, 1883; Moran, *Sending Out Ireland's Poor*, 212–213.

57. *Cork Examiner*, July 12, 1883.

58. *Cork Examiner*, July 25, 1883.

59. Massachusetts, *Seventh Annual Report of the State Board of Health, Lunacy, and Charity of Massachusetts*, 1886, Public Doc. 17, xlii.

60. Massachusetts, *Fifth Annual Report of the State Board of Health, Lunacy, and Charity of Massachusetts*, 1884, Public Doc. 17, xii–xiii.

61. *Boston Globe*, July 18, 1883; Massachusetts, *Fifth Annual Report of the State Board of Health, Lunacy, and Charity of Massachusetts*, xiii.

62. Massachusetts, *Fifth Annual Report of the State Board of Health, Lunacy, and Charity of Massachusetts*, li–lii.

63. Letter from C. S. Fairchild to H. H. Hart, December 29, 1887, Press Copies of Letters Sent by Miscellaneous Division, Vol. 1, Records of the Department of the Treasury (RG 56), National Archives-College Park.

64. *Cork Examiner*, August 9, 1883.

65. Moran, *Sending Out Ireland's Poor*, 215–218.

66. *Annual Report of the State Board of Charities, for the Year 1885* (Albany: Weed, Parsons and Company, 1886), 62.

67. John Higham, *Strangers in the Land: Patterns of American Nativism, 1860–1925* (1955; New York: Atheneum, 1970), 99–100; Evans, "'Likely to Become a Public Charge,'" 94–108. For the history of Ellis Island, see Thomas M. Pitkin, *Keepers of the Gate: A History of Ellis Island* (New York: New York University Press, 1975); Vincent J. Cannato, *American Passage: The History of Ellis Island* (New York: HarperCollins, 2009); Ronald H. Bayor, *Encountering Ellis Island: How European Immigrants Entered America* (Baltimore: Johns Hopkins University Press, 2014).

68. An Act in Amendment to the Various Acts Relative to Immigration and the Importation of Aliens under Contract or Agreement to Perform Labor, 26 Stat. 1084 (1891). Congressional debates do not reveal the reason for the addition of people with contagious diseases and polygamists to the federal law's excludable

category in 1891. Immigration scholars attribute the addition to the inadequacy of quarantine procedures under state jurisdiction and the public outcry over the practice of plural marriage among the Mormons in Utah in the late nineteenth century. See Alan M. Kraut, *Silent Travelers: Germs, Genes, and the "Immigrant Menace"* (Baltimore: Johns Hopkins University Press, 1995), 50–51; Hutchinson, *Legislative History of American Immigration Policy*, 421–422.

69. *Fifteenth Annual Report of the Board of Commissioners of Public Charities of the State of Pennsylvania* (Harrisburg: Lane S. Hart, 1885), 288–289.

70. *Baltimore Sun*, May 4, 1888.

71. Pitkin, *Keepers of the Gate*, 14–15; Marian L. Smith, "Immigration and Naturalization Service," in *A Historical Guide to the U.S. Government*, ed. George Thomas Kurian (New York: Oxford University Press, 1998), 305.

72. Letter from Acting Secretary to Francis W. Rockwell, March 2, 1891, Press Copies of Letters Sent by Miscellaneous Division, Vol. 11, Records of the Department of the Treasury (RG 56).

73. Massachusetts, *Thirteenth Annual Report of the State Board of Lunacy and Charity of Massachusetts*, 1892, Public Doc. 17, 20; Massachusetts, *Fourteenth Annual Report of the State Board of Lunacy and Charity of Massachusetts*, 1893, Public Doc. 17, 22.

74. Letter from Assistant Secretary to G. A. von Lingen, May 2, 1891, letter from Assistant Secretary to Samuel G. Davis, May 11, 1891, Press Copies of Letters Sent by Miscellaneous Division, Vol. 12, Records of the Department of the Treasury (RG 56).

75. Kraut, *Silent Travelers*; Amy L. Fairchild, *Science at the Borders: Immigrant Medical Inspection and the Shaping of the Modern Industrial Labor Force* (Baltimore: Johns Hopkins University Press, 2003); Mae M. Ngai, *Impossible Subjects: Illegal Aliens and the Making of Modern America* (Princeton, NJ: Princeton University Press, 2004); Cannato, *American Passage*; Erika Lee and Judy Yung, *Angel Island: Immigrant Gateway to America* (New York: Oxford University Press, 2010); Kelly Lytle Hernández, *Migra! A History of the U.S. Border Patrol* (Berkeley: University of California Press, 2010).

76. For the LPC clause, see Evans, "'Likely to Become a Public Charge.'"

77. William C. Van Vleck, *The Administrative Control of Aliens: A Study in Administrative Law and Procedure* (New York: Commonwealth Fund, 1932), 54; Cannato, *American Passage*, 195.

78. An Act in Amendment to the Various Acts Relative to Immigration and the Importation of Aliens under Contract or Agreement to Perform Labor, 26 Stat. 1084 (1891); Salyer, *Laws Harsh as Tigers*, 26–32. On the plenary power doctrine, see Motomura, *Americans in Waiting*, 15–37. Matthew Lindsay has analyzed plenary power in relation to European immigration in the late nineteenth century and the concept of national security. Matthew J. Lindsay, "Immigration as Invasion: Sovereignty, Security, and the Origins of the Federal Immigration Policy," *Harvard Civil Rights-Civil Liberties Law Review* 45, no. 1 (2010): 1–56. For due process in American immigration policy, see Anna O. Law, *The Immigration Battle in American Courts* (New York: Cambridge University Press, 2010), 188–230.

79. *New York Irish-American*, May 1889.

80. Salyer, *Laws Harsh as Tigers*, 26–28.

CONCLUSION

1. John Higham, *Send These to Me: Immigrants in Urban America*, rev. ed. (Baltimore: Johns Hopkins University Press, 1984), 71–77.

2. *Immigrants—Landing and examination of,* September 1, 1885, *Synopsis of the Decisions of the Treasury Department on the Construction of the Tariff, Navigation, and Other Laws, for the Year Ending December 31, 1885* (Washington, DC: US Government Printing Office, 1886), 359–360; letter from Charles S. Fairchild to W. F. McAllister, June 12, 1888, Letters from the Treasury Secretary, Box 55, Records of the United States Customs Service (RG 36), National Archives-San Bruno.

3. Letter from William Windom to Mahlon H. Dickinson, July 8, 1889, Letters Received, Box 1, Folder 1889, Records of the Office of the Commissioner of Immigration, Records of the Immigration and Naturalization Service (RG 85), National Archives-Philadelphia.

4. Letter from William Windom to John Weber, June 24, 1890, Press Copies of Letters Sent by Miscellaneous Division, Vol. 8, Records of the Department of the Treasury (RG 56), National Archives-College Park.

5. Letter from William Windom to Thomas Drumm, November 4, 1890, Press Copies of Letters Sent by Miscellaneous Division, Vol. 10, Records of the Department of the Treasury (RG 56).

6. Vincent J. Cannato, *American Passage: The History of Ellis Island* (New York: HarperCollins, 2009), 95–106.

7. *America against the world!*, Broadside Collection, American Antiquarian Society.

8. Three years later, the Foran Act was amended with a deportation provision for foreign laborers whose contracted status was identified within one year of arrival. Torrie Hester, "'Protection, Not Punishment': Legislative and Judicial Formation of U.S. Deportation Policy, 1882–1904," *Journal of American Ethnic History* 30, no. 1 (Fall 2010): 13–14.

9. On the legal history of belonging in nineteenth-century America, see Barbara Young Welke, *Law and the Borders of Belonging in the Long Nineteenth Century United States* (New York: Cambridge University Press, 2010).

10. Mae M. Ngai, *Impossible Subjects: Illegal Aliens and the Making of Modern America* (Princeton, NJ: Princeton University Press, 2004), 21–55.

11. Ngai, *Impossible Subjects*, 68–69. For Border Patrol, see also Kelly Lytle Hernández, *Migra! A History of the U.S. Border Patrol* (Berkeley: University of California Press, 2010).

BIBLIOGRAPHY

PRIMARY SOURCES
Manuscript Collections

American Antiquarian Society, Worcester, Massachusetts
Broadside Collection

Archdiocese of Boston Archives, Braintree, Massachusetts
John Bernard Fitzpatrick Papers

Boston Public Library, Boston, Massachusetts
Pamphlets of the Boston Society for the Prevention of Pauperism

City of Boston Archives, West Roxbury, Massachusetts
Board of Aldermen Summary Minutes with Index
Boston City Council Joint Committee on Alien Passengers Records
Common Council Summary Minutes

Cork City and County Archives, Cork, Ireland
Records of the Cork Poor Law Union

Francis A. Countway Library of Medicine, Harvard University, Boston, Massachusetts
Worcester Lunatic Hospital Records

Galway County Archives, Galway, Ireland
Galway Poor Law Union Board of Guardians Minute Books
Mountbellow Poor Law Union Board of Guardians Minute Books

Historical Society of Pennsylvania, Philadelphia, Pennsylvania
Statements of the Accounts of the Guardians of the Poor

Liverpool Records Office, Liverpool, United Kingdom
Records of the Liverpool Board of Guardians
Records of the Rainhill Hospital

Massachusetts Archives, Boston, Massachusetts
Board of Health, Lunacy, and Charity Records
Board of State Charities Records
Bridgewater State Almshouse Records
Histories of Alien Residents of Almshouses and Other Institutions, 1852–1857
Monson State Almshouse Records
Rainsford Island State Hospital Records
Registers of Passengers Arriving in Mass. Port, 1848–1891
Tewksbury State Almshouse Records

Massachusetts Historical Society, Boston, Massachusetts
Boston Overseers of the Poor Records
Theodore Parker Papers

National Archives, College Park, Maryland
Records of the Department of the Treasury (RG 56)

National Archives, Kew, United Kingdom
FO5/473, Consul at Boston, 1847, Records of the Foreign Office
FO5/516, Letters of Consuls, 1850, Records of the Foreign Office
FO5/625, Letters of Consuls, 1855, Records of the Foreign Office
FO5/717, Letters of Consuls, 1859, Records of the Foreign Office
HO45/478, Registered Papers, Records of the Home Office
HO45/1080B, Registered Papers, Records of the Home Office
HO45/6849, Registered Papers, Records of the Home Office
HO45/7253, Registered Papers, Records of the Home Office

National Archives of Ireland, Dublin, Ireland
North Dublin Poor Law Union Admission and Discharge List
North Dublin Poor Law Union Board of Guardians Minute Books

National Archives, Philadelphia, Pennsylvania
Records of the Immigration and Naturalization Service (RG 85)

National Archives, San Bruno, California
Records of the United States Customs Service (RG 36)

National Library of Ireland, Dublin, Ireland
Fitzwilliam Estate Papers
Prior-Wandesforde Papers

New York Historical Society, New York, New York
Annual Reports of the New York Association for Improving the Condition of the Poor

New York Municipal Archives, New York, New York
Records of the Office of the Mayor

New York State Archives, Albany, New York
Records of the State Board of Charities

New York State Library, Albany, New York
State Board of Charities. Minutes of the Board's Meetings from July 11, 1867, to January 3, 1878.
State Board of Charities. Minutes of the Board's Meetings from February 5, 1878, to December 17, 1885.

Philadelphia City Archives, Philadelphia, Pennsylvania
Records of the Guardians of the Poor

Provincial Archives of New Brunswick, Fredericton, Canada
Saint John Alms House Records

Public Record Office of Northern Ireland, Belfast, United Kingdom
Belfast Board of Guardians Minute Books
Lissadell Papers
Sample Family Emigrant Papers
Shirley Papers

Rare Book and Special Collections Division, Library of Congress, Washington, DC
Broadside Collection

State Library of Massachusetts, Boston, Massachusetts
Journals of the House of Representatives
Journals of the Senate

American, British, and Irish Government Reports and Publications

Acts and Laws of the Commonwealth of Massachusetts. Boston: Wright and Potter, 1895.

The Acts and Resolves, Public and Private, of the Province of the Massachusetts Bay. 1692–1780.

Census of the State of New-York, for 1855; Taken in Pursuance of Article Third of the Constitution of the State, and of Chapter Sixty-Four for the Laws of 1855. Compiled by Franklin B. Hough. Albany: Charles Van Benthuysen, 1857.

The Charters and General Laws of the Colony and Province of Massachusetts Bay. Boston: T. B. Wait, 1814.

City of Boston. *Annual Reports of the Overseers of the Poor.* 1865–1882.

City of Boston. *Report of the Board of Visitors of the Boston Lunatic Hospital, Containing a Statement of the Condition of That Institution, and Transmitting the Annual Report of the Superintendent for 1850.* 1850. City Doc. 48.

Massachusetts Constitutional Convention. *Official Report of the Debates and Proceedings in the State Convention, Assembled May 4th, 1853, to Revise and Amend the Constitution of the Commonwealth of Massachusetts.* 3 vols. Boston: White & Potter, 1853.

Report of the Joint Special Committee of the Census of Boston, May, 1855, Including the Report of the Censors, with Analytical and Sanitary Observations. Compiled by Josiah Curtis. Boston: Moore & Crosby, 1856.

The Seventh Census, of the United States: 1850. Compiled by J. D. B. DeBow. Washington, DC: Robert Armstrong, 1853.

State of California. *Journals of the Senate and Assembly.* 1852–1882.

State of California. *The Statutes of California.* 1852–1882.

State of Louisiana. *Reports of the Commissioners of Emigration to the General Assembly of Louisiana.* 1870, 1871.

State of Massachusetts. *Acts and Resolves Passed by the General Court of Massachusetts.* 1792–1882.

State of Massachusetts. *Address of His Excellency Henry J. Gardner, to the Two Branches of the Legislature of Massachusetts, January 9, 1855.* 1855. Senate Doc. 3.

State of Massachusetts. *Address of His Excellency Henry J. Gardner, to the Two Branches of the Legislature of Massachusetts, January 3, 1856.* 1856. Senate Doc. 3.

State of Massachusetts. *Address of His Excellency Henry J. Gardner, to the Two Branches of the Legislature of Massachusetts, January 9, 1857.* 1857. Senate Doc. 3.

State of Massachusetts. *Annual Reports of the Board of State Charities.* 1864–1878.

State of Massachusetts. *Annual Reports of the Commissioners of Alien Passengers and Foreign Paupers.* 1851–1863.

State of Massachusetts. *Annual Reports of the Inspectors of the Hospital at Rainsford Island.* 1854–1869.

State of Massachusetts. *Annual Reports of the Inspectors of the State Almshouse at Bridgewater.* 1854–1883.

State of Massachusetts. *Annual Reports of the Inspectors of the State Almshouse at Monson.* 1854–1878.

State of Massachusetts. *Annual Reports of the Inspectors of the State Almshouse, at Tewksbury.* 1854–1883.

State of Massachusetts. *Annual Reports of the State Board of Health, Lunacy, and Charity of Massachusetts.* 1879–1892.

State of Massachusetts. *Annual Reports of the Superintendent of Alien Passengers for the Port of Boston.* 1849–1863.

State of Massachusetts. *Annual Reports of the Trustees of the State Lunatic Hospital at Northampton.* 1856–1883.

State of Massachusetts. *Annual Reports of the Trustees of the State Lunatic Hospital at Taunton.* 1854–1878.

State of Massachusetts. *Annual Reports of the Trustees of the State Lunatic Hospital at Worcester.* 1854–1883.

State of Massachusetts. *The General Laws of Massachusetts, from the Adoption of the Constitution, to February, 1822.* 2 vols. Boston: Wells & Lilly and Cummings & Hilliard, 1823.

State of Massachusetts. *The General Laws of Massachusetts. From June 1822, to June 1831.* Boston: Hilliard, Gray, Little, and Wilkins, 1832.

State of Massachusetts. *Report on Insanity and Idiocy in Massachusetts.* 1855. House Doc. 144.

State of Massachusetts. *Report of the Joint Special Committee on Alien Passengers.* 1847. Senate Doc. 109.

State of Massachusetts. *Report of the Joint Special Committee on Alien Passengers and Paupers.* 1848. Senate Doc. 46.

State of Massachusetts. *Report of the Joint Special Committee on Alien Passengers and Paupers.* 1852. Senate Doc. 127.

State of Massachusetts. *Report of the Special Joint Committee Appointed to Investigate the Whole System of the Public Charitable Institutions of the Commonwealth of Massachusetts, during the Recess of the Legislature in 1858.* 1859. Senate Doc. 2.

State of Massachusetts. *Report on Orders Relating to Foreign Immigration and Support of State Paupers.* 1851. House Doc. 152.

State of Massachusetts. *Report on Pauper Immigration.* 1855. House Doc. 255.

State of Massachusetts. *Report Regarding the Prevention of Introduction of Foreign Paupers.* 1836. House Doc. 66.

State of Massachusetts. *Report of the Select Committee to Whom Was Referred the Subject of the Practicability of Preventing the Introduction of Foreign Paupers into the State.* 1835. House Doc. 60.

State of Massachusetts. *Laws of the Commonwealth of Massachusetts, Passed by the General Court, in the Years 1837 and 1838.* Boston: Dutton and Wentworth, 1839.

State of Massachusetts. *The Revised Statutes of the Commonwealth of Massachusetts, Passed November 4, 1835.* Boston: Dutton and Wentworth, 1836.

State of Massachusetts. *The General Statutes of the Commonwealth of Massachusetts: Revised by Commissioners Appointed under a Resolve of February 16, 1855, Amended by the Legislature and Passed December 28, 1859.* Boston: Wright and Potter, 1860.

State of New York. *Annual Reports of the Commissioners of Emigration of the State of New York.* 1847–1892.

State of New York. *Annual Reports of the State Board of Charities.* 1874–1890.

State of New York. *Laws of the State of New York.* 1785–1880.

State of New York. *Communication from the Governor relative to the Commissioners of Emigration.* 1876. Senate Doc. 69.

State of New York. *Report of the Delegates to the Emigration Convention, Held at Indianapolis.* 1871. Assembly Doc. 25.

State of New York. *Report of the select committee on the resolutions of the State of Rhode Island, on the introduction of foreign paupers and criminals.* 1855. Assembly Doc. 134.

State of New York. *The Revised Statues of the State of New York.* 3 vols. Edited by Montgomery H. Throop. Albany: Banks & Brothers, 1882.

State of Pennsylvania. *Annual Reports of the Board of Commissioners of Public Charities of the State of Pennsylvania.* 1870–1892.

Statistical View of the United States. Compiled by J. D. B. DeBow. Washington, DC: Beverley Tucker, 1854.

Synopsis of the Decisions of the Treasury Department on the Construction of the Tariff, Navigation, and Other Laws, for the Year Ending December 31, 1885. Washington, DC: US Government Printing Office, 1886.

UK Parliament, House of Commons. *Annual report of the commissioners for administering the laws for relief of the poor in Ireland, including the twenty-third report under the 10 & 11 Vic., c. 90, and the eighteenth report under the 14 & 15 Vic., c. 68; with appendices.* 1870 (C.156).

UK Parliament, House of Commons. *Copy of a letter addressed to Her Majesty's Secretary of State for the Home Department, by Edward Rushton, Esquire, Stipendiary Magistrate of Liverpool, bearing date 21st April 1849.* 1849 (266).

UK Parliament, House of Commons. *Destitute Irish (Liverpool). Copies of, or extracts from, any correspondence addressed to the Secretary of State for the Home Department, relative to the recent immigration of destitute Irish into Liverpool.* 1847 (193).

US Congress. *A Bill to Prevent the Introduction into the United States of Foreign Criminals and Paupers.* HR 124. 34th Cong., 1st sess., 1856.

US Congress. *Chinese Immigration.* 46th Cong, 2d sess., 1880. House Rep. 572.

US Congress. *Foreign Criminals and Paupers.* 34th Cong., 1st sess., 1856. House Rep. 359.

US Congress. *Foreign Paupers and Naturalization Laws.* 25th Cong., 2d sess., 1838. House Rep. 1040.

US Congress. *Reports of the Immigration Commission: Abstracts of Reports of the Immigration Commission.* Volume 2. 61st Cong., 3d sess. 1910. Senate Doc. 747.

US Congress. *Reports of the Immigration Commission: Immigration Legislation.* 61st Cong., 3d sess. 1910. Senate Doc. 758.

US Department of Treasury. *Arrivals of Alien Passengers and Immigrants in the United States from 1820 to 1892.* Washington, DC: US Government Printing Office, 1893.

Published Primary Documents

Annual Reports of the Commissioners of Emigration of the State of New York, from the Organization of Commission, May 5, 1847, to 1860, inclusive: Together with Tables and Reports, and Other Official Documents, Compiled and Prepared under Resolution Adopted by the Board, August 29, 1860. New York, 1861.

Basler, Roy P., ed. *The Collected Works of Abraham Lincoln.* 8 vols. New Brunswick, NJ: Rutgers University Press, 1953.

Boston Board of Trade. *Report on Congressional Bill (H.R. 3853), Proposing to Levy a National Head-Money Tax, and Otherwise to Interfere with the Freedom of Immigration.* Boston, 1877.

Boston Society for the Prevention of Pauperism. *Annual Reports.* 1851–1891.

Brightly, Frank F. *A Digest of the Laws and Ordinances of the City of Philadelphia.* Philadelphia: Kay & Brothers, 1887.

Brooks, Erastus. *American Citizenship and the Progress of American Civilization: An Oration Delivered before the Order of United Americans, at the Academy of Music, February 22d, 1858.* New York: C. E. Gildersleve, 1858.

Busey, Samuel C. *Immigration: Its Evils and Consequences.* New York: DeWitt and Davenport, 1856.

Dickens, Charles. *American Notes.* 1842. Reprint, New York: Modern Library, 1996.

Ely, Alfred B. *American Liberty, Its Sources—Its Dangers—Its Preservation: An Oration.* New York, 1850.

Foreign Pauperism in Philadelphia: A Memorial to the Legislature of Pennsylvania, Exhibiting Reasons for the Amendment of Certain Laws in Relation to the Poor and to Foreign Emigrants, with the Bill Annexed. Philadelphia, 1851.

Grattan, Thomas Colley. *Civilized America.* Two volumes. London: Bradbury and Evans, 1859.

Griscom, John H. *The Sanitary Condition of the Laboring Population of New York.* New York: Harper & Brothers, 1845.

Hale, Edward Everett. *Letters on Irish Emigration.* Boston: Phillips, Sampson, 1852.

Hill, Hamilton A., Thomas Russell, and E. H. Derby. *Arguments in Favor of the Freedom of Immigration at the Port of Boston, Addressed to the Committee on State Charities of the Massachusetts Legislature, April, 1871.* Boston: Wright & Porter, 1871.

Hone, Philip. *The Diary of Philip Hone, 1828–1851.* Edited by Allan Nevins. 1927. Reprint, New York: Kraus Reprint, 1969.

Kapp, Friedrich. *Immigration and the Commissioners of Emigration of the State of New York.* New York: The Nation Press, 1870.

The Know Nothing Almanac and True Americans' Manual. New York: DeWitt and Davenport, 1854, 1855, and 1856.

Melville, Herman. *Redburn: His First Voyage.* 1849. Reprint, New York: Penguin, 1986.

Mitchel, John. *The Last Conquest of Ireland (Perhaps).* Glasgow: R. & T. Washbourne, [1861].

Morse, Samuel F. B. *Foreign Conspiracy against the Liberties of the United States.* 7th ed. New York: American and Foreign Christian Union, 1855.

Nicholls, George. *A History of the English Poor Law, in Connection with the Legislation and Other Circumstances Affecting the Condition of the People.* London: John Murray, 1854.

Nicholls, George. *A History of the Irish Poor Law, in Connection with the Condition of the People.* London: John Murray, 1856.

Northend, Charles, ed. *Elihu Burritt; A Memorial Volume Containing a Sketch of His Life and Labors, with Selections from His Writings and Lectures, and Extracts from His Private Journals in Europe and America.* New York: D. Appleton, 1879.

Parker, Theodore. *The Material Condition of the People of Massachusetts.* Boston: Geo. C. Rand & Avery, 1860.

Pashley, Robert. *Pauperism and Poor Laws.* London: Longman Brown Green and Longmans, 1852.

Proceedings of a Conference Between Representatives of the Massachusetts State Board of Health, Lunacy and Charity, and the State Board of Charities of New York. Held in New York City, November 12, 1879. Albany: Weed, Parsons, 1880.

Proceedings of the Conference of Charities, Held in Connection with the General Meeting of the American Social Science Association, Detroit, May, 1875. Boston: Tolman & White, 1875.

Proceedings of the Conference of Charities, Held in Connection with the General Meeting of the American Social Science Association, at Saratoga, September, 1876. Albany: Joel Munsell, 1876.

Report of the Delegation Appointed by the Philadelphia Emigrant Society of the Emigration Laws in the State of New York: Together with a Memorial to the Legislature of Pennsylvania Praying That Honorable Body to Enact Similar Laws. Philadelphia: Merrihew and Thompson, 1854.

Report of the Executive Committee to the Board of Directors of the Emigrant's Friend Society, Established, April, 1848.

Report of a General Plan for the Promotion of Public and Personal Health, Devised, Prepared and Recommended by the Commissioners Appointed under a Resolve of the Legislature of Massachusetts, Relating to a Sanitary Survey of the State. Boston: Dutton & Wentworth, 1850.

Rules for the Government of the Board of Guardians of the Poor in the City of Philadelphia, Adopted May, 1851. Philadelphia: King and Baird, 1851.

Rules for the Government of the Board of Guardians of the Poor in the City of Philadelphia. Philadelphia, 1883.

Sanborn, F. B. "The Poor-Laws of New England." *North American Review* 106, no. 2 (1868): 483-514.

Sanborn, F. B., ed. *Proceedings of the Eighth Annual Conference of Charities and Correction, Held at Boston, July 25–30, 1881.* Boston: A. Williams, 1881.

Sanborn, F. B., ed. *Proceedings of the Seventh Annual Conference of Charities and Correction, Held at Cleveland, June and July, 1880.* Boston: A. Williams, 1880.

Sanborn, F. B., ed. *Proceedings of the Sixth Annual Conference of Charities, Held at Chicago, June, 1879.* Boston: A. Williams, 1879.

Shattuck, Lemuel. *Report to the Committee of the City Council Appointed to Obtain the Census of Boston for the Year 1845, Embracing Collateral Facts and Statistical Researches, Illustrating the History and Condition of the Population, and Their Means of Progress and Prosperity.* Boston: John H. Eastburn, 1846.

Trench, W. Steuart. *Realities of Irish Life.* London: Longmans, Green, 1869.

Tuke, J. H. *A Visit to Connaught in the Autumn of 1847. A Letter Addressed to the Central Relief Committee of the Society of Friends, Dublin.* 2nd ed. London: Charles Gilpin, 1848.

Weiss, John, ed. *Life and Correspondence of Theodore, Parker, Minister of the Twenty-Eighth Congregational Society, Boston.* 2 vols. New York: D. Appleton, 1864.

Whitney, Thomas R. *A Defence of the American Policy, as Opposed to the Encroachments of Foreign Influence, and Especially to the Interference of the Papacy in the Political Interests and Affairs of the United States.* New York: De Witt & Davenport, 1856.

Newspapers and Periodicals

American Celt (Boston)
American Patriot (Boston)
Atlantic Monthly
Baltimore Sun
Belfast News-Letter
Boston Atlas
Boston Daily Advertiser
Boston Daily Bee
Boston Daily Courier
Boston Daily Evening Transcript
Boston Globe
Boston Herald
Boston Pilot
Boston Post
Charleston Mercury

Congressional Globe
Congressional Record
Cork Constitution
Cork Examiner
Frank Leslie's Illustrated Newspaper (New York)
Freeman's Journal (Dublin)
Galway Vindicator
Halifax Christian Messenger
Harper's New Monthly Magazine
Harper's Weekly
Illustrated London News
Irish Times
Know-Nothing and American Crusader (Boston)
Liberator (Boston)
Liverpool Daily Post
Liverpool Mercury
Lowell Daily Citizen and News
Morning Chronicle (London)
National Era (Washington, DC)
New York Citizen
New York Commercial Advertiser
New York Daily Tribune
New York Evening Express
New York Herald
New York Irish Citizen
New York Irish-American
New York Times
New Orleans Picayune
Newburyport Herald
North American Review
Pall Mall Gazette (London)
Philadelphia Public Inquirer
Philadelphia Public Ledger
Puck
Quebec Mercury
Sacramento Weekly Union
Saint John Morning News
San Francisco Bulletin
Times (London)
Tralee Chronicle
Worcester National Aegis

SELECT SECONDARY SOURCES

Abbott, Edith. "Federal Immigration Policies, 1864–1924." *University Journal of Business* 2, no. 2 (March 1924): 133–156.

Abbott, Edith. *Historical Aspects of the Immigration Problem*. Chicago: University of Chicago Press, 1926.

Abbott, Edith. *Immigration: Select Documents and Case Records*. Chicago: University of Chicago Press, 1924.

Aleinikoff, T. Alexander. *Semblances of Sovereignty: The Constitution, the State, and American Citizenship.* Cambridge, MA: Harvard University Press, 2002.

Allen, Austin. *Origins of the* Dred Scott *Case: Jacksonian Jurisprudence and the Supreme Court, 1837–1857.* Athens: University of Georgia Press, 2006.

Anbinder, Tyler. *Five Points: The 19th-Century New York City Neighborhood That Invented Tap Dance, Stole Elections, and Became the World's Most Notorious Slum.* New York: Plume, 2002.

Anbinder, Tyler. "From Famine to Five Points: Lord Lansdowne's Irish Tenants Encounter North America's Most Notorious Slum." *American Historical Review* 107, no. 2 (April 2002): 350–387.

Anbinder, Tyler. "Lord Palmerston and the Irish Famine Emigration." *Historical Journal* 44, no. 2 (2001): 441–469.

Anbinder, Tyler. "Moving Beyond 'Rags to Riches': New York's Irish Famine Immigrants and Their Surprising Savings Accounts." *Journal of American History* 99, no. 3 (December 2012): 741–770.

Anbinder, Tyler. *Nativism & Slavery: The Northern Know Nothings & the Politics of the 1850s.* New York: Oxford University Press, 1992.

Ayers, Edward L. *The Promise of the New South: Life After Reconstruction.* New York: Oxford University Press, 1992.

Baker, Jean H. *Ambivalent Americans: The Know-Nothing Party in Maryland.* Baltimore: Johns Hopkins University Press, 1977.

Baseler, Marilyn C. *"Asylum for Mankind": America, 1607–1800.* Ithaca, NY: Cornell University Press, 1998.

Baum, Dale. *The Civil War Party System: The Case of Massachusetts, 1848–1876.* Chapel Hill: University of North Carolina Press, 1984.

Baynton, Douglas C. "Defectives in the Land: Disability and American Immigration Policy, 1882–1924." *Journal of American Ethnic History* 24, no. 3 (Spring 2005): 31–44.

Bayor, Ronald H. *Encountering Ellis Island: How European Immigrants Entered America.* Baltimore: Johns Hopkins University Press, 2014.

Beckert, Sven. *The Monied Metropolis: New York City and the Consolidation of the American Bourgeoisie, 1850–1896.* New York: Cambridge University Press, 2001.

Belchem, John. *Irish, Catholic and Scouse: The History of the Liverpool-Irish, 1800–1939.* Liverpool: Liverpool University Press, 2007.

Bennett, David H. *The Party of Fear: The American Far Right from Nativism to the Militia Movement.* Rev. ed. New York: Vintage Books, 1995.

Benton, Josiah Henry. *Warning Out in New England, 1656–1817.* Boston: W. B. Clarke Company, 1911.

Berger, Max. "Irish Emigrant and American Nativism as Seen by British Visitors, 1836–1860." *Pennsylvania Magazine of History and Biography* 70, no. 2 (April 1946): 146–160.

Bernstein, Iver. *The New York City Draft Riots: Their Significance for American Society and Politics in the Age of the Civil War.* New York: Oxford University Press, 1990.

Berthoff, Rowland. "Southern Attitudes Toward Immigration, 1865–1914." *Journal of Southern History* 17, no. 3 (1951): 328–360.

Bilder, Mary Sarah. "The Struggle Over Immigration: Indentured Servants, Slaves, and Articles of Commerce." *Missouri Law Review* 61, no. 4 (Fall 1996): 743–824.

Billington, Ray Allen. *The Protestant Crusade, 1800–1860: A Study of the Origins of American Nativism.* 1938. Reprint, Chicago: Quadrangle Books, 1964.

Boyer, Paul. *Urban Masses and Moral Order in America, 1820–1920.* Cambridge, MA: Harvard University Press, 1978.

Branscombe, Martha. "The Courts and the Poor Laws in New York State, 1784–1929." Chicago: University of Chicago Press, 1943.

Bredbenner, Candice Lewis. *A Nationality of Her Own: Women, Marriage, and the Law of Citizenship.* Berkeley: University of California Press, 1998.

Bremner, Robert H. *The Discovery of Poverty in the United States.* 1956. Reprint, New Brunswick, NJ: Transaction, 1992.

Bremner, Robert H. *The Public Good: Philanthropy and Welfare in the Civil War Era.* New York: Knopf, 1980.

Bric, Maurice J. *Ireland, Philadelphia and the Re-invention of America, 1760–1800.* Dublin: Four Courts Press, 2008.

Bruce, Susannah Ural. *The Harp and the Eagle: Irish-American Volunteers and the Union Army, 1861–1865.* New York: New York University Press, 2006.

Brundage, David. *Irish Nationalists in America: The Politics of Exile, 1798–1998.* New York: Oxford University Press, 2016.

Burrows, Edwin, and Mike Wallace. *Gotham: A History of New York City to 1898.* New York: Oxford University Press, 1999.

Cannato, Vincent J. *American Passage: The History of Ellis Island.* New York: HarperCollins, 2009.

Canny, Nicholas P. "The Ideology of English Colonization: From Ireland to America." *William and Mary Quarterly* 30, no. 4 (October 1973): 575–598.

Chang, Kornel. *Pacific Connections: The Making of the U.S.–Canadian Borderlands.* Berkeley: University of California Press, 2012.

Clark, Dennis. *The Irish in Philadelphia: Ten Generations of Urban Experience.* Philadelphia: Temple University Press, 1973.

Clement, Priscilla Ferguson. *Welfare and the Poor in the Nineteenth-Century City: Philadelphia, 1800–1854.* Cranbury, NJ: Associated University Presses, 1985.

Cohen, Patricia Cline. *The Murder of Helen Jewett: The Life and Death of a Prostitute in Nineteenth-Century New York.* New York: Vintage Books, 1999.

Cohn, Raymond L. *Mass Migration Under Sail: European Immigration to the Antebellum United States.* New York: Cambridge University Press, 2009.

Coleman, John F. *The Disruption of the Pennsylvania Democracy, 1848–1860.* Harrisburg: Pennsylvania Historical and Museum Commission, 1975.

Conforti, Joseph A. *Imagining New England: Explorations of Regional Identity from the Pilgrims to the Mid-Twentieth Century.* Chapel Hill: University of North Carolina Press, 2001.

Cowan, Mimi. "Immigrants, Nativists, and the Making of Chicago, 1835–1893." PhD diss., Boston College, 2015.

Cox, Thomas H. *Gibbons v. Ogden, Law, and Society in the Early Republic.* Athens: Ohio University Press, 2009.

Crossman, Virginia. *Local Government in Nineteenth-Century Ireland.* Belfast: The Queen's University of Belfast for the Ulster Society of Irish Historical Studies, 1994.

Crossman, Virginia. *Politics, Pauperism and Power in Late Nineteenth-Century Ireland.* Manchester: Manchester University Press, 2006.

Crossman, Virginia. *The Poor Law in Ireland, 1838–1948.* Dublin: Dundalgan Press, 2006.

Crossman, Virginia. *Poverty and the Poor Law in Ireland, 1850–1914.* Liverpool: Liverpool University Press, 2013.

Crossman, Virginia, and Peter Gray, eds. *Poverty and Welfare in Ireland, 1838–1948*. Dublin: Irish Academic Press, 2011.

Crowley, John, William J. Smyth, and Mike Murphy, eds. *Atlas of the Great Irish Famine*. New York: New York University Press, 2012.

Cummings, John. "Poor-Laws of Massachusetts and New York: With Appendices Containing the United State Immigration and Contract Labor Laws." *Publications of the American Economic Association* 10, no. 4 (July 1895): 15–135.

Curran, Thomas Joseph. "Know Nothings of New York State." PhD diss., Columbia University, 1963.

Curtis, L. Perry Jr. *Apes and Angels: The Irishman in Victorian Caricature*. Rev. ed. Washington, DC: Smithsonian Institution Press, 1997.

Daniels, Roger. *Guarding the Golden Door: American Immigration Policy and Immigrants Since 1882*. New York: Hill and Wang, 2004.

Dayton, Cornelia H., and Sharon V. Salinger. *Robert Love's Warnings: Searching for Strangers in Colonial Boston*. Philadelphia: University of Pennsylvania Press, 2014.

Delahanty, Ian. "Immigrants in a Time of Civil War: The Irish, Slavery, and the Union, 1845–1865." PhD diss., Boston College, 2013.

De Nie, Michael. *The Eternal Paddy: Irish Identity in the British Press, 1798–1882*. Madison: University of Wisconsin Press, 2004.

Dickson, R. J. *Ulster Emigration to Colonial America, 1718–1775*. London: Routledge and Kegan Paul, 1966.

Diner, Hasia R. *Erin's Daughters in America: Irish Immigrant Women in the Nineteenth Century*. Baltimore: Johns Hopkins University Press, 1983.

Dolan, Jay P. *The Immigrant Church: New York's Irish and German Catholics, 1815–1865*. 1975. Reprint, Notre Dame: University of Notre Dame Press, 1983.

Dolan, Jay P. *The Irish Americans: A History*. New York: Bloomsbury Press, 2008.

Donnelly, James S. Jr. *The Great Irish Potato Famine*. Phoenix Mill, UK: Sutton Publishing, 2001.

Driver, Felix. *Power and Pauperism: The Workhouse System, 1834–1884*. Cambridge: Cambridge University Press, 1993.

Duberman, Martin. *Charles Francis Adams, 1807–1886*. Stanford: Stanford University Press, 1960.

Duffy, John. *A History of Public Health in New York City 1625–1866*. New York: Russell Sage, 1968.

Duffy, Patrick J. "Assisted Emigration from the Shirley Estate, 1843–1854." *Clogher Record* 14, no. 2 (1992): 7–62.

Duffy, Patrick J., ed. *To and From Ireland: Planned Migration Schemes, c. 1600–2000*. Dublin: Geography Publications, 2004.

Dunn, Mary Lee. *Ballykilcline Rising: From Famine Ireland to Immigrant America*. Amherst: University of Massachusetts Press, 2008.

Ellis, Eilish. *Emigrants from Ireland, 1847–1852: State-Aided Emigration Schemes from Crown Estates in Ireland*. 1960. Reprint, Baltimore: Genealogical Publishing, 1993.

Erie, Stephen P. *Rainbow's End: Irish-Americans and the Dilemmas of Urban Machine Politics, 1840–1985*. Berkeley: University of California Press, 1988.

Ernst, Robert. *Immigrant Life in New York City, 1825–1863*. 1949. Reprint, Syracuse: Syracuse University Press, 1994.

Evans, Patricia Russell. "'Likely to Become a Public Charge': Immigration in the Backwaters of Administrative Law, 1882–1933." PhD diss., George Washington University, 1987.

Fahey, John H. "James Irwin: Irish Emigrant Agent, New York City, 1846–1858." *New York History* 93, no. 3 (Summer 2012): 219–245.

Fairchild, Amy L. *Science at the Borders: Immigrant Medical Inspection and the Shaping of the Modern Industrial Labor Force*. Baltimore: Johns Hopkins University Press, 2003.

Fehrenbacher, Don E. *The Dred Scott Case: Its Significance in American Law and Politics*. New York: Oxford University Press, 1978.

Fitzgerald, David Scott, and David Cook-Martín. *Culling the Masses: The Democratic Origins of Racist Immigration Policy in the Americas*. Cambridge, MA: Harvard University Press, 2014.

Fitzgerald, Maureen. *Habits of Compassion: Irish Catholic Nuns and the Origins of New York's Welfare System, 1830–1920*. Urbana: University of Chicago Press, 2006.

Fitzpatrick, David. *Irish Emigration, 1801–1921*. Dundalk, Ireland: Economic and Social History Society of Ireland, 1984.

Flaherty, Sandra, and Catherine Lavelle. "The State-Aided Emigration from the Crown Estates of Boughill and Irvilloughter, 1848–1849." *Galway Roots: Journal of the Galway Family History Society* 3, Famine Edition (1995): 77–86.

Foner, Eric. *Free Soil, Free Labor, Free Men: The Ideology of the Republican Party Before the Civil War*. 1970. Reprint, New York: Oxford University Press, 1995.

Foner, Eric. *Gateway to Freedom: The Hidden History of the Underground Railroad*. New York: Norton, 2015.

Foner, Eric. *Reconstruction: American's Unfinished Revolution, 1863–1877*. New York: Harper & Row, 1988.

Formisano, Ronald P. *The Transformation of Political Culture: Massachusetts Parties, 1790s–1840s*. New York: Oxford University Press, 1983.

Fox, James W. Jr. "Citizenship, Poverty, and Federalism: 1787–1882." *University of Pittsburgh Law Review* 60, no. 2 (Winter 1999): 421–577.

Franchot, Jenny. *Roads to Rome: The Antebellum Protestant Encounter with Catholicism*. Berkeley: University of California Press, 1994.

Franzen, Katharine Mary Grigsby. "Free to Leave: Government Assisted Emigration Under the 1834 Poor Law." PhD diss., University of Virginia, 1996.

Fraser, Derek, ed. *The New Poor Law in the Nineteenth Century*. New York: St. Martin's, 1976.

Freyer, Tony Allan. *The Passenger Cases and the Commerce Clause: Immigrants, Blacks, and States' Rights in Antebellum America*. Lawrence: University Press of Kansas, 2014.

Gallman, J. Matthew. *Receiving Erin's Children: Philadelphia, Liverpool, and the Irish Famine Migration, 1845–1855*. Chapel Hill: University of North Carolina Press, 2000.

Gardner, Martha. *The Qualities of a Citizen: Women, Immigration, and Citizenship, 1870–1965*. Princeton, NJ: Princeton University Press, 2005.

Garis, Roy L. *Immigration Restriction: A Study of the Opposition to and Regulation of Immigration into the United States*. New York: Macmillan, 1927.

Gienapp, William E. *The Origins of the Republican Party, 1852–1856*. New York: Oxford University Press, 1987.

Gleeson, David T. *The Irish in the South, 1815–1877*. Chapel Hill: University of North Carolina Press, 2001.

Glickstein, Jonathan A. *American Exceptionalism, American Anxiety: Wages, Competition, and Degraded Labor in the Antebellum United States*. Charlottesville: University of Virginia Press, 2002.

Glickstein, Jonathan A. *Concepts of Free Labor in Antebellum America*. New Haven, CT: Yale University Press, 1991.

Golash-Boza, Tanya Maria. *Deported: Immigrant Policing, Disposable Labor, and Global Capitalism*. New York: New York University Press, 2015.

Goldberg, Chad Alan. *Citizens and Paupers: Relief, Rights, and Race, from the Freedmen's Bureau to Workfare*. Chicago: University of Chicago Press, 2007.

Gray, Peter. *Famine, Land and Politics: British Government and Irish Society, 1843–1850*. Dublin: Irish Academic Press, 1999.

Gray, Peter. *The Irish Famine*. New York: Harry N. Abrams, 1995.

Gray, Peter. *The Making of the Irish Poor Law, 1815–1843*. Manchester: Manchester University Press, 2009.

Green, David R. *From Artisans to Paupers: Economic Change and Poverty in London, 1790–1870*. Aldershot: Scolar Press, 1995.

Green, David R. *Pauper Capital: London and the Poor Law, 1790–1870*. Burlington, VT: Ashgate, 2010.

Green, Elna C. *This Business of Relief: Confronting Poverty in a Southern City, 1740–1940*. Athens: University of Georgia Press, 2003.

Griffin, Patrick. *The People with No Name: Ireland's Ulster Scots, America's Scots Irish, and the Creation of a British Atlantic World, 1689–1764*. Princeton, NJ: Princeton University Press, 2001.

Grob, Gerald N. *Mental Institutions in America: Social Policy to 1875*. New York: Free Press, 1973.

Grob, Gerald N. *The State and the Mentally Ill: A History of Worcester State Hospital in Massachusetts, 1830–1920*. Chapel Hill: University of North Carolina Press, 1966.

Gyory, Andrew. *Closing the Gate: Race, Politics, and the Chinese Exclusion Act*. Chapel Hill: University of North Carolina Press, 1998.

Hadden, Sally E., and Alfred L. Brophy, eds. *A Companion to American Legal History*. Malden, MA: Blackwell, 2013.

Halperin, Terri Diane. *The Alien and Sedition Acts of 1798: Testing the Constitution*. Baltimore: Johns Hopkins University Press, 2016.

Handlin, Oscar. *Boston's Immigrants: A Study in Acculturation*. Rev. ed. New York: Atheneum, 1968.

Hansen, Marcus Lee. *The Atlantic Migration 1607–1860: A History of the Continuing Settlement of the United States*. 1940. Reprint, New York: Harper & Brothers, 1961.

Hardesty, Jared Ross. *Unfreedom: Slavery and Dependence in Eighteenth-Century Boston*. New York: New York University Press, 2016.

Harding, Walter, and Carl Bode, eds. *The Correspondence of Henry David Thoreau*. New York: New York University Press, 1958.

Helbich, Wolfgang, and Walter D. Kamphoefner. "The Hour of Your Liberation is Getting Closer and Closer ..." *Studia Migracyjne—Przeglad Polonijny* 35, no. 3 (2009): 43–58.

Hernández, Kelly Lytle. *Migra! A History of the U.S. Border Patrol*. Berkeley: University of California Press, 2010.

Herndon, Ruth Wallis. *Unwelcome Americans: Living on the Margin in Early New England*. Philadelphia: University of Pennsylvania Press, 2001.

Hester, Torrie. "'Protection, Not Punishment': Legislative and Judicial Formation of U.S. Deportation Policy, 1882–1904." *Journal of American Ethnic History* 30, no. 1 (Fall 2010): 11–36.

Higham, John. *Send These to Me: Jews and Other Immigrants in Urban America*. Rev. ed. Baltimore: Johns Hopkins University Press, 1984.

Higham, John. *Strangers in the Land: Patterns of American Nativism, 1860–1925*. 1955. Reprint, New York: Atheneum, 1970.

Hirota, Hidetaka. "'The Great Entrepot for Mendicants': Foreign Poverty and Immigration Control in New York State to 1882." *Journal of American Ethnic History* 33, no. 2 (Winter 2014): 5–32.

Hirota, Hidetaka. "The Moment of Transition: State Officials, the Federal Government, and the Formation of American Immigration Policy." *Journal of American History* 99, no. 4 (March 2013): 1092–1108.

Hirota, Hidetaka. "Nativism, Citizenship, and the Deportation of Paupers in Massachusetts, 1837–1883." PhD diss., Boston College, 2012.

Hofstra, Warren R., ed. *Ulster to America: The Scots-Irish Migration Experience, 1680–1830*. Knoxville: University of Tennessee Press, 2012.

Hoglund, A. William. *Finnish Immigrants in America, 1880–1920*. Madison: University of Wisconsin Press, 1960.

Hollett, David. *Passage to the New World: Packet Ships and Irish Famine Emigrants, 1845–1851*. Abergavanny, UK: P. M. Heaton, 1995.

Holt, Michael F. *The Political Crisis of the 1850s*. New York: Norton, 1978.

Huston, James L. *The Panic of 1857 and the Coming of the Civil War*. Baton Rouge: Louisiana State University Press, 1987.

Hutchinson, E. P. *Legislative History of American Immigration Policy, 1798–1965*. Philadelphia: University of Pennsylvania Press, 1981.

Isenberg, Nancy. *Sex and Citizenship in Antebellum America*. Chapel Hill: University of North Carolina Press, 1998.

Jacobs, Meg., William J. Novak, and Julian E. Zelizer, eds. *The Democratic Experiment: New Directions in American Political History*. Princeton, NJ: Princeton University Press, 2003.

Jacobson, Matthew Frye. *Barbarian Virtues: The United States Encounters Foreign Peoples at Home and Abroad, 1876–1917*. New York: Hill and Wang, 2000.

Jacobson, Matthew Frye. *Whiteness of a Different Color: European Immigrants and the Alchemy of Race*. Cambridge, MA: Harvard University Press, 1998.

Janis, Ely M. *A Greater Ireland: The Land League and Transatlantic Nationalism in Gilded Age America*. Madison: University of Wisconsin Press, 2015.

Jeffery, Keith, ed. *'An Irish Empire'? Aspects of Ireland and the British Empire*. Manchester: Manchester University Press, 1996.

Johnson, Herbert A. *Gibbons v. Ogden: John Marshall, Steamboats, and the Commerce Clause*. Lawrence: University Press of Kansas, 2010.

Johnson, H. J. M. *British Emigration Policy, 1815–1830: 'Shovelling out Paupers'*. Oxford: Oxford University Press, 1972.

Jones, Douglas Lamar. "The Strolling Poor: Transiency in Eighteenth-Century Massachusetts." *Journal of Social History* 8, no. 3 (Spring 1975): 28–54.

Jung, Moon-Ho. *Coolies and Cane: Race, Labor, and Sugar in the Age of Emancipation*. Baltimore: Johns Hopkins University Press, 2006.

Kanazawa, Mark. "Immigration, Exclusion, and Taxation: Anti-Chinese Legislation in Gold Rush California." *Journal of Economic History* 65, no. 3 (September 2005): 779–805.

Kanstroom, Daniel. *Aftermath: Deportation Law and the New American Diaspora*. New York: Oxford University Press, 2012.

Kanstroom, Daniel. *Deportation Nation: Outsiders in American History*. Cambridge, MA: Harvard University Press, 2007.

Katz, Michael B. *In the Shadow of the Poorhouse: A Social History of Welfare in America.* Rev. ed. New York: Basic Books, 1996.

Katz, Michael B. *Poverty and Policy in American History.* New York: Academic Press, 1983.

Katz, Michael B. *The Undeserving Poor: America's Enduring Confrontation with Poverty.* 2nd ed. New York: Oxford University Press, 2013.

Kelly, Patrick J. *Creating a National Home: Building the Veterans' Welfare State, 1860–1900.* Cambridge, MA: Harvard University Press, 1997.

Kelso, Robert W. *The History of Public Poor Relief in Massachusetts, 1620–1920.* Boston: Houghton Mifflin, 1922.

Kenny, Kevin. *The American Irish: A History.* New York: Longman, 2000.

Kenny, Kevin. "Diaspora and Comparison: The Global Irish as a Case Study." *Journal of American History* 90, no. 1 (June 2003): 134–162.

Kenny, Kevin. "Immigration." In *A Companion to Abraham Lincoln,* edited by Michael Green. Malden, MA: Blackwell, forthcoming.

Kenny, Kevin, ed. *Ireland and the British Empire.* Oxford History of the British Empire. Oxford: Oxford University Press, 2004.

Kenny, Kevin. *Making Sense of the Molly Maguires.* New York: Oxford University Press, 1998.

Kenny, Kevin. *Peaceable Kingdom Lost: The Paxton Boys and the Destruction of William Penn's Holy Experiment.* New York: Oxford University Press, 2009.

Kerber, Linda K. *No Constitutional Right to be Ladies: Women and the Obligations of Citizenship.* New York: Hill and Wang, 1998.

Kettner, James H. *The Development of American Citizenship, 1608–1870.* Chapel Hill: University of North Carolina Press, 1978.

Keyssar, Alexander. *Out of Work: The First Century of Unemployment in Massachusetts.* New York: Cambridge University Press, 1986.

Keyssar, Alexander. *The Right to Vote: The Contested History of Democracy in the United States.* New York: Basic Books, 2000.

Kinealy, Christine. *Charity and the Great Hunger in Ireland.* New York: Bloomsbury, 2013.

Kinealy, Christine. *This Great Calamity: The Irish Famine, 1845–52.* Boulder, CO: Roberts Rinehart, 1995.

Klebaner, Benjamin J. "The Myth of Foreign Pauper Dumping in the United States." *Social Service Review* 35, no. 3 (September 1961): 302–309.

Klebaner, Benjamin J. "Public Poor Relief in America, 1790–1860." PhD diss., Columbia University, 1952.

Klebaner, Benjamin J. "State and Local Immigration Regulation in the United States Before 1882." *International Review of Social History* 3, no. 2 (1958): 269–295.

Knighton, Andrew Lyndon. *Idle Threats: Men and the Limits of Productivity in Nineteenth Century America.* New York: New York University Press, 2012.

Knobel, Dale T. *"America for the Americans": The Nativist Movement in the United States.* New York: Twayne Publishers, 1996.

Knobel, Dale T. *Paddy and the Republic: Ethnicity and Nationality in Antebellum America.* Middletown, CT: Wesleyan University Press, 1986.

Kraut, Alan M. *Silent Travelers: Germs, Genes, and the "Immigrant Menace."* Baltimore: Johns Hopkins University Press, 1995.

Kulikoff, Allan. "The Progress of Inequality in Revolutionary Boston." *William and Mary Quarterly* 28, no. 3 (July 1971): 375–412.

Kurian, George Thomas, ed. *A Historical Guide to the U.S. Government.* New York: Oxford University Press, 1998.

Laurie, Bruce. *Artisans into Workers: Labor in Nineteenth-Century America.* New York: Hill and Wang, 1989.

Laurie, Bruce. *Beyond Garrison: Antislavery and Social Reform.* New York: Cambridge University Press, 2005.

Law, Anna O. *The Immigration Battle in American Courts.* New York: Cambridge University Press, 2010.

Law, Anna O. "Lunatics, Idiots, Paupers, and Negro Seamen—Immigration Federalism and the Early American State." *Studies in American Political Development* 28 (October 2014): 107–128.

Lears, Jackson. *Rebirth of a Nation: The Making of Modern America, 1877–1920.* New York: HarperCollins, 2009.

Lee, Erika. *At America's Gates: Chinese Immigration during the Exclusion Era, 1882–1943.* Chapel Hill: University of North Carolina Press, 2003.

Lee, Erika. "The 'Yellow Peril' and Asian Exclusion in the Americas." *Pacific Historical Review* 76, no. 4 (November 2007): 537–562.

Lee, Erika, and Judy Yung. *Angel Island: Immigrant Gateway to America.* New York: Oxford University Press, 2010.

Lee, J. J., and Marion R. Casey, eds. *Making the Irish American: History and Heritage of the Irish in the United States.* New York: New York University Press, 2006.

Levine, Bruce. "Conservativism, Nativism, and Slavery: Thomas R. Whitney and the Origins of the Know-Nothing Party." *Journal of American History* 88, no. 2 (September 2001): 455–488.

Levine, Bruce. "'The Vital Element of the Republican Party': Antislavery, Nativism, and Abraham Lincoln." *Journal of the Civil War Era* 1, no. 4 (December 2011): 481–505.

Lew-Williams, Beth. "Before Restriction Became Exclusion: America's Experiment in Diplomatic Immigration Control." *Pacific Historical Review* 83, no. 1 (February 2014): 24–56.

Leyburn, James G. *The Scotch-Irish: A Social History.* Chapel Hill: University of North Carolina Press, 1962.

Lindsay, Matthew J. "Immigration as Invasion: Sovereignty, Security, and the Origins of the Federal Immigration Policy." *Harvard Civil Rights-Civil Liberties Law Review* 45, no. 1 (2010): 1–56.

Lindsay, Matthew J. "Preserving the Exceptional Republic: Political Economy, Race, and the Federalization of American Immigration." *Yale Journal of Law and the Humanities* 17, no. 2 (Summer 2005): 181–251.

Litwack, Leon F. *Been in the Storm So Long: The Aftermath of Slavery.* New York: Vintage Books, 1980.

Litwack, Leon F. *North of Slavery: The Negro in the Free States, 1790–1860.* Chicago: University of Chicago Press, 1961.

Lord, Robert H., John E. Sexton, and Edward T. Harrington. *History of the Archdiocese of Boston in the Various Stages of Its Development, 1604 to 1943.* 3 vols. New York: Sheed & Ward, 1944.

Lyne, Gerard J. *The Lansdowne Estate in Kerry Under the Agency of William Steuart Trench, 1849–1872.* Dublin: Geography Publications, 2001.

MacDonagh, Oliver. "The Economy and Society, 1830–45." In *A New History of Ireland V, Ireland Under the Union, I, 1801–70,* edited by W. E. Vaughan, 218–241. Oxford: Clarendon Press, 1989.

MacDonagh, Oliver. "The Irish Famine Emigration to the United States." *Perspectives in American History* 10 (1976): 357–446.

MacKay, Donald. *Flight from Famine: The Coming of the Irish to Canada.* Toronto: McClelland & Stewart, 1992.

MacRaild, Donald. *The Irish Diaspora in Britain, 1750–1939.* New York: Palgrave Macmillan, 2011.

Mageean, Deirdre M. "Emigration from Irish Ports." *Journal of American Ethnic History* 13, no. 1 (Fall 1993): 6–30.

Maltz, Earl M. *Fugitive Slave on Trial: The Anthony Burns Case and Abolitionist Outrage.* Lawrence: University of Kansas Press, 2010.

McClain, Charles J. *In Search of Equality: The Chinese Struggle Against Discrimination in Nineteenth-Century America.* Berkeley: University of California Press, 1994.

McKeown, Adam. *Melancholy Order: Asian Migration and the Globalization of Borders.* New York: Columbia University Press, 2008.

McMahon, Cian T. *The Global Dimensions of Irish Identity: Race, Nation, and the Popular Press, 1840–1880.* Chapel Hill: University of North Carolina Press, 2015.

McPherson, James M. *Battle Cry of Freedom: The Civil War Era.* New York: Oxford University Press, 1988.

Meagher, Timothy J. *The Columbia Guide to Irish American History.* New York: Columbia University Press, 2005.

Meltsner, Heli. *The Poorhouses of Massachusetts: A Cultural and Architectural History.* Jefferson, NC: McFarland, 2012.

Milano, Kenneth W. *The Philadelphia Nativist Riots: Irish Kensington Erupts.* Charleston, SC: History Press, 2013.

Miller, Kerby A. *Emigrants and Exiles: Ireland and the Irish Exodus to North America.* New York: Oxford University Press, 1985.

Miller, Randall M. "The Enemy Within: Some Effects of Foreign Immigrants on Antebellum Southern Cities." *Southern Studies* 24, no. 1 (1985): 30–53.

Mohl, Raymond A. *Poverty in New York, 1783–1825.* New York: Oxford University Press, 1971.

Moloney, Deirdre M. *American Catholic Lay Groups and Transnational Social Reform in the Progressive Era.* Chapel Hill: University of North Carolina Press, 2002.

Moloney, Deirdre M. *National Insecurities: Immigrants and U.S. Deportation Policy Since 1882.* Chapel Hill: University of North Carolina Press, 2012.

Montgomery, David. *Beyond Equality: Labor and the Radical Republicans, 1862–1872.* New York: Knopf, 1967.

Moran, Gerard. *Sending Out Ireland's Poor: Assisted Emigration to North America in the Nineteenth Century.* Dublin: Four Court Press, 2004.

Moran, Gerard. *Sir Robert Gore Booth and His Landed Estates in County Sligo, 1814–1876: Land, Famine, Emigration and Politics.* Dublin: Four Court Press, 2006.

Motomura, Hiroshi. *Americans in Waiting: The Lost Story of Immigration and Citizenship in the United States.* New York: Oxford University Press, 2006.

Mulkern, John R. *The Know-Nothing Party in Massachusetts: The Rise and Fall of A People's Movement.* Boston: Northeastern University Press, 1990.

Murphy, Angela F. *American Slavery, Irish Freedom: Abolition, Immigrant Citizenship, and the Transatlantic Movement for Irish Repeal.* Baton Rouge: Louisiana State University Press, 2010.

Murphy, Peter D. *Poor Ignorant Children: Irish Famine Orphans in St John, New Brunswick.* Halifax: Saint Mary's University, 1999.

Mushkat, Jerome. *Fernando Wood: A Political Biography.* Kent, OH: Kent State University Press, 1990.

Neal, Frank, *Black '47: Britain and the Famine Irish.* London: Newsham Press, 1998.

Nellis, Eric, and Anne Decker Cecere, eds. *The Eighteenth-Century Records of the Boston Overseers of the Poor*. Charlottesville: University of Virginia Press, 2007.

Neuman, Gerald L. *Strangers to the Constitution: Immigrants, Borders, and Fundamental Law*. Princeton, NJ: Princeton University Press, 1996.

Ngai, Mae M. "Chinese Gold Miners and the 'Chinese Question' in Nineteenth-Century California and Victoria." *Journal of American History* 101, no. 4 (March 2015): 1082–1105.

Ngai, Mae M. *Impossible Subjects: Illegal Aliens and the Making of Modern America*. Princeton, NJ: Princeton University Press, 2004.

Novak, William J. *The People's Welfare: Law and Regulation in Nineteenth-Century America*. Chapel Hill: University of North Carolina Press, 1996.

O'Connor, John. *The Workhouses of Ireland: The Fate of Ireland's Poor*. Dublin: Anvil Books, 1995.

O'Connor, Thomas H. *The Boston Irish: A Political History*. Boston: Northeastern University Press, 1995.

O'Connor, Thomas H. *Fitzpatrick's Boston, 1846–1866: John Bernard Fitzpatrick, Third Bishop of Boston*. Boston: Northeastern University Press, 1984.

O'Mahony, S. C. "Emigration from the Limerick Workhouse, 1848–1860." *Irish Ancestor* 14, no. 2 (1982): 83–94.

O'Malley, Brendan P. "Protecting the Stranger: The Origins of U.S. Immigration Regulation in Nineteenth-Century New York." PhD diss., City University of New York, 2015.

O'Sullivan, Patrick, ed. *The Meaning of the Famine* (Irish World Wide Vol. 6). London: Leicester University Press, 1997.

Ó Gráda, Cormac. *Black '47 and Beyond: The Great Irish Famine in History, Economy, and Memory*. Princeton, NJ: Princeton University Press, 1999.

Overdyke, W. Darrell. *The Know-Nothing Party in the South*. Baton Rouge: Louisiana State University Press, 1950.

Page, Thomas W. "Some Economic Aspects of Immigration Before 1870: I." *Journal of Political Economy* 20, no. 10 (December 1912): 1011–1128.

Page, Thomas W. "The Transportation of Immigrants and Reception Arrangements in the Nineteenth Century." *Journal of Political Economy* 19, no. 9 (November 1911): 732–749.

Parker, Kunal M. "From Poor Law to Immigration Law: Changing Visions of Territorial Community in Antebellum Massachusetts." *Historical Geography* 28 (2000): 61–85.

Parker, Kunal M. *Making Foreigners: Immigration and Citizenship Law in America, 1600–2000*. New York: Cambridge University Press, 2015.

Parker, Kunal M. "State, Citizenship, and Territory: The Legal Construction of Immigrants in Antebellum Massachusetts." *Law and History Review* 19, no. 3 (Autumn 2001): 583–643.

Pegler-Gordon, Anna. *In Sight of America: Photography and the Development of U.S. Immigration Policy*. Berkeley: University of California Press, 2009.

Pfaelzer, Jean. *Driven Out: The Forgotten War Against Chinese Americans*. New York: Random House, 2007.

Pirraglia, Rose May. "The Context of Urban Pauperism: Foreign Immigration and American Economic Growth, 1815–1855." PhD diss., Columbia University, 1984.

Pitkin, Thomas M. *Keepers of the Gate: A History of Ellis Island*. New York: New York University Press, 1975.

Proper, Emberson Edward. *Colonial Immigration Laws: A Study of the Regulation of Immigration by the English Colonies in America*. New York: Columbia University Press, 1900.

Purcell, Richard J. "The New York Commissioners of Emigration and Irish Immigrants: 1847–1860." *Studies: An Irish Quarterly Review* 37, no. 145 (1948): 29–42.

Quigley, David. *Second Founding: New York City, Reconstruction, and the Making of American Democracy*. New York: Hill and Wang, 2004.

Read, Gordon. "Liverpool—The Flood-Gate of the Old World: A Study in Ethnic Attitudes." *Journal of American Ethnic History* 13, no. 1 (Fall 1993): 31–47.

Rees, Jim. *Surplus People: The Fitzwilliam Clearances, 1847–1856*. Cork: Collins Press, 2000.

Ricci, David M. *Good Citizenship in America*. New York: Cambridge University Press, 2004.

Richardson, Heather Cox. *The Death of Reconstruction: Race, Labor, and Politics in the Post-Civil War North, 1865–1901*. Cambridge, MA: Harvard University Press, 2001.

Richardson, Heather Cox. *The Greatest Nation of the Earth: Republican Economic Policies During the Civil War*. Cambridge, MA: Harvard University Press, 1997.

Robertson, Craig. *The Passport in America: The History of A Document*. New York: Oxford University Press, 2010.

Roediger, David R. *The Wages of Whiteness: Race and the Making of the American Working Class*. Rev. ed. New York: Verso, 1999.

Rose, Michael E. *The English Poor Law 1780–1930*. Newton Abbot: David & Charles, 1971.

Rose, Michael E., ed. *The Poor and the City: The English Poor Law in Its Urban Context, 1834–1914*. New York: St. Martin's, 1985.

Rothman, David J. *The Discovery of the Asylum: Social Order and Disorder in the New Republic*. Rev. ed. New Brunswick, NJ: Aldine Transaction, 2002.

Rugemer, Edward Bartlett. *The Problem of Emancipation: The Caribbean Roots of the American Civil War*. Baton Rouge: Louisiana State University Press, 2008.

Ruswick, Brent. *Almost Worthy: The Poor, Paupers, and the Science of Charity in America, 1877–1917*. Bloomington: Indiana University Press, 2013.

Saloutos, Theodore. *They Remember America: The Story of the Repatriated Greek-Americans*. Berkeley: University of California Press, 1956.

Salyer, Lucy E. *Laws Harsh as Tigers: Chinese Immigrants and the Shaping of Modern Immigration Law*. Chapel Hill: University of North Carolina Press, 1995.

Samito, Christian G. *Becoming American Under Fire: Irish Americans, African Americans, and the Politics of Citizenship During the Civil War Era*. Ithaca, NY: Cornell University Press, 2009.

Saxton, Alexander. *The Indispensable Enemy: Labor and the Anti-Chinese Movement in California*. Berkeley: University of California Press, 1971.

Scally, Robert James. *The End of Hidden Ireland: Rebellion, Famine, and Emigration*. New York: Oxford University Press, 1995.

Scally, Robert James. "Liverpool Ships and Irish Emigrants in the Age of Sail." *Journal of Social History* 17, no. 1 (Autumn 1983): 5–30.

Schmidt, James D. *Free to Work: Labor Law, Emancipation, and Reconstruction, 1815–1880*. Athens: University of Georgia Press, 1998.

Schneider, David M. *The History of Public Welfare in New York State, 1609–1866*. Chicago: University of Chicago Press, 1938.

Schneider, David M., and Albert Deutsch. *The History of Public Welfare in New York State, 1867–1940*. Chicago: University of Chicago Press, 1941.

Schneider, Dorothee. *Crossing Borders: Migration and Citizenship in the Twentieth-Century United States*. Cambridge, MA: Harvard University Press, 2011.

Schoeppner, Michael Alan. "Navigating the Dangerous Atlantic: Racial Quarantines, Black Sailors and United States Constitutionalism." PhD diss., University of Florida, 2010.

SenGupta, Gunja. *From Slavery to Poverty: The Racial Origins of Welfare in New York, 1840–1918*. New York: New York University Press, 2009.

Shepperson, Wilbur S. *Emigration & Disenchantment: Portraits of Englishmen Repatriated from the United States*. Norman: University of Oklahoma Press, 1965.

Silverman, Jason H. *Lincoln and the Immigrant*. Carbondale: Southern Illinois University Press, 2015.

Sim, David. *A Union Forever: The Irish Question and U.S. Foreign Relations in the Victorian Age*. Ithaca, NY: Cornell University Press, 2013.

Skocpol, Theda. *Protecting Soldiers and Mothers: The Political Origins of Social Policy in the United States*. Cambridge, MA: Harvard University Press, 1992.

Smith, Rogers M. *Civic Ideals: Conflicting Visions of Citizenship in U.S. History*. New Haven, CT: Yale University Press, 1997.

Smith, Stacey L. *Freedom's Frontier: California and the Struggle over Unfree Labor, Emancipation, and Reconstruction*. Chapel Hill: University of North Carolina Press, 2013.

Snay, Mitchell. *Fenians, Freedmen, and Southern Whites: Race and Nationality in the Era of Reconstruction*. Baton Rouge: Louisiana State University Press, 2007.

Snell, K. D. M. *Parish and Belonging: Community, Identity and Welfare in England and Wales, 1700–1950*. Cambridge: Cambridge University Press, 2006.

Stanley, Amy Dru. *From Bondage to Contract: Wage Labor, Marriage, and the Market in the Age of Slave Emancipation*. New York: Cambridge University Press, 1998.

Stansell, Christine. *City of Women: Sex and Class in New York, 1789–1860*. Urbana: University of Illinois Press, 1987.

Stolarik, M. Mark, ed. *Forgotten Doors: The Other Ports of Entry to the United States*. Cranbury, NJ: Associated University Presses, 1988.

Steinfeld, Robert J. *Coercion, Contract, and Free Labor in the Nineteenth Century*. New York: Cambridge University Press, 2001.

Steinfeld, Robert J. "Property and Suffrage in the Early Republic." *Stanford Law Review* 41, no. 2 (January 1989): 335–376.

Stephenson, Kathryn. "The Quarantine War: The Burning of the New York Marine Hospital in 1858." *Public Health Reports* 119, no. 1 (2004): 79–92.

Svejda, George J. *Castle Garden as an Immigrant Depot, 1855–1890*. Washington, DC: National Park Service, 1968.

Tichenor, Daniel J. *Dividing Lines: The Politics of Immigration Control in America*. Princeton, NJ: Princeton University Press, 2002.

Torpey, John. *The Invention of the Passport: Surveillance, Citizenship, and the State*. New York: Cambridge University Press, 2000.

Trattner, Walter I. *From Poor Law to Welfare State: A History of Social Welfare in America*. 6th ed. New York: Free Press, 1999.

Tuerk, Edward F. "The Supreme Court and Public Policy: The Regulation of Immigration, 1820–82." Master's thesis, University of Chicago, 1951.

Ueda, Reed, ed. *A Companion to American Immigration*. Malden, MA: Blackwell, 2006.

Van Vleck, William C. *The Administrative Control of Aliens: A Study in Administrative Law and Procedure*. New York: Commonwealth Fund, 1932.

Vaughan, W. E., ed. *A New History of Ireland V, Ireland Under the Union, I, 1801–70.* Oxford: Clarendon Press, 1989.

Vaughan, W. E., and A. J. Fitzpatrick, eds. *Irish Historical Statistics: Population, 1821–1971.* Dublin: Royal Irish Academy, 1978.

Von Frank, Albert J. *The Trials of Anthony Burns: Freedom and Slavery in Emerson's Boston*. Cambridge, MA: Harvard University Press, 1998.

Wagner, David. *The Poorhouse: America's Forgotten Institution.* Lanham, MD: Rowman & Littlefield, 2005.

Welke, Barbara Young. *Law and the Borders of Belonging in the Long Nineteenth Century United States*. New York: Cambridge University Press, 2010.

Williams, E. Russ Jr. "Louisiana's Public and Private Immigration Endeavors: 1866–1893." *Louisiana History* 15, no. 2 (Spring 1974): 153–173.

Wilson, David A. *United Irishmen, United States: Immigrant Radicals in the Early Republic*. Ithaca, NY: Cornell University Press, 1998.

Woodham-Smith, Cecil. *Great Hunger: Ireland, 1845–1849*. New York: Harper and Row, 1962.

Woodward, C. Vann. *Origins of the New South, 1877–1913*. Baton Rouge: Louisiana State University Press, 1955.

Wyman, Mark. *Round-Trip America: The Immigrants Return to Europe, 1880–1930*. Ithaca, NY: Cornell University Press, 1996.

Young, Elliott. *Alien Nation: Chinese Migration in the Americas from the Coolie Era Through World War II*. Chapel Hill: University of North Carolina Press, 2014.

Zesch, Scott. *The Chinatown War: Chinese Los Angeles and the Massacre of 1871*. New York: Oxford University Press, 2012.

Zolberg, Aristide R. *A Nation by Design: Immigration Policy in the Fashioning of America*. Cambridge, MA: Harvard University Press, 2006.

INDEX

immigration levels in, 97, 146

Irish immigrants in, 1, 4, 17–18, 23, 27, 33, 36–38, 49, 51, 58–63, 65, 75, 98, 100–101, 104, 116, 122–23, 193, 195, 198–99

Know-Nothing movement in, 96, 102, 125

Lunatic Hospital in, 80

North End neighborhood in, 51

Panic of 1857 and, 126

passenger law enforcement in, 72, 78

South Boston neighborhood in, 95

Superintendent of Alien Passengers in, 62–63, 65–68, 70–72, 75, 77–79, 96, 112, 133, 158

Whig Party in, 50

Boughill (Crown estate in Ireland), 29

"Boy and Girl at Cahera" (illustration), 38

Boyle, Edward, 1

Brady, Elisa, 1

Brady, William V., 64

Braydon, Honor and Thomas, 35

Brennan, Denis, 33

Brennan, Mary, 196–97

"Bridget O'Donnel and Children" (illustration), 39

Bridgewater state almshouse (Massachusetts)

compulsory labor at, 142

deportations from, 106–7, 117, 199

as facility for vagrants, 141–43, 147–48, 199

illustration of, 81

Irish immigrants in, 1, 28, 106–7, 117

women at, 148

Briggs, George N., 74

British Poor Law Commissioners, 34, 170

British West Indies, 54

Brooks, Erastus, 103

Brownlee, William C., 50

Bullock, Alexander H., 134

Burlingame Treaty (1868), 90–91, 131, 145, 189

Burns, Anthony, 112–13, 115

Burritt, Elihu, 23

Butler, Abbey, 169

Butler, Benjamin, 193

Cahill, D. (member of Cork Board of Guardians), 167

Cahirciveen (Ireland), 180, 199

California

Asian women banned from immigration (1870) to, 145

Chinese immigrants in, 9–10, 88–91, 145–46, 184, 189–90

Chinese Police Tax (1862) in, 90

Commissioner of Emigration in, 89–91, 207

Foreign Miners' Tax (1854) in, 89

gold discovery (1848) in, 88

immigration policies in, 2–3, 10, 71, 83, 88–91, 145, 207

Know-Nothing movement in, 102

passenger laws in, 88–90, 145, 184, 187

State Supreme Court in, 90, 146

Canada

assisted immigration opposed in, 200–201

deportation of immigrants from United States to, 2, 12–13, 69, 106, 133, 144, 149, 187

immigration to United States from, 33–34, 36, 78–79, 107, 124, 150–51

Irish immigrants in, 17, 24–25, 27–29, 32–33, 165

workhouses in, 36

Canny, Nicholas, 48

Carley, Patrick, 26

Carr, Hugh, 115–18, 127, 159

Carrigan, Andrew, 66

Carroll, Hugh, 117–18

Castle Garden (immigration facility in New York City)

Commissioners of Emigration's management of, 108–9, 189, 197–98

deportations from, 180, 195–98

Ellis Island and, 202

establishment of, 108

illustration of, 109

immigration levels at, 109

Manhattan residents' opposition to, 108

state-federal joint administration of, 201

voluntary returns arranged by, 83, 97, 140, 160–61, 176
Commissioners of Woods, Forests and Land Revenues (British agency), 29–30
Congress of the United States
  Act to Encourage Immigration (1864) and, 131
  Chinese Exclusion Act of 1882 and, 9, 189–90
  citizenship and naturalization laws as purview of, 118–19
  Civil Rights Act of 1866 and, 142
  Expatriation Act (1868) and, 129–30, 132
  Gibbons v. Ogden on powers of, 53–54
  Hartford Convention's proposals regarding, 49–50
  Henderson case on passenger regulation authority of, 184–85, 187
  Immigration Act of 1882 and, 181, 186–87, 189–92
  Immigration Act of 1891 and, 199, 201–2, 204
  immigration policy as purview of, 5, 90, 203
  Know-Nothing movement and, 102–3
  Passenger Cases on authority of, 72–73
  report on pauper immigration (1838) at, 56–57
  states' advocacy for federal immigration policies at, 185–86, 201–2
Connacht (province in Ireland), 20, 156
Connecticut, 43, 101–2
Conway, Mary, 167–68
Cork (city in Ireland)
  Board of Guardians in, 167, 169–70, 173–75
  emigration from, 24–25, 62–63
  immigrants' postdeportation experiences in, 156, 166–72, 175
  workhouse in, 156, 166–70, 175
Cork (county in Ireland)
  emigration from, 17, 23–25, 28–29, 31, 62–63, 70, 166
  famine (1840s) in, 16, 23, 31

immigrants' postdeportation experiences in, 156, 166–72, 175, 197
Poor Law Union in, 35, 167
workhouses in, 17, 156, 166–70, 175
Crossman, Virginia, 177
Crown estates (Irish territories owned by British monarchy), 19, 29–30, 37
Cruger, August, 148
Culberson, Jean, 44
Cullen, Mary, 169
Cunagh, Mary, 167–68

Daly, Esther, 169
Davis, Catherine, 117
Davis, Henry, 116–17
Davis, John, 51
Davis, Margaret, 116–17
Deer Island (Massachusetts), 27, 60, 62, 78, 104, 106
Delaware, 43, 47
Democratic Party
  free labor ideology and, 136
  Irish immigrants' support for, 6, 65, 97–98
  Jacksonian Democrats and, 120
  limited central government advocated by, 120
  in Massachusetts, 8
  in New York City, 65, 97–98, 108
  in New York State, 8, 65–66, 97–98, 108
  in Pennsylvania, 153
  Reconstruction policies opposed by, 153
  slavery and, 6, 95–96
  southern states and, 55, 86
deportation
  Alien and Sedition Acts and, 49
  almshouses and, 8, 95, 106–7, 114, 117, 127, 141, 143–44
  of American citizens of Irish descent, 4, 11, 93–94, 101, 108, 114–18, 128, 163, 197
  to Canada, 2, 12–13, 69, 106, 133, 144, 149, 187
  federal standard established (1891) for, 199, 201–2

Printed in the USA
CPSIA information can be obtained
at www.ICGtesting.com
BVHW040812150823
668546BV00003B/10